GOD IN THE FRAY

W9-BXG-459

Walter Brueggemann

GOD IN THE FRAY

A TRIBUTE TO
WALTER BRUEGGEMANN

EDITED BY
TOD LINAFELT AND
TIMOTHY K. BEAL

BS
1192.6
•G66
1998

Regis College Library
15 ST. MARY STREET
TORONTO, ONTARIO, CANADA
M4Y 2R5

WITHDRAWN

Fortress Press   Minneapolis

GOD IN THE FRAY
A Tribute to Walter Brueggemann

Copyright © 1998 Augsburg Fortress. All rights reserved. Except for brief quotations in critical articles or reviews, no part of this book may be reproduced in any manner without prior written permission from the publisher. Write to: Permissions, Augsburg Fortress, Box 1209, Minneapolis, MN 55440-1209.

Biblical quotations are from the New Revised Standard Version of the Bible, copyright 1989 by the Division of Christian Education of the National Council of the Churches of Christ in the USA. Used by permission. All rights reserved.

Cover design: Craig Claeys
Text design: ediType

Library of Congress Cataloging-in-Publication Data
ISBN 0-8006-3090-4

The paper used in this publication meets the minimum requirements of American National Standard for Information Sciences—Permanence of Paper for Printed Library Materials, ANSI Z329.48–1984.

Manufactured in the U.S.A.   AF 1-3090

02   01   00   99   98   1   2   3   4   5   6   7   8   9   10

Contents

Part Three
GOD IN THE PROPHETS

Part Four
GOD IN THE WRITINGS

Part Five
CONTINUING THE DIALOGUE

Abbreviations

AB	Anchor Bible
ABD	*Anchor Bible Dictionary*
ANET	J. B. Pritchard, ed., *Ancient Near Eastern Texts Relating to the Old Testament*
AOAT	Alter Orient und Altes Testament
ATANT	Abhandlungen zur Theologie des Alten und Neuen Testaments
BBET	Beiträge zur biblischen Exegese und Theologie
BETL	Bibliotheca ephemeridum theologicarum lovaniensium
BI	*Biblical Interpretation*
BibOr	Biblica et Orientalia
BJRL	*Bulletin of the John Rylands Library of Manchester*
BKAT	Biblischer Kommentar: Altes Testament
BSOAS	*Bulletin of the School of Oriental and African Studies*
BTB	*Biblical Theology Bulletin*
BWANT	Beiträge zur Wissenschaft vom Alten und Neuen Testament
BZAW	Beihefte zur Zeitschrift für die alttestamentliche Wissenschaft
CBQ	*Catholic Biblical Quarterly*
CBQMS	Catholic Biblical Quarterly Monograph Series
CJT	*Canadian Journal of Theology*
ConBOT	Coniectanea biblica, Old Testament
Ebib	Etudes bibliques
ET	English Text
FOTL	Forms of the Old Testament Literature
FRLANT	Forschungen zur Religion und Literatur des Alten und Neuen Testaments
GNB	Good News Bible
HAR	*Hebrew Annual Review*

HAT	Handbuch zum Alten Testament
HBT	*Horizons in Biblical Theology*
HSM	Harvard Semitic Monographs
HUCA	*Hebrew Union College Annual*
IB	*Interpreter's Bible*
ICC	International Critical Commentary
IDBSup	*The Interpreter's Dictionary of the Bible, Supplementary Volume*
Int	*Interpretation*
IRT	Issues in Religion and Theology
JAAR	*Journal of the American Academy of Religion*
JAARSup	JAAR Supplement
JB	Jerusalem Bible
JBL	*Journal of Biblical Literature*
JJS	*Journal of Jewish Studies*
JPOS	*Journal of the Palestine Oriental Society*
JPS	Jewish Publication Society
JR	*Journal of Religion*
JRE	*Journal of Religious Ethics*
JSOT	*Journal for the Study of the Old Testament*
JSOTSup	JSOT Supplement
JSS	*Journal of Semitic Studies*
KAT	Kommentar zum Alten Testament
KJV	King James Version
LCBI	Literary Currents in Biblical Interpretation
LXX	Septuagint
MT	Masoretic text
NAB	New American Bible
NCB	New Century Bible
NEB	New English Bible
NIB	*New Interpreter's Bible*
NICOT	New International Commentary on the Old Testament
NIV	New International Version
NJPS	New Jewish Publication Society Version

NovT	*Novum Testamentum*
NRSV	New Revised Standard Version
NTS	*New Testament Studies*
OBO	Orbis Biblicus et Orientalis
OBT	Overtures to Biblical Theology
OT	Old Testament
OTL	Old Testament Library
OTS	Oudtestamentische Studiën
PTMS	Pittsburgh Theological Monograph Series
RB	*Revue biblique*
RHPR	*Revue d'histoire et de philosophie religieuses*
RSR	*Recherches de science religieuse*
RSV	Revised Standard Version
SBLDS	Society of Biblical Literature Dissertation Series
SBT	Studies in Biblical Theology
SR	*Studies in Religion*
ST	*Studia theologica*
SUNT	Studien zur Umwelt des Neuen Testaments
TDNT	*Theological Dictionary of the New Testament*
TEV	Today's English Version
ThStud	*Theologische Studien*
TS	*Theological Studies*
TSK	*Theologische Studien und Kritiken*
TToday	*Theology Today*
TZ	*Theologische Zeitschrift*
VT	*Vetus Testamentum*
VTSup	Vetus Testamentum Supplements
WBC	Word Biblical Commentary
WMANT	Wissenschaftliche Monographien zum Alten und Neuen Testament
ZAW	*Zeitschrift für die alttestamentliche Wissenschaft*
ZNW	*Zeitschrift für die neutestamentliche Wissenschaft*

Contributors

Samuel E. Balentine is Professor of Hebrew and Old Testament at Southeastern Baptist Theological Seminary.

James Barr is Professor of Hebrew Bible at Vanderbilt Divinity School.

Timothy K. Beal is Assistant Professor of Religious Studies at Eckerd College.

David R. Blumenthal is Jay and Leslie Cohen Professor of Judaic Studies, Emory University.

Walter Brueggemann is William Marcellus McPheeters Professor of Old Testament at Columbia Theological Seminary.

Ronald E. Clements is Samuel Davidson Professor of Old Testament Studies at Kings's College, London.

David J. A. Clines is Professor of Old Testament at the University of Sheffield.

James L. Crenshaw is Professor of Old Testament at Duke University Divinity School.

Terence E. Fretheim is Professor of Old Testament at Luther Northwestern Seminary.

Norman K. Gottwald is Professor Emeritus of Biblical Studies at New York Theological Seminary.

David M. Gunn is A. A. Bradford Professor of Religion at Texas Christian University.

Clayton H. Hulet is Reference Librarian at the John Bulow Campbell Library at Columbia Theological Seminary.

Nancy C. Lee is a Ph.D. candidate at Union Theological Seminary (Virginia) and was recently a Fulbright Scholar in Croatia.

Tod Linafelt is Assistant Professor of Biblical Studies at Georgetown University.

Patrick D. Miller is Charles T. Haley Professor of Old Testament at Princeton Theological Seminary.

R. W. L. Moberly is a Lecturer in Theology at the University of Durham.

Kathleen M. O'Connor is Professor of Old Testament at Columbia Theological Seminary.

Dale Patrick is Endowment Professor of the Humanities at Drake University.

Rolf Rendtorff is Professor Emeritus of Old Testament at the University of Heidelberg.

Samuel Terrien is Professor Emeritus of Old Testament at Union Theological Seminary (New York).

Phyllis Trible is Associate Dean and Professor of Hebrew Bible at the Divinity School at Wake Forest University.

Claus Westermann is Professor Emeritus of Old Testament at the University of Heidelberg.

Acknowledgments

We gratefully acknowledge the encouragement and guidance of Mary Miller Brueggemann, Patrick Miller, and Terence Fretheim, who have been instrumental in carrying through this project from the beginning. We are also thankful for the support of Columbia Theological Seminary, Eckerd College, and Georgetown University. We thank in particular Greg Briggs and Shirley Ruggles at Eckerd for editorial assistance, and Jet Harper of Columbia Seminary for providing the photograph of Walter Brueggemann. Clayton Hulet's remarkable skills as a reference librarian (and as a theological scholar in his own right) proved equal to the daunting task of preparing a nearly exhaustive bibliography of Walter Brueggemann's writings to date. Finally, thanks go to Marshall Johnson, former Editorial Director at Fortress Press, for trusting us with this opportunity to honor a mutual friend and colleague.

Introduction

In the Fray and at Risk

Timothy K. Beal and Tod Linafelt

> The Prophets Isaiah and Ezekiel dined with me, and I asked them how they dared so roundly to assert that God spake to them; and whether they did not think at the time, that they would be misunderstood, & so be the cause of imposition.
>
> Isaiah answer'd. I saw no God nor heard any...as I was then perswaded & remain confirm'd; that the voice of honest indignation is the voice of God, I cared not for consequences but wrote.
>
> Then I asked: does a firm perswasion that a thing is so, make it so?
>
> He replied. All poets believe that it does, & in ages of imagination this firm perswasion removed mountains; but many are not capable of a firm perswasion of any thing.
>
> ...I heard this with some wonder, & must confess my own conviction.
>
> —WILLIAM BLAKE, *The Marriage of Heaven and Hell*

This passage from the late-eighteenth-century apocalyptic poet William Blake is astonishing for a number of reasons, but mostly because of its prophetic audacity. The setting is a dinner party with the prophets Isaiah and Ezekiel. What would one discuss with such intimidating dinner guests? Blake wastes no time with formalities but asks the pair straight out how they dare to assert the fact of revelation. The answer given by Isaiah is perhaps no less astounding than his presence at Blake's table: "I saw no God nor heard any...I cared not for consequences but wrote." Revelation for Blake's Isaiah is not an event that precedes its writing, but instead is bound up with the act of writing itself. Isaiah's God takes shape only in the writing—a writing that is a matter of both risk ("I cared not for consequences") and firm persuasion. The risk lies in the conviction, which "all poets believe," that a firm persuasion, put into writing, has the power to "make a thing so." That is, the poet has the risk-ridden power to make available through the written word that which was not previously available.

Walter Brueggemann's work as a scholar and teacher of the Bible resonates with this passage from Blake. It was as a teacher that the two of

1

us first encountered Professor Brueggemann. In a not soon forgotten seminary class on the Pentateuch—and later as intimidated guests at the dinner
table—we quickly came to appreciate his boldness and imagination, as
well as his willingness to treat even novice students as potential scholars
and colleagues. Our first reading assignment, we recall, was Gerhard von
Rad's important essay, "The Form-Critical Problem of the Hexateuch." No
greater testimony to Walter Brueggemann's gifts as a teacher could be offered than to say that under his guidance this dense piece of scholarship
seemed to us, for the space of a few weeks at least, the most fascinating
thing one could ever hope to read and became an inspiration to pursue
biblical criticism further. In the classroom, Brueggemann was able to bring
the biblical literature and even specialized biblical scholarship to life, at
times taking on the very personae of the figures we were discussing. Indeed, he *became* those figures. Imagine the vexed wonderment of first-year
seminary students as this prominent scholar careened between impressions
of the matriarch Sarah (reacting to Abraham's attempts to pawn her off as
his sister), the nineteenth-century biblical critic Julius Wellhausen (taking a
Sunday morning stroll by the local church in his bathing suit), and no less
than God's own self (struggling mightily with the question, "What kind of
god will I be today?"). But such classroom drama was more than just a way
to get the attention of seminarians, although that did happen; rather, it was
intrinsically connected to large and important questions about the ongoing
significance of these ancient texts and the scholars who have struggled with
them. We heard all of this with some wonder and must confess our own
conviction, as well as our growing awareness of the consequences and risks
of doing biblical theology.

   Having been introduced to Professor Brueggemann as a teacher, we soon
came to realize his stature as a scholar as well. Indeed, he is certainly one
of the most prolific and widely respected, and simultaneously controversial (Blake would approve!), biblical scholars of this century, as the selected
bibliography prepared by Clayton Hulet for this volume clearly attests. Beginning with his doctoral dissertation in 1961, written at Union Theological
Seminary (New York) under the now-legendary teacher James Muilenburg,
Brueggemann has produced a steady stream of influential publications. He
has established an impeccable scholarly reputation via his publication of
numerous critical articles, which have appeared in virtually every major
journal in biblical studies. He also has demonstrated an uncanny gift for
communicating the results of such critical scholarship to a more general
audience, as exemplified by the popularity of such widely read monographs
as *The Prophetic Imagination.*

   If there were risks and consequences for the poet-prophet Isaiah, there are certainly also risks and consequences for the writer who today wishes to take the biblical literature seriously. No one—not even his strongest opponents—could accuse Brueggemann of not being "capable of a firm persuasion of any thing." On the contrary, he has cared not for consequences but has written boldly and with a passionate conviction that echoes Blake as well as Isaiah. Consider, for example, the following excerpt from his most recent major work, *Theology of the Old Testament*:

> I shall insist, as consistently as I can, that the God of Old Testament theology as such lives in, with, and under the rhetorical enterprise of this text, and nowhere else and in no other way. This rhetorical enterprise operates with ontological assumptions, but these assumptions are open to dispute and revision in the ongoing rhetorical enterprise of Israel.[1]

The implication here is that God is available in the rhetoric: as God is put into writing, embodied in biblical texts, and as we engage those texts in our own reading, writing, and arguing about them. Rhetoric—the fabric and texture of language itself—renders God readable and writable, in biblical literature and in our discourses on it.

Of course no text (let alone book, let alone collection of books such as the Bible) is ever univocal or homogeneous, saying the same thing consistently or in total agreement with itself. This has profound implications for any biblical theology sensitive to the rhetoric or literary art of the texts. For if there are tensions and ambivalences between and within biblical texts, then there must also be tensions and ambivalences within the God who is rendered in, with, and under those texts. When one begins to pay close attention to God as rendered in the literature of the Bible these profound tensions cannot be avoided. As Brueggemann writes,

> The substance of Israel's testimony concerning Yahweh, I propose, yields a Character who has a profound disjunction at the core of the Subject's life. This disjunction, moreover, is the engine that drives Israel's testimony; it is the splendor of Israel's odd faith and the source of the deep vexation that marks Israel's life.[2]

Biblical testimony—and countertestimony—never admits to a God who is "above the fray." On the contrary, this God is always entangled in history, astonishingly transformative, and impinged upon by the voice of suffering. Biblical testimony yields a God who is " 'in the fray' and at risk."[3]

On the one hand, such a claim presents itself as a most outlandish threat to any theology, whether characteristically "liberal" or "conservative," that

---

1. Walter Brueggemann, *Theology of the Old Testament: Testimony, Dispute, Advocacy* (Minneapolis: Fortress Press, 1997) 66.
2. Ibid., 268.
3. Ibid., 83.

attributes a fundamental oneness and transcendence to the God attested in biblical literature; such a God could only be imagined as existing above the fray and never at risk. On the other hand, the claim that the God who moves in, with, and under the biblical literature is an *embodiment of disjunction* may present itself as a powerful resource for speaking to human experiences of profound tension and ambivalence, whether in our world or in ourselves. Such a construal of God has the potential to speak to the core of a human existence that, as Brueggemann has articulated so clearly in his work on the Psalms, is characterized by the constant inbreaking of disorientation.[4] It is a disorientation that one tends to resist, clinging to the old and reassuring patterns of orientation, those modes of living and thinking that assume the world makes sense. In a society that trades on the illusion of a reliable and controllable world—we think, for example, of the constant barrage of advertising that assures one that any crisis or discomfort can be remedied by attaining the right car, or the right beer, or the right toothpaste, or the newest computer software—the candid admission that something has gone awry, be it in the most intimate spheres of our lives or in the massive sphere of public policy, becomes a difficult and potentially radical act. The dismantling of a supposedly safe and reliable world opens one to "a rush of negativities, including rage, resentment, guilt, shame, isolation, despair, hatred, and hostility."[5] Such dismantling, however, may also permit the ingress of unforeseen passions, unanticipated newness, and a radically open future. In short, disorientation encompasses both threat and promise, and it is impossible to have one without the other.

In response to such disorientation, one can attempt to hold one's ground, banking on a God of harmony and accord who stands apart from such negativities and, by implication, apart from the unexpected. If the idea of God as the ground and guarantor of stability can serve to anchor or validate the human desire for order and reliability, however, then certainly the idea of God as disjunctive at the core likewise not only speaks to but validates the very real human experience of disorientation. It is not finally the case that one must choose between these construals of God, or between competing desires for the reassurance of order and the exhilaration of unpredictability. The Bible certainly refuses to choose and, apparently, so does the God of the Bible. The refusal to choose constitutes the fundamental ambivalence of God, an ambivalence that is never resolved in some middle-ground synthesis but instead reels back and forth between the two. Walter Brueggemann has understood more than anyone that this tension, this fiercely imagined

---

4. See esp. *The Message of the Psalms* (Minneapolis: Augsburg, 1984); and *Psalms and the Life of Faith* (ed. Patrick D. Miller; Minneapolis: Fortress Press, 1995).

5. Brueggemann, *Message of the Psalms*, 20.

disjunction, is what drives the life of the divine; and he has insisted more than anyone that a theology worthy of the name "biblical" must reckon with divine ambivalence as both the "splendor" of Israel's faith and the "deep vexation" of Israel's life with (and at times without) its God.

*   *   *

The present volume is intended to honor Walter Brueggemann on the occasion of his sixty-fifth birthday by offering engagements of biblical literature as well as engagements of Brueggemann's own writings on biblical literature. It includes contributions from an internationally renowned group of scholars in Old Testament and Hebrew Scriptures, all focusing on the character of the biblical God as a site of theological tension and even ambivalence. In two programmatic articles in which he began to sketch out a possible "shape" for Old Testament theology, Brueggemann presented biblical faith in terms of this fundamental tension: on the one hand, one finds affirmations of stability and orientation (what he identifies as "structure legitimation"); on the other hand, one finds the powerfully disruptive and transformative countervoices of chaos and disorientation (what he identifies as "embrace of pain").[6] This fundamental tension becomes, in Brueggemann's new *Theology of the Old Testament,* the drive behind not only Israel's *faith* but the very inner life of Israel's *God* as well.[7] *God in the Fray* is intended to be a companion to Professor Brueggemann's magisterial *Theology of the Old Testament,* providing well-known colleagues from around the world the opportunity to address this theme from their own perspectives and based on their own research interests.

Walter Brueggemann has spent his career teaching at theological seminaries, first at Eden Seminary in St. Louis and then at Columbia Theological Seminary in Decatur, Georgia. Most of his students have gone on to positions in ministry, leaving fewer in the academic study of the Bible than one might expect from a scholar of his stature. Nevertheless, three former students are represented here (Beal, Lee, and Linafelt) and, we are pleased to note, a former teacher as well (Terrien). The remaining contributors are all

---

6. Walter Brueggemann, "A Shape for Old Testament Theology, I: Structure Legitimation," *CBQ* 47 (1985) 28–46; and "A Shape for Old Testament Theology, II: Embrace of Pain," *CBQ* 47 (1985) 395–415.

7. One can see this theme already in much of Brueggemann's earlier work, for example, "David and His Theologian," *CBQ* 30 (1968) 156–81; "The Formfulness of Grief," *Int* 31 (1977) 263–75; and "Israel's Social Criticism and Yahweh's Sexuality," *JAARSup* 45 (1977) 739–72. It was in the series edited by Professor Brueggemann, Overtures to Biblical Theology, that this theme was first addressed in a sustained manner: see Dale Patrick, *The Rendering of God in the Old Testament* (Philadelphia: Fortress Press, 1981); and Terence E. Fretheim, *The Suffering of God* (Philadelphia: Fortress Press, 1984). For a more recent popular discussion of this theme, see also Jack Miles, *God: A Biography* (New York: Knopf, 1995).

celebrated scholars and teachers: they include colleagues and former colleagues at Columbia Seminary (Gunn, Hulet, and O'Connor), authors of
books in Brueggemann's series Overtures to Biblical Theology (Balentine,
Crenshaw, Fretheim, Moberly, Patrick, Rendtorff, and Trible), and some
who have simply been in close conversation with Brueggemann and his
work over the years (Barr, Blumenthal, Clements, Clines, Gottwald, Miller,
and Westermann).

God in the Fray begins in Part One with three essays that engage Professor Brueggemann's biblical theology directly, focusing in particular on
the unsettled nature of the character of God. Following this "opening" in
Part One—which opens the present volume while at the same time opening
and reading Brueggemann's own biblical theology—the subsequent contributions, while also engaging Brueggemann's scholarship, are theological
discussions centered around particular biblical texts or topics. Thus Part
Two includes essays focusing on the character of God in the Torah, Part
Three on the Prophets, and Part Four on the Writings.[8] Finally, Part Five
includes Brueggemann's own "Prompt Retrospect" (written without having
read the other essays in this volume), along with a nearly comprehensive bibliography of Brueggemann's work to date (prepared by Clayton H.
Hulet). The reader will find that each essay stands on its own as an authoritative yet readable treatment of its text or topic, even as it contributes to
the larger portrait of Israel's God constructed by the volume as a whole.

Before the reader moves on to this rich and disparate portrait of the biblical God, a few words of clarification are in order, about both the term
biblical and the term *God*. To speak of *the* biblical or *the* Bible as a single book or entity is more than a little disingenuous. To begin with, the
Bible, as we noted above, is not a book so much as a collection or anthology of books. Furthermore, the books collected therein differ a great
deal according to which Bible one happens to be reading. The most obvious difference is perhaps between Christian and Jewish Bibles. What is
called in most Christian Bibles "the Old Testament" is more or less coter-
minous with the Jewish Bible, often called the Hebrew Bible or *Tanakh*
(an acronym based on the Hebrew terms for the three sections of Torah,
Prophets, and Writings). Protestant Bibles (for example, the KJV, NIV, or
RSV) not only preserve a different order and different versification for the
books of the Jewish Bible, but, of course, they supplement it with the New
Testament, bringing the number of books included in the collection from

---

8. The terms *Torah, Prophets,* and *Writings* designate the three main divisions of the Hebrew Scriptures. In the Old Testament of Christian Bibles such as the KJV and the NRSV,
however, these divisions are not strictly followed.

39 to 66. And Roman Catholic and Eastern Orthodox Bibles (for example, the NAB or JB) contain certain books and passages that are not in Protestant Bibles (these are called by Protestants "the Apocrypha"). The contributors to this volume will refer to this collection of books variously as "the Bible," the "Hebrew Bible," the "Hebrew Scriptures," the "Old Testament," or simply "Scripture." Individual authors may use their own translations of the biblical and other ancient texts, or they may refer to more familiar English versions.

As for the character of God, here too the reader will find a variety of names. Within the Bible itself, there are numerous ways of referring to the divine. The name of God in the Bible is tantalizingly unreadable: the scribes who preserved the Hebrew texts, in order to discourage the pronouncing of the holy proper name of the divine, preserved only the consonants, y-h-w-h (known as the tetragrammaton). To this day, no one knows precisely how the name of God was originally pronounced: the name "Jehovah" in older English Bibles was a failed attempt that combined the consonants of one word with the vowels of another; the name "Yahweh" is a more recent scholarly reconstruction that may or may not be correct. The authors in *God in the Fray* will employ various terms for the divine, including "YHWH" (a transliteration of the Hebrew consonants), "the LORD" (which stands in for YHWH), "Yahweh," "God," or simply "the divine."

If all this sounds complex, it is. The Bible itself is complex, though richly so, and the God to which it bears witness is no small reason for this complexity. To engage these texts and this God should never be considered a simple thing; it takes not only "a firm perswasion" but finesse and, not the least, imagination. No scholar has combined these qualities more effectively than Walter Brueggemann. And no teacher is more deserving of the honor that we hope is conveyed by the presentation of this volume, which can be no more than a tiny defrayal of the debt that we owe him. It is a debt that Walter, in his generosity, would no doubt refuse to acknowledge; but it is one that we profess freely and, indeed, with some pride.

Part One

Engaging Brueggemann's Theology

– 1 –

Rhetorical, Historical, and Ontological Counterpoints in Doing Old Testament Theology

Norman K. Gottwald

> Interdisciplinary work, so much discussed these days, is not about con-
> fronting already constituted disciplines (none of which, in fact, is willing to let
> itself go). To do something interdisciplinary it's not enough to choose a "sub-
> ject" (a theme) and gather around it two or three sciences. Interdisciplinarity
> consists in creating a new object that belongs to no one.
>
> —ROLAND BARTHES[1]

In my judgment, Walter Brueggemann has produced what is likely to be the
most seminal Old Testament theology since Eichrodt and von Rad, something approaching "a new object" of which Barthes speaks.[2] By adopting
a rhetorical strategy in analyzing God-talk in the Hebrew Bible, he offers
a daringly original reading of the diverse, often sharply conflicted, Israelite
and Jewish renderings of deity. In the process, he has capitalized on precisely the bewildering diversity of views that has long hamstrung most
efforts at doing a comprehensive Old Testament theology.

The Legitimacy of Old Testament Rhetorical Theology

At the 1986 annual meeting of the Society of Biblical Literature, I floated
a proposal for Old Testament theology that Brueggemann's work now
substantially implements in a manner that my sketchy remarks merely ad-
umbrated. In context, I was inquiring as to what form a theology of the

---

1. Translated quotation by J. Clifford in *Writing Culture: The Poetics and Politics of
Ethnography* (ed. J. Clifford and G. E. Marcus; Berkeley: Univ. of California Press, 1984)
1, from R. Barthes, "Jeunes Chercheurs," in *Le Bruissement de la langue* (Paris: Seuil, 1984)
97–103 (no page cited by Clifford).

2. W. Brueggemann, *Theology of the Old Testament: Testimony, Dispute, Advocacy*
(Minneapolis: Fortress Press, 1997).

Old Testament might take if it wished to attend to literary-critical practice. My answer was as follows:

> It seems to me that a proper beginning point for a theology of the Hebrew Bible is to take account of everything that the Bible says about God, everything that God says, and everything that people say to God. This would be to follow radically and faithfully the course of the text. It would be an enormous task of registering and grouping the data. Unless and until this is done, however, theological criticism will continue to build very selectively on narrow bases of God-talk and perhaps often with assumptions about how that language functions which a fresh look might alter. Of course a mere adding up of all the theological formulations according to some classification system will not produce theology, but interpretation would, I think, be better founded and more consistently answerable to a wider range of data than is now the case.[3]

In formulating my rudimentary remarks about an Old Testament rhetorical theology, I frankly failed to reckon with the quantitative magnitude of biblical rhetoric about God (as I soon discovered, when I began to make lists of scriptural references to deity), nor did I hazard any notion of how one might proceed to give order and coherence to the manifold theological rhetoric.

Brueggemann has addressed both of the thorny methodological challenges that my suggestion skirted: how to select among the plenitude of theological data, and how to give shape to the data selected. He chooses to focus on what he judges to be "characteristic" (i.e., typical or representative) theological rhetoric as argued for contextually by an array of trenchant textual exegeses. Nor does he flinch at admitting rhetoric saturated in patriarchy and violence, as well as rhetoric that foregrounds the intemperate "self-regard" of Israel's deity. Furthermore, he employs a number of ordering devices to organize his exposition: the semantic function of verbal sentences, adjectives, and nouns; pervasive themes that are typically in tension and often contradictory; types of institutional mediation between the human and the divine, and so on. The result is an exceedingly rich tapestry of argument in which theological utterances are viewed in their interconnection from a variety of angles.

By focusing single-mindedly on what Yahweh says, on what is said about Yahweh, and on what is said to Yahweh, Brueggemann highlights and explores the dialogical character of Old Testament theological assertions in all their astonishing and puzzling variety without insisting on forcing them

---

3. N. K. Gottwald, "Literary Criticism of the Hebrew Bible: Retrospect and Prospect," in *The Hebrew Bible in Its Social World and in Ours* (Atlanta: Scholars Press, 1993) 219. Reprinted from *Mappings of the Biblical Terrain: The Bible as Text=Bucknell Review* 37/2 (ed. V. L. Tollers and J. Maier; Lewisburg, Pa.: Bucknell Univ. Press, 1990) 27–44.

into a single harmonious unity. In particular, he resolves not to invoke history or metaphysics as organizers or arbiters of Israel's theological talk, a crucial point that I shall return to in the body of this paper. He wants to adhere closely to the linguistic-aesthetic shape of Old Testament assertions and, by doing so, to preclude the strong modernist temptation to extract a theological content that can be judged apart from the rhetorical situation in which Israel's words about God are spoken and heard. It is critical to note that in taking a stance against "modernism," Brueggemann is not reverting to "premodernism" but attempting to locate his approach in a "postmodern" intellectual and cultural milieu. He imagines that what Israel has to say about God is given in a tumult of voices requiring each reader and each reading community to listen attentively and to interpret imaginatively. The "jagged" and "elusive" Old Testament claims about God are no easy read, for they irritatingly resist settled conclusions.

As a methodological strategy to bring out the rich and conflictual character of Old Testament theological rhetoric, Brueggemann's approach largely succeeds in letting the Old Testament voices speak with forceful ardor and jarring dissonance, precisely as "testimony," without interrupting them prematurely with the kinds of questions and judgments that spring to our minds as contemporary readers and scholars. Instead, the questions and judgments to which Brueggemann does give prominence are the objections and caveats that other voices in the Old Testament interject as "countertestimony." Thus we are enabled to overhear heated differences of experience and belief concerning Israel's God arising precisely among the Israelites themselves. This approach generates the metaphor of a courtroom trial as the venue for Old Testament theology. Within the rhetorical situation of witnesses addressing a jury, we encounter theological advocacy and dispute played out across the broad canvas of biblical texts. Brueggemann cautions us not to force closure to this ongoing courtroom scene by anxiously introducing arguments that do not rise within the trial itself. He instructs us to accept our role as members of the jury who must give our undivided attention to the witnesses before we render a verdict.

Brueggemann's impressive construal of Old Testament theology is subtle and complex. While not persuaded by all his judgments, I heartily approve of his decision to *begin* with rhetoric and to *stay* with rhetoric as far as it can be taken. I think it is a fruitful procedure for at least three reasons: because it honors the distinctive speech patterns and genres in which Israel does its theological reportage; because it shows how literary criticism can contribute significantly to theological understanding; and because it documents and underscores the perplexing "oddity" of Israel's God as the central Character of the Old Testament.

Rhetoric vs. History and Ontology in Old Testament Theology

With the above fundamental agreements in mind, the aspect of Bruegge-mann's work that I want to query and explore for its adequacy is his resolute insistence on categorically excluding "history" and "ontology" from the purview of Old Testament theological discourse. To put it suc-cinctly, I do not think that everything falling under the rubrics of "history" and "ontology" can be so confidently dismissed from Old Testament theol-ogy, and I furthermore believe that this is demonstrated by Brueggemann's own implicit, and occasional overt, appeal to historical and ontological categories.

Brueggemann's clearest programmatic statement on the exclusion of his-tory and ontology from Old Testament theology, reiterated in various ways throughout his work, reads as follows:

> Note well that in focusing on speech, we tend to bracket out all questions of historicity. We are not asking: "What happened?" but "What is said?" To inquire into the historicity of the text is a legitimate enterprise, but it does not, I suggest, belong to the work of Old Testament theology. In like man-ner, we bracket out all questions of ontology, which ask about the "really real." It may well be, in the end, that there is no historicity to Israel's faith claim, but that is not a position taken here. And it may well be that there is no "being" behind Israel's faith assertion, but that is not a claim made here. We have, however, few tools for recovering "what happened" and even fewer for recovering "what is," and therefore those issues must be held in abeyance, pending the credibility and persuasiveness of Israel's testimony, on which everything depends.[4]

Viewing his theological project as a whole, it seems to me that the func-tion of this emphatic break between rhetoric, on the one hand, and history and ontology, on the other, is twofold:

1. *Concerning the immediate task of Old Testament theology.* Neither conceptions of history nor categories of ontology should be allowed to preselect the data or predetermine the categories of interpretation in Old Testament theology, as was so often the case in previous Old Testament theologies. Theological utterances should be allowed their full integrity and force regardless of how the interpreter evaluates the history alluded to in the text or presumed to lie behind the text. Likewise theological utterances should be allowed their full integrity and force irrespective of how coher-ent or adequate they may be, or may not be, according to one or another philosophical system or church doctrine. In terms of his courtroom trial metaphor, Brueggemann wants to make sure that the biblical witnesses are

---

4. Brueggemann, *Theology,* 118.

not muzzled because of prejudgments about "what happened" or about "the way things really are." Without this safeguard, our verdicts are likely to be reached on the basis of truncated or censored testimony.

2. *Concerning the appropriation of Old Testament theology in dialogue with contemporary historical and ontological perspectives.* Although he does not state it with programmatic precision, it appears that when it comes to the appropriation of Old Testament rhetorical theology Brueggemann is cautioning us that some versions of history and ontology entertained by contemporary readers are far more congenial to Old Testament theology than others. Forms of history in a positivist mode and forms of ontology in an essentialist mode have dominated both the shaping and the appropriation of Old Testament theology. But in Brueggemann's judgment they are precisely the modes least able to come to terms with biblical theological utterance, as they are also the modes of understanding undergoing sustained critique in our postmodern era. In terms of his courtroom trial metaphor, Brueggemann wants to preclude that, having initially resisted rigid historical and ontological constraints on allowable testimony, we might in the end, when "the chips are down," fall back upon just such historical and ontological preconceptions to cancel out or radically distort what we have heard. Without such vigilance, our verdicts are in danger of ignoring or misconstruing the testimony in all its fullness.

In so "defending the turf" of Old Testament theology, I am in sympathy with both of Brueggemann's points if I have understood him correctly. It seems to me, however, that this issue of the intersection of rhetoric, history, and ontology is both such a "hornet's nest" of debate and such a "dismal swamp" of confusion that he could have said a good deal more on the subject, especially since Brueggemann himself breaches the letter of his own prohibition, although I think not the spirit. In spite of his principled determination to keep history and ontology out of the theological arena, I find it striking that in practice historical and ontological concerns keep making their appearance in the course of his rhetorical exposition. I think it is important to note that these concerns appear not exclusively as unwelcome interlopers who are rebuked, but often as commentators and interrogators invited into the discourse, even if on limited terms and for brief moments.

I shall comment briefly on some of these historical and ontological insertions. Before I do so, I want to be clear about one thing: I am not faulting Brueggemann for allowing these historical and ontological "intrusions," since I cannot imagine any persuasive rhetorical theology that would categorically bar them. Thus my more modest complaint is this: that in his formal account of how he is doing theology, Brueggemann has not accounted sufficiently for the dialogical emergence of historical and ontological concerns that function as interactive "counterpoints" to the theological rhetoric—indeed, the very emergence that his own practice frequently honors.

Historical Counterpoints to Rhetorical Theology

"History," at best a slippery protean concept, may be examined in two respects: first, the history out of which theological rhetoric was spoken; second, the texture of historicity with respect to the interplay of documentation and imagination.

The history out of which Israel speaks of God is directly identified by Brueggemann when he states that *"The Old Testament in its final form is a product of and a response to the Babylonian exile,"* and, more precisely, *'the literature is put together in order to exhibit and to explore the tension between verbal testimony and circumstance."*[5] The fulcrum on which the corpus of testimony turns, and sometimes teeters precariously, is conceived as a series of historical events and processes labeled "the Babylonian exile." This assertion can be generalized into the claim that the dialogical referent of Israel's God-talk is "circumstance," that is, the particulars of Israel's history that stand in generative but problematic relationship to Israel's theological rhetoric. Even more tellingly, he notes that "we know too much about the history of Israelite religion to ignore the changes, transformations, and adjustments that have taken place in Israel's rhetoric."[6]

Another way that the historical counterpoint to rhetoric is brought out is Brueggemann's articulation of the salience of power and justice in the public realm as the locus of Israel's theology. This not only brings exile and restoration into the theological sphere, but also, in principle, draws the earlier phases of Israel's history into the same orbit. The way in which Brueggemann treats rhetoric ostensibly rooted in tribal and monarchic settings shows a similar focus on power and justice in the social and political order. Irrespective of our assessments of the accuracy of Israelite memories about preexilic events, what Israel recounts in its narrative discourse, from Moses onward, is a series of stories about the contestation for power: externally, vis-à-vis Egypt, Philistia, Syria, Assyria, and Neo-Babylonia, and internally, among rival individuals and groups. The events and circumstances so recited are freighted with vexing theological claims and counterclaims. The primary "testimony" about God refers to a deity

---

5. Brueggemann, *Theology,* 74, 210.
6. Ibid., 87.

fully "in the fray" of Israel's history, and the answering "countertestimony" responds with variant readings of God's presence in, or absence from, that same vortex of events and circumstances.

The creative interplay of documentation and imagination that constitutes much contemporary historical theory introduces a multidimensionality into our reconstructions of history, vigorously challenging the typical positivist orientation of prevailing treatments of Israel's history. It is this restrictive view of history, regarded as a fixed series of "facts proven beyond a shadow of doubt" and basically self-explanatory in their causal interactions, that Brueggemann is renouncing as an organizer and arbiter of Israel's theological rhetoric, and appropriately so. It is evident from his hermeneutical posture and the wide range of contemporary authors he cites, however, that Brueggemann is widely conversant with broader conceptions of history as communally lived and imaginatively remembered experience. It is increasingly recognized that historical documentation, necessarily under close scrutiny and in constant debate, does not pass unmediated into a historical narrative. The diverse kinds of historical "evidence" interact and combine in an imaginative construal that is thoroughly transformative and cannot be accounted for as the transparent reading of an accumulation of data grouped and ranked according to veracity and pertinence to the subject.

The dynamic that has broken the monopoly of positivist historiography is the developing synergistic relations among literary and cultural criticism, historical studies, and anthropology, such that many practitioners in these fields share common perspectives and methodologies. The import of this synergism for how we see the relation of rhetoric and history in biblical studies is that history is viewed as accessible only through speech and its construal as historiography is recognized as a rhetorical project. Hayden White argues that all history writing entails imaginative figurations, such as modes of emplotment (romantic, tragic, comic, satirical) and literary tropes (metaphor, metonymy, synecdoche, irony).[7] Dominick LaCapra, challenging the unity and order that historiography commonly imposes on the past, argues for multilayered dialogue between divergent voices from the past and the voice(s) of the historian who constructs a negotiated, and always partial, narrative of the past.[8] On this way of conceiving historical inquiry, "The fictive, imaginary dimension in all accounts of events does not mean

---

7. H. White, *Metahistory: The Historical Imagination in Nineteenth-Century Europe* (Baltimore: Johns Hopkins Univ. Press, 1973). His schema, explained in the introduction, is then applied successively to Hegel, Ranke, Tocqueville, Burckhardt, Marx, Nietzsche, and Croce.

8. D. LaCapra, *Rethinking Intellectual History: Texts, Contexts, Language* (Ithaca: Cornell Univ. Press, 1983); *History and Criticism* (Ithaca: Cornell Univ. Press, 1985).

that the events did not actually happen, but does mean that any attempt to *describe* events (even as they are occurring) must rely on various forms of imagination."[9] Put in other terms, Lynn Hunt remarks that the discipline of history is "an ongoing tension between stories that have been told and stories that might be told. In this sense, it is more useful to think of history as an ethical and political practice than as an epistemology with a clear ontological status."[10] One implication of this literary mode of looking at history writing is that the theological rhetoric of ancient Israel, so heavily committed to narrativity, represents a potential resource for doing Israelite historiography

But within this interdisciplinary synergism, the traffic is multidirectional, not only from literature to historiography but also from historical theory to the offshoots of literary and cultural theory in anthropology. Clifford Geertz's influential cultural analysis as "thick description" (a term to which Brueggemann is indebted for his reference to the "density" of Israel's theological rhetoric) is criticized by many fellow anthropologists for a drift toward static "timelessness" in his symbolic decoding of "local knowledge," severed from the dynamic interaction with wider history that brings irreversible change to local systems.[11] Eric Wolf, for example, has illuminated the way European expansion from 1400 on affected and altered "primitive" societies in Africa, Asia, and the Americas by incorporating them in a worldwide political economy in so far-reaching a manner that it is idle romanticism to picture these peoples as discrete and homogeneous survivals existing "outside of history."[12] Marshall Sahlins, focusing on one sector of Wolf's panorama, shows how the coming of Captain Cook to Hawaii effected a profound alteration in the indigenous population as their social practices and communal values were reinterpreted and refashioned to accommodate the political and economic intrusions of colonialism. Hawaiians managed to keep a culture intact, but it was definitely not identical with their precontact culture.[13] One implication of this historical mode of

---

9. L. S. Kramer, "Literature and Historical Imagination: The Literary Challenge of Hayden White and Dominick LaCapra," in *The New Cultural History* (ed. L. Hunt; Berkeley: Univ. of California Press, 1989) 101.

10. L. Hunt, "History as Gesture; or, the Scandal of History," in *Consequences of Theory: Selected Papers from the English Institute* (ed. J. Arac and B. Johnson; Baltimore: Johns Hopkins Univ. Press, 1991) 103.

11. C. Geertz, *The Interpretation of Cultures* (New York: Basic Books, 1973); idem, *Local Knowledge: Further Essays in Interpretive Anthropology* (New York: Basic Books, 1983); A. Biersack, "Local Knowledge, Local History: Geertz and Beyond," in *New Cultural History,* 72–96.

12. E. R. Wolf, *Europe and the People Without History* (Berkeley: Univ. of California Press, 1982).

13. M. Sahlins, *Islands of History* (Chicago: Univ. of Chicago Press, 1985).

looking at the self-understanding of peoples, including their rhetorical symbolism, is that the historical vicissitudes of ancient Israel, both vis-à-vis its neighbors and in its own social development, constitute a potential datum for doing Old Testament rhetorical theology.

Ontological Counterpoints to Rhetorical Theology

Ontology, an off-putting term without the popular currency enjoyed by the word *history,* may be examined in two respects: first, the traces of proto-ontology evident in Israel's theological rhetoric; second, the kinds of contemporary ontology, and their systematic theological counterparts, that might facilitate the incorporation of Old Testament theological perspectives into current ecclesial and secular discourses without "taking the edge off" the explosive biblical rhetoric.

There is a virtual consensus that speculative or critical philosophy does not appear in the theological rhetoric of the Hebrew Bible, beyond the possibility that wisdom literature may contain a few terms with a semantic coloration derived from Hellenistic metaphysics. Nonetheless, this does not in itself argue for the irrelevance of ontology for Old Testament theology. I think one can claim that Israel's theology is proto-ontological in two regards. First, Yahweh, the central character of the Old Testament, is regarded by Israel as the ultimate reality framing and sustaining the fundamental conditions of human existence and the more specific terms of Israel's life, and Brueggemann's paired motifs of divine "sovereignty" and divine "solidarity" express this proto-ontology in the personalized idiom of Israel's theological utterances. Second, insofar as Israel's "testimony" and "countertestimony" are frequently at odds, a lengthy (and lengthening?) "shadow of doubt" is cast on the certainty and reliability of Israel's most confident assertions of divine governance. The proto-ontological question is thus posed: Is there an actual orderliness in the world to which we may confidently conform our lives? Or, as theologically phrased, is Yahweh really the Creator and Redeemer as alleged? Does Yahweh deliver on the divine promises? As the vagaries of historical experience persist, the proto-epistemological question also arises: How are we to know the connection between appearance and reality? Which appearances are solidly based in reality, and which are ephemeral or illusionary? Or, as theologically phrased, how do we know that what Yahweh says, or what is said of Yahweh, is really so?

Brueggemann is sensitive to the probing, questioning dimension of Israel's theological rhetoric that verges on ontology. He can even refer to "ontological assumptions" in biblical rhetoric, by which he appears to mean "the assumptions of narrative" offering "alternative worlds."[14] Biblical narrativity expresses strongly felt needs for intervention in human distress satisfiable only by divine deliverance (sovereignty active in solidarity!). Yet Brueggemann remains cool toward ontology because he wants to hold fast to Israel's "hot" theological idiom, which he finds totally inconsistent with the mainstream of idealist or transcendental philosophies. In his treatment of wisdom cosmology and ethics, where one might have expected him to note proto-ontological leanings, he steers clear of such comparisons. Even at the point of Israel's most radical questioning of divine justice, which generates a "theodic" mode of protest, he is loath to see the seeds of ontology. Nonetheless, ambivalence and ambiguity about ontology hover over Brueggemann's theological project, as expressed in the tantalizing undeveloped remark with which he concludes one section, "When an affirmative decision is made [in favor of Israel's testimony], a real world of ontological substance follows."[15]

I am of the opinion that Brueggemann's most pointed nod in the direction of ontology occurs with the sentence, "In its deepest vexation, then, Israel makes a distinction between Yahweh and the reality of justice."[16] This strikes me as a strong admission of a deep split between appearance and reality at the heart of the rhetoric. Yahweh's claim to be "real" over against what "appears" to be injustice is inverted by the suspicion, even allegation, that injustice is "the real" and Yahweh is "the appearance" who, in life's extremities, deludes and forsakes Israel. At least at those moments of radical doubt, justice is seen as a higher order of reality that can (or should?) "bring Yahweh to heel." This is certainly the brew from which the acid of speculative and critical philosophy is made, yet still wrapped in the mythic imagery of premetaphysical discourse.

The greatest fear that Brueggemann harbors towards metaphysics, as also toward Enlightenment historicism, is apparently his assumption that it "sacrifices risk."[17] Doubtless he is correct that a guarded preoccupation with ontology as abstract speculation can block risk-taking. And the same inhibition to risk may result from a guarded preoccupation with positivist or antiquarian history. But is it not equally true that a guarded preoccupation with rhetoric as clever or artful speech can have exactly the same paralyzing effects on human venturesomeness?

In short, there does not seem to be anything intrinsic to the disciplines of ontology, history, or rhetoric that either maximizes or minimizes risk-

---

14. Brueggemann, *Theology,* 66–69.
15. Ibid., 725.
16. Ibid., 740.
17. Ibid., 707–13.

taking. I would venture to say that the only time we are willing to risk is when rhetoric is felt to correspond to or reverberate with a history that we are helping to make and an ontology that gives us a sense of what is most assuredly and reliably real. My impression is that just such a fruitful conjunction of rhetoric, history, and ontology is what moves and sustains Brueggemann in his quest to articulate Israel's theological rhetoric as a resource for risky living in today's world.

Lastly, I offer some observations on twentieth-century ontologies, and their theological implicates, that are possibly compatible with one or more aspects of biblical theological rhetoric. I do so without trying to rank them or to advocate any one in particular, but with the intent of reminding ourselves that there are a good many ontological and systematic theological options other than the static idealist types that Brueggemann chiefly associates with ontology.

Notions of a limited deity engaged in a struggle to prevail against resistant or contrary forces run against the grain of the classic claim of divine omnipotence, yet such an "unfinished" deity echoes Brueggemann's recognition that the Old Testament at times hints at conditions and forces beyond Yahweh's control (Samuel Alexander, Pierre Teilhard de Chardin).[18] Then there are conceptions of a God who acutely feels human pain and enters into our suffering in defiance of classic claims to divine "passionlessness," a view that accords with Yahweh's tempestuous relationship with Israel so forcefully argued by Brueggemann (Jürgen Moltmann, Carter Heyward, Gustavo Gutiérrez).[19]

Process philosophy, distinguishing between the primordial and the consequent natures of deity, or claiming the dialectical paradox that divine supremacy and absoluteness are revealed in God's indebtedness and relatedness to all lesser beings, strives to illuminate the enigmas of Israel's God that Brueggemann has convincingly laid bare (Alfred North Whitehead, Charles Hartshorne).[20] Indeed, some biblical scholars have applied a process hermeneutic to their exegetical work (e.g., Gerald Janzen on Job, George Pixley on Exodus).[21] Moreover, Janzen has published a much-neglected article on

---

18. S. Alexander, *Space, Time, and Deity* (2 vols.; London: Macmillan, 1920); P. Teilhard de Chardin, *The Divine Milieu* (New York: Harper & Row, 1960).

19. J. Moltmann, *The Crucified God* (trans. R. A. Wilson and J. Bowden; New York: Harper & Row, 1974); I. C. Heyward, *The Redemption of God: A Theology of Mutual Relation* (Lanham: Univ. Press of America, 1982); G. Gutiérrez, *On Job: God-Talk and the Suffering of the Innocent* (trans. M. J. O'Connell; Maryknoll, N.Y.: Orbis, 1987).

20. A. N. Whitehead, *Process and Reality: An Essay in Cosmology* (ed. D. R. Griffin and D. W. Sherburne; corrected ed.; New York: Free Press, 1978); C. Hartshorne, *The Divine Relativity: A Social Conception of God* (New Haven: Yale Univ. Press, 1948).

21. J. G. Janzen, *Job* (Interpretation; Atlanta: John Knox, 1985); G. V. Pixley, *On Exodus: A Liberation Perspective* (Maryknoll, N.Y.: Orbis, 1987) 76–80.

Old Testament theology viewed from the perspective of process thought
that goes a long way toward addressing Langdon Gilkey's fierce critique of
the ontological naivete of biblical theology.[22] On recent re-reading, I conclude that Janzen's proposals show a considerable affinity with the drift of
Brueggemann's theological constructs.

In close parallel with Brueggemann's commitment to theological rhetoric, there are various forms of hermeneutical ontology that focus on the
word as constitutive of reality, either philosophically (Charles Sanders
Peirce) or theologically (Paul Ricoeur).[23] We need also to take note of
the full-blown postmodernists who, while undermining all sorts of stable
meanings based on science and common sense, nevertheless discern genuine
possibilities for human authenticity rooted in self-knowledge and humility
in the face of a multiplicity of shifting identities and meanings (Jean Baudrillard, Jacques Derrida).[24] Although at first glance these theorists seem
far removed from theological discourse, it is noteworthy that Brueggemann
himself, confronting the contradictions of Old Testament discourse, ex-
claims, "In the tradition of Job (and of Derrida), I suggest, Yahweh is held
to justice, and if Yahweh cannot subscribe to this earthly passion, then the
claims of heaven must be deconstructed."[25]

Finally, there are those "masters of suspicion," Marx and Nietzsche,
who—contrary to repeated press reports—are far from deceased. There is a
vital Marxian historical-materialist tradition of praxis as the locus of self-
understanding and social transformation, modified and extended by literary
and cultural considerations unavailable to or overlooked by Marx himself
(Jürgen Habermas, Ernesto Laclau and Chantal Mouffe, Frederic Jameson).[26] Nietzsche's tradition of genealogy of knowledge and will to power,
cannily literary well in advance of his time, remains an abiding resource for
ontology and theology (Michel Foucault, Gilles Deleuze and Felix Guat-

---

22. J. G. Janzen, "The OT in 'Process' Perspective: Proposal for a Way Forward in Bib-
lical Theology," in *Magnalia Dei: The Mighty Acts of God* (ed. F. M. Cross, et al.; Garden
City, N.Y.: Doubleday, 1976) 480–509; L. Gilkey, "Cosmology, Ontology, and the Travail of
Biblical Language," *Journal of Religion* 41 (1961) 194–205.

23. C. S. Peirce, *Peirce on Signs: Writings by Charles Sanders Peirce* (ed. J. Hope; Chapel
Hill: Univ. of North Carolina Press, 1991); P. Ricoeur, *Interpretation Theory: Discourse and
the Surplus of Meaning* (Forth Worth: Texas Christian Univ. Press, 1976).

24. J. Baudrillard, *Symbolic Exchange and Death* (London: Sage, 1993); J. Derrida, *Writing
and Difference* (trans. Alan Bass; Chicago: Univ. of Chicago Press, 1978).

25. Brueggemann, *Theology,* 74.

26. J. Habermas, *Theory and Practice* (Boston: Beacon, 1973); idem, *The Theory of Com-
municative Action* (2 vols.; Boston: Beacon, 1984–87); E. Laclau and C. Mouffe, *Hegemony
and Socialist Strategy: Towards a Radical Democratic Politics* (New York: Verso, 1985);
F. Jameson, *Postmodernism, or, The Cultural Logic of Late Capitalism* (Durham, N.C.: Duke
Univ. Press, 1991).

tari, Thomas J. J. Altizer).[27] In both Marx and Nietzsche, power realities are central, as Brueggemann judges them to be in Old Testament theological discourse: Who has power over whom and with what consequences? Is it a mere coincidence that large sections of the writings of Marx and Nietzsche speak with the imaginative figuration, iconoclastic rigor, and high moral tone of much of Israel's theological utterance?

This cursory sample of ontologies, performative in at least certain respects in the manner of Old Testament theological rhetoric, is neither exhaustive nor prescriptive. My basic point is that just as our notions of history are moving more and more beyond simplistic positivism, so our ontological options are less and less confined to transcendental theories and increasingly committed to the immanence of human existence. Of course, as practical-minded North Americans, we tend not to fret excessively about global views of history and philosophy. Moreover, facing a daunting array of contested historiographic and ontological options, we may lack sufficient cultural or intellectual incentive and curiosity to go deeper into either field. Nevertheless, as meaning-seeking and time-enmeshed humans, we do bring historical and ontological inclinations and sensibilities to our biblical interpretation.

Brueggemann has deliberately strung a series of "trip wires" across our path to warn us about dogmatic or unwitting importations of history and ontology into a discipline that needs to stay focused on the specificity of linguistic utterances. If my reasoning is correct, he will not succeed in keeping our views of history and ontology totally out of the picture when we as jurors render our various verdicts on Old Testament theological utterance, any more than he has entirely suppressed his own views on those subjects. But he may give us a healthy boost in the direction of greater self-awareness about the implicit interplay of rhetoric, history, and ontology in our own theological utterance, and he may save us from a lot of superficial judgments and outright interpretive blunders as we continue to grapple with that "odd" witness about an "odd" and "unsettling"—even "unsettled"— God, concerning whom, as Brueggemann concludes, "the jury only trickles in—here and there, now and then."[28]

---

27. M. Foucault, "Nietzsche, Genealogy, History," in *Language, Counter-Memory, Practice* (trans. D. Bouchard and S. Simon; ed. D. Bouchard; Ithaca: Cornell Univ. Press, 1977) 139–64; G. Deleuze and F. Guattari, *Anti-Oedipus: Capitalism and Schizophrenia* (New York: Viking, 1977); T. J. J. Altizer, *Genesis and Apocalypse: A Theological Voyage Toward Authentic Christianity* (Louisville: Westminster/John Knox, 1990).

28. Brueggemann, *Theology*, 750.

– 2 –

Some Reflections on Brueggemann's God

Terence E. Fretheim

I am delighted to contribute to this volume honoring Walter Brueggemann. He has been a colleague, mentor, and friend. He has informed my work by his tenacious attention to specific texts, his relentless pursuit of theological issues, his fresh use of language, his voracious reading, and his concern to link biblical thought and contemporary life.

My intent here is to reflect on some (!) aspects of his understanding of the God of the Old Testament. I trust it will be evident that his proposals have considerable evocative and provocative power. Getting a firm grasp of his theology is not an easy task, not least because his publications never quit and, despite much consistency, his understandings are always on the move. For purposes of this essay I will center on two programmatic pieces and draw on his magisterial *Theology of the Old Testament*, which I have studied in manuscript form.[1] First of all, I offer some more general observations.

For Brueggemann "the primal subject of an Old Testament theology is of course God" (*TOT*, 117), evident not least in the sheer volume of his treatment of God in his *TOT*. But to speak of Israel's God is for him not simply a matter of describing an ancient faith. "Everything depends on our confession of God.... Let none among us imagine that the right discernment of God does not matter... there will be no community on earth until there is a fresh articulation of who God is. What the church can be depends on that. There will be no new community on earth so long as we rally round old God-claims of self-sufficiency and omnipotence."[2] The pas-

---

1. Quotations from Brueggemann's *Theology of the Old Testament: Testimony, Dispute, Advocacy* (Minneapolis: Fortress Press, 1997) will be cited as *TOT* within the text. The two other essays are "A Shape for Old Testament Theology, I: Structure Legitimation," *CBQ* 47 (1985) 28–46; and "A Shape for Old Testament Theology, II: Embrace of Pain," *CBQ* 47 (1985) 395–415. These articles now appear with related essays in his *Old Testament Theology: Essays on Structure, Theme, and Text* (ed. Patrick D. Miller; Minneapolis: Fortress Press, 1992) 1–21, 22–44, respectively.

2. "Covenant as a Subversive Paradigm," in *A Social Reading of the Old Testament: Pro-*

sion and urgency evident in this statement suffuse his work. I enter into this conversation because I share these commitments and concerns.

Brueggemann's understanding of Israel's God does not fit neatly into any systematic categories, not least because he allows himself to be pushed and pulled around by specific texts, and the texts will not sit still any more than he will. The lack of univocity in the biblical witness to God is a virtual refrain in his work; but this pluralism is not simply a matter of information, it is *theologically* important in itself. "Biblical faith, of course, is not static. It is not a set of statements that are always and everywhere true; therefore, contemporary biblical theology must not be reductionist in order to make all of the Old Testament fit together."[3] Israel does not offer a finished portrayal of God. For Brueggemann, theological pluralism has been canonized. Thus, any approach or flat thematization that diminishes this pluralism in the interests of congruence with, say, a systematic theology is suspect. He warns against the Western and churchly propensity to universalize at the expense of the particular, to smooth out the rough edges of the testimony. He admits that the Bible itself moves toward certain generalizations about God, but he views them as provisional and they may be challenged by countertestimonies.

At the same time, the biblical theologian must be conversant with systematic and philosophical efforts, and Brueggemann often calls upon such scholars to elucidate the text and to shape his own work (e.g., Paul Ricoeur, Karl Barth, the Yale school). His own identification with the Christian tradition in its Reformed expression plays an important role in his reflection. The Reformed centering in the sovereignty of God is always near at hand, and in it he seems to rest when his theological back is up against the wall. Though he breaks out of traditional understandings of sovereignty in many ways (e.g., attributes such as impassibility and immutability), his not uncommon appeal to such matters as divine intervention, control, irresistibility, and "unlimited" sovereignty shows that this tradition is still important for him (e.g., *TOT,* 66–67). One is given to wonder whether he has sufficiently followed through on his own emphases. Even more, I think that, at the end of the day, his emphasis upon an unsettled and an unsettling God is a *postmodern restatement of sovereignty* (see below).

For Brueggemann, Israel's God is dependent on speech, on Israel's "testimony" and the utterance of the texts produced. "The God of Old Testament theology . . . lives in, with, and under the rhetorical enterprise of this text, and nowhere else and in no other way" (*TOT,* 66). Even more, there

---

phetic Approaches to Israel's Communal Life (ed. Patrick D. Miller; Minneapolis: Fortress Press, 1994) 43, 46–47. Published originally in *The Christian Century* 97 (1980) 1094–99.

3. "Embrace of Pain," 23.

is a rhetorical "restlessness and openness" in Israel's God-talk that has to do not simply with the task of theological formulation but with God's own self. God himself has chosen to be caught up in this dialogue and has been affected thereby so that God's very self is "in process."

Within this testimony Brueggemann makes a distinction between "core testimony" and "countertestimony," and has major treatments of each. The core testimony is Israel's "characteristic" and "habituated" speech about God (*TOT,* 122). The countertestimony consists of themes and texts (e.g., divine hiddenness, the lament) that challenge or protest the more "normative" speech. Yet this testimony does not have a second-class status, but makes the core testimony "fuller and richer" and shows forth the "dialectical, resilient, disputatious quality that is definitional for this faith" (400). The net effect, however, is that the line between these testimonies becomes blurred. For example, violence "belongs to the very fabric of this faith" (381) and "savageness... belongs to the core claims of Yahweh" (276).

Brueggemann focuses on narrative, especially verbal sentences, which feature Yahweh as "actor and agent"; these "were Israel's first and foremost strategy for making available the character of Yahweh." (It is not clear to me why and how nominal sentences become secondary [see *TOT,* 123–24 n. 17], but it may be related to his theological commitments; as with his neglect of the psalms of orientation, they reveal a less unsettled God.) The density of this narrative, irreducible to simple or coherent formulations, reveals "the density of its God who refuses every exhaustible domestication." This narrative is a "theo-drama," mediating a God who cannot be controlled or made safe, who "deabsolutizes and destabilizes" what the world regards as given; this God is complex, elusive, and even "odd" (*TOT,* 69–71).

Brueggemann may be too easily settled in a narrative theology (under the influence of the Yale school). Though he is not uncritical, such a theology finally stands somewhat at odds with the God he himself finds in the Scriptures. I pursue one point here (on genre issues, see below). He acknowledges that textual "exposition is always conducted in the presence of two audiences," the believing community and the larger public. But this larger public seems only to be "listening"; Israel's rhetoric is only a speaking *"to"* this public (*TOT,* 87–88). But more must be said here. The God of the Bible, according to its own witness, is actively engaged in the world outside Israel; this work has good effects and shapes Israel's own testimony. God's continuing activity in that extrabiblical story is of such a character as to bring a potentially critical word to bear on the Bible and its testimony regarding God (one thinks of patriarchy) and to enable its readers to hear more clearly where *the Bible itself* is being self-critical, where the

Bible would say no to one or another element in its own testimony. Difficult issues of discernment and criteria are quickly at hand, but we cannot
in the face of those difficulties retreat into the narrative world of the Bible,
so that the text is thought to absorb every human story into its own. God,
and certainly the God of Brueggemann's analysis, could never simply be
"at home" in such a narrative retreat.

I now take a closer look at the two programmatic articles revealing of
Brueggemann's approach to and understanding of the biblical God. These
articles are basic for his *TOT*. I begin by noting his conclusion:

> The God portrayed here is an *ambiguous* one, *always in the process of decid-
> ing*. For Israel, the issue is whether to be "like the nations" or to be a "holy
> people." Israel dared to say that its God, Yahweh, *lived* in the same *ambigu-
> ity: whether to be* "like the other gods" or to be a holy God, "the Holy One
> in our midst," who had *learned* from Abraham fresh subversive notions of
> ṣĕdāqâ and mišpāṭ.[4]

I have emphasized the word *ambiguity*. The word refers not to God's
external acts and Israel's understanding thereof, but to the divine "interi-
ority,"[5] to God's own unresolved interior life and decision making. This
ambiguity refers not to one moment of decision, nor is it just that God
"noted, responded to, and embodied the pain that Israel was also to embody."[6] God *"lived"* in ambiguity, was *"always* in the process of deciding,"
"whether to be" a certain kind of God.

Brueggemann frames this divine decision-making process by positing
a dialectical interaction of "structure legitimation" and the "embrace of
pain." Another pair of phrases he uses: God is "above the fray" and "in
the fray." This distinction seems to correspond to the traditional distinction
between transcendence and immanence.[7] These formulations are problematic. The biblical God is transcendent *within* relationship (never "above"
it); the God active "in the fray" and "embracing pain" is so engaged as the
immanent *and* transcendent one. The godness of God is revealed precisely
in *that* God wills—once and for all (see below)—to enter into the fray and
by *the way in which* God embraces the pain: steadfast in love, faithful to
promises, and unwaveringly willing the salvation of Israel and world. This
God is so committed to full participation in a genuine relationship with Israel and the world that God no longer has the option of finally pulling back

---

4. "Embrace of Pain," 43–44 (emphasis added).
5. "Structure Legitimation," 35; cf. 44; "Embrace of Pain," 408.
6. "Embrace of Pain," 415.
7. This is also Leo Perdue's interpretation of this point in Brueggemann's work in *The
Collapse of History: Reconstructing Old Testament Theology* (OBT; Minneapolis: Fortress
Press, 1994) 287. In his *TOT*, "mutuality" may speak "against" transcendence or is associated
with fidelity but not sovereignty, both problematic formulations.

from it. But we cannot factor out what it takes for God to be this kind of God; God will make surprising, unsettling, and sharply judgmental moves, particularly in the encounter with creaturely resistance. But all such divine moves occur *from within* this resolve.[8]

For Brueggemann a "common theology" of the Near East has taken root in Israel, evident in creational and covenantal understandings that issue in "structure legitimation" and "contractual theology." This "tight system of deeds and consequences" allows "no slippage, no graciousness, no room for failure."[9] Such a perspective is reality for both Israel and God. But because "it lacks a human face," it needs to be submitted to sharp critique.[10] I believe that this "system" is much looser than he supposes; it does not function mechanically, even in Deuteronomic theology (e.g., Deut 4:31; Judg 2:1; 1 Sam 12:2; 2 Sam 7). The language of "contractual theology" will simply not do for the God-Israel relationship in any Old Testament tradition, though it had its adherents in popular understanding, then as now (e.g., the friends of Job). We should not forget that "covenant" is used metaphorically, carrying both a yes and a no with respect to the sociopolitical analogue.

For Brueggemann, this contract is one to which Israel's God is committed. Yet Israel's life experience intrudes upon this settled structure and issues in various forms of protest—the laments of the psalmists, the "alternative consciousness" of the prophets, and Job. Changes in this structure are generated not from God's side but from the human side; indeed, the human experience of pain "forces" change on God's part.[11] Israel's prayers "evoke from God a new posture of relationship."[12] This experience (and the extent to which Brueggemann understands experience to figure in Israel's changing theological formulations is notable) occasions an "in-house struggle," between the "common theology" and "mutations which seek to transform" it.[13] But, and this is a key point, these "mutations" are not simply expressed by Israel's theologians; rather they are "going on in the very person of God," disclosing "God's own life, which is troubled, problematic, and unresolved."[14]

Another way in which Brueggemann speaks of the God who is "lodged in a 'common theology' " with Israel is that "two moves are underway at

---

8. For a more complete statement, see Terence E. Fretheim, *The Suffering of God: An Old Testament Perspective* (OBT; Philadelphia: Fortress Press, 1984), esp. 70–71.

9. "Embrace of Pain," 405; "Structure Legitimation," 42.

10. "Structure Legitimation," 42.

11. "Embrace of Pain," 402, 404.

12. Ibid., 404.

13. "Structure Legitimation," 34, 43.

14. Ibid., 35, 44.

the same time, and in opposite directions." One move is "an *intensification of Yahweh's anger and impatience*"[15] at Israel's waywardness that finally issues in the destruction of Jerusalem. In this common theology, "the outcome of judgment for Jerusalem is tightly tied to disobedience." A second and *concurrent* move within God is "an enormous patience, a holding to promises, even in the face of disobedience, a resistance to the theological categories which conventionally give God self-definition."[16] This movement within God (apart from Israel's response) occasions a divine "reluctance" about simply being an "enforcer" of the contract; indeed God *"wills"* to be other than this. This occasions an "unbearable incongruity" in God. God is "committed to a structure of sanctions, and yet with a *yearning* for a [renewed?] *relationship* with this disobedient partner." Again and again, God must decide "how much he must implement its [the contract's] claims, and how much he can resist."[17]

This second movement, however, seems to me to be not an integral aspect of the common theology, but already stands over against it. The point is an important one: Israel discerned such "resistance" and "reluctance" in God *apart from* Israel's prayers or appeals to God. Israel understood that its God was not a simple upholder of the contract come what may. Israel could appeal to God precisely because God was discerned to be already open to, "yearning for," such a direction. In any case, why this situation should be described as an "unbearable incongruity"[18] for God is not clear to me. Brueggemann suggests where God's "will" is in all of this, namely, in being other than simply an enforcer of the contract; this use of "will" language would seem to make clear that this is for God more than simple "reluctance." Is it not a positive willing, which assumes a relationship with Israel that has its best interests at heart ("an enormous patience, a holding to promises")? Yet Brueggemann also states that Israel had only a *"hunch* that this God does not want to be an unchallenged structure...and tests the hunch."[19] On what grounds is this only a "hunch"? When Moses, for example, makes his plea to God, he appeals to God's promise to Abraham (Exod 32:13). God's being "committed to a structure of sanctions" does not ever fully comprehend the divine will for Israel. Generally, the *will* of God is a neglected theme in Brueggemann's theology.[20]

---

15. "Embrace of Pain," 397.
16. Ibid., 397.
17. Ibid., 398.
18. Ibid., 397.
19. Ibid., 401 (emphasis added).
20. For my own reflections on this theme, see "Will of God in the OT," *ABD* (New York: Doubleday, 1992) 6:914–20.

Brueggemann's statement about the "will" of God stands in no little tension with his comments that "God *may wish* to be 'above the fray,'" or that "Israel's laments *force* God to recharacterization," indeed "a new identity."[21] Brueggemann even speaks of God's response to such prayers as a "galling" experience; at one point he speaks of "the transformative power of Yahweh, of which Yahweh is indisputably capable, *depends upon* the triggering power of the human agent" (*TOT,* 472–73, emphasis added). Indeed, "Israel's vigorous protest has moved Yahweh *back to fidelity*" (*TOT,* 440, emphasis added). Brueggemann claims that Israel's laments and acts of protest to God stand "in deep tension with the reality of God's sovereign freedom to be who God *chooses* to be."[22] But if God's choosing to be, which must include God's willing, already moves beyond a commitment to structure before any lament is heard, then it seems incongruous to speak of incongruity. In other words, there is within God a leaning toward Israel and being *for* Israel by virtue of the divine purpose and promises (see below). God's decision-making and actions toward Israel and the world will always be informed by that loving purpose and those promises.

This is true even in judgment, the exercise of God's "ferocious sovereignty." Brueggemann's exposition of the theme of divine anger and judgment suggests otherwise, however. His treatment of Exod 34:6–7, with its combination of divine love and graciousness and yet taking violators seriously, is taken as an example of such "incongruity," though there is no signal in the text of its being so (both come into play again in Numbers 14).[23] Why should love be inconsistent with "just judgment"? Why is divine judgment an act of unfaithfulness? Why cannot judgment be in the service of graciousness? Why is a word or act "against Israel" by Yahweh incongruous with God's will "for Israel"? I would claim that divine judgment is *always* in the service of God's loving and saving purposes, and their juxtaposition in Exod 34:6–7 says precisely this.

I offer some reflections regarding judgment along these lines. God's anger is an exercise of the *circumstantial* will of God, which always stands in the service of God's *absolute* will for life and blessing.[24] Or, from another angle, wrath (unlike love) is never for Israel considered to be an attribute of God; if there were no sin, there would be no wrath and no judgment. Wrath issuing in judgment is a contingent response to a specific situation. Wrath/judgment is never God's final word for Israel or the world (though

---

21. For the first quotation see "Embrace of Pain," 403; cf. "above the fray" on 406. For the others see ibid., 402, 404, 407 (emphasis added).

22. Ibid., 402 (emphasis added).

23. Ibid., 414; pursued with much detail in his *TOT,* e.g., 215–24.

24. On this distinction within the will of God, see Fretheim, "Will of God," 915.

Israel may wonder about that, especially when untrusting of the promises). But, precisely in order to be faithful, God *must* judge. Fidelity calls for a harsh sovereignty in some situations.

Israel may not *know* how God is working out the divine will in such circumstances, and deeply question God, but that does not mean that God has a divided will with regard to the divine purpose. Several times in his *TOT* Brueggemann will say something like this: Yahweh's exercise of power is linked to Yahweh's fidelity "but not always" (276). Or, Yahweh may act in any circumstance in gracious fidelity "and often does" (271). The "not always" and "often" would mean that Yahweh's faithfulness or saving purposes have been bracketed out in certain divine activities. At times Brueggemann places such an emphasis on "sovereign freedom" that Yahweh can even "cancel the commitment" to Israel (*TOT*, 410). Sovereignty clearly takes priority over fidelity in such formulations. This direction of thought opens up the possibility that the interpreter can decide where and when God is acting faithfully to the divine purpose and promises. Moreover, if God is not always faithful, then *all* God's words and deeds are in question, and one has to do with a "however" theology. "God is faithful, however...." " "God is loving, but...." " This is not love or faithfulness in any genuine sense. I would appreciate a closer study of the relationship of divine love, saving will, and grace to wrath and judgment.[25]

To return to a level of Brueggemann's thought noted above, these texts make available an unsettled God, who is uncertain, indecisive, ambiguous, and conflicted. His thesis as stated in his *TOT*:

> Yahweh is a Character and Agent who is evidenced in the life of Israel as an Actor marked by unlimited [!] sovereignty and risky solidarity, in whom this sovereignty and solidarity often converge, but for whom, on occasion, sovereignty and solidarity are shown to be in an unsettled tension or in an acute imbalance. *The substance of Israel's testimony concerning Yahweh, I propose, yields a Character who has a profound disjunction at the core of the Subject's life.* (268)

He even claims this unsettledness within Yahweh to be "the central datum of the character of Yahweh" (282), belonging "definitionally to the character of Yahweh" (303). This unsettledness is grounded in Yahweh's "excessive self-regard," or "singular preoccupation with self," which is "massive, savage, and seemingly insatiable" (272–79, 293, 556). These comments constitute a *rationale* for Yahweh's unsettling actions, an "explanation" for the fact that "Yahweh has not yet got it right" (331). Again,

---

25. Abraham Heschel's *The Prophets* (New York: Harper & Row, 1962) 279–306, has influenced my thinking in this area.

any concern that Yahweh may have for the relationship with Israel and the world is given a secondary place, as is the will of God. This unresolved tension is finally to claim that the sovereignty of God (see his "definition-ally") is the centering metaphor for an Old Testament theology. Though, at one point in his *TOT* (312) Brueggemann will say: "in the end, from the perspective of the final form of the text, fidelity dominates the vision of Israel."

I do not say that God never has any decisions to make in view of the interaction with Israel's laments and protests, or that God cannot ag-onize regarding such decisions. Brueggemann is right in so forthrightly lifting up these themes. Yet the texts make distinctions among divine de-cisions. For example, God does make once-for-all decisions, *within which* other decisions are made. Not every divine deciding constitutes a return to ground zero.

Three such divine decisions are especially momentous—once-for-all de-cisions that shape God's relating to the future of both the world and Israel. First, in Gen 8:21–22 (and 9:8–17) God decides never again to visit the earth in floodlike ways; God will go with the world come what may. This promise grounds certain prophetic texts having to do with *Israel* amid the experience of exile (Jer 31:35–37; 33:19–26; Isa 54:4–10). Lamentations 3:22–33 puts this divine resolve and Israel's experience together in its claim that, while God has "rejected" God's people, God's steadfast love for Israel persists through exile.[26] Second, in Gen 15:7–21, God passes through the fire in committing the divine self to the promises to Abraham (reaffirmed in the covenant with David); God places God's own life on the line on behalf of those promises. Third, in a text parallel to Genesis 8–9, God makes a comparable decision regarding the future of Israel (Exod 34:10), grounded in the Abrahamic covenant (32:13) and in the very nature of God (34:6–7).

To reiterate, these decisions that God makes *for* the world and Israel are once-for-all decisions; God will never go back on the promises to Noah and to Abraham-Israel, even in the midst of the fires of judgment. At the same time, people can reject God and remove themselves from the sphere of the promise, a move that God will honor if not finally be settled with. The texts that speak of God before and during the making of these once-for-all decisions cannot necessarily be used to characterize the God who acts after

---

26. Brueggemann considers several of these texts (though not Lam 3:22–33) in "A Shat-tered Transcendence? Exile and Restoration," in *Old Testament Theology*, 183–202. The issue of the relationship between divine love/will/purpose and judgment/rejection emerges also in this article. When Brueggemann states that *"the transcendence of God is placed in deep jeop-ardy* by the exile" (199), it is not clear to me what the word *transcendence* entails. Taken at its face value, this would mean that God could cease to be God.

them. Moreover, those once-for-all decisions are grounded in an ultimate or fundamental divine will *for* Israel and the world. Hence it seems clear that each decision-making moment does not entail God's deciding "what kind of God to be,"[27] as if God had an option not to be a God of, say, steadfast love and faithfulness. In summary, we might speak of three levels of divine decision making: God's ultimate will; three (at least) once-for-all decisions that implement that will; and various circumstantial decisions. God's *ongoing* "ambivalence" is related only to the last.

From another angle, this interpretation is not "incongruous" with our understanding of relationships more generally (Brueggemann's discussion of God in relationship comes late in his *TOT* and does not decisively shape his discussion). In parental and marital relationships (two primary metaphors used for the God-Israel relationship), a commitment to structure *and* an openness to change are integral to genuine relationship. To be true to such relationships one must be committed concurrently to both constancy and change. This is not "incongruity," but revealing of the heart of what it means to be in a relationship of consequence. God is one who enters into such relationships with integrity. On the one hand, God will be steadfast in love, constant in saving will for the world, and faithful to promises made. On the other hand, God will move with the world, interacting in view of developments in the relationship and changing times and places, disciplining and judging, responding to prayers of lament, and (not) repenting of *specific* directions taken in view of that interaction. In traditional language, God is both mutable and immutable; which term one uses depends on the topic under discussion. God's transcendence is revealed in both such moves.

We return to Brueggemann's concern to address entrenched theologies of various sorts. For him, the texts of God's heavy-handedness and destructive judgments are problematic for "normative theology." In the steady reference throughout his *TOT* to Israel's testimony to Yahweh as both unsettled and unsettling, the range of descriptors used for God is remarkable: savage, odd, abusive, mean-spirited, wild, self-indulgent, unreliable, unstable, capricious, irascible, irrational, sulky, and more (none of them biblical words any more than much churchly language for God has been). Again, this language suggests that, whatever is said about divine fidelity, sovereignty admits of no qualification by the relationships with Israel and the world into which God has entered. Brueggemann does speak of partial qualifications of divine sovereignty by the divine fidelity in some texts, but these seem not to be hermeneutically significant for the larger biblical picture. Countertestimony finally has just as much standing as core testimony.

---

27. "Embrace of Pain," 410.

But does every text and every metaphor carry equal weight in considering Israel's understanding of God (see below)?

Brueggemann may insufficiently recognize that there are some theologians (whether evangelical or orthodox) who appeal precisely to these unsettling judgment themes to keep the troops in line with an image of a scary God! Brueggemann's relentless attention to unsettling images for God speaks against settled establishment types who champion a "settled 'establishment' Yahweh," the better to maintain control over life and thought. Not in his purview (from a personal conversation) is a significant theological establishment for whom an unsettling God is precisely the trump card to keep matters settled. Such a portrayal of God "on the loose" is designed to keep people on edge, always looking over their shoulders wondering what God is going to do next if they do not toe the mark. This is another form of sovereignty, and of a hardened sort, for it often has none of the restraints and constraints that genuine relationship entails. In other words, Brueggemann's God may be used in ways that are just as controlling as any other, and I know several folks who will be delighted to be able to appeal to him to substantiate their version of orthodoxy. What guards Brueggemann's work from being so understood and used? The "antidote" can in fact intensify the problem that Brueggemann is rightfully concerned to address.

A further issue may be raised in this connection. What counts as being "unsettling" with respect to God? Does this include the portrayal of God in terms of patriarchy—integral even to Israel's core testimony? For moderns, this is indeed an unsettling aspect of the testimony to Yahweh. But is it an appropriate unsettling? I understand that Brueggemann does not treat patriarchy as an appropriate dimension of the Bible's portrayal of God, though he uses the word *reliable* for the biblical testimony. Brueggemann does, however, in several publications (including his *TOT*), consider violence an appropriate unsettling matter in Israel's God-talk; in fact, he speaks of violence as belonging to the "very fabric" of Israel's faith, as "situated in God's own will and purpose" (381, 497). Again, no distinctions are made within the divine will; it is as if love and violence belong eternally together in God (an eternal dualism is close at hand).

Violent images (e.g., God as warrior) do disrupt traditional attempts to domesticate God. But on what grounds is God's exercise of violence (and other testimonies to "irascible" and "irrational" divine behavior) understood to be appropriately unsettling, but not patriarchy? Moreover, does this include every violent image? One thinks of the common prophetic witness to a God who lifts up Israel's skirts and exposes her genitalia (e.g., Isa 3:16–17). Another unsettling image! But appropriately so? Criteria must be developed to sort out these testimonies, to make distinctions regarding appropriateness among images of God. Without this, *all* talk about Israel's unsettling testimony regarding God is called into question.

The Bible itself recognizes this issue. One might speak of a biblical capacity to be self-critical regarding its imaging of God. Some studies have shown that certain texts have a subversive role to play regarding patriarchy; the same could be said about violence.[28] Other (implicitly) critical voices regarding various matters are to be found (e.g., Gen 18:25). These testimonies to an internal critique regarding unsettling divine activity need to be more explicitly developed. Such a study will have implications for contemporary usage, not least giving readers permission to ask into the continuing appropriateness of its unsettling testimony without being charged with escapism. We have an inner-biblical warrant to be comparably critical (though we do not finally stand on neutral ground in making this observation). Bible readers should deal with and be confronted by every text, allowing them to be "in our face," but this does not necessarily affirm that every image of God is appropriately unsettling. Some unsettling images for God ought not put the fear of God in anyone![29]

Another way into this discriminating enterprise in view of inner-biblical warrants is through an analysis of genre and other narratological features. In conclusion, I raise questions in three areas, but focus especially on the issue of genre.

1. *Point of view.* In drawing upon Israel's testimonies to God, Brueggemann explicitly makes no important distinction between Israel's speech *about* God and the word spoken *by* God to Israel; this is surprising given his emphasis on the word and its rhetorical shaping. This decision diminishes a rhetorical feature such as "point of view" in assessing the text's testimony regarding God and makes possible a claim that words placed in the mouth of God have no special standing in Israel's God-talk.

2. *Character.* It has become commonplace to consider God a character just like other characters in the narrative, and Brueggemann generally speaks as if this were the case. But are there no differences to be taken into account? Might the differences between Yahweh and other gods (e.g., theogony) be compromised by a collapse of character differences? What difference does it make that all language for God is analogical? In thinking

---

28. For example, Phyllis Trible, *God and the Rhetoric of Sexuality* (OBT; Philadelphia: Fortress Press, 1978); on violence, see Erich Zenger, "The God of Exodus in the Message of the Prophets as Seen in Isaiah," in *Exodus—A Lasting Paradigm* (ed. B. van Iersel and A. Weiler; Edinburgh: T. & T. Clark, 1987) 22–33.

29. For a study of the appropriateness and reliability of God images in the Old Testament, see my *The Bible as Word of God in a Postmodern Age* (Minneapolis: Fortress Press, 1998), with Karlfried Froehlich.

about such matters as divine anger or divine speech, one must take into account both a yes and a no with respect to the human analogue. With respect to every divine "character trait," indeed every divine action, one must seek to discern where the yes and the no lie. Is not the distinction between the textual God and the actual God somewhat different from the textual-actual distinction with other characters? Does not the narrative itself present God as one who transcends the narrative in ways distinct from other characters? God does enter deeply "into the fray," but not in such a way that God ceases to be God. These are questions that, to my knowledge, have not been adequately addressed in recent literature about God. I would eagerly appreciate an effort by Brueggemann to do just this; he is one of the few biblical theologians who could handle the issue in a theologically sophisticated way.

3. *Genre.* To my knowledge, Brueggemann does not address the issue of genre with respect to God-talk in any sustained way.[30] What effect does the identification of genre have on the readerly move to theological construction? Take the laments and protests. How does one "translate" the language of these genres into theological formulations? People (then and now) say all kinds of things about God when they are in dire straits, but would never so speak in a carefully formulated theological statement. One thinks of bargaining or the use of hyperbolic language or the use of metaphors designed to get attention. How does one assess the theological value of such outbursts? When the psalmist complains, "Why do you sleep, O Lord? . . . Why do you forget?" (Ps 44:23–24, NRSV) is one to conclude that he thought that God was actually sleeping or forgetting? Is he speaking hyperbolically? Even more, that these expressions occur in *poetry* is important for theological reflection. One must sort out the rhetorical function of this language and its metaphorical character before discerning how to use it in theological formulation.

Another case in point: What does it mean that Israel gathered claims about God into creedal formulations? They are present in two primary forms, historical recital (Deut 26:5–9) and more abstract confessions (Exod 34:6–7; Deut 10:17–18). Echoes of these credos are found in numerous texts, especially hymnic literature (which gathers the "leaner" forms of Israel's faith), and they are woven into narratives. They would seem to say: This is the kind of God with whom Israel has to do in every circumstance. Just *how* God will be this kind of God in any moment cannot be predicted in advance, nor how Israel will appropriate this material, or even contest it

---

30. For fuller discussion, esp. of creedal genres, see my "God Who Acts: An Old Testament Perspective," *TToday* 54 (1997) 6–18. For an earlier effort regarding the import of generalizing genres for theological formulation, see my *Suffering of God,* 24–29.

(Jonah 4:2). But such generalizing genres would seem to provide an inner-biblical basis for interpreting the God who appears in narrative.[31] They represent some kind of centering amid the Bible's theological pluralism, so that "core testimony" does have a distinctive theological value.

Brueggemann does seem aware of this genre issue at various points in his discussion. For example: "Israel does not always stay within the rhetoric of specificity... Israel transforms its testimony about Yahweh from specificity to a larger, more general claim" (*TOT*, 213). The question then becomes: What rhetorical function does this move from specifics to generalizations have within the larger narrative? And what import do the generalizing genres have for the theological interpretation of the specifics of the narrative? Brueggemann does say they are "provisional," and we can observe additions to both the historical recitals (e.g., creation in Nehemiah 9) and the more abstract confessions (e.g., divine repentance in Jonah 4:2; Joel 2:13), though their core claims remain essentially intact. But are they any more provisional than, say, the Apostle's Creed is for Christians? He cites Psalm 136 as a prime example of this generalizing move: "the concrete verbal action of Yahweh cited [in the first half of each verse] permits the larger sweeping affirmation" (*TOT*, 214). Yet the connecting *kî*, "for" (which he neglects), suggests that the move is actually more complex: God acted in this way *because* God's "steadfast love endures forever." God will be steadfast in love wherever God is speaking or acting in any such specific situation. While God's specific actions may well have given rise to such generalizations, and continue to be important to support them, the latter now become a general testimony that can be confessed apart from an immediate experience of such action (as does, say, Lam 3:22–33).

Narrative readings will continue to challenge the core confessions, probing their continuing adequacy in a "theology in process" and resisting an easy settledness. Brueggemann has attended to this challenge in particular in a way that leaves us all profoundly indebted to his work.

---

31. I lay out three criteria for discerning the "confessional" status of certain claims about God (pervasiveness, genre, and tradition) in "The Repentance of God: A Key to Evaluating Old Testament God-Talk," *HBT* 10 (1988) 47–70.

– 3 –

Confronting the Character of God
Text and Praxis
David R. Blumenthal

Text

> Therefore, impress these my words upon your heart and upon your very be-
> ing: bind them as a sign...teach them to your children...and inscribe them
> on the doorposts...to the end that your days and the days of your children
> may be many in the land that the LORD swore to your forefathers to give to
> them—as the days of heaven are over the earth. (Deut 11:18–21)

The theme that God swore to give the land to the Jewish people is firmly
entrenched in Deuteronomic theology (it occurs there more than twenty
times)[1] as well as in the prophetic writings. Later it was incorporated into
rabbinic Judaism where the passage quoted above was added to the Shema
and has been recited as part of rabbinic liturgy at least twice a day for
centuries. Several questions arise: Where does God actually swear to do
this? Why would God swear, not just promise or give God's word? How
does God swear? Is there anything else that God swears to do?

The last two questions are easier to answer: There are three linguistic
usages by which God swears: (1) *ḥay-ʾānî*, "by my life";[2] (2) *nāśāʾtî ʾet-yādî*,
"I have lifted my hand";[3] and (3) *nišbaʿ*, especially in the form, *bî nišbaʿtî*,
"I swear by myself."[4] In addition to swearing to give them the land, God
swore to sustain the Jewish people, particularly with the blessings of seed
(that is, continuous existence) and abundant sustenance.[5]

---

1. Deut 1:35; 6:10, 18, 23; 7:13; 8:1; 9:5; 10:11; 11:9, 21 (cited here); 19:8; 26:3, 15;
28:11; 30:20; 31:7, 20, 21, 23; 34:4; etc.
2. Num 14:21, 28, and 20 times in the prophets, esp. in Ezekiel.
3. Exod 6:8; Num 14:30; and four times in Ezekiel.
4. Gen 22:16 and later in Isa 45:23; Jer 22:5; 49:13.
5. Exod 6:8; 13:5, 11; 32:13 (seed); 33:1; Num 11:12; 14:17, 23; 32:11; Deut 4:31;
7:8–9, 12; 8:18; 13:18 (seed); 28:9; 29:12. The reference in Isa 54:9 is poetic and does not
correspond to the language in Genesis.

As to the roots of the theology of God swearing, a look at the sources shows that it is grounded in biblical consciousness well before Deuteronomy. The theme appears in Exodus and Numbers.[6] It is especially prominent in Numbers 14, where God takes a counteroath not to let those who followed the advice of the spies enter the land that God had previously sworn to give to the Jewish people.[7]

Since the swearing form[8] almost always invokes the forefathers, one would expect this motif to occur in Genesis, and so it does. In ensuring that his family will return his bones to the land for burial, Joseph invokes the moment when God swore: "I am going to die, but God will surely recall you and bring you up from this land to the land that God swore to Abraham, Isaac, and Jacob" (Gen 50:24). God invokes this moment when speaking to Isaac: "Do not go down to Egypt...I will be with you and I will bless you...and I will fulfill the swearing that I swore to Abraham your father" (26:2–3). Abraham, too, invokes this moment of God swearing in his instructions to his faithful servant: "The LORD, God of heaven, who took me from the house of my father and from the land of my birth and who spoke to me and who swore to me saying..." (24:7). Where does it all begin? Where does God first swear, and why?

All the references in the Torah to God having sworn to do something for the forefathers go back to one instance. Indeed, all subsequent references to God having sworn, whether in the prophets or in the rabbinic sources, go back to that same moment, forming thereby a mighty tradition.[9] The text is as follows:

> The angel of the LORD called to Abraham from the heavens a second time. He said: "The LORD has declared: 'I swear by myself that, because you have done this thing and have not held back your son, your only one, I shall surely bless you, and I shall surely multiply your seed like the stars in the heavens and like the grains of sand on the shore of the sea, and your seed will inherit

---

6. Exod 6:8; 13:5, 11; 32:13; 33:1; Num 11:12; 32:11. I note, but do not know why, this motif does not occur in Leviticus.

7. Num 14:17, 23, for God's oath to give the land; and Num 14:21, 28, 30, for God's counteroath. See also Num 32:10–12; Deut 2:14; 1:35.

8. In English one "swears an oath." In Hebrew there is a difference between an "oath" (*neder, nĕdābā*) and a "swearing" (*šĕbûʿāh* drawn from the verb, *šbʿ*). In almost all the passages cited, the Hebrew uses forms of *nišbaʿ*, and I have chosen, therefore, to avoid "oath" and to use forms of "swear."

9. A parallel tradition of God swearing to punish evildoers goes back to Numbers 14, and is developed and extended by the prophets. That is not our concern here. It does not have the same theological power precisely because it is within, and is a reflection of, what Walter Brueggemann calls "contractual theology."

the gates of their enemies. All the nations of the earth shall be blessed by your seed because you have hearkened unto my voice.' " (Gen 22:15–18)

This moment of God swearing contains the threefold blessing of seed, land, and blessedness. It is the blessing with which God and Abraham begin their journey together (Gen 12:1–3,7). Land is repeated to Abraham in the covenant of the pieces (15:18), seed and land are repeated before the covenant of circumcision (17:2, 6–8), and land is recalled by Abraham in his instructions to his faithful servant (24:7). The actual moment of God swearing is recalled by God and the threefold blessing is renewed, separately, to Isaac (26:2–5). In the complicated story of the "stolen" blessing, neither Jacob nor Esau gets the threefold sworn blessing from their father (chap. 27); it is only when he is leaving his father's home that Jacob gets the blessings of seed and land (28:3–4). Jacob finally receives the full threefold sworn blessing directly from God at Bethel (28:13–14).[10] On his deathbed, Jacob invokes the Bethel blessing and divides it among his sons, counting the first two of Joseph's sons as his own (48:3–6). With this, the threefold sworn blessing is given to the whole Jewish people, and it remains that way in biblical, rabbinic, and some Christian theology. In the foreshadowing and in each and every repetition, however, God speaks (*wayyōʾmer/ wayyōʾmar/lēʾmōr*) but God does not swear (*nišbaʿ*). Only in 22:16 does God swear. Why?

The nineteen-sentence story of the Akeda (the "binding of Isaac") is one of the richest in all human literature. It is an endless source for interpretation in commentary, in literature, and in art.[11] One can look at this story from the point of view of Isaac: Was he an innocent or a full participant? Did he agree willingly ("Father, bind me well that I not tremble") or was he a victim, bound against his will ("Who will save me from the hand of my father")?[12] Was he, in fact, sacrificed ("O, do Thou regard the ashes of Father Isaac heaped up on top of the altar, and deal with Thy children in accordance with the Mercy Attribute"), or only bound?[13] One can, and should, also look at this story from the point of view of Sarah: Was she,

---

10. On the "stolen" and "true" blessings, see Thomas Mann's *Joseph and His Brothers* (New York: Knopf, 1945).

11. See the very thorough study of Jon Levenson, *The Death and Resurrection of the Beloved Son* (New Haven: Yale Univ. Press, 1993), who mentions God swearing (141) but who missed the centrality of this swearing in the Akeda story. On art and the Akeda, see J. Milgrom, *The Akedah* (Berkeley: Bibal, 1988).

12. Midrash cited in my *Facing the Abusing God: A Theology of Protest* (Louisville: Westminster/John Knox, 1993) 181. See also Levenson, *Death*, chap. 12.

13. Midrash cited in S. Spiegel's classic study of the Akeda, *The Last Trial* (reprinted Woodstock, Vt.: Jewish Lights, 1993) 38ff. On the liturgical appeal to the merit of the binding, see my *Facing*, 290–91. See also Levenson, *Death*, chap. 14.

too, tested?[14] Did she reject Abraham for this?[15] One can look at the story from the point of view of God: What did God achieve with this test? A proof of Abraham's total loyalty and faith; yes, but is that all?

It is, however, from the point of view of Abraham that the story of the Akeda is most perplexing. Why did he do it? To prove his own utter loyalty to, and faith in, God? Perhaps; but there may be more. Elie Wiesel, remarking that God does not like human beings to come before God in resignation, sees the Akeda as a double-edged test. God starts it, but Abraham understands the true opportunity. "As though Abraham had said: I defy You, Lord. I shall submit to Your will, but let us see whether You shall go to the end, whether You shall remain passive and remain silent when the life of my son—who is also Your son—is at stake."[16] Wiesel then points to three victories Abraham achieves in this "brinkmanship with legitimated structure."[17] First, God changed God's mind and relented on the command to sacrifice Isaac. Second, God had to cancel the order Godself, as it says, "the Lord has declared."[18] Third, God had to agree that, whenever the children of Israel would be sinful, they need only retell the story to invoke God's mercy.[19] To this, I add: as it says, "I swear by Myself."

The Akeda, then, is a story of protest, of challenge to authority. Abraham's goal is to prod God beyond God's own word, to force God beyond God's own promise.[20] The purpose of the story is to record that God swore, by God's very own self, that God will always remember God's people for the threefold now-sworn blessing of seed, land, and blessedness. The Akeda is an act of "embracing of pain"—the pain of Isaac, Sarah, and Abraham; indeed, the pain of all Jewish suffering. The Akeda is also, however, an "assault on the throne of God" that once spoken, "cannot be recalled." It "pushes the relationship to the boundary of unacceptability, for the sake of

---

14. C. Thompson, "Imagining Sarah," *Kerem* (Winter 1994) 81–85; H. Gotkowitz, "A Midrash on Genesis, Chapter 22," in *Taking the Fruit* (ed. J. Zones; La Jolla, Calif.: Woman's Institute for Continuing Jewish Education, 1981) 51–58.

15. E. Umansky, "Re-visioning Sarah," in *Four Centuries of Jewish Women's Spirituality* (Boston: Beacon, 1992) 235.

16. E. Wiesel, *Messengers of God* (New York: Summit, 1976) 91.

17. W. Brueggemann, "A Shape for Old Testament Theology, II: Embrace of Pain," *CBQ* 47 (1985) 404.

18. On the interchangeability of God and God's angels, though not required in this passage, see Levenson, *Death*, 46.

19. Wiesel, *Messengers of God*, 91–93.

20. Levenson, reading with the midrash, understands that God's previous promises are rooted in God's grace while this one is rooted in Abraham's act (*Death*, 138–39). I think this is not quite the meaning; rather, the text conceives the transition as being from promise to swearing, from grace to obligation. Further, though this transition is indeed rooted in the act of the Akeda, I think it is Abraham's courage in challenging God, not his obedient loyalty, that is the key act, as Moses and others challenged God at crucial moments. Note that Num 30:3 makes it a sin to renege on something one has sworn.

a new kind of obedience rooted in faith."[21] The proof—after this, there is nothing left to say. God and Abraham never speak again.

Text

Rabbi Simeon began by saying: There are two verses. It is written, "For the Lord your God is a devouring fire" (Deut 4:24) and it is also written, "And you that cleave to the Lord your God are alive, all of you, today" (Deut 4:4). We have reconciled these verses in several places, but the companions have a [deeper] understanding of them.... Whoever wishes to understand the wisdom of the holy unification, let him look at the flame that rises from a glowing coal, or from a burning lamp, for the flame rises only when it takes hold of some coarse matter.

Come and see. In the rising flame there are two lights: one is a radiant white light and one is a light that contains black or blue. The white light is above and it ascends in a direct line. Beneath it is the blue or black light and it is a throne for the white. The white light rests upon it and they are connected together, forming one whole. The black light, [that which has] blue color, is the throne of glory for the white. And this is the mystic significance of the blue.

This blue-black throne is joined to something else, below it, so that it can burn and this stimulates it to grasp the white light.... This [blue-black light] is connected on two sides. It is connected above to the white light and it is connected below to what is beneath it, to what has been prepared for it so that it might illuminate and grasp [that which is above it].

This [blue-black light] devours continuously and consumes whatever is placed beneath it; for the blue light consumes and devours whatever is attached to it below, whatever it rests upon, since it is its habit to consume and devour. Indeed, the destruction of all, the death of all, depends upon it and therefore it devours whatever is attached to it below. [But] the white light which rests upon it does not devour or consume at all, and its light does not change. Concerning this, Moses said, "For the Lord your God is a devouring fire," really devouring, devouring and consuming whatever rests beneath it....

Above the white light rests a concealed light which encompasses it. Here is a supernal mystery and you will find all in the ascending flame. The wisdom of the upper realms is in it. (*Zohar* 1:50b–51b).[22]

The *Zohar,* a medieval theosophical work, begins this passage in classical midrashic style by showing a contradiction between two verses, one of

---

21. Brueggemann, "Embrace of Pain," 399–401.

22. Modified from F. Lachower and I. Tishby, *The Wisdom of the Zohar,* vol. 1 (trans. D. Goldstein; Oxford: Littman Library and Oxford Univ. Press, 1989) 319–20. The *Zohar,* although it exists in translation, is not comprehensible without an explication. Tishby's three volumes do that. For a shorter presentation of Tishby's method, see my *Understanding Jewish Mysticism,* vol. 1 (New York: Ktav, 1978) 101–91.

which speaks of God as a consuming fire while the other advocates cleaving to God. It goes on to draw an analogy to the common flame that is attached to dark coal, which it must consume in order to burn. The flame itself is composed of two parts: a blue-black center, which is attached to the wick or coal; and a white periphery, which encompasses and rises above the blue-black center.

According to the *Zohar,* God is made up of ten dimensions, called *sefirot* (singular, *sefira*). These *sefirot* are not extradeical hypostases, nor are they intramental attributes. Rather, they are extramental, intradeical dimensions of God's very being; that is, they are real, external to our minds, but also they are inside God's very being. Furthermore, the *sefirot* are not static; they interact with one another. Thus God's *Ḥesed* (grace) interacts with God's *Gevura* (power to draw lines, set standards, and make judgments). Thus, too, God's *Tif'eret* (compassion, mercy) draws on God's *Ḥesed* and God's *Gevura.* All three draw on God's *Ḥokma* (knowability) and God's *Bina* (intuitive understanding), as well as upon God's *Keter* (ineffability). God's *Malkut* (ruling ability) is God's Face to creation; it is the point of contact between God and creation; it is where the spiritual energy of humanity and of God interact.

In this passage, the *Zohar* depicts the central *sefira,* which is *Tif'eret,* as the white part of the flame. It rests upon the *sefira,* is the point of contact with creation, *Malkut,* here depicted as the blue-black part of the flame. At the end of this passage, the *Zohar* calls attention to the invisible part of the flame—the zone of invisible heat that surrounds every flame—and interprets it as *Keter* (God's ultimate ineffability).

Finally, the *Zohar* notes that the blue-black part of the flame, *Malkut* (God's ruling ability), consumes the coal or wick to which it is attached. The coal and wick are material; they depict creation, particularly humanity.

Having decoded the symbolism of the passage, we can address the theology.[23] The *Zohar* teaches here that God's compassion is interactive with God's providence for, or governance of, creation; there can be no flame without both a blue-black and a white light. Energy flows from compassion to governance and also from governance to compassion. God is in discussion with Godself, so to speak, on the issue of how best to act in creation. The *Zohar* also teaches here that God's very energy depends on creation; without the wick or coal there can be no flame. This means that God's providence is fed by human action and, further, that that energy is passed on even to God's compassion. To put it differently, spiritual energy gen-

---

23. For a good explication of the difference between symbol decoding and theological interpretation, see my *Understanding Jewish Mysticism.*

erated in creation rises up into God's self. This human-generated spiritual energy, according to the *Zohar,* actually sustains the dimensions of God's very being, God's providence and compassion, as the wick or coal sustains the blue-black, the white, and the invisible parts of the common flame.

Finally, the *Zohar* teaches that, for most of creation, this feeding of energy to the divine is consuming; that is, that it results in the death of created beings. This death-into-God is the purpose of most of creation and it fits well with the following midrash: "The Torah says, 'And God saw that it was very good' (Gen 1:31). The word 'very' would seem superfluous, how can the rest of God's own handiwork be anything less than 'very good'?" The word "very," then, according to the rabbis, includes death and, indeed, death is good for creation. The *Zohar* extends this and teaches that death is not only part of the natural action of God's governance, but also that death adds energy to God.

> Come and see. The only stimulus that causes the blue light to burn and to grasp the white light is that which comes from Israel, who cleave to it below.
>
> Come and see. Although it is the way of the blue-black flame to consume whatever is attached to it beneath, Israel, who cleave to it beneath, survive as they are. This is the meaning of "And you that cleave to the Lord your God are alive"...to the blue-black light that devours and consumes whatever is attached to it beneath and yet you who cleave to it survive as is written, "alive, all of you, today."[24]

Here the *Zohar* takes another theological step and identifies the stimulus that sustains the flame as being the Jewish people.[25] They, in their proper zoharic observance of the commandments, feed spiritual energy first to *Malkut* and then to *Tif'eret.* Performing the *miṣwōt* (commandments) with the proper zoharic intent allows the Jewish creature consciously to direct energy to God. It allows the Jew to interact directly with God, not just in dialogue but in interaction, in a conscious directing of spiritual energy to God. This ability to feed spiritual energy back to God through the zoharic observance of God's commandments is the height of interactivity with God. It is the purpose of Jewish existence. It gives Jews life; hence the verse from Deut 4:4 that contrasts with Deut 4:24 in which contact with the Godhead results in death.

The theology of the spiritual interaction of humanity and the dimensions of God's very being is repeated and extended in another passage.

> Rabbi Judah said: When the righteous increase in the world, the Assembly of Israel exudes a sweet perfume, and she is blessed by the Holy King and

---

24. Ibid.

25. The *Zohar* did not envision non-Jews (and Jewish women) as participating in this process.

her face shines. But, when the wicked increase in the world, the Assembly of Israel does not exude sweet perfumes, so to speak, but she tastes of the bitter "other side." Then is it written, "He has cast down earth from heaven" (Lam 2:1) and, then, her face is darkened. (*Zohar* 3:74a)[26]

To decode this passage, one must know that "Assembly of Israel" is not the Jewish people; rather, it is *Malkut* (God's face to creation). Similarly, the "Holy King" is not God but is *Tiferet* (God's compassion).[27] To "exude sweet perfume" is to radiate positive spiritual energy. To have a "face shine" is to experience joy, bliss. Finally, "earth" is *Malkut* and "heaven" is *Tiferet*.

The theology of this passage is deceptively clear. It teaches that the righteous, by their righteousness—that is, by their zoharic observance of the commandments, especially prayer—consciously return energy to God, and then God (i.e., *Malkut,* the dimension of God that governs creation) radiates positive spiritual energy and God experiences bliss (!). The new idea here is that the wicked, by their wickedness—which includes, but is not limited to, their nonzoharic observance of the commandments—return negative energy to God. This, in turn, means that God (i.e., *Malkut*) then does not radiate positive spiritual energy and does not experience bliss. Rather, when the wicked prosper, God is drawn toward the "other side," the dark side, of God's own being, and then God experiences darkness, which is absence of bliss, anger, and dangerous power. When the wicked prosper, God is fragmented; as the passage says, "earth" is separated from "heaven," that is, *Malkut* is severed from *Tiferet.* To put it succinctly: When the righteous prosper, God's governance and compassion act together and God is in bliss. But when the wicked are ascendant, God's ability to govern is severed from God's compassion, and God is subject to the dark side of God's nature and is depressed and dangerous. This is a remarkable theological statement: that God is influenced by the actions of humans, for better but also for worse; that the human capacity consciously to direct energy to God can have bad, as well as good, consequences not just in this world but also inside God.[28] As Walter Brueggemann has noted: "Thus, we need to consider not only mutations in the social processes, or mutations in the articulations of God

---

26. Tishby, *Zohar,* 364.

27. Part of the great art of the *Zohar* is that most of its passages can be read on a simple midrashic level referring to God and the Jewish people. "Texting" by double entendre is an art lost to contemporary theological writing.

28. This passage does not spell it out but other passages draw a further conclusion: that, when the wicked prosper, God actually radiates negative spiritual energy to creation, with disastrous consequences.

which serve the social processes, but *mutations that are said to be going on in the very person of God.*"[29]

Philosophical theology in the Jewish, Christian, and Islamic traditions effected a major change in the way we think. Philosophical theology introduced the God of "omni-" adjectives, of conceptuality, and of consistency.[30] In doing so, however, philosophical theology abandoned the anthropopathic language of Scripture, of midrash, of liturgy, and of the *Zohar*. Heschel fought this tendency with his emphasis on the "divine pathos"; so did Kadushin with his "normal mysticism."[31] Muffs has also taken the anthropopathic position: "By mirroring back to God His underlying love at the hour of His anger, the prophet paradoxically restores the divine balance of emotion."[32] I follow these sources and thinkers, firmly believing that the anthropopathic language of the nonphilosophical tradition is closer to the language of the sacred texts, as well as far more imaginative, truer to the full range of human experience, theologically more flexible, and liturgically more powerful.[33]

Praxis

A text and a question generated my book *Facing the Abusing God*. The text was Psalm 44. It is one of the most angry moments in biblical literature, so angry that the rabbis repressed its liturgical recitation.[34] The prevailing emotion is one of rage. One can understand this only if one reads the psalm out loud—in rage and not in good pulpit, responsive-reading style. The question was the theological nightmare of the twentieth century: Where was God during the Holocaust? There have been many answers to that question but most of them are echoes of the friends of Job—not an approved (or a good) response.

One day, while teaching Psalm 44, I asked a student to read it. After several attempts, she understood that it needed to be read with power. I asked her to read it once more, setting it in winter 1945, Auschwitz (just before the liberation). The young woman, who later became a minister, prayed it so powerfully that I could not talk when she finished. I still find it difficult to resume speech when I recall that moment. The act of praying

---

29. Brueggemann, "Structure Legitimation," 35

30. See J. C. Murray, *The Problem of God* (New Haven: Yale Univ. Press, 1964) for a concise and very positive view of this step.

31. See my *Facing*, 12, with the notes to Heschel and Kadushin.

32. Y. Muffs, "His Majesty's Loyal Opposition: A Study in Prophetic Intercession," *Conservative Judaism* 33.3 (1980) 35.

33. See my *Facing*, 252, 301.

34. *b. Soṭa* 48a, cited in *Facing*, 106.

this psalm in the context of the Holocaust is an act of "embracing pain,"[35] almost infinite pain. Praying is praxis in theology.

When lecturing on the psalms of anger before publication of the book, I used only to teach and read the text. One day, in the discussion, a psychiatrist asked, "Rabbi, are you trying to tell us God is an Abuser? If so, it will be easier on you, and on us, if you just say it outright." So I did. Abuse is the use of force that is disproportionate to whatever it is that the other is reputed to have done wrong. Parents who overreact to a child's error, men who physically or sexually abuse women, and police who brutalize criminals practice abuse. So do many others in our society. The essence of abuse is that the victim is innocent of the intensity of the force used against her or him; perhaps not totally innocent, but certainly blameless of the degree of violence utilized. If the Holocaust is excessive force, that is, violence against a people innocent of that degree of punishment—which the Holocaust was; and, if God is our God and is active in our history, not just a cosmic impersonal force—which God is; then, how did God permit the Holocaust to happen? So I said it: The Holocaust was abuse, and, in a theology of divine providence, God is an abuser. I trembled from head to toe to say it—I still do—knowing that "the unthinkable has now been thought."[36] "Truth is the seal of God."[37] Speaking truth is praxis in theology.

Part One of *Facing the Abusing God* is a theological prolegomenon, with many interesting insights, but not dangerous. Part Two is a series of texts, among them Psalm 44. This part is really very subversive but, because it is the biblical texts that speak, it "passes." Part Three is a response to the texts. It is also subversive but, because it contains some tough criticism of the central motif of the book, it too seems less dangerous than it really is. But Part Four sets out the theology of the abusing God and the proper response to that. It is terrifying. I admit that, before I sat down to write this "assault on the throne of God," I was physically ill for two days. I knew what I had to do, and did not want to do it. Even now, when I pick up the text of this section, I wonder: Did I write this? How did I have the nerve to think, write, and then publish such thoughts? Writing truth is praxis in theology.

I did write Part Four, including the inserts into the Jewish penitential liturgy. I have had Orthodox friends tell me that the book is "bad," but not really "bad" until they reach the liturgical inserts. They are right. Praying the liturgy is terrifying, each and every time I use it. "Playing brinkmanship

---

35. Brueggemann, "Embrace of Pain," 395ff.
36. Ibid., 410.
37. *b. Šabb.* 59a, dealt with in *Facing*, 237–39.

with legitimated structure"[38] is not for the weakhearted. Can you imagine bringing yourself into the presence of God Almighty and then telling God that God must ask forgiveness from us for what God has done?[39] Confronting God in thought and prayer is praxis in theology.

The book went to Westminster/John Knox, the press of the Presbyterian Church (USA). After careful consideration, they decided to "embrace this pain" and they, courageously, published the book, knowing that the conservative segment of the church would not be happy and having no idea of who would buy and read such a book.[40] Publishing truth is also praxis in theology.

The book has been reviewed almost twenty times but not often by Jews. Jewish colleagues who usually review almost everything I write have told me, "I'll get to it." Friends in the rabbinate and academy who usually follow my work have not reviewed it, or have read it and cannot finish it, or know what it is about but do not invite me to talk about it in their respective settings. Of course, there are exceptions. Some Jewish colleagues gathered at a professional meeting to discuss the book and did so with great care, even love. One local rabbi, with some courage, invited me to lecture on it. Several have indeed reviewed it, always favorably even though critically. Christian colleagues have received the book very favorably, reviewing it frequently. They have even organized several conferences on it. Somehow, Christians have had an easier time of it. Is this, perhaps, because the Jew is expected to confront God in a way the Christian is not—a vicarious theology of rage? The psychotherapeutic community, which greeted my initial presentations with enthusiasm because they legitimated rage even against God, has also fallen silent since publication of the book, at least to the best of my knowledge. I admit to being puzzled by the reaction of this group of colleagues more than the others.[41] There seems to be a general need among readers and colleagues in all areas to distance themselves from this theology. As Brueggemann has put it: "A theology of contractual coherence must excommunicate all the pained and pain-bearers as having violated the common theology.... Visible pain-bearers...assert that the legitimated

---

38. Brueggemann, "Embrace of Pain," 404.

39. "Our Father, our King, You have sinned before us.... Our Father, our King, ask forgiveness and forbearance for all Your purposeful sins" (*Facing*, 291–93); and the Christian version to be inserted into the Lord's Prayer at the proper place: "Ask forgiveness of us, as we ask forgiveness of those whom we have wronged" (*Facing*, 297, n. 21, where, by a Freudian slip, the wrong text is given).

40. When they asked me who the audience was, I responded "God." To which someone at the press demurred, "But God won't buy very many copies."

41. The most vigorous response has been from the fringe, particularly those who say that God is not abusing; he is just punishing the Jews for rejecting Jesus. I keep a file of this material.

structures are not properly functioning."[42] I like to hope that those who listen do so because, like the prophets of old, this theology "pushes the relationship to the boundaries of unacceptability"[43] while still remaining within fidelity to the covenant. Reading truth is praxis in theology.

Facing the Abusing God is really about healing. I did say that. In fact, I devoted one of the four texts and a good part of the concluding theology to this motif.[44] But no one has seen it, or at least no one has commented on it. Naming the Abuser has captured the center when, for me, it was only a step. For me, the rectilinear image of getting "beyond" rage did not seem realistic or even morally proper. Rather, the image of tacking with the wind in order to advance, as one sails a boat into the wind, was the better paradigm. One rages and protests vigorously and honestly. Then one tacks to a liturgy of joy and blessing. One turns yet again to a theology of courageous challenge. Then one tacks again to a theology of belonging and empowerment.[45] To put it differently: A sculpture must be seen from all sides and this cannot be done simultaneously but must be done sequentially; one must walk around a sculpture again and again to see it fully. Like sailing, then, seeing a sculpture is a better image of what life is, and ought to be. Healing and protest alternate in sculpting one's life, not once but repeatedly. I did write this but I should have been clearer about it, highlighted it, cited more sources, perhaps devoted a whole section to naming the Abuser as only one step toward healing.

In the rush to name the Abuser, readers have also thought that I meant to shelter humans from responsibility. Nothing could have been further from my mind, and I did state that explicitly.[46] I now use the following analogy: When I give the car keys to my teenage son and he injures someone, both he and I are responsible—in different ways, but both responsible. So it is with human affairs. Humans act and are fully responsible, even while God is ultimately also responsible. Neither party's obligations exempt the other. Again, the shock of embracing the pain overwhelmed the sense for the proper distribution of responsibility. I should have been more forceful about this, too.

The impulse to name the Abuser, or rather not to name the Abuser, led to two other objections to the book. First, many object to the anthropopathic language in general. The use of passions to describe God seems inappropriate. I made my position on this, too, clear—that I follow

---

42. Brueggemann, "Structure Legitimation," 44.
43. Brueggemann, "Embrace of Pain," 400.
44. See my *Facing,* index, s.v. "healing."
45. See ibid., index, s.v. *"seriatim."*
46. Ibid., 261–62.

scriptural, liturgical, and midrashic usage as do Heschel, Kadushin, and others[47]—but I was not strong enough in stating my views. Second, many people prefer the abstract, omnibenevolent God who cannot, and does not, do evil. Here, too, I stated my views—that such a God is, as Freud says, a projection of the human psyche, an "illusion" that we create to help us deal with a hostile universe. In its place, I suggested, together with the classic sources, a God who is capable of error, who is interactive with us, who can address us, and to whom we can speak. Instead of an "illusion," I proposed, together with the tradition, a mature understanding of our Father (Parent) and a mature understanding of ourselves.[48] This, too, however, required more argumentation.

There is one recurrent criticism of *Facing the Abusing God* that I accept, though I did, and do, respond to it as thoughtfully as I can. The analogy of the human and divine abuser implies that we should separate ourselves firmly from God as we do from human abusers; that we should not pray to an abusing God but reject such a God fully and justifiedly.[49] Some people do precisely this and, in survivors at least, such a move is understandable. Still, I have argued that the nature of covenant allows us to continue facing God, but only in protest that alternates with acceptance. Indeed, covenant requires us not to reject God but to protest as strongly as our courage will admit, as our ancestors did, and yet to remain faithful to the basic relatedness. I use the analogy of one's human parents who remain parents even if they are abusing or even if they are dead.[50] In retrospect, I understand better the objection though I still do not accept it. Writing as praxis in theology sometimes produces very uneven results, and correcting one's errors is also praxis in theology.

"At the end, when everything has been heard, fear God and observe God's commands, for this is the whole of human existence" (Eccl 12:13). Thinking the unthinkable, saying the unsayable, and praying the unprayable had a curious effect on me. It strengthened my faith. Truth really is the seal of God and living this truth was good—for God, for the Jewish people, for the covenant, and for me. It cleared the air of a terror that arose in the aftermath of the Holocaust, even though speaking that truth was itself terrifying, especially in prayer. Faith grows from being in God's presence, from being afraid to speak to God and nonetheless speaking directly and clearly the great pain we feel, always rooting ourselves within the relationship that binds us together. Covenantal love includes confronta-

---

47. See above.
48. *Facing,* 201, 257–58.
49. Ibid., 198–99.
50. See ibid., index, s.v. "God, not reject."

tion with God, indeed requires it—not for oneself, but for God, for God's people, indeed for all of God's creation.[51] Brueggemann see clearly that this is part of serious biblical piety:

> It requires deep faith, but not only deep—it requires faith of a new kind. It takes not only nerve but a fresh hunch about this God. The hunch is that this God does not want to be an unchallenged structure but one who can be frontally addressed.... The outcome of such challenge is not known in advance, until the risk is run to test the hunch... this bold speech of assault is in fact received at the throne not as disobedience but as a new kind of obedience... that this ultimately legitimated structure is indeed open to the embrace of pain, open both for Israel and for God. That can never be known theoretically. It can only be known concretely.[52]

I would agree. Confronting the character of God requires not only text but praxis of many types; otherwise, theology is only fun and games.

I agree, too, that praxis creates a new form of obedience: protest.

> The usual response [to the Holocaust] has been to blame the victim (ourselves), to exonerate the perpetrator (God), and to affirm the love of the abuser even when it is contrary to the evidence. There is [however] also a long and noble tradition of protest which does none of the above; rather, it names the event for what it is—abuse, though that word was not in the vocabulary of the liturgists and poets... and the tradition is, as Laytner has clearly displayed,[53] long and recklessly clear in its naming of abuse and its holding God responsible for the evil that has befallen us.[54]

Openness to suffering, embracing the pain of the other, and responding in protest and healing constitute the charge we are given from God; they are the focus of meaning in our lives.

---

51. See "My Faith Is Deeper Now," *Jewish Spectator* (Spring 1995) 40–43.
52. Brueggemann, "Embrace of Pain," 401.
53. A. Laytner, *Arguing With God: A Jewish Tradition* (Northvale, N.J.: Jason Aronson, 1990), reviewed by me in *Modern Judaism* 12.2 (1992) 105–10.
54. "My Faith Is Deeper Now," 40.

Part Two

God in the Torah

– 4 –

Was Everything That God Created Really Good?

A Question in the First Verse of the Bible

James Barr

Walter Brueggemann's proposal for Old Testament theology "seeks to present the faith both as in the fray and above the fray."[1] Is he a God of order or a God involved in negative elements like pain and suffering? The present essay will cover only a small area and cannot answer these large questions, but will hope to furnish something that is at least relevant to them. God's relation as creator to his world is a supremely important indicator of his character. As it happens, the first verse of the Bible—long known as a topic of controversy—may have something to contribute here.

"In the beginning God created the heaven and the earth" (KJV) is one of the great sentences of the Bible. But within its apparently simple form it conceals intriguing hermeneutical problems. There are, it seems, three main options for understanding it:

Option 1: it describes an initial act of creation, previous to the creation of light in v. 3 which is the first event of the seven-day scheme of the chapter.

Option 2: it is actually a temporal expression, something like "in the beginning of God's creating heaven and earth," and thus attached to the description of a chaotic state in v. 2.

Option 3: it is a summary of the total work of creation, placed at the beginning and followed by the detailed account that goes back over the same process of creation in seven days.

Option 1 is of great historical importance. It reads the text as follows: In the beginning God created the rude, unformed matter of the world. Verse 2 describes this chaotic state. Then from v. 3 onward God creates the *formed*

---

1. Walter Brueggemann, *Old Testament Theology* (ed. Patrick D. Miller; Minneapolis: Fortress Press, 1992) 4.

world, both creating new things (light, firmament, etc.) and using them to separate out and organize the various chaotic elements (water, darkness). This idea seems to underlie Wis 11:17, "thy almighty hand, which created the world *out of formless matter*" (NEB), and this text seems to be the key place within the biblical tradition for this approach. These concepts are fully discussed by Augustine (*Confessions* 12), for whom of course Wisdom of Solomon was fully canonical Scripture, often cited by him as proof of this doctrine.[2] This approach provides, among other things, a basic creation *out of nothing* (v. 1), and an apparent rationale for the chaos of v. 2. Option 1 was very influential in supporting traditional Christian doctrines.

Nevertheless, option 1 must be regarded as mistaken, for several reasons. First, it produces a sort of double creation: the precreation of matter, and the subsequent creation of formed things. Thus the Calvinist Archbishop Ussher dated the "beginning of time" with this precreation on the Saturday evening, followed on the first Sunday morning by the creation of light.[3] It is doubtful if there is any evidence elsewhere for any such idea of a double creation among the Hebrews of biblical times. The dramatic creation of light, on the first day, is badly spoiled if an even more remarkable act of creation, making matter out of nothing, had already taken place. Second, and more seriously, option 1 depends entirely on the distinction between matter and form inherited from the Greco-Roman world, which was probably entirely absent from the Old Testament. No biblical accounts of creation (following the Protestant canon of the Old Testament and thus excluding Wisdom of Solomon) appear to have an interest in the creation of *matter*: they are interested in the creation of distinct *things*, such as seas, stars, animals. Man was created (in part) from dust (Gen 2:7), but there seems to be no interest in how dust itself came into existence. It was common for authors to say that the Lord was the maker *of all things* (Sir 43:33, etc.), but usually, or always, they were thinking of visible and identifiable entities, not of stuff like matter or energy. At a recent discussion, we were talking about the creation of Adam and a friend pointed out that, if Adam was made from the dust, even the dust had been created by God. I doubt if this is relevant, in that, in Old Testament times (unless the very latest, which would bring us down to Wisdom of Solomon, etc.), they seem never to have thought of *the dust* as being created: it was just something that was lying around, an insignificant and worthless substance that God used for

---

2. See the copious footnotes of Augustinian quotations in the large edition of Wisdom in the Old Latin Bible: W. Thiele, ed., *Sapientia Salomonis* (Vetus Latina 11/1; Freiburg: Herder, 1977–85) 445–46 (Wis 11:17).

3. See J. Barr, "Why the World Was Created in 4004 BC: Archbishop Ussher and Biblical Chronology," *BJRL* 67 (1985) 592.

the fashioning of Adam. Third, most serious of all, option 1 fails to take account of the essential literary form of the chapter, which is dominated by the seven-day scheme and in which the dramatic command "Let there be light!" on the *first* day is clearly the *first* act of creation.

Option 1 must therefore be rejected. But, as soon as it is rejected, new problems appear, and in particular two: First, what then is the role of the chaos described in v. 2? Second, what then is the function of v. 1 itself? These considerations move us to look at option 2.

According to option 2, Gen 1:1 is really a temporal expression and the resultant meaning is something like: "In the beginning of God's creating heaven and earth, the earth was void, there was darkness over the ocean," and so on, and then God said "Let there be light." This appears in numerous modern Bible translations, either as the main text or as a marginal alternative. The first reason in its favor is that many creation stories begin in this way, thus Gen 2:4: "In the day that the Lord God made the earth and the heavens," followed by a description of the desolate state of the earth, followed by the first action taken by God. So also the Mesopotamian *Enuma Elish* begins: "When above the heaven had not been named," then a description of the desolate land, then the formation of the first gods. This is a significant consideration, though not an absolutely decisive one. Genesis 1 does not necessarily have to conform to these other patterns. In particular, we might consider this possibility: that the story in its origin did indeed conform to these patterns, so that it did at an earlier stage indeed have "in the beginning of God's creating, . . . " but that at a later stage this was altered, for reasons that will have to be determined.

Second, it is sometimes argued that the Hebrew grammar supports option 2. "Beginning" (*rē'šît*) does not have an article. Therefore, it is said, it is likely to be a construct, with a function like "in the beginning of." If this is so, the next word "create" might be handled in either of two ways: (a) revocalize as the infinitive *bĕrō'*, which is really a change of text, even if not a very drastic one; or (b) take it as a construct followed by a verb clause, "beginning of he created," as it were, which is said to have some good parallels, especially in Hos 1:2 ("beginning of the Lord spoke"). Either of these possibilities *could* be right. This, however, does not mean that they *are* necessarily right. Even the parallel in Hos 1:2 is not very convincing: the text might be questioned there too; and even if it is sound, a grammatical link that is acceptable in the unusual idiolect of Hosea is not therefore automatically plausible for the much more standard and normal diction of the stratum to which Genesis 1 belongs.

Actually, there is no grammatical evidence that "beginning" is a construct here. Since in this word, as in many others, absolute and construct are identical in form, the argument depends on the absence of the article. But one can easily show that terms for remote time and cosmic elements commonly take no article or, when they do have it, it makes no difference to meaning: so always with *qedem,* "beginning," and most tellingly with *rō'š,* "head," in the sense of "beginning," in *mērō'š,* "from [the] beginning" (Isa 41:4, 26; 48:16; Prov 18:23; Eccl 3:11; and *never* with article). One must conclude that absence of the article in this usage is normal not exceptional. There is therefore no grammatical reason to suppose that "beginning" is a construct in Gen 1:1.

One reason why option 2—which seems intrinsically unlikely—has been favored is that something like it is said by the important medieval commentator Rashi. Read it as if it was *běrō',* he advised. But many of those who have quoted Rashi in favor of option 2 have failed to quote, or to see, the reasons why he said this. Though Rashi is often esteemed as a good literal expositor, at this point he is distinctly following an allegorical line. He was involved in the typical midrashic line of argument which suggested that *šāmayim,* "heaven," was actually made up from *šām,* "there," and *mayim,* "water," giving the meaning "water is there," or even that it was made up from *'ēš,* "fire," and *mayim,* "water," meaning "fire and water [were both included in the term 'heaven']." In other words, Rashi's exegesis in this respect was not at all based on the linguistic characteristics of the text, but was a semi-allegorical attempt to deal with a theological problem: when and how was the water, later divided into two by the firmament, created? In this regard Rashi was actually arguing for a position like that of option 1: the statement of 1:1 was a sort of precreation of water (and fire?). Rashi's apparent support does not therefore provide serious justification for option 2. It is worth noting that no ancient Jewish sources—LXX, Targums, Jubilees, and (I think) Philo—show evidence of following option 2 or being influenced by it.

So we come to option 3. By option 3, Gen 1:1 is a general statement of the total work of creation, prefixed to the entire detailed account. It does not tell of something that happened *before* the creation of light on the first day, but it is a summary of the entire creative activity from 1:3 up to 2:4a. If this is so, what are the problems that arise? May it be that the prefatory verse was put there precisely in order to deal with some of these problems? As I have said, it may well be that in an earlier stage Gen 1:1—along with 1:2—was indeed a temporal expression, as option 2 maintains, but under option 3 it has been slightly altered so as to function as a summary of the whole. Or else one may simply say that 1:1 was never a temporal expression anyway but was, from the beginning, a general statement of creation as it now, in the present text, is.

What then are these problems? They lie in two areas: first, the existence, within the created world, of elements that are apparently not created; and second, the place of the dark and watery chaos of v. 2. The two questions are closely related. On the first day God created the light and separated it from the darkness. These then become alternating constituents of the world, day and night. Darkness was not created, but darkness or night is part of our world, the created world. If light was a pure creation of God, as seems the natural understanding, where did the darkness come from? Most obviously, one may say, it came from the darkness that was over the face of the deep in v. 2, in other words, from the precreation chaos. An analogous problem arises with water. Nothing is said about God creating water. In vv. 6–8 God creates the firmament that divides the waters into two segments, those above the firmament and those below. In vv. 9ff. the latter are gathered into one lot and become the seas, while the dry land is equally separated off. This is quite clear. But why was there no *creation* of the water? Most naturally, because the water came from the precreation chaos, as the darkness did. Indeed, there is no explicit creation of the *land* either. God does not, at this point anyway, bring the land or earth into being: he separates the sea from the land, so that both come into existence as discrete entities, but he does not *create* the substance of either of them. Just as the water of v. 6ff. most naturally comes from the waters of v. 2, so the land, now to be separated from the sea, comes from the land that was empty and chaotic in v. 2.[4]

There were, then, elements within the created world that were not absolutely *created*, not totally brought into being, by God. They were already in some sense there: "creation" for them meant that they were set against something different, demarcated by that other, separated. This is the keynote of the main creation narrative (Gen 1:3–2:4a): the keynote is not absolute existence, as against nonexistence, but separation into ordered relations and categories. Thus we note familiar elements such as: the different "kinds" of plants and animals; the distinction between plants and trees; the distinct functions of sun and moon; the special place of humanity, including specification of the coordinate and simultaneous creation of male and female.[5] "Creation by separation" is a good term to describe the major

---

4. I cannot take seriously the handling of this problem by Karl Barth, *Kirchliche Dogmatik*, III/1, 152. He treats the chaos of v. 2 as an "impossible possibility," not a reality. It was "the world which God had not willed and not created." Where then did the waters, which were separated by the firmament, come from? God had created another lot of water. His creation of a "separation between the waters" *implied* the creation of this water. The artificiality of this explanation is only too obvious.

5. I write "simultaneous" here because it is the common opinion for chap. 1 (though naturally not so for chap. 2). Elsewhere, however, in a paper not yet published, I argue that this

thrust of the passage. The main emphasis is not on a process from nothing to something, from nonexistence to existence, but on a process from confusion to distinction, from chaos to order. Some of the things created do appear to be absolutely created, as if out of nothing, like the light; others seem to "emerge naturally," like the plants, which the earth "brings forth"; others again seem to have been there from the beginning and simply to have been demarcated, like the land and sea. And the chaos of 1:2 seems to have been not just a negation of existence but to have been a source from which certain elements in the created world were drawn.

Now the question that next arises from this concerns the *goodness* of the world as created. It may be only a curiosity that the declaration of goodness is not made on every single day: the MT does not have it on day 2 though the LXX has it, which might be taken either way text critically, and which might be significant or might be unimportant. In any case "God saw everything that he had made, and behold it was very good" (v. 31) gives a final judgment of goodness to the whole.

Yet how much is meant by this "goodness" of creation? It seems that the created world, as it emerged from the process of creation, still contained equivocal elements. The Old Testament in general regards darkness as a negative element in comparison with light, and, though water in smallish quantities is a good thing, large masses of water—oceans, seas, and the heavenly waters—are negative and dangerous, signs of chaos. The separation of the waters by the heavenly firmament is a striking example, because it is not long before these waters overwhelm the earth in the flood of Genesis 6–8. After this there is a promise (9:11) that this will not happen again, but the fact remains that the waters were there, a dangerous and destructive element, and later on people feared that something analogous and even worse might ensue (2 Pet 3:5–7). Reversion of the earth to chaos ("waste and void," the same words as Gen 1:2, in Jer 4:23) might be feared, along with loss of light, destabilization of the earth, disappearance of all birds, and so on. When it was said that all that God made was good, did this mean that the entire universe, as created, was good, or only that the structure as set up by God was good—good in that it controlled and limited those elements that were not directly brought into existence by him?

Moreover, what exactly was meant by "good" in this context? Perhaps it has often been taken to mean "perfect," "containing no defects at all," and if so this may be too much to accept as valid. Perhaps it means something more like "satisfactory," suitable for the tasks that are required. Moreover,

---

is doubtful for chap. 1 also. This is not directly relevant for the present question; but it is relevant for the more general question, that of the relation between likely "original" meaning and final form.

there remained the question whether absolutely *everything* in the universe could be regarded as "good"—poisons, for instance, or the organisms that created disease and plague, were they really "good"? To this the probable answer is that the writers had not thought of such a problem. To them creation was the creation of visible and tangible entities like sun and moon, trees, sheep and cows. Disease was not a "thing" in the same sense.

This was one of a series of antinomies that the first chapter of Genesis presented, in comparison with some other parts of the Hebrew Bible. All that God created was good: there was, it seems, no evil in it, no fault. But elsewhere the story was different:

> I form light and create darkness
> I make peace and create evil. (Isa 45:7)

Or:

> Does evil befall a city
> and the LORD has not done it? (Amos 3:6)

In Isaiah, God "creates" darkness as well as light; in Genesis 1, all that God creates or "does" is good; but in Isaiah and Amos, God creates evil also. These are not necessarily contradictions, but they could certainly form puzzles to the average reader, difficulties that redactors might wish and seek to overcome.

These then are issues that the core of Genesis 1 did not fully clarify. To them can be added another, a very obvious, question: What about death? In Genesis 1 God creates living beings, animal and human; he gives them life and asks them to multiply. There is no explicit mention of death. Does this mean that they are, all alike, to go on living forever? If so, and if they multiply as required, they will surely soon fill the earth! "God did not make death," wrote Wis 1:13, doubtless meditating upon Genesis, for Genesis 1 said nothing about the creation of death, and so, he went on, "he created all things for Being" (*ektisen gar eis to einai ta panta*). But is it realistic to think that Genesis 1 contemplated a world in which there was absolutely no death, in which not only every human, but every animal and insect would live forever? God in the Old Testament is indeed a God of life, but can that really mean that all beings should live forever, without limit? Hardly so, for the Old Testament itself expresses a quite contrary other side. God is also portrayed as the author of death; indeed some passages mention his causing death before they mention his giving life: "I kill and I make alive" (Deut 32:39; a boast of difference as against the other, inactive, gods); "the LORD kills and makes alive" (1 Sam 2:6, in Hannah's song). Particularly important is Ps 104:27–30, because it is a sort of creation story, perhaps of earlier provenance than Genesis 1, and it makes clear that it is normal for God to bring about death.[6] When God takes away the breath of the living creatures they die and return to their dust, and when he sends forth his Spirit they are restored (literally "created"). This last depicts what is normal: living things have life, but in the end God takes away that life. God is the giver of life, but he does not give life without limit: the limitation of life is assumed as normal in the culture of the Old Testament. Thus there is a whole dimension of creaturely existence that is not made explicit in Genesis 1.

Taken as a general hermeneutical problem, where does Genesis 1 stand in relation to people's beliefs? As I have argued, the main structure of the chapter is built upon the seven-day scheme. That scheme, however, is based upon separation and demarcation rather than on mere existence as against nothingness. One way to go is to say that this is the true biblical emphasis: Genesis is interested in an organized world, as against a chaotic world, and not in the metaphysical question of something against nothing. On the basis of Genesis alone, one could argue that creation out of nothing is not a biblical interest—not, at least in the (Protestant) canonical books. The strongest expression of creation out of nothing would appear to be 2 Macc 7:28: "God did not make them out of things that existed" (*ouk ex ontōn epoiēsen auta ho theos*)—another passage much cited in the ancient church.[7] The mother of the seven martyred sons uses the argument from the mysterious creative acts of God to give confidence in the hope of resurrection and new life. But the emphasis on creation *out of nothing* is seldom seen in the older Hebrew books of the Old Testament. This does not necessarily mean that it is negligible, as we shall see in a moment.

It seems to me likely that the very first verse of the Bible was a deliberate expression that sought to overcome some of these problems. We may perhaps accept that probably at an earlier stage it had been a temporal expression: In the beginning of God's creating the heaven and the earth, there was a chaos (as described), and then God said "Let there be light." But, whether this was so or not, the first verse as it now stands is a transformation of that into a different function. First, it has the important function of a summary that states the full reality in brief and lapidary style: this is what

---

6. I once talked about this subject to a rather conservative Christian audience and was a little nervous that they would be critical of this argument, on the ground that by orthodox doctrine death came in as a result of sin, and I would be damaging this conviction by suggesting that death must have been there all the time. I was saved from such opposition, however, by a good professor there present, who pointed out that, after the offense of Adam and Eve, God had made them clothes of skins, which must have come from dead animals, proving that death must have been in the world even before Adam's fall. Genesis has resources to deal with every problem!

7. There is a further question here: Should we understand "God did not make them out of things that existed" or "God made them out of things that did not exist"? The two possibilities are recognized by a version like RSV. Perhaps it is significant, perhaps not.

we are going to tell you, in essence: God created the heaven and the earth. The seven-day narrative that is the main body of text is systematic but also has a certain diffuseness about it in places: not everyone is equally interested in the difference between the plants that produce seed according to their kinds and the trees that bear fruit containing seed according to their kinds. This kind of detail is held together and made relevant on the larger scale by the fact that the reader already knows, from v. 1, that this is the story of God's total creation. Even when we come to the end of the passage, at 2:4a, even the fine summary with which it closes is immensely strengthened by the fact that the essential point was already announced in 1:1.

Second, the verse does something to defuse the problem of the chaos of v. 2. Though the story may well have begun, at an earlier stage, with a perception of the chaos, such a start to the most important creation story of the Bible and to the Pentateuch as a whole might have seemed improper. Better, surely, to begin with God's great action of creation. As I have said, I think it a misunderstanding to suppose that God first created the chaotic elements and then out of these made the ordered world; but that misunderstanding is a not unreasonable development out of the motivation that did lie behind the present form of the first verse. What actually happened was that the chaos was made less prominent and its problems less pressing. The chaos could not easily be eliminated, after all, because it was needed: needed as the source for the darkness and the waters that appear in the core of the seven-day story.

That this kind of adjustment of the story could have taken place is indicated by the rewriting of it as found in Jubilees 2. This has the seven-day scheme as in Genesis but it claims twenty-two distinct acts of creation in all, seven of them falling on the first day. These were: the heavens; the earth; the waters; the angelic spirits (of various kinds); the chaos and darkness; evening and night; and light, dawn and day. In other words, Jubilees has solved the problem by pulling in the heaven and earth of Gen 1:1, the waters, chaos, and darkness of v. 2, and placing them within the first day of creation along with the actual light or day of v. 3, adding in the angelic spirits (about which Genesis had said nothing and which were clearly felt to be an omission).

It is often said that the entire universe was corrupted through the sin of humanity. Is there biblical evidence of this? The New Testament has passages like Rom 8:21–23: creation is in "bondage to decay," it "groans in travail" for redemption. There may well be evidence in the Old Testament, say in prophetic passages, that is relevant (e.g., in depictions of a future return to paradise as in Isaiah 9 and 11). But is there evidence in Genesis? In particular, does the creation story of Genesis show any awareness of this interest? When it says that God saw all his work, that it was good, is this something that was to be changed when humanity fell into disobedience? If so, it seems to have us in a cleft stick! For, if the goodness of creation was destroyed through human sin, then how does it help us to know that creation was (originally) good but no longer is so?

I have already talked about a possible "double creation," produced through an interpretation of Genesis 1 by option 1. There is, however, another sort of double creation, produced by the story of Noah and his flood. Noah's flood has an effect on our assessment of Genesis 1. For, clearly, the "goodness" of the creation in Genesis 1 did not prevent the overwhelming of the world by the flood. But the world we live in is in many ways more Noah's world than Adam's world. Adam's world was vegetarian and no animal flesh was eaten; the killing of animals was unheard of. With Noah's world the killing of animals becomes normal. The only restriction is that blood must not be consumed. Moreover, bloodshed perpetrated upon humans, whether by animal or by humans, is to be punished by blood (Gen 9:5–7), because man was made in the image of God. All existing humans, according to the biblical picture, are descendants of Noah: all others were wiped out. Now it is with Noah's flood that we do hear of the corruption of "the earth"—Gen 6:11–12. But that corrupt world is destroyed: we do not hear that it continues so after the flood. Thus we have two paradoxes: On the one hand the goodness of Adam's world does not prevent the corruption of the world in Noah's time, which suggests that we cannot rely too heavily on that goodness of the original world; on the other hand the corruption of Noah's time seems to be expiated in the flood, so that it is no longer to be considered, at least as normal, thereafter. So there is definitely an uncertainty how far the "goodness" of the world as first created provides an assurance for things long afterward.

Two basic religious questions seem to emerge from this. First, how far does the "goodness" of the created world, as emphasized in Genesis 1, constitute a basis for religious confidence by which to live? There is no doubt that the goodness of the world has been an important part in traditional Christianity (and Judaism), and some forms of theology and piety could be said to be entirely centered in that goodness of creation. But is this aspect meant to be so totally relied on? The world of Genesis 1 appears to contain certain partial exceptions. Jon Levenson refers to the belief in the total perfection of the original created world as only a "gross overgeneralization from the conventional optimistic reading of Genesis 1."[8] The

---

8. Jon D. Levenson, *Creation and the Persistence of Evil* (San Francisco: Harper & Row, 1988) 50.

issue involved in this is one that our religious traditions have not adequately faced.[9]

Second, we come back to the theme of creation out of nothing. We have seen that this is not the main theme of Genesis 1, and perhaps of any canonical Old Testament passage. In Genesis, some things, like light, are created out of nothing; others, like land and water, seem to be there already. If so, we may say that creation out of nothing is not a central affirmation of the passage. Traditional theology, I have suggested, affirmed it mainly through exegesis by option 1 and dependence on documents that are now (for Protestants) noncanonical. Is creation out of nothing, then, only a piece of unthinking theological conservatism? Not necessarily. There may be another side. Professor Maurice Wiles wrote a decade ago that, for a doctrine of creation to be meaningful, it must be creation out of nothing, for only this answers the question, Why should there be anything at all?[10] Why should there be a world? Why should there not be just God himself? What does it mean that he chose to create a world such as we live in? This might mean that, if a doctrine of creation is to be meaningful, it has to extend itself beyond the limits of a strict exegesis of Genesis 1, and include a wider range of considerations. Possibly, one may suggest—just possibly, not more—that the existence of the first verse of the Bible, in the form in which we now have it, is an indication that the tradition of Israel was already moving in its thinking in this same direction. To say that Genesis actually asserted creation out of nothing, by option 1 in its traditional form, is wrong; but to see that Gen 1:1 provides a pointer in that direction, when taken more sophisticatedly, is perhaps very suggestive. As an exercise in hermeneutical complications, the whole matter is of great interest.

It is a pleasure to dedicate these thoughts as a mark of appreciation to Walter Brueggemann for his catholic interest in the problems of biblical theology and his support to all the rest of us who work in the same area.

---

9. For fuller discussion in a wider context, see my Gifford Lectures, *Biblical Faith and Natural Theology* (Oxford: Clarendon, 1993) 179ff.

10. M. F. Wiles, *God's Action in the World* (London: SCM, 1986) 16: "Creation is creation out of nothing or it is nothing. An indispensable element in any contemporary defence of theistic belief is the sense of mystery as to how it comes about that there is anything at all."

– 5 –

Genocide's Lament

Moses, Pharaoh's Daughter, and the Former Yugoslavia[1]

Nancy C. Lee

Was there one moment when the woman
who's always lived next door turned stranger to you?
...Did the way she laughed, or shook out her mats make you
suddenly feel as though she'd been nursing a dark side to her difference,
and bring that word, in a bitter rush to the back of the throat
   —*Croat/Muslim/Serb*—
the name, barbed, ripping its neat solution through common ground?
...One morning, will you ignore her greeting....
And as they drive her away, will her face be unfamiliar, her voice, bearable:
a woman crying from a long way off?[2]

Unbearable was the sound of the baby's crying in the ears of Pharaoh's daughter—she, an Egyptian. Unbearable not because it pierced the silence of the imposed ban on Hebrew babies, but unbearable because the child was suffering. With compassion and recognition she said, "this must be one of the Hebrews' children" (NRSV). Refraining from using the term *Hebrew* derisively, she rejects her father's propaganda about this other people and risks her own welfare. In easy defiance she reaches down and spares his life, standing on common ground with the child, as though nothing were at stake, as though *everything* were at stake. Pharaoh's daughter symbolizes a

---

1. This paper was completed as part of a 1996/97 Fulbright Fellowship in Croatia and originally presented to the National Association of Professors of Hebrew group at the 1996 SBL annual meeting. I am grateful to be able to express a measure of my profound debt and appreciation to my teacher, Walter Brueggemann, and my appreciation to colleagues in the former Yugoslavia for their inspiration, especially Marija Koprivnjak and Dr. Davor Peterlin at Evangelical Seminary in Osijek.
2. Selection from "Striking Distance," by Carole Satyamurti in *Klaonica: Poems for Bosnia* (ed. K. Smith and J. Benson; Newcastle upon Tyne: Bloodaxe Books, 1993) 110–11. *Klaonica* means "slaughterhouse" in Croatian and Serbian.

recurring theme in the Bible: a human or messenger of God acts on behalf of a child in jeopardy and embodies God's response to lament.[3]

Recent feminist readings have aptly noted the activity of women, including Pharaoh's daughter, in the Exodus story.[4] With a sociological reading, however, I aim to propose that, beyond gender roles and beyond understanding Exodus as Israel's paradigmatic story of lament[5] and redemption, Exodus 1–2 also treats the sociopolitical reality of a people threatened with genocide.[6] Can this text provide a "model" for illuminating and responding against genocide? This study finds that an answer in the affirmative is not easily granted. Yet the matter is urgent. The time is late. As the century draws to a close, across haunting landscapes, including Bosnia and Croatia, entire villages sit ruined and silent, once full of people. I offer a reading of Exodus in light of the context of the recent war and genocide in the former Yugoslavia, by an outsider-in-residence. I will include texts from voices there that show parallels to the Exodus story.[7]

This essay has two purposes: (1) to consider Exodus 1–2 as a hopeful

---

3. Children in jeopardy in the Bible include Ishmael, Isaac, Joseph, Moses, and with Elijah, the unnamed son of the unnamed Phoenician widow of Zarephath. Jesus is in jeopardy at his birth, and extrabiblically the prophet Muhammad is endangered when bereft of his parents. The horrible exception of Jephthah killing his daughter is all the more tragic because of the larger biblical emphasis upon the esteem of children and the theme of their rescue (though this is not to overlook the Bible's patriarchal favoritism toward sons). I shall return to this tragic theme below as it occurs in Exodus.

4. See Phyllis Trible, "The Pilgrim Bible on a Feminist Journey," *Princeton Seminary Bulletin* 11 (1990) 237–39; Renita J. Weems, "The Hebrew Women Are Not Like the Egyptian Women: The Ideology of Race, Gender and Sexual Reproduction in Exodus 1," *Semeia* 59 (1992) 25–34; J. Cheryl Exum, " 'You Shall Let Every Daughter Live': A Study of Exodus 1:8–2:10," *Semeia* 28 (1993) 63–82; and *A Feminist Companion to Exodus–Deuteronomy* (ed. Athalya Brenner; Sheffield: Sheffield Academic Press, 1994).

5. While the Hebrews' cry of suffering in Exodus was not directed to God (as in lament psalms), the story suggests the paradigm of human cries answered by God that later takes the shape of *lament* psalms or prayer. This paper will use the term "lament" to refer both to expressions of suffering that appeal directly to God and to expressions that merely voice suffering and grief. This distinction is of paramount importance in the book of Lamentations.

6. Brevard Childs labeled Pharaoh's policy to have the people kill all Hebrew baby boys as "the genocide tradition" (*The Book of Exodus* [OTL; Philadelphia: Westminster, 1974] 10). More recently see Zev Garber, *Shoah: The Paradigmatic Genocide* (Lanham: Univ. Press of America, 1996); idem, ed., *Genocide: Critical Issues of the Holocaust* (Los Angeles: Simon Wiesenthal Center, 1983).

7. I gathered these texts in the former Yugoslavia in the year after the war ended. They are not intended to reconstruct historical events of the war. For various views, see the following works: Laura Silber and Allan Little, eds., *Yugoslavia: Death of a Nation* (New York: TV Books, 1995); Robert J. Donia and John V. A. Fine, *Bosnia and Hercegovina: A Tradition Betrayed* (New York: Columbia Univ. Press, 1994); Branka Magaš, *The Destruction of Yugoslavia: Tracking the Break-up 1980–92* (London: Verso, 1993); Noel Malcolm, *Bosnia: A Short History* (New York: NYU Press, 1994); Roy Gutman, *A Witness to Genocide* (New York: Macmillan, 1993); Michael A. Sells, *The Bridge Betrayed: Religion and Genocide in Bosnia* (Berkeley: Univ. of California Press, 1996). Reading the biblical text with a concern for inhabitants of the former Yugoslavia does not preclude the need to undertake the same task in relation to other peoples suffering genocide, where there may be contextual parallels.

paradigm for *human response to genocide;* and (2) to highlight what is rarely suggested: that in the book of Exodus (4:21–23; 11:4–8; 12:12–30) *the divine response to genocide*—the killing of Egyptian firstborn children—is highly problematic ethically, limited by ancient social practices, open to dangerous application, and should finally be critiqued rather than glossed over in this paradigmatic story.

The Paradigm of Human Response to Genocide

Exodus 1–2 presents four key social elements important for the human task of interpreting and responding against genocide. First, Exodus presents a *critique* of a certain social arena in which a political leader employs rhetoric to cast aspersions upon another people (Exod 1:9–10), imagining them as a threat, making them a scapegoat and object of oppression (1:11–14).[8] Brevard Childs notes Calvin's insight that Pharaoh actually uses only "an alleged threat" as rationale for his policy against the Hebrews. Pharaoh's rationale "turns on a series of hypothetical situations: 'Were they to continue to multiply, and were enemies to come . . . then if the Hebrews were to join them. . . . ' "[9] Moreover, Renita Weems points out that Pharaoh exploits alleged racial/ethnic, gender, and biological "differences" between the Hebrews and Egyptians.[10] Umberto Cassuto suggests that it is the Hebrews' prosperity and increase that arouse Pharaoh's envy and hatred, such that he stirs up his own people's fears against them.[11]

As a result of Pharaoh's rhetoric and policy, the Egyptians come to "dread" the Hebrews (1:12).[12] Pharaoh's paranoid scapegoating of the Hebrews, then, is the ground for his policy of genocide; to implement it, he implicates his own people and believes he will have their support in carrying it out (1:22). For all this, however, Pharaoh cannot eradicate the perceived menaces to his power and people. Pharaoh's name is never given; he is a "type" whose portrait foreshadows politicians today using genocide (see below).

Theologian Miroslav Volf's *Exclusion and Embrace,* written within the context of the 1991–95 war in the former Yugoslavia, treats the phe-

---

8. Cf. Herod's analogous actions against Jesus in Matthew 2.

9. Childs, *Exodus,* 15.

10. Weems, "Hebrew Women," 28, 30.

11. Cassuto, *A Commentary on the Book of Exodus* (trans. I. Abrahams; Jerusalem: Magnes, 1967) 9. J. G. Williams uses a Girardian analysis of Exodus to analyze the scapegoating in *The Bible, Violence, and the Sacred* (San Francisco: HarperSanFrancisco, 1991).

12. That a climate of dread preoccupies Egyptian society is perhaps suggested by its rhetorical location at the center of the large *inclusio* in Exod 1:11–14, as noted by Exum, "You Shall Let Every Daughter Live," 44–45.

nomenon of scapegoating there within larger ideologies of ethnoreligious "exclusion," practiced not only among ordinary people, but by some intellectuals, politicians, and religious leaders.

> "Economists" [give] accounts of present exploitation and great economic potentials; "political scientists" add the theme of the growing imbalance of power, of steadily giving ground, of losing control over what is rightfully ours; "cultural anthropologists" bring in the dangers of the loss of identity; ... "politicians" pick up all four themes and weave them into a high-pitched aria about the threats to vital interests posed by the other who is therefore the very incarnation of evil.[13]

Paul Mojzes notes also the practice of some journalists and media in the former Yugoslavia to support political leaders by creating "a barrage of misinformation" and waging a "vitriolic campaign against alleged 'enemies.'"[14] Such rhetoric creates rather than critiques a social arena in which scapegoating becomes acceptable and lays the necessary groundwork for genocide.

A second key social element in Exodus 1–2 is the response of the oppressed to Pharaoh's ideology: the human expression of suffering in *"lament" speech* (2:23–25), not only to evoke God and the human community to intervene and alleviate suffering but also to critique the unjust actions of the oppressor. Claus Westermann and Walter Brueggemann have brought the biblical lament tradition to the fore in scholarship in recent years.[15] Brueggemann especially has noted the contemporary neglect of lament as a form of speech in society and in liturgy (in lectionaries and where "praise" hymns predominate):

> We have yet to ask what it means to have this form [lament] available in the social construction of reality. What difference does it make to have faith that permits and requires this form of prayer?...[A] theological monopoly is re-enforced, docility and submissiveness are engendered, and the outcome in terms of social practice is to re-enforce the political-economic...status quo....In regularly using the lament form, Israel kept the justice question visible and legitimate. It is this justice question in the form of lament that energizes the Exodus narrative. Indeed, it is the cry of Israel...which mobilizes Yahweh to action that begins the history of Israel. The cry initiates history.[16]

---

13. M. Volf, *Exclusion and Embrace* (Nashville: Abingdon, 1996) 57, 88.

14. P. Mojzes, *Yugoslavian Inferno: Ethnoreligious Warfare in the Balkans* (New York: Continuum, 1994) 55–58, 69–70.

15. E.g., C. Westermann, *Praise and Lament in the Psalms* (trans. K. Crim and R. N. Soulen; Atlanta: John Knox, 1981); idem, *Lamentations: Issues and Interpretation* (trans. C. Muenchow; Minneapolis: Fortress Press, 1994); W. Brueggemann, "The Costly Loss of Lament," *JSOT* 36 (1986) 57–71; idem, *Israel's Praise* (Philadelphia: Fortress Press, 1988); idem, "The Book of Exodus," *NIB* (Nashville: Abingdon, 1994) 1:683–707.

16. Brueggemann, "Costly Loss," 59–63.

Building on Brueggemann's work, Samuel Balentine has recently connected the neglect of lament by Western and European biblical scholars (and churches) in the early part of the twentieth century to their highly tragic failure to respond against genocide in World War II.[17]

Given these arguments, have biblical scholars, theological educators, liturgists, and clergy changed their stances regarding lament since World War II and in the present context of genocide in the former Yugoslavia? While this matter must be examined, another question is posed: Have the voices of the people suffering injustice and genocide in the former Yugoslavia been raised? Indeed, hundreds of poems and accounts of suffering were composed by people in the war, many of whom were driven from their homes, but only a few were translated for the print media and rarely given voice in international electronic media.[18] Borislav Arapović of Hercegovina in 1991 described the siege of the city of Osijek in Croatia in his poem "Telefax from Croatia":

> night midnight fire slaughter hell
>
> ....
> ...993580......991202.......991212........
> ...dialing........dialing........dialing..........
> ...london........paris..........stockholm.....
> ...helsinki......washington...new york......
> ....
>
> —lines dead—no connection—
>
> but I would like to transmit to them by fax
> the zigzag flight of the frightened starlings
> disoriented by bullets from planes
> and the city pigeons' hoarse cooing
> between thundering explosions
> and the nightly crashing of growling mortar shells
> through the roofs into streams of blood
> and the flight of rats from fleeing feet
> through moldy cellars
> —once the sky was our ally
> —now it's the netherworld
> then the bloodied kitten's meows
> sniffing along a glass-strewn street....

17. S. Balentine, *Prayer in the Hebrew Bible* (OBT; Minneapolis: Fortress Press, 1993) 3–12, 24–259.

18. See the acknowledgments in *Klaonica* for some of the periodicals that ran war lament poetry. See also *U ime oca...zbornik duhovne poezije nastale u danima rata u Hrvatskoj* [*In the name of the Father....A collection of spiritual poetry created during days of war in Croatia*] (ed. Danko Tomanić; Sisak: MG "Getsemani," 1992) [in Croatian]. With regard to the number of poems, Brueggemann's book *Finally Comes the Poet* (Minneapolis: Fortress Press, 1989) strikes one as prophetic.

and the labor of a birthing mother in a hospital on fire
and holes in the children's clinic walls
and voices never born
and a head without eyes
and legs without arms
and arms without legs. . . .
hurriedly frenetically leafing searching turning
....
...99472.......99396........993170.......99422...... . . .
...dialing.oslo.rome........the hague........prague.........
...budapest.....bucharest...brussels......vienna.....
...bern..........berlin........bonn.........and all....
...the baals.and.gods of this world....................
....

not a sound—no connection

oh God in Heaven
is there a fax anywhere
from madrid to moscow
that is not blocked by traders' quotes
assailed by lies of our killers
that could receive the message
from a shelter full of dread
from a deathly silent classroom

osijek croatia september 17 1991[19]

Another voice of lament was that of Marija Koprivnjak, who fled from Mostar when the war shifted from Croatian territory into Bosnia. Moved by her own reading of the book of Lamentations, her poems from May 1992 directly address a personified Bosnia and Mostar. Like the poet of Lam 2:13, she speaks to her destroyed city, Mostar, that needs comforting; and mourning its suffering, she encourages it, remarkably, to remember the biblical text.

"MOSTAR, THE VUKOVAR OF HERCEGOVINA"

To Mostar—my beloved town,
    about whom Ivo Andrić said, long ago,
    "town of sun and light."
Where is your light now?
The dark clouds of war,
    destruction and decay have covered you.
And could not God find even ten righteous men within your walls
    for whose sake he would save you from this evil?
My town of spring flowers, of beautiful blossom and scented rose!

---

19. "Telefaks iz Hrvatske," in *Ratni blagoslovi* [*War blessings*] (ed. Marija Koprivnjak; Osijek: Izvori, 1996) 28–31 [in Bosnian/Croatian]. Poem translated by Ivana and Marc Jerić.

The beauty of spring is now cloaked in black. It weeps and sobs.
Who cares now for the words of your great poet, Aleks Santić,
     whose birthplace was until recently the meeting place
     of God's people of all nations,
     and which is now being looted by lawless men?
Your son Aleks wrote, in truth, that we are all brothers,
     three nations—three branches—of one tree.
See—within you brother has risen up against brother....
Mostar, my beloved town!
Can you find anywhere words of encouragement, comfort, and hope?
You will find them in God's word, which says:[20]

> He has made my teeth grind on gravel,
>   and made me cower in ashes;
> My soul is bereft of peace;
> I have forgotten what happiness is;
> So I say, 'Gone is my glory,
>   and all that I had hoped for from the LORD.'
> The thought of my affliction and my homelessness
>   is wormwood and gall!
> My soul continually thinks of it
>   and is bowed down within me.
> But this I am calling to mind,
>   and therefore I am hoping:[21]
> The steadfast love of the LORD, indeed, has not ceased,
>   his mercies have not ended;[22]
>   they are new every morning;
>   great is your faithfulness.
> "The LORD is my portion," says my soul,
>   "therefore, I am hoping in him."[23]
> The LORD is good to those who wait for him,
>   to the soul that seeks him.
> Good (to the one) that is hoping—at peace—[24]
>   for the salvation of the Lord." (Lam 3:16–26).[25]

---

20. NRSV followed here, except where noted. It is obviously different from the Croatian Bible translation, *Biblija* (Zagreb: Kršćanska Sadašnjost, 1994).

21. Author's translation of the Hebrew imperfect form of *yḥl* (cf. v. 18).

22. The translation reflects a shift in the Hebrew here to the perfect form of the verb.

23. Imperfect of *yḥl* once again.

24. The phrase "at peace" translates the Hebrew *wĕdûmām* as a *Qal* participle from *dmm* and follows the suggestion of the Croatian translation, which renders *miru* "peace," "quiet," or "calm" (see Ps 131:2) rather than the verb's other connotation of "silence." The poet(s) of Lamentations has been anything but silent. Having voiced his or her complaint and finally hope in God's love and mercy, the poet experiences a state of still calm or peace, while waiting for God's larger intervention. Cf. this with v. 17 just above: "my soul is bereft of peace [*šālôm*]."

25. Marija Koprivnjak, ed., *Ratni blagoslovi* [*War blessings*] 138–39; poem translated by Janet Berković and Ružica Pađen; first published in the religious magazine *Izvori* (1992) 10.

As in the Bible, women in the former Yugoslavia have played an important role in expressing mourning songs or dirges.[26] Kata Šolji, a mother from Vukovar, Croatia, lost four sons in the war and lamented:

> Into the Danube, Mother, throw the white flower,
> Let the whole world know, down the length of the river
> Of your grief and of your pain....
> Decorate the unknown grave of your children![27]

The laments of children in the former Yugoslavia have been rarely expressed. Some of their voices were finally published in *The Suitcase: Refugee Voices from Bosnia and Croatia:*

> "WHY ME?"
> (by Majana, Burazovic, 12 years old,
> of Bosnia-Hercegovina, March 1995)

> Sometimes I ask myself:
> ... Why am I the one to whom it is normal
> to see dead bodies on the street and the one
> who in the cellars listens to
> the sound of bombs....

> Why am I the one who has to queue in the street
> for a tin and the one whose bed
> is a thin blanket on a cold floor? ...[28]

The siege of cities in the former Yugoslavia was indiscriminate in taking lives. In the eight-month siege of the ancient Croatian town of Dubrovnik on the Adriatic in 1991 and 1992, the first death was of the Serbian poet Milan Milišić. During the siege, Catholic Bishop Želimir Puljić and other priests spoke to the people by radio while shells fell on the town.[29] The following excerpts reveal their laments in both prayer and sermon:

> In this sleepless night, while we are still shocked by everything that is hap-
> pening around us, and while we are trembling at the thought of how we will
> live through it all until tomorrow, I am thinking about all of you, praying

---

26. Biblical figures include Miriam, Deborah, Jephthah's daughter, the mourning women with Jeremiah, and Rachel. In Montenegro Orthodox women still perform ritual mourning songs; Muslim women in the former Yugoslavia still lead funeral songs; and in parts of Croatia in this century, women sang lament psalms from memory in Catholic church services. Moreover, during the war, a women's group in Belgrade called "Women in Black" has been active, symbolically expressing the connection between their grief and social protest.

27. From "I Forgive the Enemy, but I Cannot Forget the Pain!" *Izvori* 3/4 (1996) 32.

28. *The Suitcase* (ed. Julie Mertus, Jasmina Tesanovic, Habiba Metikos and Rada Boric; Berkeley: Univ. of California Press, 1997) 136.

29. The radio addresses of Bishop Puljić, as well as poetry by Luko Paljetak, were later recorded and performed with a musical composition in "The Truth About the City of Liberty" (CD-D-K 5065098, HDS/BIEM Hrvatska naklada zvuka i slike, Croatia Records, 1995; music by Đelo Jusić).

for you, sharing all the pain, anxiety, hardship, and misfortune in this time of
our great national distress. I feel all the more that we have both as individuals
and as a people immersed in the mystery of the Cross.... We are cut off from
the world; there are no telephone or television links. But we are not cut off
from heaven.

> ...Take heart! Pray to God and cry for help!
> Have faith in Christ! Place your trust in him!
>
> Forgive them, God, for they know not what they do!
> You be the judge, you hold the sword!
> Look down on us from up above,
> Have mercy on our pain and cries,
> Turn your eternal and kind eyes,
> And give us faith, love and strength.[30]

While human lament and divine hearing and intervention may be a
central emphasis in Exodus (2:23–25), a third social element appears.
Individuals appear who take bold action to intervene with help for the
children in jeopardy,[31] to derail the dictator's dreadful train of genocide.
They may be "insiders" within the oppressed ethnoreligious community,
like the Hebrew midwives, Miriam, and Moses' mother, Jochebed. Or they
may be "outsiders," like Pharaoh's daughter, not part of the oppressed
community.[32] She must cross dangerous social and ethnic boundaries to
help, regardless of her father's pervasive policy. Her radical action cannot be overstressed. In the ancient Near East, this common literary figure
who reaches out to save the child in jeopardy is not depicted as belonging to a different ethnic group, rarely is it a figure of royalty, and rarely
a woman.[33] In Exodus 1–2 individual insiders and outsiders are united in

---

30. Ibid. Excerpts from sermons and prayers by Bishop Puljić.

31. See Donald Redford, "The Literary Motif of the Exposed Child," *Numen* 14 (1967)
209–28; also the infancy legends in Louis Ginzberg, *The Legends of the Jews* (7 vols.;
Philadelphia: JPS, 1909–38) 2:262–72.

32. Exod 1:1–8 implies that in the earlier time of Joseph, ethnic division between Hebrews
and Egyptians was not problematic. Likewise, in the former Yugoslavia, ethnoreligious identity and divisions were not such a grave issue as they have become just before and during
the recent war. Indeed, "multiethnic" families were common and communities mixed. Nonetheless, lingering grievances about historical injustices, especially twentieth-century sufferings
(ethnic division and fighting caused by World War II and the rise and fall of communism) left
serious divisions suppressed; see P. Mojzes, *Yugoslavian Inferno*, 45–124.

33. The figure who rescues the child is usually a shepherd, some powerless figure, or even
an animal (Redford, "Literary Motif," 225–26). Note the pattern of insiders and outsiders
crossing boundaries in Exodus: Pharaoh's daughter; Miriam, by boldly approaching Pharaoh's
daughter; Moses, as an Egyptian intervening for his Hebrew kindred, then as a Hebrew for the
Midianite women. Brueggemann's comment is apropos: "One becomes an outsider by making
choices to continue as savior on the side of the marginated, in order to break the cycles of
brutality" ("Exodus," 705).

saving lives. Since God is still behind the scenes, it is primarily through these boundary-breaking figures that the deity responds against genocide.

In the context of the former Yugoslavia, an example of this third social element, the intervening individual, is found in a rare account given by a Muslim woman and her daughter, of Sarajevo, who were rescued by a Serb there.

> MOTHER: I knew that somehow I had to get my children out of there. One day, I found two cars that worked and I found some gas. Then, I saw a Serb on the street. He was about thirty years old and he had a long scar on his face—he was pretty ordinary looking. I had never seen him before and I didn't even know his name, but he had a good face, a kind face. I approached him and asked him for help. He said, "Come tomorrow and pack your things."

> DAUGHTER: The next day, we went to this man with my brothers and sisters. He was waiting in the car. All of us kids got in, but Mother had to stay behind because there wasn't any room.

> MOTHER: They put me in prison in a basement. There were ten women in one room—two were older women, and the rest were between the ages of thirty and forty.... There was no light in the basement so we all sat in darkness. And it was so cold, we all began to get sick.... I kept thinking that at least my children were in a better place. I wasn't sure where they were, but I knew it was better.... After two months in the basement like that, I was saved. The Serb who had helped my children came in the middle of the night and stole me from the prison. He threw me in the trunk of a car and drove me off. I still don't even know his name.[34]

The fourth social element in Exodus, rooted in the oral, then written, transmission of the text, is *the telling* of the story within the oppressed community of the amazing victories of individuals with God's help over the oppressors who threaten them (Exodus 1–15).[35] The telling of the victories of the slaves, the midwives, Moses' mother and sister shapes the historical event, until finally all laments in the community give way to praise as depicted in the triumphal song of Exodus 15. The general text presents a rhetorical model of telling, shaped by the genres of lament and praise, for subsequent generations faced with oppression or genocide.

Thus a challenge before us, whether scholars or religious leaders, is to encourage the telling of the "Exodus" story (of suffering and escape) within faith communities by those to whom it is now happening once again, in whatever new shape it takes. "Pharaoh's" alternative rhetoric continues unabated. But what of the modern-day midwives and Miriams and Moseses?

---

34. From "My Daughter's Eyes: A Mother/Daughter Story," in *The Suitcase*, 23–26.
35. See also Weems, "Hebrew Women," 26.

Where are they and why are they silent? Why are their voices not eagerly sought anew in communal gatherings, as key players in the liturgical
drama? Who is responsible for recognizing these familiar figures with new
faces, if not we?

The Problem of Divine Response to Genocide

While the story of Exodus presents a paradigm for *human* response to
genocide through the four social elements outlined above, let us now consider *God's response,* for it contains a most troubling element. For God,
extremely concerned to best Pharaoh and set the Hebrew people free at any
cost, will also kill Egyptian children as the ultimate plague to teach Pharaoh
a lesson. In Exod 4:22–23, God says, "You shall say to Pharaoh,...'Israel
is my firstborn son.' I said to you, "Let my son go that he may worship
me." But you refused to let him go; now I will kill your firstborn son.' "[36]
The ethic of YHWH's response in threatening to kill Pharaoh's own firstborn
is obviously at radical odds with the story's concern for defending Hebrew
children and showing compassion for the victims. The contradiction is that
God resorts to the same practice, the killing of children, that Pharaoh uses
in his abuse of power.

Yet this action of God in the text is usually glossed over and not critically assessed by commentators. The usual treatment is the traditional (and
legitimate) claim that God entered into a relationship of covenant with
Israel in order to enter a world of suffering humanity to redeem it. The
implicit corollary, though rarely given critical attention, is that God's extension of goodness toward the Hebrews involves God's violence toward
the "other" peoples along the way who do not know or live according to
God's commandments. It is implied that this is a necessary and unpleasant
evil if all people are to benefit from God's blessing in the long run. Even
if one accepts this premise, should it then lead to a one-sided focus upon
Israel in the Exodus story to the total neglect of those who suffer or die
from God's violence? For example, emphasizing creation theology Terence
Fretheim summarizes the Exodus conflict in this way:

> The God who redeems has been at work in life-giving ways all along the
> journey...it is activity which brings forth and fosters life and blessing....It
> is ironic that this marvelous creative activity occurs *in Egypt....* How sig-

---

36. Jon Levenson discusses the ancient Near Eastern traditions of the firstborn son sacrificed
by gods (*The Death and Resurrection of the Beloved Son* [New Haven: Yale Univ. Press, 1993]
25–35). J. G. Williams stresses Eric Voegelin's observation of the Egyptian Pyramid Texts in
which the god refers to the king as "my son, my firstborn" (*Bible, Violence, and the Sacred,*
76).

nificant a work is here carried out by the "non-chosen" to provide life and blessing for the "chosen." ... How seldom it has been acknowledged![37]

Indeed, how seldom has the suffering of the Egyptians because of God's violence been taken seriously, as though they would have gladly said, "Kill our babies, so that your people may be blessed!" Fretheim's glowing and sentimental picture of God's "creative" work benefiting Israel bypasses (even more than the biblical text) the Egyptians, thereby implicitly excluding them. It easily ignores the text's portrayal of God's ambiguous dark side.

The realist storyteller of Exodus, however, leaves intact troubling ambiguities. While Pharaoh's daughter could "cross over" a gravely serious social boundary to rescue a Hebrew child, despite Pharaoh's power, God is neither able nor willing in the end to show mercy and cross this boundary to secure the safety of Egyptian as well as Hebrew children. Yet, while Pharaoh's daughter circumvented Pharaoh's power, the story suggests he was still oppressing the Hebrews and ordering the killing of children. Showing mercy to Pharaoh would not likely persuade him to change his policy. Realistically, only the show of power in opposition to such a tyrant is effective. The ethical issue, however, is not simply whether God should use violence, but what *kind* of violence is acceptable, given the character of God. It is extremely problematic to say that because God has a special commitment to the Hebrews, then the *means* God chooses for delivering them is beyond question.

Alongside the *ethical* question of God's response is the *literary* element, as David Gunn has put it, that as a character God "is depicted as risking insecurity because that is the price of allowing ... [human] freedom ... [creating] external pressures on God which in turn circumscribe ... [God's] own action."[38] Moreover, *sociologically,* as Brueggemann has put it, since texts "are always acts of advocacy ... God is a party to social conflict and social interest."[39] Thus, in terms of story and social context, God is severely limited by human action.

Yet God's actions in Exodus can also be explained by limitations from the larger ancient social context. James Williams draws on René Girard's anthropological insights to suggest that in Exodus God entered a unique relationship with Israel but also entered a point in history when violence

---

37. Fretheim, *Exodus* (Interpretation; Louisville: John Knox, 1991) 25–26.
38. D. Gunn, "The 'Hardening of Pharaoh's Heart': Plot, Character and Theology in Exodus 1–14," in *Art and Meaning: Rhetoric in Biblical Literature* (ed. David J. A. Clines, David M. Gunn, and Alan J. Hauser; JSOTSup 19; Sheffield: JSOT Press, 1982) 89.
39. Brueggemann, "Exodus," 681–82.

and sacrifice played a powerful, systemic role in the ancient Near East.[40] Williams follows Girard's view that humans were and are caught up in a social crisis of "mimesis, rivalry, and collective violence." The crisis is "managed only by the killing or expelling of a victim," a "scapegoat" that represents the rival. While this violence and victimization are present in biblical texts, so, according to Girard, is its critique. In Exodus and elsewhere, Williams suggests, there is "the revelation...of a God who does not want victims, a God who is disclosed in the action of those who take the side of the victims."[41]

Williams notes, however, that this "process of...the disclosure of the innocent victim and the God of victims does not come about quickly and easily." The rivalry between the Egyptians and Hebrews is still part of the old cycle of violence and revenge. While God aims to break this cycle and expose the scapegoat mechanism, God's own use of the plagues and killing Pharaoh's firstborn are part of the old cycle.[42] Yet Williams concludes, "The model of this confrontation between the old sacral order and the emergent Israelite vision is captured in Exod 4:21–23."[43] Whether this specific text (with God's announcement to kill Pharaoh's firstborn!) "models" such a transition is debatable, but what is essential to confront here is that the text offers a poor "model" for divine or human behavior. Shall we not finally critique this notion found in Exod 4:21–23 that the vengeful killing of children or anyone as a kind of punishment, particularly by people of faith in the name of God, might somehow facilitate their own rescue or redemption?[44]

In the context of the former Yugoslavia, the misappropriation of such a text threatens to perpetuate the practice of genocide. Moreover, if, as is

---

40. Williams, *Bible, Violence, and the Sacred*, 1–31, 71–103.

41. Ibid., 6–13.

42. Ibid., 71–77. God's actions do differ from Pharaoh's in that God's threat to Pharaoh's firstborn comes as a warning to persuade Pharaoh to relent. As such, YHWH's announcement of death is contingent on Pharaoh's behavior.

43. Williams, *Bible, Violence, and the Sacred*, 76. Williams suggests that the narrative radically tries to break this old cycle by focusing on the innocent victim in a way unparalleled in the ancient Near East and by aiming to diminish the violence against both the Egyptians and the innocent since only Egypt's firstborn would be killed, as compared to all Hebrew male newborns (Exod 4:21–23). One could argue, however, that what first appeared to be a warning against only Pharaoh's firstborn son (4:23) later expands to include all Egyptian firstborn (Exodus 11 and 12). Moreover, by taking all firstborn Egyptians (regardless of age), God likely kills not only a greater number of individuals but the more valued ones. It is difficult to see how this development helps break the cycle of violence. More to the point, Williams also suggests that "the victims of oppression do not wish to retaliate, but to leave" (78).

44. While reasonable people may think such a critique is tacit and unnecessary, consider that some reasonable individuals in the former Yugoslavia whose children have been under threat, when asked, find this text reprehensible.

commonly and legitimately claimed regarding the conflict in Exodus, "God is a God who takes sides,"[45] then any one group in the former Yugoslavia might irresponsibly claim that God is always *only* on their side.[46]

The potential danger latent in this Exodus text is evident in light of the rhetoric of one of the indicted war criminals in the former Yugoslavia charged with genocide against Muslims and others. In a 1995 interview in an official publication of the church of which he is openly a part, he readily employs religious rhetoric. He refers to how his people have been the victim in history for centuries, have been kept in "subordination" and servitude by the other groups. But now, in a "national rebirth," he believes he has helped restore freedom to his people: "Our deaths, suffering, and endurance we accept as God's grace, that he gave us the gift of destiny to accomplish this." Like a kind of "suffering servant" he claims to be the defender of "our tribe and our Church hoping to God that we used only as much force as was necessary... God graced me to do something in my life that is significant, so significant that I think it was worth being born, live, and die to help my people.... Not a single important decision was made without the Church."[47] Indeed, the church publication that ran this interview in no way critiqued or condemned his implicit theology or complicity in atrocities.[48] In co-opting religious traditions, such leaders exploit the people's real suffering and God's concern for them by claiming that God is only on their side and so justify their own genocidal response against the perceived oppressor. Such co-opting tacitly selects some biblical texts while conveniently ignoring all others that would place serious ethical restraints on such behavior.

Prospects for the Reader's Response to Genocide

The Exodus portrayal of the means God uses against the Egyptians (death of the firstborn) is problematic for two reasons. The first reason concerns God. Could it ever be deemed ethical or justified for God to kill Egyptian children? The second concerns human behavior. The notion of an oppressed, chosen people who have God on their side, while certainly legitimate for the Hebrews as part of their unique, early historical context, is

---

45. Fretheim, *Exodus*, 31; see also Weems, "Hebrew Women," 26.

46. For critiques of religious leadership making such claims, see Volf, *Exclusion and Embrace*, 88; and Mojzes, *Yugoslavian Inferno*, 125–46.

47. Interview reprinted in the August 1995 issue (vol. 15) of the journal *Religion in Eastern Europe*, ed. Paul Mojzes, 17–22; originally published as "The Resurrection of the Crouching Soul: A Conversation with Mr. Radovan Karadžić," *Svetigora* 4 (1995) 14–23.

48. Noted by Paul Mojzes, *Religion in Eastern Europe* 15 (1995) 21.

now manipulated and results in contemporary injustices. In the former Yugoslavia, the notion of religious chosenness has given license to dangerous
leaders, as noted above, to claim this "chosen" spot for their people and
then to justify any manner of exclusionary and genocidal practices against
their neighbor.

The need is not to rewrite the Bible or change the canon, but rather for
its *readers*—its scholars, religious leaders, and congregations—to be more
responsible, less naive, and more critically outspoken about the social use
and misuse of biblical texts.

In the former Yugoslavia, it also becomes apparent that greater critical
responsibility is needed with the social use of lament. In the region's history,
sociopolitical laments of people on all sides over severe suffering at times
went unexpressed, unheard, or unanswered. Such lament gone awry has
been recently exploited by irresponsible leaders. The lament issue is about
the burden of choice. How does one choose to respond when there is only
ambiguous silence to one's lament, when there comes no intervention in
the midst of cruel suffering and grief? "My God, my God, why have you
forsaken me?!" (Ps 22:1 [MT 2]). The biblical tradition never finally gives
up on God or on lament, but persists with *more* lament and waits (as in
the lament psalms, Job, and Lamentations).

It is in the waiting for God's intervention that one's choice becomes
crucially operative. How does one respond to the other's evil? Having
lamented the injustice, one may choose to pursue vengeance, but this is
not the way of biblical lament, whose natural angry imprecations against
the enemy still leave such vengeance to God. The biblical tradition loads lament with an even greater burden, expecting *God* to resolve the ambiguity.
Alleviation of one's suffering, justice, and forgiveness are all sought from
God. But there is more to this than meets the eye, for this intercession is
also *for the children*. By refraining from blood vengeance, with mercy, the
Suffering One is reaching out for the children, for *all* children in jeopardy,
even for the next generation—for in this act of lament prayer, of refusing violence, is their rescue from the futile cycle of revenge, suffering, and
genocide. It is an action that chooses life not just for one's own "chosen
people," but for all people.

A woman of the former Yugoslavia, a victim of rape in war, depicted
in the play "The Legend About the End of the World," is another such
suffering one:

> It would be very difficult for me to avenge all those who should be avenged,
> because my revenge would be just another part of the same inexorable rite.
> I have to break that terrible chain. I want to think that *my task is life,* and
> that my mission is not to prolong hatred, while I wait for better times to

come, while I carry this child in my womb, the daughter of so many rapes or perhaps his, but above all, my own daughter. (emphasis added)[49]

In the book of Exodus, God's killing of Egyptian children is rooted in a theology in which God inflicts upon children suffering as punishment for the sins/injustices of their parents (Exod 20:5; cf. Jer 31:29–30). The ambiguity of God, who is also merciful in this text, leaves a burden of responsibility upon us to choose how we will respond to injustice. In the eyes of Pharaoh's daughter, Moses' infant life, floating on the Nile, hung in the balance. What would she choose? Miriam watched to see. About Pharaoh's daughter, a university student in Osijek, Croatia, remarked poignantly "The daughter of Pharaoh 'saves the situation.' She pays, both literally and figuratively, for the sins of her father. When Moses was grown, he fought injustice in his own way, by revenge."[50] She pays by risking to break the cycle of vengeance and scapegoating. It is exceedingly unjust and unmerciful that she, who helped rear Moses, would have then paid if her own firstborn Egyptian child were to die in God's final plague.

Pharaoh's daughter and the women of Exodus 1–2 embody the human *and divine* paradigmatic response to genocide, by rescuing lives rather than taking revenge. As Brueggemann has aptly put it: "the women have displaced the providence of God and are the ones who assure the baby's future."[51] Indeed, their actions implicitly *critique* God's taking of lives and implicitly *fulfill* God's own desire—"by you all the nations of the earth shall be blessed" (Gen 12:3).

Pharaoh's daughter and the young student mentioned above give hope to those who despair of ever finding a lasting answer to the recurring horrors of genocide. For when the sins of the parents persist in the widespread suffering of children, hope still resides in the will of the children. Consider the following Jewish tradition concerning the postmessianic world:

The children of the wicked who had to die in infancy on account of the sins of their fathers will be found among the just, while their fathers will be ranged on the other side. The babes will implore their fathers to come to them, but God will not permit it. Then Elijah[52] will go to the little ones, and teach them

---

49. "The Legend About the End of the World," a play performed and directed by five women of Dah Theatre of Belgrade, Serbia (performed in Atlanta in connection with the 1995 Summer Olympics and in other U.S. cities).

50. Lidija Matorić was one of my students in an introduction to Old Testament class at the Josip J. Strossmayer University in Osijek in the fall of 1996, less than a year after the war in the region had stopped. I am indebted to all of the students for their insights into the biblical text.

51. Brueggemann, "Exodus," 701.

52. Elijah was identified in Jewish tradition as rescuer of those threatened by the "Angel of Death." Also, as the forerunner of the Messiah, he would "utter a lament over the devastation of the Holy Land, and his wail will be heard throughout the world. The last words of his elegy

how to plead in behalf of their fathers. They will stand before God and say: "Is not the measure of good, the mercy of God, larger than the measure of chastisements? If, then, we died for the sins of our fathers, should they not now for our sakes be granted the good, and be permitted to join us in Paradise?" God will give assent to their pleadings, and Elijah will have fulfilled the word of the prophet Malachi: "Lo, I will send you the prophet Elijah before the great and terrible day of the LORD comes. He will turn the hearts of parents to their children and the hearts of children to their parents" (Mal 4:5, NRSV).[53]

---

will be: 'Now peace will come upon earth!' " See Ginzberg, *Legends of the Jews*, 4:227–29 and 6:333–34.

53. For a list of sources see Ginzberg, *Legends of the Jews*, 4:235.

– 6 –

The Sojourner Has Come to Play the Judge

Theodicy on Trial

James L. Crenshaw

The dramatic confrontation between Lot and the citizens of Sodom takes a turn for the worse when they accuse the sojourner of playing the role of judge (Gen 19:9).[1] Refusing his overtures of comradeship—the initial linking of himself with them as brothers and the subsequent offer of two virginal daughters for their pleasure—the men of Sodom threaten a worse fate for Lot than "sodomy."[2] The concept of judging[3] also lies at the center of the episode leading up to this story of conflicting wills, Abraham's intercession for Sodom and Gomorrah. In it, a sojourner par excellence utters

---

1. Hermann Gunkel, *Genesis* (trans. Mark E. Biddle; Macon Ga.: Mercer Univ. Press, 1997) 202, follows Wellhausen in understanding Abraham's intercession for Sodom as a late interpolation into the Yahwistic narrative, primarily because of the way it deals with the problem of divine justice in the abstract. Classical prophets, he points out, saw no difficulty with the total punishment of a given community. Gerhard von Rad accepts Gunkel's general understanding of the two episodes in terms of the history of religions but goes on to emphasize theological dimensions of the narrative (*Genesis* [trans. John H. Marks; rev. ed.; OTL; Philadelphia: Westminster, 1972] 216ff.). Terence E. Fretheim's sensitivity to the religious dimensions of the text stands out among the several commentaries consulted ("Genesis," in *NIB* [Nashville: Abingdon, 1994], 1:473–79). The attitude expressed by the people of Sodom has been replicated hundreds of times when confronted by "sojourners": an African American professor who assails the culture that welcomed him, a new congresswoman who attacks those doing things the traditional way, a new clerk in a law firm who dares to raise objections to company policy, a novice minister who challenges ecclesiastical procedure, and so forth.

2. The term *sodomy* derives from this biblical story and should not be projected onto the narrative, hence the quotation marks. In vv. 7–9 the expressions for brotherhood, *'aḥay*, and evil behavior, *tārē'û. . . . kattôb bĕ'ênêkem,* links this text with Judg 19:23–24, where citizens of Gibeah demand a visitor for homosexual purposes and are offered a virgin daughter and a concubine instead.

3. In ancient Egypt the notion of divine judgment led to the picture of scales on which were placed at death the human heart and a feather symbolizing justice. This powerful ethical motivation was familiar throughout the ancient Near East, as the frequent epithets for divine judge demonstrate.

the unimaginable, although stating it interrogatively: "Shall not the Judge of the whole earth act justly?" (Gen 18:25). No better paradigm exists for the effort to defend divine justice, theodicy, inasmuch as human beings are quintessentially sojourners.[4]

At least two things make such "playing at judge" extraordinary. A sojourner brings a different perspective to bear on the situation, for other experiences and friendships have shaped that alien viewpoint than those responsible for the ethos prevailing in an adopted environment.[5] Moreover, anyone who has merely taken up residence among strangers but dares to pronounce judgment on their value system displays a high degree of chutzpah. When that shameless audacity extends to its ultimate expression, theodicy, the sole justification may rest in the existential fact of life's brevity. This sobering reality, the death sentence proclaimed over the entire human race, inspires courage in the face of awareness that a sojourner's understanding is different and that resident aliens lack authority.[6]

Indeed, the patriarch's venture in this realm comes as a result of the deity's initiative. Reflecting on the special relationship with Abraham and his vocation with respect to the nations, Yahweh ponders the advisability of informing him of the possibility, or probability, that the wickedness of the two cities signals their ruin. Like a true sojourner, Abraham approaches the Lord with empty pockets, but the lack of a bargaining chip does not deter Abraham from inventing one and imposing it on the sovereign visitor. Lying behind the poignant question, "Shall not the Judge of the whole earth do justly?" is the assumption that Yahweh must abide by a moral code of human devising.[7] Unless the deity acts in accord with the divine nature as

---

4. John Bunyan's classic, *Pilgrim's Progress,* gave expression to the idea that human beings merely pitch their tents on earth, that earthly existence offers opportunity to form character for life in eternity. Given the brevity of human life, whatever understanding that accrues is limited from the temporal and the spatial viewpoints. Criticizing the Eternal One from a transitory perspective demands considerable nerve, as Immanuel Kant noted: "It is arrogant to attempt to defend God's justice; it is still more arrogant to assail the deity" ("Über das Misslingen aller philosophischen Versuche in der Theodizee," *Werke,* ed. W. Weischedel [Darmstadt: Insel-Verlag, 1964] 6:103–24).

5. We shape our own culture and then become subject to its claims. Ethos thus owes its origin to human beings even when it sits in judgment on its originators.

6. The ancient *gēr* came under royal protection, at least in ideology (Norbert Lohfink, "Poverty in the Laws of the Ancient Near East and the Bible," *ThStud* 52 [1991] 34–50; and Leonidas Kalugila, *The Wise King* [ConBOT 15; Lund: Gleerup, 1980]). According to the sapiential tradition, one type of sojourner, the foreign woman (*nokrîyāh; 'iššāh zārāh*), flaunted her outsider status for seductive advantages.

7. Considerable debate has raged over the extent, if any, of Yahweh's subjection to an external order: whether, in Klaus Koch's words, Yahweh did midwife service for the principle of deed/consequence, or was thought to rule in majestic indifference to the concept. Walter Brueggemann, *Genesis* (Interpretation; Atlanta: John Knox, 1982) 171, recognizes the centrality of divine character in this argument. The character of Yahweh, not equity in history, is the issue here.

moral, human beings have no reason to exercise justice. Abraham's argument implies that the deity should, at a minimum, aspire to the same level of morality as that achieved on earth.[8]

The decisive issue concerns indiscriminate sweeping away of the innocent alongside the guilty—the Dostoevskian concern for the tears of children—as if virtue means nothing. An earlier sweeping away, with which this text has remarkable similarities, was less inclusive, for Noah and his extended family escaped the deluge. Hence the emphatic "indeed"—"Will you indeed sweep away the righteous with the wicked?" Will the same principle apply in this new irruption of divine judgment? Abraham's bold overture mixes an accusatory tone with self-effacing language: for example, "Far be it from you . . . I who am dust and ashes . . . Let not the Lord be angry if I speak just once more" (Gen 18:25–32).[9]

Stung—or pleased—by the sojourner's perspective, Yahweh accedes to his wishes. The principle of a minority functioning to save the majority has been established through a combination of human and divine solicitousness. "For the sake of fifty, I will forgive the entire population" (Gen 18:26). Now it falls to Abraham to ascertain the limits of such forbearance, and he proceeds by gradations of five, then ten, until arriving at the point at which a group dissolves into individuals.[10] From the perspective adopted thus far in this analysis, the narrator's concluding words in this episode carry double force: "and Abraham returned to his place." The sojourner-judge reverts to the status of alien resident while simultaneously going home. The wheels of justice begin to grind more rapidly, at least for the city of Sodom.

Lot's munificence as host failed to rival that of his uncle—until pressed by extenuating circumstances. Both sojourners demonstrated a determination to abide by the existing moral code, specifically the requirement of hospitality.[11] Having demonstrated a willingness to entertain a new principle of justice, the deity acts on the basis of an old one, already in effect

---

8. The biblical deity often engages in dubious practices, from the modern perspective, a point that provokes provocative comments from Jack Miles, *God: A Biography* (New York: Knopf, 1995), esp. 308–28, dealing with God as fiend.

9. Contrast this accusing mood with the prophetic intercession in Amos 7 ("Lord, Yahweh, please forgive! How can Jacob stand, for he is small?"). Here, too, the intercession stops short, for after two successful attempts to stay divine judgment, Amos abandons the effort.

10. Claus Westermann, *Genesis 12–36* (Continental Commentaries; trans. J. J. Scullion; Minneapolis: Augsburg, 1985) 292. Other possibilities, however, come to mind—reluctance to become too precise; the recognition that the smallest military units consisted of ten; Abraham has made his point and to press it further would be useless.

11. That, not homosexuality, is the specific offense that comes in for censure, although the text also denounces the people for the way in which they broke the code.

on the occasion of the deluge. Still, none who heard about the destruction of the cities could accuse Yahweh of sweeping away the innocent with the guilty. Neither the exact accounting, spelled out with rational exactitude by the prophets Jeremiah (18:8–11) and Ezekiel (14:12–20; 18:1–32), nor the newly won principle of a saving minority comes into play here, unless the sparing of the little village of Zoar—and of Lot's daughters—qualifies as the latter. The narrator assiduously avoids any specific identification of Lot as righteous.[12]

We may surmise that the calamity befalling the cities of the plain in persistent memory served paradigmatically for the similar fates of Samaria and Jerusalem. The haunting question, "If there, why not here?" must have burned itself into the minds of thinking people. Why had Yahweh acted to spare the only individuals in Sodom with the slightest claim to goodness while sweeping away the righteous with the wicked in the case of a chosen people?[13] If any comfort is to be had, it must come from a firm conviction that the Lord does not desire the death of anyone, to quote Ezekiel. Abraham the sojourner had elicited that concession at considerable risk.

Another link between the two episodes in Genesis 18 and 19 illustrates the danger when sojourners treat the divine word lightly. From a place of apparent concealment, Sarah laughed on hearing that she would once more "find pleasure" and conceive a son, and Lot's future (?) sons-in-law considered his dire warning a mere jest.[14] Whoever dares to sit in judgment over divine ways does well to ponder the implications of a vantage point accessible only to the deity, before whom every lying protest comes to light and every belittling of serious warning issues in disaster—if, that is, the deity bows before the moral law. The story reckons, however, with randomness, an ignoring of human merit, or lack of it, that allows the wicked to escape, for nothing suggests that everyone in Zoar was blameless. Perhaps the unspoken answer to Yahweh's question, "Is anything too hard for the LORD?" is yes. Holding together the qualities of mercy and justice comes to mind.[15]

In the patriarch's intercession for condemned cities, the reader encoun-

---

12. For that matter, Abraham never appeals to his kinship with Lot as a bargaining chip. The story offers no hint that Lot would be a salvific influence over the people of Zoar.

13. Anger over Yahweh's sparing of a wicked but repentant Nineveh moves Jonah to morbid thoughts that death would be better under the circumstances. The natural question, "Why did Yahweh relent in this instance but not in the case of Israel and Judah?" lies under the surface (Terence E. Fretheim, "Jonah and Theodicy," *ZAW* 90 [1978] 227–37).

14. The initial story, a mirror image of an earlier episode involving Abraham, involves a pun on the name Isaac.

15. James L. Crenshaw, "Who Knows What YHWH Will Do? The Character of God in the Book of Joel," in *Fortunate the Eyes That See: Essays in Honor of David Noel Freedman in Celebration of his Seventieth Birthday* (eds. A. B. Beck, et al.; Grand Rapids: Eerdmans, 1995) 185–96.

ters a rare feature within ancient Near Eastern theodicies.[16] The complaint of the human sojourner takes the form of direct address to the culpable (?) deity. Normally, such accusation assumes a less confrontative mode, the speaker taking shelter in descriptive narrative. The aggrieved one complains about the deity, or deities, rather than engaging in dialogue with the originator of physical, intellectual, and religious dismay. A pharaoh observes that the shepherd has neglected the sheep, demonstrating reckless disdain for life and social order;[17] an innocent sufferer accuses the creators of concealing their will;[18] and another tells a faithful friend that the gods gave deception to human beings.[19] These critics of the gods acknowledge a measure of human fault, but they deny that it is met with commensurate punishment. The gods have stacked the deck, as it were, making it impossible to ensure a life of well-being by adhering to a moral code.[20]

Biblical critics of Yahweh complain to the deity, as if face to face, sometimes in language just short of irreverent. "How long?" and "Why?" ring out from prophetic challengers of humans and God. Jeremiah goes farthest of all, accusing Yahweh of spiritual seduction and rape, whereas Habakkuk soberly reminds the Lord of moral standards regulating human society.[21] Sometimes the accuser appeals to an ideal past as a basis for complaining about the disagreeable present. The judge Gideon reminds Yahweh's messenger that the hardships of the moment create a cloud of disbelief over cherished stories about more favorable treatment by the deity. Similarly, Job contrasted earlier days of divine favor with his daily misery at even-

---

16. Ronald J. Williams, "Theodicy in the Ancient Near East," *CJT* 2 (1956) 14–26; Wolfram von Soden, "Das Fragen nach der Gerechtigkeit Gottes im Alten Orient," in *Bibel und Alter Orient* (ed. Hans-Peter Müller; BZAW 162; Berlin and New York: de Gruyter, 1985) 57–76; J. J. Stamm, *Das Leiden des Unschuldigung in Babylon und Israel* (ATANT 10; Zurich: Zwingli, 1946); Rainer Albertz, "Der sozial geschichtliche Hintergrund des Hiobsbuches und der 'Babylonischen Theodizee,'" in *Die Botschaft und die Boten; Festschrift für Hans Walter Wolff* (ed. J. Jeremias and L. Perlitt; Neukirchen-Vluyn: Neukirchener Verlag, 1981) 349–72; Moshe Weinfeld, "Job and Its Mesopotamian Parallels: A Typological Analysis," in *Text and Context: Old Testament and Semitic Studies for F. C. Fensham* (ed. W. Claassen; JSOTSup 48; Sheffield: JSOT Press, 1988) 217–26.

17. "The Admonitions of Ipuwer." Often believed to be intrusive, this brief section gives the impression of a society in considerable disarray.

18. This text, "Ludlul" ("I Will Praise the God of Wisdom") has recently been translated by Benjamin R. Foster under the title, "Poem of Righteous Sufferer" in *From Distant Days: Myths, Tales, and Poetry of Ancient Mesopotamia* (Bethesda: CDL Press, 1995) 300–313.

19. "The Babylonian Theodicy," in *From Distant Days*, 316–23

20. Magic was not the only instrument for controlling the gods; subjecting them to a human concept of order arose from a similar desire. At least the author of "Ludlul" recognized the impossibility of knowing what the gods liked or hated. Some biblical authors also emphasized the incomprehensibility of Yahweh.

21. For the former see James L. Crenshaw, *A Whirlpool of Torment: Israelite Traditions of God as an Oppressive Presence* (OBT; Philadelphia: Fortress Press, 1984) 31–56. For the latter, Donald E. Gowan, *The Triumph of Faith in Habakkuk* (Atlanta: John Knox, 1976) 20–50.

tide.[22] When the occasion arises for him to challenge Yahweh face to face, however, his earlier courage fades—or his trust triumphs—and issues in silence.[23]

Some accusers of Yahweh refuse to pull their punches, having completely departed from belief in providence. Their voices usually reach us indirectly, either by way of a prophet's citation of their view only to refute it,[24] or concealed within liturgical condemnation of unacceptable religious talk. On one occasion the doubting thoughts comprise a stage in a psalmist's spiritual journey from envying the prosperous people devoid of ethics to a new awareness of what constitutes the goodness of the Lord.[25] Others speak freely because they enjoy a buffer zone provided by an angel, who zealously defends Yahweh's actions even when they fall in the realm of the imponderable. Thus Ezra takes the Lord to task for inaugurating the whole process that we may loosely call the human experiment, since the rules of the game condemn most inhabitants of the earth to eternal damnation.[26]

In light of such boldness, persons eager to defend Yahweh's justice seize every available opportunity to do so, oblivious to the implications for a biblical anthropology. The Deuteronomistic history represents a monumental theodicy with a single message: the calamity that struck the people of the Lord came as punishment for the nation's wickedness only after persistent prophetic warning and divine forbearance. Impatient with dissenting views, the prophet Ezekiel engages in a shouting match with those who rejected Yahweh's justice, insisting that they, not he, lied.[27] Even radical changes in worldview presaged by a growing emphasis on the individual rather than the group did not deter this prophet from maintaining traditional dogma in new circumstances regardless of the gyrations forced on him.

Contemporary interpreters of this ancient literature belong to the cate-

---

22. W. A. M. Beuken, ed., *The Book of Job* (BETL 114; Leuven: Leuven Univ. Press, 1994), indicates the rich diversity of opinion regarding this provocative text.

23. Job's silence has not generated comparable reticence among interpreters, who view the text from vastly different perspectives. Does he find reconciliation as a result of the divine speeches, or does he express hidden contempt for such a deity? Are his words sincere, or does he resort to irony? What does he actually say?

24. James L. Crenshaw, "Popular Questioning of the Justice of God in Ancient Israel," *ZAW* 84 (1970) 380–95, reprinted in Crenshaw, *Urgent Advice and Probing Questions: Collected Writings on Old Testament Wisdom* (Macon, Ga.: Mercer Univ. Press, 1995) 175–90.

25. Martin Buber, "The Heart Determines (Psalms 73)," in *On the Bible* (New York: Schocken, 1968) 199–210; Crenshaw, *Whirlpool of Torment*, 93–109.

26. Michael Edward Stone, *Fourth Ezra* (Hermeneia; Minneapolis: Fortress Press, 1990) and A. L. Thompson, *Responsibility for Evil in the Theodicy of IV Ezra* (SBLDS 29; Missoula, Mont.: Scholars Press, 1977).

27. This chapter (Ezekiel 18) has long been seen as the watershed of individualism, but it more correctly may be viewed as the prophetic insistence that Yahweh deal with Israel on the basis of its actions, whether good or evil.

gory of sojourners in a twofold manner. Besides being temporary residents on earth, they try to imagine life as it unfolded millennia ago. Then they sit in judgment on the deity, the writers, and a society about which they know very little. As one of these critics, I readily acknowledge this fact, at the same time refusing to concede that the guild's approach to theodicy is flawed from the outset.[28] That charge of neglecting the social dimension comes from a scholar wielding enormous influence and merits serious consideration.

The three categories of evil (natural, moral, and religious) can by no stretch of the imagination be rejected as inadequate because they leave out the social dimension. What else does moral evil mean? If by religious evil one refers to the vertical relationship, moral evil must surely cover the horizontal dimension of life in society. That is why I could write about two types of theodicy, one for the oppressed and another for the oppressor.[29] This survival technique on the part of widely different groups has profound social implications. Rulers devise a theodicy to justify their power and status, and to encourage subjects to submit to this view of reality; the powerless invent quite different arguments, often based on revolutionary or eschatological concepts.

Furthermore, corporate solidarity in early Israel excluded individualistic morality by definition. The rise of a wealthy class and urban culture seriously compromised the older sense of a family that linked the larger nation, but the emerging idea of vicarious suffering held in tension the new individualism and the waning solidarity. This balancing of competing notions continues in Psalm 73, which begins by focusing on the social dimensions of theodicy and concludes by concentrating on the existential realities connecting the individual worshiper with the Transcendent One.

The choice of the three categories did not arise from any desire to cover up social processes, nor did it constitute a sort of social contrivance.[30] Because the actual causes of human misery—Philistines, Canaanites, Assyrians, Babylonians, land-grabbing Israelites, corrupt religious and political figures in Judah—were so obvious that stating it seemed unnecessary,[31] the social context may not have received its due. That neglect, however,

---

28. Walter Brueggemann, "Theodicy in a Social Dimension," *JSOT* 33 (1985) 13.

29. Crenshaw, "The Shift from Theodicy to Anthropodicy," in *Theodicy in the Old Testament* (IRT; Philadelphia: Fortress Press, 1983) 1–16, repr. in *Urgent Advice and Probing Questions*, 141–54 (especially 144).

30. Brueggemann, "Theodicy in a Social Dimension," 8.

31. The incessant denunciation of Israel and Judah in the Deuteronomistic history and in prophetic literature, together with confessions in liturgical prayers, have had unfortunate consequences, for they give the impression that God's people were intractable from the very beginning. The problem arises when outsiders fail to acknowledge the context of such denunciation and take a further step toward anti-Semitism.

resulted from conviction that modern interpreters know next to nothing about social factors governing ancient Israel, despite the voluminous speculation prompting a single question, "Where is the proof?" Form critics have long sought to recognize the social location of each particular literary type, with minimal results. Modesty in this endeavor strikes me as essential in the wake of elaborate hypotheses based largely on cultural anthropology or political theory.

The accusation of supernaturalism[32] rests on a misunderstanding of descriptive analyses of biblical texts. These may give the impression of supernaturalism, for they accept the imaginary world of the authors, who definitely believed in an interventionalist deity. By no means does that openness to an alien worldview suggest personal acceptance of it. Israelites naturally attributed everything to divine initiative, and discussions of theodicy were no exception. Even when Job goes from pariah to his former status, the narrator attributes the change to Yahweh before going on to credit relatives and friends with the restoration. Interpreters have not been blind to this latter feature of the story; instead, they have struggled to integrate such an epilogue into the larger literary context.[33]

The suggestion that interpreters have ignored social processes because they belong to the "haves" rather than the "have nots" takes up an argument leveled against the foreign sage Agur.[34] This curious view assumes that all affluent people lack compassion for those less fortunate than they, which is palpably untrue. Anyone who hazards a guess about an author's social status on the basis of attitudes to rich and poor ignores the remarkable diversity at all levels of society. Moreover, some contemporary scholars who fall into the category of "haves" remember vividly earlier days of impoverishment. Past experience has taught them compassion for the "have nots."

What about the essential brief with members of the guild? Are they guilty of stressing *theos* rather than *dikē?*[35] The first thing that comes to mind concerns the meaning of *theodicy.* The word must have primary reference to *theos,* and that has guided interpreters in their treatments of the

---

32. Brueggemann, "Theodicy in a Social Dimension," 13, 19.

33. The incongruity of the epilogue has commanded the attention of many interpreters, who see the ending as undercutting the essential insight in the poem. Having pressed forward to the conclusion that one's external circumstances do not signify one's inner being, the book now has Yahweh deal with Job in a manner predicated on the assumption that goodness must be rewarded in tangible ways.

34. Brueggemann, "Theodicy in a Social Dimension," 13, 21. On Agur see James L. Crenshaw, "Clanging Symbols," in *Justice and the Holy* (ed. D. A. Knight and P. J. Paris; Philadelphia: Fortress Press, 1989) 51–64, repr. in *Urgent Advice and Probing Questions,* 371–82.

35. Brueggemann, "Theodicy in a Social Dimension," 18–21.

problem. The other half of the word, *dikē*, also refers to divine action. The insistence that it be restricted to social processes has no linguistic basis. To be sure, biblical writers understood the evil repercussions of certain social processes, and these frequently provoked theodicies, but the blame fell on Yahweh as supreme ruler and shepherd. In the view of the writers, the Lord was ultimately responsible for social processes. The more sophisticated biblical authors may have realized that individuals make their own choices, but they still attributed actions to Yahweh.

Modern interpreters understand events differently, but they err when projecting their own views on biblical texts. The ancients believed that Yahweh provided the impetus of social process, acting as its norm and as the agent for its transformation.[36] They may even have been comfortable with the claim that Yahweh guided the process through human instruments.

The changing of the question from "Why do the innocent suffer?" to "How does history work?" solves nothing as long as Yahweh is thought to orchestrate human events.[37] The interpreter may concentrate on the deity's malfeasance or on human social processes, but theodicy requires that one pronounce judgment on Yahweh, whatever else may be said about societal responsibility.

In short, the enthusiasm generated by recent sociological interpretations of the Bible should be tempered by an awareness of our profound ignorance. When did individualistic thinking first surface, and when did it reach the point that it forced thinkers to offer a theodicy exonerating Yahweh for apparent injustices? What periods of history made this issue one that could not be ignored? When did the question become abstract, a matter for erudite speculation rather than a struggle to maintain religious faith?[38] At what time did someone first entertain the thought that Yahweh was either immoral or impotent? When did biblical thinkers begin to take refuge in the belief that Yahweh concealed the truth while revealing limited insights to humans?[39] What enticed biblical thinkers to attribute fault to human

---

36. Ibid., 21.

37. David Noel Freedman, "Son of Man, Can These Bones Live?" *Int* 29 (1975) 185–86. Gerhard von Rad, "The Joseph Narrative and Ancient Wisdom," in *The Problem of the Hexateuch and Other Essays* (trans. E. W. T. Dicken; Edinburgh and London: Oliver & Boyd, 1966) 297, uses the image of God as puppeteer ("God has all the threads firmly in his hands even when men are least aware of it").

38. Ludwig Schmidt, *"De Deo": Studien zur Literaturkritik und Theologie des Buches Jona, des Gesprächs zwischen Abraham und Jahwe in Gen 18:22ff. und von Hi 1* (BZAW 143; Berlin and New York: de Gruyter, 1976), attributes Gen 18:17–18, 22b–33 to a single hand and understands the late text as an expression of new collective thinking. He considers such an attitude impossible in preexilic Israel, for its main concern is not "that God is just" but "why God is just"—an abstract problem. Schmidt thinks the author of this story came from the same circle as the person responsible for the book of Jonah.

39. For discussion of limits to knowledge, see James L. Crenshaw, "Wisdom and the Sage:

beings rather than assailing the deity? Why did later sages internalize the signs of divine retribution?[40] In response to these and similar questions, a stinging *kî tēdāʿ* shimmers with irony.

If the unknown poet responsible for Deutero-Isaiah correctly perceived the vast chasm separating divine and human ways, as well as thoughts, every effort at theodicy may indeed be an arrogant exercise in futility. Nevertheless, stories like those concerning Abraham's intercession for Sodom and its sequel encourage the attempt. As sojourners we lift our voices in protest when society fails to implement justice. We may put the blame on the ultimate source of authority, but that does not overlook human transgression, which evoked the complaint in the first place. Theodicy may indeed be on trial today, but not because its practitioners have overlooked the social dimension. Rather, modern society's self-absorption has eroded the transcendent dimension of reality, condemning the present world to a single option, the secular, and in the process erasing *theos*.[41] In such a world, theodicy has indeed shifted to anthropodicy.[42]

On Knowing and Not Knowing," in *Proceedings of the Eleventh World Congress of Jewish Studies: Division A, The Bible and Its World. Jerusalem 1994* (Jerusalem: World Union of Jewish Studies, 1995) 137–44, and chap. 10, "Probing the Unknown: Knowledge and the Sacred," in my forthcoming book, tentatively entitled *Across the Deadening Silence: Education in Ancient Israel*, scheduled for publication in 1998 by Doubleday in the Anchor Bible Reference Library.

40. Both Ben Sira and Wisdom of Solomon added psychological and philosophical arguments to the conventional ones in discussions of theodicy (James L. Crenshaw, "The Problem of Theodicy in Sirach: On Human Bondage," *JBL* 94 [1975] 49–64, repr. in *Urgent Advice and Probing Questions*, 155–74).

41. Seyyed Hossein Nasr, *Knowledge and the Sacred* (Albany: SUNY Press, 1989). These Gifford Lectures by a renowned Islamic scholar argue powerfully against the hegemony of secularism.

42. As I argue in "The Shift from Theodicy to Anthropodicy," the usual defenses of divine justice come at considerable expense to human dignity. In such a context, defense of humankind may be appropriate, but it is not theodicy.

– 7 –

God's Commandment

Dale Patrick

The collections of laws in the Pentateuch are typically referred to by plural category nouns like *mišpāṭîm, ḥuqqîm, ʿēdôt,* and *miṣwōt,* but occasionally the singular *miṣwāh* is used (e.g., "and it will be righteousness for us, if we are careful to do all this *miṣwāh* before YHWH our God, as he has commanded us"; Deut 6:25). This latter usage suggests a concept of "commandment-ness," of some essence or idea that transcends and includes all particular prohibitions, prescriptions, judgments, and so on. It is this concept I propose to search out in this essay.

If any portion of biblical literature fits Walter Brueggemann's category of "structure legitimation,"[1] it would be law. Indeed, law has lent its name to the sociological concept from which Brueggemann derives his theological category.[2]

What does it mean for law to be promulgated as the commandment of God? How can anything new be said on this topic? It is one of the most discussed subjects in the theological and philosophical tradition. Perhaps, though, each new generation has to scale the mountain for itself. Who knows, maybe we will scale it a bit differently than our ancestors.

Socrates posed a fundamental dilemma that faces all theological ethics: Is an act good or holy because a god commanded it, or does the god command it because it is good?[3] The latter alternative accords an act an intrinsic goodness or rightness, and assumes that reason, or perhaps some other faculty, can know it apart from its being commanded. This is Socrates' preference. The orthodox traditions of Judaism and Christianity

---

1. "A Shape for Old Testament Theology, I: Structure Legitimation," *CBQ* 47 (1985) 28–46; on law in particular, cf. 36–38.

2. I first encountered the term and concept of "legitimation" in Peter Berger's *Sacred Canopy* (Garden City, N.Y.: Doubleday, 1967); it is defined on 29–31, and then used constantly.

3. An abstract extension of *ara to hosion, hoti hosion estin, phileitai hypo tōn theōn, hē hoti phileitai, hosion estin* (Plato *Euthyphro* 10a.2).

have tended to defend God's authority. It is the fact that God has commanded something that makes it good, and that God has prohibited it that makes it evil. This "divine command" model of ethics[4] seems to be the proper way to honor God as creator and sovereign, actively engaged in the affairs of creation. Its corollary is that Scripture is given authority over reason, custom, or intuition as the communication of ethical norms.[5]

It may be that we can engage Socrates' dilemma from another angle and discover other possibilities. I propose to do this through the lens of J. L. Austin's theory of performative utterance.[6] He believes that the philosophical tradition has viewed language too narrowly as a description of phenomena, and has been caught in fruitless debates over how it "mirrored" the world.[7] Human discourse in fact does more than describe objects of consciousness—it constructs relationships between speaker and audience. Indeed, all utterances do that to some degree, and some are primarily, perhaps wholly, devoted to constructing or maintaining relationships.

Commandments are clearly relationship-constructing utterances, or "performative utterances," to use Austin's coinage. Will this identification generate new ways to address Socrates' dilemma? Will the concept of a relationship constructed through language be able to avoid the seemingly authoritarian and irrationalist implications that have dogged "divine command" ethics? Can reason, experience, and affections be enlisted as a support rather than a competitor with authority?

I

Austin's distinction between performative and declaratory language is relatively easy to grasp. A declaration is an assertion about something that the addressee can check out if there is any doubt regarding its truth. The truth of the statement depends on its correspondence to the state of af-

---

4. For a discussion of the classical expression, consult Eliezer Schweid, "The Authority Principle in Biblical Morality," *JRE* 10:1 (1982) 1–21; for a philosophic expression, see Robert Merrihew Adams, "A Modified Divine Command Theory of Ethical Wrongness," in *Religion and Morality* (ed. Gene Outka and John P. Reeder Jr.; Garden City, N.Y.: Anchor, 1973) 318–47; and idem, "Divine Command Meta-ethics Modified Again," *JRE* 7:1 (1980) 66–79.

5. Many theologians and theistic philosophers have sought to strike a middle ground to avoid the arbitrariness of divine fiat. Scripture itself gives support for ascribing moral "limits" to God's freedom: in the Psalms, for example, God exemplifies goodness, justice, compassion, and loyalty (e.g., Pss 33:4–5; 97:6–12; 98:3, 9; 100:5; also Exod 34:6–9). This means that believers can trust that what God wills is benevolent, just, and merciful.

6. See "Performative Utterances," in *Philosophical Papers* (Oxford: Oxford Univ. Press, 1979) 233–52; and *How to Do Things with Words* (Cambridge: Harvard Univ. Press, 1975).

7. *How to Do*, 1–4.

fairs referred to. When the description involves logical implications, the truth depends on coherence as well. But language does a lot more than describe or assert. It also does something for speaker and addressee. When humans greet each other, the informative function of language takes a back seat to the forging or maintaining of social bonds. When a speaker offers descriptions of a highly metaphorical character, the descriptive and logical function is displaced by the sharing of emotions and intuitions about what is described and perhaps about something else the statement alludes to. Austin calls these nondeclarative aspects of speaking and listening "illocutionary" and "perlocutionary": what the speaker does in the saying, and how the listener takes what is said.

Performative language consists primarily or entirely of illocutionary and perlocutionary acts. When individuals agree on some project, the "reference" of the language is to actions that they have obligated themselves to perform. Of course, there is some reference to physical conditions outside the acts, but the force of the agreement concerns the actions of the speakers/ addressees.

A command is a performative. The speaker exercises authority over the addressee to obligate the latter to an action. If the addressee recognizes the authority of the speaker, or sees the point of the action in the same light as the speaker, we have a *transaction* between the parties.[8] If the addressee does not recognize the speaker's authority or does not see the point of the action, the speaker's act is "aborted," we might say. If the addressee does owe the speaker obedience and refuses to obey, however, then we have insubordination, which may issue in another performative, a judgment.

Austin describes the various kinds of performatives with face-to-face discourse in mind. He hints occasionally at less personal types of exchanges, such as signs saying "No Trespassing," but he does not really bring law and judicial acts into his discussion. Obviously they do belong. The act of a legislature signed by the proper executive has, in the United States, the force of a command. The citizens of the society are duty-bound to obey the law, and noncompliance involves judicial remedy.

---

8. Much of the effort of speech-act theorists has been devoted to describing how statements are given a particular illocutionary force and how actors receive their power or authorization to perform from their discourse communities. I will be concentrating more on the transaction between speakers and addressees, that is, what takes place between them in the utterance. In commandment, the addressee's relationship to the speaker and to the larger discourse community is changed "before" the addressee responds (the perlocutionary act). This change is effected by the illocutionary act. *Rhetoric,* as I use the term, has to do with how discourse constructs an illocutionary act to elicit a particular response, and how an addressee/ interpreter can construe the discourse in order to respond appropriately.

II

The question is, can the biblical texts that communicate divine command-ments, and other types of law, be categorized as performative? Austin specifically excludes exchanges between imaginary characters and audience as performatives.[9] How could a performative utterance within a narrative world apply to an audience? How can a character who has been created by narrative art enter into relationship with persons "outside" that world? How could a performative transaction between characters within the nar-rative world have force for an audience that is not a part of the event depicted?

When Austin proposed to describe how we "do things with words," he totally ignored the literary artist, who creates an imaginary world with words. In fact, there is something strikingly similar between a play or nar-rative and the ritual by which some performatives are enacted. Each create a "world" through language. The difference is that the performative ritual changes the "real world" status of the participants, whereas a play is only "make-believe."

But what if the imaginary world is the history of one's family and na-tion? That past history can be rendered as an imaginary world may present philosophical conundrums, but in fact it is a common mode of present-ing history. The Pentateuch—beginning with Abraham and Sarah—does present itself as Israel's story. Here the recognition factor is not, or not pri-marily, the audience's humanity, but its own identity as members of this people. Now we are in the realm of performatives that impinge on the audience, for its identity as a people is constituted by specific performa-tive acts. The audience's ancestors participated in some identity-creating performative transactions that continue to bind the people together.

There is a second difficulty for interpreting this narrative as having performative force for the reader: Can God be regarded as a speaker of genuine performative utterances? One could grant that original partici-pants believed that they were encountering this being and that "Israel" is constituted by sole recognition of Yhwh as its God and sovereign, yet ques-tion whether there was/is a "real being" with whom to transact. Israelite identity may well be based on a fiction.

Yhwh is the Creator and Lord of human destiny who lays claim to Is-rael as his people. This description arises in the very accounts that purport to have rhetorical force for the audience of the text. One really cannot separate out the question concerning the reality of the divine persona en-

---

9. *How to Do,* 22

tering into a performative transaction with Israel from the reality of the transaction. The reality of the biblical God cannot be known apart from responding to the utterances of the persona.[10]

In the background of this thesis is a monograph on Old Testament God-language for a series, Overtures to Biblical Theology, a series edited by Walter Brueggemann.[11] In it I proposed that biblical God-language renders God as a character, which means that the identity of God is communicated in the depiction of a dramatis persona who is present to the audience. The narratives and histrionic utterances of prophets and psalmists not only say things about God, but have God actually meet the reader in person, so to speak. At the time, I tended to envisage the rendering as creating an "imaginary world" that the reader was invited to enter, to make her own.

Since I wrote that book, I have become more and more conscious of the rhetoric of the text, that is, how the text is designed to achieve certain objectives with its "inscribed" audience.[12] At first, I thought that the overarching rhetorical objective of Scripture was to persuade the reader to enter or appropriate the textual world. I then began to realize that something transactional was happening: The text was actually creating a relationship between God and the readers—the Israelite people in particular—in the very presentation of the stories, oracles, and prayers of the text. The language that specifically accomplished this rhetorical objective was performative utterances that reached out from the narrative world to address the reader.

God's commandments certainly address the readers of the text along with the Israel depicted in the text. Subsequently, every generation of Jews stands again at the foot of Sinai. Christians have had a more mediated relationship to these laws because of the critique of the Gospels and Paul; but at least the Ten Commandments have been so heard. If commandments create the relationship they describe—if they have performative force—the readers do not come to the knowledge of God at "second hand," but must exist in it to know its truth.[13]

---

10. The narrative of the Pentateuch, and much of the rest of biblical literature, can be understood as a persuasive argument for the reality of the distinctive relationship of the Creator and Lord of creation with the audience, Israel. The narrative and histrionic mode of the argument actually evokes the presence of the divine persona and seeks to elicit the relationship argued for. Revelation occurs when the transaction takes place.

11. *The Rendering of God in the Old Testament* (OBT; Philadelphia: Fortress Press, 1982).

12. See the book I wrote with Allen M. Scult, *Rhetoric and Biblical Interpretation* (Sheffield: Almond, 1990).

13. An observation derived from Søren Kierkegaard, *Philosophical Fragments* (trans. Howard and Edna Hong; Princeton: Princeton Univ. Press, 1985) 89–110.

III

What is meant by "God's commandment"? One must distinguish between commands issued in specific situations to specific persons and those issued to all Israel for all time to come. On the one hand, particular commands, such as Yʜwʜ's command to Abraham to "go from your country and your kindred and your father's house to the land that I will show you" (Gen 12:1), concern the personage in the textual world, and can be appropriated by the text's audience only by analogy. This particular one has had quite a fruitful history in synagogue and church. On the other hand, the commandments of the Decalogue are as pertinent to and binding on the reader as they are to the people in the textual world. The audience must interpret them, and analogy plays a role in that practice, but the "thou shalt not..." is unmediated: interpretation becomes the fulfillment of the obligation created by the addressee.

The rabbinic tradition has found commandments and moral and legal doctrine throughout the Pentateuch, but I think we are justified in restricting the term *commandment* to the formal promulgation of law for Israel at Mount Horeb. It is in these texts that the authority of Yʜwʜ to command and Israel's duty to obey is negotiated and ratified, and the exercise of this authority takes speech forms recognized by form criticism as rules of law. Textually, this means the prescriptive material in Exodus 20 through Numbers 10, supplemented by scattered prescriptions in Numbers 11–35. Here we find the Decalogue (Exod 20:1–17), the Book of the Covenant (Exod 20:21–23:19), instructions for the construction of the Tabernacle (Exod 25:1–31:17), the so-called cultic Decalogue (Exod 34:11–28), rules for sacrifice (Leviticus 1–7), rules for maintaining purity in the community (Leviticus 11–15), institution of the Day of Atonement (Leviticus 16), and the Holiness Code (Lev 17:1–26:2; 27:1–34).[14] Numbers adds prescriptions occasioned by the issues that come up as the people prepare to leave Sinai (e.g., Num 5:1–6:21), during the forty-year sojourn in the wilderness (e.g., 15:1–41) and the beginnings of the conquest (e.g., 35:1–34).

Not all of this material is commandment in the linguistic sense of prescriptions and prohibitions addressed directly to the textual audience. After the Ten Commandments, we find this type of formulation scattered through the various legal collections, mixed in with impersonally formulated laws, material addressed to community officials, commands concerning the Exodus generation, and so on. One of the questions is how widely the term

---

14. While some scholars have recently expressed doubts about the existence of an independent legal corpus in Leviticus 17–26, large portions of those chapters stand out sufficiently from Priestly law to legitimate the judgment that there may be.

commandment should be extended. This question is compounded by the tendency of traditio-historical and form critics to consider the impersonal formulations to be artificially placed in the mouth of Yhwh. Even if we accept the extant text as the object of our exposition, impersonal statements of law do not forge the kind of relationship between speaker and addressee attributable to personally addressed commandments and prohibitions.

How is that relationship to be described? A personally addressed commandment or prohibition is, to borrow from Martin Buber, an "I-Thou" encounter.[15] The speaker is not only offering a rule of conduct, but expressing a concern about the good of the addressee, who is made personally responsible to the speaker for fulfilling the relationship. When parents communicate commandments covering moral conduct to their children, the receptive child understands this as an expression of love and seeks to return that love by "pleasing" her parents. It is not uncommon for people to gauge their whole lives according to whether they have lived up to their parents' expectations. When God addresses Israelites in the commandments—quite likely through parents—the same sort of relationship is formed.[16]

The impersonal laws of the collections do not bear the same import. They bear the authority of God, but not the personal encounter and sense of concern for the recipients' welfare. Moreover, they govern the decisions of public officials—judges, priests, heads of households, royal administrators. Even in an organic society, where everyone is involved in everyone else's business, lines of authority are maintained. Perhaps personally addressed prescriptions and proscriptions governing official acts (e.g., Exod 23:1–3, 6–8) had the same force for the officials as the commandments had for all Israelites in all aspects of their lives; but these legal collections for officials would be heard differently by outsiders.

I have not mentioned the Deuteronomic law (Deuteronomy 12–26). Since Moses is the speaker, it does not have the same performative force as the law with God as speaker. Nevertheless, it does address readers in such a way as to make them responsible to Yhwh for compliance with its injunctions. Indeed, no other corpus has the degree of personal appeal that this one has. The human word of Moses, the interpreter of God's will par excellence, has the force of God's own address. Its laws are to be proclaimed to Israel generation after generation (Deut 31:9–14). The authority of Yhwh stands behind it and will enforce it (Deut 12:1, 28, 31; and cf. chap. 28).

---

15. As developed in *I and Thou* (trans. R. G. Smith; New York: Charles Scribner's Sons, 1958).

16. Perhaps there is less immediacy, at least for the child, but greater authority and one that remains constant in adulthood. Parents themselves, acutely aware of their own fallibility and need for rhetorical power, welcome God's authority behind character-forming injunctions.

Perhaps this is one of the roots of the rabbinic tradition that produced the Mishnah and Talmuds.[17]

It is hard to say what this means for the thesis of this article that the commandments create a personal relationship between speaker and addressee. At the least, it casts a shadow over it. Within Deuteronomy, God's direct address of law to Israelites is restricted to the Ten Commandments (so chap. 5; also 4:9–14); the rest is human interpretation, applying the comprehensive code of conduct to particular subjects. Within the Pentateuch, the Ten Commandments do enjoy a pride of position, but God follows them up with codes and pronouncements covering a broad spectrum of moral and legal topics, with Deuteronomy performing the function of inaugurating the interpretive tradition.

Jews and Christians part ways on the question of how broadly to extend the term *commandment,* or at least which texts continue to bear the full weight of commandment for the religious community. Everyone agrees on the Ten Commandments, but Jewish tradition tends to accord the laws contained in the codes and collections equal status, whereas Christians have demoted them—though to varying degrees according to differing rationales. These differing responses, reflecting ambiguous signals in the text itself, justify leaving the question open.

IV

Now we are in a position to return to Socrates: Is an act good, or righteous, because a god commanded it, or did the god command it because it is right and good? We have seen that, and in what sense, God commands the laws of the Pentateuch. Now we must ask: What difference does that make to the law?

There is no question that the Israelite audience for which the legal collections were written and the Pentateuch assembled was expected to learn and obey the law because God commanded it. We read exhortations frequently to do all that YHWH commands. This type of exhortation, however, does not preclude the proposition that God commands it because it is good. If a commandment or judicial rule conforms to the audience's moral convictions and legal conceptions, or can be supported by arguments of a general moral or legal character, it may be that its intrinsic quality of rightness is what makes it authoritative. The prohibitions of killing, committing adultery, and stealing within the Ten Commandments are well-nigh universal norms; clearly, God commands them because they are right.

---

17. The style of Deuteronomic literature is much different from the Mishnah and Talmuds, but both speak divine Torah in a human voice.

In cases like this, God's will has been identified with what can be called "natural law." We need not get bogged down in the philosophical issue of whether there is such a thing. That is, we do not need to prove that there are some universal moral and legal principles; a given society, or even broader cultural sphere, has a generally agreed upon set of moral, social, legal and political values and concepts. The value scheme involving honor and shame, for example, may not be of great force in modern urban society, but it certainly was potent in ancient Near Eastern societies. This value scheme was "natural" in that it was not created by authority, but assumed by it.[18]

An interpreter can reconstruct the apologetic situation of a law or body of law in various ways. Just in reading the laws themselves one can sense when their rightness was taken for granted, or had to be established by motives clauses, or came down to the authority of God the lawgiver. Most of the law appeals to the moral judgment of the audience and thus can be classified as the expression of "natural law."

Another piece of evidence that biblical laws are expressions of natural law is found in several stories in which mediators submit arguments to God about what God should do, or how the law should be modified (e.g., Gen 18:22–33; Num 27:1–11); these arguments involve general moral reasoning.

Finally, we can, I think, take the descriptions of the kind of men who should be selected as judges—"able, God-fearing, trustworthy, honest" (Exod 18:21)—as an indication that the interpretation and application of the law was to be guided by principles of piety, justice, and prudence, norms that are accessible to a common human wisdom.[19]

Biblical scholarship has supplemented this internal check with studies of parallels in the ancient Near East. When pentateuchal laws are the same as, or very similar to, laws of surrounding societies, we can assume that we have a "natural" law, a law whose rightness was accepted before or without reference to a particular god's commandment to a particular people.

---

18. James Barr works with this rather sociocultural idea of natural law in "Biblical Law and the Question of Natural Theology," in *The Law in the Bible and in Its Environment* (ed. T. Veijola; Göttingen: Vandenhoeck & Ruprecht, 1990) 1–22. Natural law theorists, and their opponents, would prefer precise definitions and distinctions, but for the purposes of my argument a loose and eclectic definition is preferable.

19. It is human finitude and sinfulness, according to the most consistent versions of this position, that require special revelation in the first place, and those who have been granted knowledge of God will have in principle been freed from the limitations of natural, sinful humanity. Otherwise, they could not recognize the truth in the relationship created and knowledge communicated. See A. MacIntyre, *Three Rival Versions of Moral Enquiry: Encyclopaedia, Genealogy, and Tradition* (Gifford Lectures 1988; Notre Dame: Univ. of Notre Dame, 1990) 82–103, on Augustine's theological conception of moral inquiry.

All but the first two commandments of the Decalogue can be considered to conform to the moral and religious convictions of most ancient Semitic societies.[20] Many parallels can be found, moreover, to the judicial law of the Book of the Covenant, as well as many provisions of the other collections. Indeed, it is standard interpretive procedure in the study of biblical law to search out parallels.

One could conclude from this evidence that God's commanding only adds motivational force to common moral convictions. God's role in law and morals is to encourage us to do what we already know is right. One of the distinguishing features of pentateuchal law is the amount of "motive clauses" and "parenesis" interspersed among the commandments and rulings. This grows with time.[21] Religious conviction is obviously playing the role we often assign to "rhetoric." The appeal is to emotions and imagination to supplement the "rational" language of law.

A deeper view of rhetoric will, however, accord the rhetorical transaction of commanding and hearing an independent force. The command creates a relationship between the speaker and addressee that does not exist apart from it. Obedience to the commandment is a triangular transaction: the addressee does what he or she knows is right because there is an obligation to God, a responsibility one may prize for itself because one loves God. The fact that one knows that the act is good or right now becomes an enhancement of one's relationship to God: God has given the law for our good (Deut 6:24–25; 10:12–13). It is not that God's commanding adds emotive force to what is good, but what is good adds moral force to God's authority.[22] Rhetorical power works in concert to enhance one's relationship to God.

The triangular relationship created by God's commanding the good is reflected in the Psalms. Access to God's presence in the temple depends

---

20. See my article, "Is the Truth of the First Commandment Known by Reason?" *CBQ* 56 (1994) 423–41.

21. In B. Gemser's classic article on motive clauses, "The Importance of the Motive Clause in Old Testament Law," in *Congress Volume, Copenhagen, 1953* (VTSup 1; Leiden: Brill, 1953) 50–66, he noted their increase in the Holiness Code and Deuteronomic Law over the Book of the Covenant and Ten Commandments.

22. James Watts's paper read to the SBL Pentateuch Section, at the SBL Annual Meeting (Nov. 25, 1996), entitled "The Legal Characterization of God in the Pentateuch," says this nicely: "The casuistic laws of the Pentateuch show [an] interest for fairness and equity, and thereby characterize their promulgator as just. The repetition of particular issues elevates them to paradigmatic illustrations of God's concerns. For example, laws protecting the welfare of resident aliens establish in the divine speeches the theme of God's equal justice for all. God's emphasis on the community's punishment of murderers demonstrates that God shares judicial authority with the leaders of the community. [Legal texts] paint a portrait of God which exemplifies the ancient Near Eastern ideal of the just king" (pp. 4–5).

on a person's moral behavior.[23] When the supplicant protests innocence or confesses guilt, moral wrongs are just as likely to be mentioned as strictly religious infractions.[24] Likewise, the supplicant's enemies are described as wicked as well as irreligious.[25]

V

The arguments submitted above should be relatively uncontroversial. None challenges the identification of God's will with the moral law, the "natural law" as embodied in a particular society. The following arguments do make that challenge, and are indeed controversial. I will set out the issues and leave the resolution open for the reader's judgment.

Deuteronomy 4 claims the *uniqueness* of Israelite law. Verses 32–33 locate the uniqueness in the theophanic experience itself: "Inquire now of the days of the past, before your time, since the day God created the human race on earth, and ask from one end of heaven to the other, whether such a great thing as this has ever happened or was ever heard of. Did any people ever hear the voice of a god speaking out of the midst of the fire, as you have heard, and live through it?" Later in the unit, it draws the conclusion: "to you it was shown, that you might know that YHWH is God; there is no other besides him" (v. 35). What are we to make of such a claim? It is a dangerous argument, for it courts the sin of spiritual pride and invites comparisons that cut the braggart down to size. In this case it seems particularly vulnerable. Theophanic appearances are a staple of ancient Near Eastern religion, and characteristic of the Canaanite god known in the Bible as Baal.[26] Contrary to what the Deuteronomic Moses says, the Sinaitic theophany is a clear manifestation of the "common ancient Near Eastern theology."[27]

One might wonder whether the author of Deuteronomy was simply ignorant of the religion of the peoples around Israel and depending for knowledge on the biblical narrative. That seems unlikely, for the mass of Israelites probably hovered somewhere between polytheism and exclusivistic Yahwism. One would certainly expect the author to know the imagery

---

23. Articulated in the two entrance torahs, Psalms 15, 24; it is also taught in less formal ways, e.g., Ps 5:4–6 (MT 5:7).

24. Confessions of sin, like Psalm 51, are too vague and poetic to sustain such a thesis. But the protests of innocence, like Ps 26:4–7, mention specific actions one might be guilty of; the fullest example of this genre is Job 31.

25. Pss 10:7–13; 14:1–4; etc.

26. See Frank Cross, *Canaanite Myth and Hebrew Epic: Essays in the History of the Religion of Israel* (Cambridge: Harvard Univ. Press, 1973) 147–77.

27. Brueggemann, "Structure Legitimation," 31–33.

associated with Y$_{HWH}$'s competitor, Baal. It occurs to me that the argument is polemical in the spirit of Amos's question, "Did you bring to me sacrifices and offerings the forty years in the wilderness, O house of Israel?" (5:25). The extant Pentateuch narratives report that they did, but Amos's rhetorical question demands a negative answer. Amos is undercutting the security of tradition.

What is "Moses" doing in asking the rhetorical question, "has such a great thing as this ever happened"? Perhaps he is denying the "reality" of the theophanies of the gods. He is certainly saying to the Israelites that the Horeb revelation makes them who they are, and should be inscribed upon their memory and appropriated as sufficient reason to recognize Y$_{HWH}$'s authority alone.

The rhetorical question does entice one to search for aspects of this tradition that are unique. It was a whole people who saw and heard, and they were not destroyed by the holy presence of God. Did other cults have this kind of remembrance? Did a whole people see and hear their god?

Perhaps the audience of the narrative makes it unique by accepting the identity imposed upon it by this narrative; the account of the event has performative force. Did any other cult create community by means of performative narrative?

An experience, however, cannot have performative force without words. According to the extant account of the revelation of Y$_{HWH}$ to Israel at Mount Sinai, the "voice out of the midst of the fire" spoke words—in fact, the Ten Commandments.[28] The commandments do not simply inform Israel of what Y$_{HWH}$ expects of his people—they put them in force. Indeed, they create a personal relationship between Y$_{HWH}$ and each Israelite by their address, making each Israelite responsible for the welfare of other Israelites and for the single-minded devotion of Israel to Y$_{HWH}$.[29]

Although this performative transaction may be unique, it remains a version of the "common ancient Near Eastern theology."[30] It would not have been possible to persuade the ancient Israelites of their obligation to laws

---

28. That is the way the narrative of Exodus 19–20 reads, and the way Deuteronomy 5 rehearses it. Exod 20:18–20 has the people ask Moses to act as mediator, as if they have only experienced numinous sounds and seen fearful things. Probably at an earlier stage in the history of the narrative, the theophany prompted the people to elect Moses to ascend the mount and receive the Ten Commandments written by the finger of God (Exod 31:18). But the text that elicited Deuteronomic thinking and has provoked many thoughts since has all Israel hear the commandments directly from God. This is the only case in the Hebrew Bible where the mass of people hear God without a mediator.

29. The people have collectively agreed to obey Yhwh (Exod 19:7–8; cf. 24:3–8); the commandments fill out what Yhwh demands, and also create a relationship with each individual Israelite.

30. Brueggemann, "Structure Legitimation," 31–33.

because they derived from God if the gods of the ancient Near Eastern did not also make demands of their worshipers. Indeed, according to *Enuma Elish,* humans were created to "serve" the gods.[31] In the Bible, the very definition of apostasy frequently employs the verb *šāmar*—the same verb used for the Israelite's proper relationship to YHWH.[32]

The Ten Commandments, however, encompass a lot more than cultic service, indeed, more than anyone would categorize as "religious" practice. Walter Harrelson breaks the content of the ten prohibitions into four parts, rather than the traditional "two tables": God's Exclusive Claims, God's Basic Institutions, Basic Human Obligations, and Basic Social Obligations.[33] Perhaps making all of life "service" to YHWH is unique in the ancient Near East. God's interests, one might say, have extended to the good of the people in all aspects of their life. Service to God includes service in behalf of a just, righteous, and holy communal life.

Again, this is not entirely novel. While the gods of the ancient Near East tend to interact with adherents at a cultic level, with service aimed at their own enhancement,[34] they are also given credit for establishing justice through law. Hammurabi, in the prologue to his code, honors Shamash for inspiring him to draw up his code.[35] While this is designed as an apologia for the monarch, it does indicate that law was experienced as having a divine origin and authority.

The collections of law found in Exodus and Leviticus, and in Deuteronomy too, are relatives of the Code of Hammurabi and similar codes. Biblical collections, with the exception of Deuteronomy, are fundamentally different, however, in that YHWH communicates them directly to the people of Israel. While Moses is the mediator, the collections are not ascribed to him and there is no apologia for "Moses' rule." The collections are formulated as YHWH's law for Israel. Whatever one thinks about the origin of these legal corpora, they are now divine "apologia." Moreover, they are concerned to establish the responsibility not only of the king but of each member of the society, according to their "station," for the justice, righteousness, and peace of the community. There is a significant "democ-

---

31. See *Enuma Elish,* Tablet VI, ll. 1–38; available in *ANET,* 68.
32. See, e.g., Exod 23:23–25, 33; Josh 24:14–24.
33. *Ten Commandments and Human Rights* (OBT; Philadelphia: Fortress Press, 1980) 51–154.
34. See *Enuma Elish,* Tablet VI, ll. 1–38.
35. At least that is how modern scholars interpret the picture on the stela from Susa; when one consults the text of the poetic prologue, it would seem that the gods have given Hammurabi power, and he is here giving an accounting to them of its exercise; available in *ANET,* 164–65.

ratization" of justice in Israelite law.[36] This may be what makes Israel's law unique.

VI

Deuteronomy 4:6–8 does claim that the content of the law sets it apart:

> Keep them and do them; for that will be your wisdom and your understanding in the sight of the peoples, who, when they hear all these statutes, will say, "Surely this great nation is a wise and understanding people." For what great nation is there that has a god so near to it as YHWH our God is to us, whenever we call upon him? And what great nation is there that has statutes and ordinances so righteous as all this law that I set before you this day?

This statement can be read as claiming a superior law, or a unique one. This claim resides in the nearness of God, presumably as the one who commands and judges the law, and in the "wisdom and understanding" it communicates to Israel. The latter claim could be for a revealed wisdom; that would be the more interesting way to take it. We could rephrase it as the question: Are there ethical and legal rules, concepts, and principles that derive from theological teaching and cannot be sustained without religious conviction? In other words, is there anything unique in biblical law, and can this uniqueness be traced to its unique religion? This question has to do with the content of the law, that is, its rulings and the concepts and principles that inform these rules of law.

The debate has the earmarks of an interminable one. Some scholars believe that one can discern unique legal principles in biblical law deriving from Israelite religion, and others insist that laws be interpreted as part of a common ancient Semitic legal culture.

A number of decades ago, Moshe Greenberg proposed that biblical law makes a fundamental distinction between crimes against persons and crimes against property. Persons cannot be assigned a monetary value, so all crimes against persons must be resolved by a proportional retribution against the perpetrator. By contrast, crimes against property involve restitution with compensation—entirely within property or monetary terms. The reason persons cannot be assessed a monetary value is that each and every human is made in the image of God, and therefore is of infinite value. Property, including animals, is lower in the hierarchy of being and therefore quite susceptible to quantification. This theological scheme is unique to biblical monotheism and was bequeathed to Europe through the Bible.[37]

---

36. Lecture by Moshe Greenberg, at Hartman Institute, Jerusalem, Spring 1990.
37. Moshe Greenberg, "Some Postulates of Biblical Criminal Law," in *Yehezkel Kaufmann Jubilee Volume* (ed. M. Haran; Jerusalem: Magnes, 1960) 5–28.

J. J. Finkelstein adopted this viewpoint in his monograph, *The Ox That Gored*.[38] The difference between Greenberg and Finkelstein is that Greenberg is a religious Jew, whereas Finkelstein was secular and saw that new foundations would have to be laid to support Western values regarding the human person. In other words, he considered the value to derive from Jewish monotheism, but that it could be sustained by other worldviews.

This line of reasoning has been contested. The most comprehensive recent alternative I know of is Raymond Westbrook's.[39] We might call his interpretive scheme a revival of pan-Babylonianism, according to which the whole of the ancient Semitic world, from 2200 to 700 BCE, shared a common legal culture. This world of legal ideas was limited and stagnant, allowing the modern interpreter to develop the reasoning on any legal topic from documents from different times and places. The casuistic laws of the Book of the Covenant (Exod 21:2–22:17 [MT 16]) are to be correlated with laws from other ancient Near Eastern codes. Nothing in them requires reference to the theological beliefs of the Israelites. We can also assume that the legal practice of Israelites conformed to the norms of the common Semitic law.

Westbrook's interpretive scheme offers many advantages to the interpreter. It allows for the development of a much larger "database," and to fill in gaps by analogy. Moreover, it aids in the reconstruction of the social mores assumed by laws. One might say that this goes hand in hand with the marshaling of anthropological evidence for recovering the mores and social structures of Israelite society because it must be "like" "premodern" societies today.

Since his scheme is genetic, it has only tangential affect on the transaction of the biblical texts with their Jewish and Christian audiences.[40] It does, however, make a difference to the interpretation of legal texts whether their legal doctrine is based intrinsically on the rendering of God in the Hebrew Bible, or whether it derives in its essentials from "natural law." Does God's commandment require a reevaluation of how those who

---

38. Transactions of the American Philosophical Society, 71/2 (Philadelphia: American Philosophical Society, 1981). Shalom Paul can also be enlisted in this group; see his *Studies in the Book of the Covenant in the Light of Cuneiform and Biblical Law* (VTSup 18; Leiden: Brill, 1970).

39. Raymond Westbrook, *Studies in Biblical and Cuneiform Law* (Cahiers de la Revue biblique 26; Paris: Gabalda, 1988); idem, *Property and the Family in Biblical Law* (JSOT-Sup 113; Sheffield: JSOT Press, 1991); and the conference volume that centered around an essay by Westbrook: *Theory and Method in Biblical and Cuneiform Law: Revision, Interpolation and Development* (ed. Bernard M. Levinson; JSOTSup 181; Sheffield: Sheffield Academic Press, 1994).

40. I have elsewhere raised objections to Westbrook's hypothesis, and will not repeat them here. See "Who Is the Evolutionist?" in *Theory and Method*, 152–59.

acknowledge God's authority seek to achieve a just and holy society, or is what is just and good determined by a universal moral reason?

Although it might seem at first glance that theology would be invested in the former, the history of theology is not that simple. Thinkers of the stature of Maimonides and Thomas Aquinas have identified God's commandment with some version or the other of natural law.[41] In contemporary critical scholarship, Martin Buss has maintained throughout his career that biblical law is best interpreted as conforming in its basic norms and legal instrumentalities to law in societies all over the world.[42] By natural law, he means a form of guidance that is understood to be "useful" or "good for life,"[43] not the will of the sovereign or the powerful. A theology which argues that God commands what is intrinsically good will differ from one which argues that the good can only be settled by God's exercise of authority, but it will be no less concerned to understand and honor God's commandment.

The issue is like a difficult case before the bar. The evidence is not decisive; for every text that seems to support one side, there is an alternative construal that would conform it to the other. A lot has to do with how one fills in the gaps. The scholarly community itself is the jury, but the jury is made up of advocates. Perhaps the debate is interminable.

VII

Can God's commandment terminate disputes over what is right and good within the community constituted by it?[44] Argument on questions of right and good is potentially interminable. That is, arguments are available on various sides of many fundamental principles and on their application to particular cases. Can God's commandment terminate an unresolved debate? This is certainly what believers have meant to do by quoting biblical texts in such debates. Is that an illicit appeal to authority or a legitimate application of divine sovereignty?

If a theologian identifies God's will with natural law, or universal moral reason, it is implied that God's sovereign power is manifested in the persuasive force of moral argumentation. God's power is the "power of truth."

---

41. See Maimonides, *Guide to the Perplexed*, III 25–49; available in an edition translated by Shlomo Pines (Chicago: Univ. of Chicago Press, 1963) 502–613; Thomas, *Summa Theologiae*, questions 90–97; available in translation in *On Law, Morality, and Politics* (Indianapolis: Hackett, 1988).

42. Cf. Buss "Legal Science and Legislation," in *Theory and Method*, 88–90; idem, "Logic and Israelite Law," *Semeia* 45 (1989) 49–65.

43. *Theory and Method*, 89–90.

44. The idea for this argument derives from Kyle Pasewark, *A Theology of Power: Being beyond Domination* (Minneapolis: Fortress Press, 1993) 236–70.

Since a given society must be in general agreement on what is oppressive, violent, crooked, petty, shameful, and disloyal, the divine commandment gains suasive power by its capacity to thematize the moral consensus. Within the cultural horizon of text and audience, this can be called the power of truth.

Every society has some issues in dispute, however, and it falls to constituted authority to rule on such matters. Does YHWH have that power within the Old Testament world? Does the divine law have that power in the religious communities that recognize its authority?

There is strong evidence in the laws and narratives of the Pentateuch that YHWH exercised the power to terminate unresolved disputes in matters of law. According to Exod 18:19–23, Moses is to "represent the people before God, and bring their cases to God" (v. 19), and allow delegated authorities to apply the law in "small matters" (v. 22a).[45] We have several accounts where this procedure is followed: a case of blasphemy by an "alien" (Lev 24:10–16, 22) and of labor on the Sabbath (Num 15:31–36). The daughters of Zelophehad bring their case to Moses in an effort to alter the legal tradition regarding inheritance, and God rules in their favor (27:1–11).[46] This latter case shows that God's decision may be acquiescence to cogent moral argument. It also exhibits the transactional character of the exercise of divine sovereignty.[47]

These texts model a tradition of interpreting God's law that ascribes to it the power both to terminate disputes and to adjust the law to the changing social conditions and moral consensus of the community for which it is authoritative. Canonization had the force of freezing the legal texts. Deut 12:32 (MT 13:1) expresses this vividly: "Everything that I command you you shall be careful to do; you shall not add to it or take from it." Nevertheless, an oral tradition carried on the task of interpreting the law to meet new conditions as they arose and to reshape the principles and concepts to maintain the law's suasive force. This tradition itself became the text of the Mishnah and Talmud. The genius of the rabbinic tradition was and still is its capacity to allow for interminable debate within the terminating authority of Torah.[48]

The Christian church has not had the same obligation to Mosaic law,

---

45. My point would be better founded if the text were taken to mean matters where no question of legal concept or principle is in dispute; see Deut 17:8.

46. One has the impression that the appellate "court" set up in Deut 17:8–13 to take the place of "Moses" did not seek divine revelation, but arrived at a divine decision by reasoning.

47. See Watts, "Legal Characterization," 12–16.

48. There was a "fundamentalist" protest against the rabbinic tradition in late antiquity, known as the Karaites. It sought to go back to the simple word of Scripture, but could not avoid many absurdities deriving from a frozen law.

nor has it had the authority to carry on an oral tradition with the force of divine law. Moral rules and fundamental principles have continued to exercise authority, however, and the Roman Catholic Church does have the authority of the confessional. Until fairly recently, the Bible, as interpreted by church authorities, had the power to terminate debate, and in many communities it still does.

Since the critical era began in the Enlightenment, the authority of Scripture to terminate disputes has been eroded from within and without the religious communities. When the human authorship of the biblical rendering of God was brought to the fore, its cultural relativity and perhaps its representation of class interests made its claims to articulate the eternal will of God implausible. For religious people, the natural law, or moral reason, progressively takes the place of Scripture as the source of the knowledge of God's will.

That is just the rub: debates that reach an impasse represent the limits of moral reason. Without an apodictic intervention, the debate will rend the community and leave its members without the firm moral guidance that makes for character. Perhaps there is something to the old idea that God's commanding is more important than what is commanded. If this sounds too authoritarian, perhaps Emmanuel Levinas's conception of obedient reason, reason that accepts God's commanding authority before it is exercised, can resolve the crisis of authority.[49] It allows the exercise of freedom in the responsibility of addressees to apply the commandment and holds us accountable for the moral quality of our application.

The question is, can community be sustained without a means of terminating debates over norms and their implementation? Consider the following midrash:

> R. Simon said: When the Holy One, blessed be He, came to create Adam, the ministering angels formed themselves into groups and parties, some of them saying, "Let him be created," whilst others urged, "Let him not be created." Thus it is written, *Love and Truth fought together, Righteousness and Peace combated each other* (Ps. LXXXV, 11): Love said, "Let him be created, because he will dispense acts of love"; Truth said, "Let him not be created, because he is compounded of falsehood"; Righteousness said, "Let him be created, because he will perform righteous deeds"; Peace said, "Let him not be created, because he is full of strife." What did the Lord do? He took Truth and cast it to the ground. Said the ministering angels before the Holy One, blessed be He, "Sovereign of the Universe! Why dost Thou despise Thy seal? Let Truth arise from the earth." Hence it is written, *Let truth spring up from the earth* (Ps. LXXXV, 12)....

---

49. See his essay, "The Temptation of Temptation," in *Nine Talmudic Readings* (Bloomington: Indiana Univ. Press, 1994) 30–50.

R. Huna the Elder of Sepphoris said: While the ministering angels were arguing with each other and disputing with each other, the Holy One, blessed be He, created him. Said He to them: "What can ye avail? Man has already been made!"[50]

Does R. Huna's termination of the debate terminate the debate?

– 8 –

"God Is Not a Human
That He Should Repent"

(Numbers 23:19 and 1 Samuel 15:29)

R. W. L. Moberly

The "repenting" of God is an aspect of the portrayal of God within Israel's Scripture that has often been something of an embarrassment to Jewish and Christian interpreters. For it has too readily appeared to be at odds with first principles about the nature of God as these have been classically formulated, not least in terms of "immutability." Such embarrassment does not, to be sure, characterize the work of Walter Brueggemann, who is happy to explore the meaning and theological significance of precisely those aspects of Israel's portrayal of God that were problematic within many traditional construals. One of the many strengths of his work has been to bring back into focus important questions about the nature of religious language in characteristic Hebrew expressions—questions that are of considerable importance for the vitality of Jewish and Christian theology and spirituality. This essay explores one small, but well-known, crux within this larger debate. It is a pleasure to offer the essay in honor of a friend who has constantly stimulated, informed, and helped reshape my theological thinking.

Divine "Repentance" as a Theological Principle

Before we discuss what it might mean that God "does not repent," it will be helpful to set the context by briefly considering some of those passages which state that God "does repent." That God "repents" (*nhm*, *Niphal*) is in fact formulated as a theological axiom in the narrative of Jeremiah at the potter's house (Jer 18:1–12). The formulation is striking, with a deliberately paradoxical logic that is easily missed.

The context, that of a potter's ability to do with clay as he wishes (v. 4), is one that stresses the power of the maker over that which is made. When applied to God (v. 6), it intrinsically suggests absolute divine power. For the logic of the imagery is not that of interpersonal relationship, which is so characteristic of Israel's Scripture (king and subjects, master and slave, husband and wife, father and son). However unequal such relationships were, they were always in principle mutual, engaging the stronger party no less than (although differently from) the weaker party. Moreover, sheer pity and compassion might renew the relationship at times when it was in danger of breaking down—as, famously, God cannot restrain compassion toward Israel (Hos 11:8–9). But with a lump of clay a potter has no relationship, no responsibilities, no feelings—it is an object to be used. When applied to God, therefore, the imagery of potter (*yôṣēr*) does not evoke mutuality in any form, but rather unilateral power. It is an idiom that is readily used in the context of God's work of creation (Gen 2:7, *yṣr*). It is hardly surprising when the imagery is used elsewhere specifically in two kinds of context: either to emphasize human weakness in contrast to divine strength (Isa 64:8–12; 2 Cor 4:7), or to discourage, indeed disallow, dissent from a divine decision that appears problematic (Isa 45:9–13; Rom 9:19–24). So when Jeremiah hears the word of YHWH at the potter's house saying that Israel in God's hand is like clay in the potter's hand, one would expect this to introduce either a picture of human weakness or some divine decree that could not be gainsaid.

The formulation that follows (vv. 7–10) is therefore remarkable. It takes up the basic commissioning of Jeremiah (Jer 1:9–10) to address "nations and kingdoms" (*gôyim, mamlākôt,* 1:10; 18:7, 9) and to speak in such a way as both "to pluck up, break down and destroy" (1:10; 18:7) and "to build and to plant" (1:10; 18:9). This commissioning is reformulated now in terms of what God does in response to people's response to such words from Jeremiah. It stresses that in neither case, whether destroying or building, is the outcome a foregone conclusion, but that all depends on how people respond; human repentance can avert a threatened disaster, while human wrongdoing can forfeit a promised good. In each case God "repents" in response to the human attitude and action. Indeed, the wording emphasizes that what God does is in some integral way dependent on the human action. This has often puzzled commentators who have missed the paradoxical logic. Typical is the observation of William McKane:

> Vv. 7–10 are not fitted for the function of interpreting a parable: they amount to a general, theological statement, with a carefully contrived structure, and they have too abstract an aspect to entitle them to be considered seriously as an interpretation of the parable of the potter and his clay.[1]

---

1. W. McKane, *Jeremiah,* I (ICC; Edinburgh: T. & T. Clark, 1986) 426.

Even Gerhard von Rad is rather weak and perplexed when discussing this text:

> In this last passage [Jer 18:1ff.], the content is somewhat obscure, and this detracts from its impressiveness. In the opening verses Jeremiah is dealing with his own people who, by being shown the immense freedom at God's disposal, are to take warning. Then, however, it suddenly passes over into general terms. If Jahweh has purposed evil against a particular nation, and it "turns," then he repents of the trouble he intended to cause; and if he has purposed good for another nation, but it is disobedient, then he will alter his design and punish it. This part, too, is meant to indicate Jahweh's freedom as he directs history, but it does this in an oddly theoretical way by giving imaginary examples which are quite contrary to the sense of the passage, for they almost make Jahweh's power dependent on law rather than on freedom. This middle passage (vv. 7–10) after which Judah is once more addressed, should probably be regarded as a theological expansion.[2]

Far from being "somewhat obscure" or "oddly theoretical," the paradoxical logic of the passage is in fact simple and clear. In a context whose imagery strongly emphasizes absolute divine power, we have as strong a statement as possible of divine responsiveness to human attitude and action. *Where God is most free to act, God is most bound in that acting.* YHWH's sovereignty is not exercised arbitrarily, but responsibly and responsively, interacting with the moral, or immoral, actions of human beings. The wording of vv. 7–10 is not some kind of denial of God's freedom, but rather specifies the morally responsive nature of that divine freedom. The shift from Israel to the nations is partly because these are the terms in which Jeremiah's commissioning as a prophet is spelled out (1:9–10), and partly to make the theological point that God's dealings with Israel/Judah are not different in their moral dynamics from God's dealings with any and every nation—as befits a God who has created all.

The theological principle thus enunciated is regularly exemplified elsewhere in Israel's scripture; and while Jeremiah formulates the principle with regard to nations, Ezekiel expresses it in terms of particular people (Ezek 33:10–16). God's "repentance" in response to human turning from evil is classically worked out in the story of Jonah (Jonah 3:1–10), and also elsewhere within the story of Jeremiah (Jeremiah 26, esp. 26:16–19). The converse, God's "repentance" of promised good in response to human wrongdoing, is equally illustrated (Gen 6:5–8; 1 Sam 2:27–30; 15:1–35).

The fundamental presupposition is that God's relationship with people is a genuine, because responsive, relationship. The relationship between God

---

2. G. von Rad, *Old Testament Theology* (trans. D. M. G. Stalker; 2 vols.; New York: Harper & Row, 1962–65) 198–99.

and people is characterized by a dynamic analogous to that of relationships between people: they are necessarily mutual, and they either develop or wither away. How people respond to God *matters* to God, and *affects* how God responds to people. This of course raises sharp problems of theological language and conceptuality. Suffice it to note that the Hebrew writers show a certain awareness of possible problems of theological language in their use of terminology. Hebrew has two different words for "repent," *šûb* and *niḥam,* and usually (though not invariably) uses *šûb* of people and *niḥam* of God. When both human and divine "repentance" are spoken of together, the terminological difference is always observed, thus implicitly recognizing a difference between what may be predicated of humanity and what may be predicated of God: when people repent (*šûb*), God "repents" (*niḥam*) (Jer 18:8; 26:3; Jonah 3:10). It is unfortunate that contemporary English has no obvious rendering for this Hebrew conceptuality—alternatives to "repent," such as "relent," "regret," or "change mind," may solve some problems, but they easily create others. The theological usage of *niḥam* may be as hard to translate as Paul's *sarx.* What matters is to understand the moral, theological, and relational conceptuality it represents, and to explain and use it accordingly.

The Denial of Divine "Repentance" as a Theological Principle

It is against this background of the consistent depiction of YHWH as "repenting" that one must set those passages which deny that YHWH "repents." If to say that God "repents" implies that the relationship of God with humanity in general, and Israel in particular, is a genuine, responsive relationship, in which what people do and how they relate to God matters to God, does the denial that God "repents" deny such mutuality of relationship? Such a denial would, prima facie, seem highly unlikely (except, perhaps, on the lips of Qohelet). For it would deny something central, rather than peripheral, to Israel's understanding of God. This suggests that the denial may be not of this central principle but of something else.

To be sure, such general unlikeliness does not rule out the possibility of such denial of a central principle. For one could easily imagine particular people at particular times or places disagreeing with the consensus construal now represented in Israel's Scripture, and it may be that such disagreement could have been preserved within Israel's Scripture despite its departure from the norm. For redactors and canonizers may have allowed reverence for tradition to overcome their own judgment, and a collection that includes Qohelet is hardly one whose boundaries were drawn according to any narrowly conceived rule of thumb. Nonetheless, as we shall see, the particular form and location of the denials that God "repents" give no reason to suppose that these texts represent a minority report that somehow managed to survive against the odds. So unless we find ourselves quite unable to make coherent sense of the texts, the disagreement/minority report hypothesis is not one to which we need resort.

The assertion that "God does not repent" (*lōʾ yinnāḥēm*) appears in conjunction with a specific oath (Ps 110:4), where the assertion clearly has the sense of underlining the irrevocable nature of a particular divine commitment; and that this commitment is to David will be seen to be consonant with 1 Sam 15:29. Similar expressions are used rhetorically to emphasize the firmness of divine action on particular occasions (Jer 4:28; 20:16; Zech 8:14). Our concern however will be with the apparently greater problem: the two passages that apparently announce as a general axiom that "God does not repent":

> God is not a man that he should deceive,
>   or a human being that he should repent,[3]
> When it is he who has spoken, will he not do it?
>   and if he has promised, will he not establish it? (Num 23:19)

> And also the Enduring One[4] of Israel does not lie and does not repent;
>   for he is not a human being that he should repent. (1 Sam 15:29)

As one looks at these two texts, two common features are readily apparent. They both amplify the statement that God does not "repent" in two similar ways. Each text, I suggest, shows awareness of the potentially problematic nature of the affirmation being made and so, by design or reflex, offers some qualification to help the reader understand what is, and is not, meant.

First, "he does not repent" is each time accompanied by another verb. In Num 23:19a, in parallel with *nḥm* (*Hithpael*), the root *kzb* (*Piel*) is used. The meaning of *kzb* is well attested: it means "lie," "deceive."[5] Interestingly, the psalmist, when alarmed (speaking in fear rather than in reflection), predicates *kzb* (*Qal*) of humanity in general: "all people are liars" (*kol-hāʾādām kōzēb*, Ps 116:11). The sense appears to be that people lie in the sense of not living up to their promises, in implicit contrast to God, who does not disappoint. This usage resonates with Num 23:19a in

---

3. The Hebrew text here uniquely uses *nḥm* in the *Hithpael* rather than *Niphal* for divine "repentance." There is most likely no difference in meaning, the only issue being the grammatical interchangeability of *Niphal* and *Hithpael* to express a reflexive sense in the case of this particular root, as also with a number of other roots.

4. The meaning of the divine epithet *nēṣaḥ yiśrāʾēl* is unclear. My rendering is influenced by the common adverbial meaning of *neṣaḥ* as "forever," and the appropriateness of an expression of divine constancy to the content that immediately follows.

5. See Ps 78:36 and Prov 14:5 for good examples of its regular usage, and Isa 58:11 for its metaphorical resonances.

that both passages suggest that lying (*kzb*) is characteristic of humanity but not of God.

In 1 Sam 15:29, immediately preceding *nhm*, we find *lō' yĕšaqqēr*, another well-known root with the sense "speak falsely." The nominal form *šeqer* is regularly used with regard to false testimony in legal contexts (Exod 20:16; Deut 19:18), and of the speech of prophets not sent by God, the content of whose message is to be disregarded (Jer 14:14; 23:25, 26). The sense of *šeqer* seems to be not primarily that of factual error (for in the case of false witnesses and false prophets such error might be far from obvious and might not even apply), but rather a self-serving, morally false use of language—a use that can transform even an otherwise accurate saying into falsehood (Jer 7:4, 8, within the context of 7:1–15). Thus both *kizzēb* and *šeqer* (which may be used in conjunction with each other, Mic 2:11; Prov 14:5) depict unreliable, untrustworthy use of speech. It is from this that the denial of divine "repenting" is distanced in Num 23:19 and 1 Sam 15:29.

The second qualification is that God "is not a human being" (*lō' 'îš/ben-'ādām*, Num 23:19a; *lō' 'ādām*, 1 Sam 15:29). In neither passage is this some kind of principle in its own right, but each time it introduces the notion of repenting as something characteristic of humanity, and it is from this that God is distanced—"not a human being that he should repent." In general terms, this is a good example of "negative theology," the denial of positive analogy between God and humanity. Although such denials, at least in overt, explicit form, are less characteristic of Hebrew Scripture than they are of much postbiblical theology, they are by no means absent;[6] and this shared feature of Num 23:19 and 1 Sam 15:29, precisely in a context where the question is of the appropriate use of language with reference to God, is striking. The point is that what "repent" (*niham*) may mean with reference to human beings does not pertain with reference to God, and this applies equally to "not repenting." There is a qualitative difference between divine and human "repentance."

When these two qualifications are taken together, the general tenor of each of our two texts is clear. The concern is to preserve what is said of God—that "God does not repent"—from possible associations of the lack of integrity and lack of faithfulness that regularly characterize human speech; God is true and faithful in a way that people are not. As a general principle, this readily coheres with much that is central to Israel's Scripture. As such it should also be apparent that it is not a denial of the principle regularly expressed by God's "repenting"—mutuality and responsiveness

---

6. I have already noted the implicit attention to such an issue in the usage of *šûb* and *niham*.

in relationship. For it is not responsiveness but insincerity and faithlessness that are specified for denial.

But why should such a principle be specified in these two passages? This brings us, at last, to a consideration of the context of each passage.

Numbers 23:19 within Numbers 22–24

The story of Balaam in Numbers 22–24 revolves around two central concerns. One is discernment, the ability to see God and what God is doing, a theme developed with unusual humor and relish. Balaam, the prophet of renown, the best that royalty and wealth can acquire, has to learn from his ass, proverbially the dullest of animals, what it means to see what is before his very eyes. For three times he blindly urges his ass on, when the ass can see death confronting them. Only when Balaam is instructed by his ass and his eyes are opened by Yhwh can he carry out his work as a prophet. When Balaam joins Balak, roles are then reversed. Three times Balak blindly urges Balaam on, being unable to see what Balaam can see: God's blessing of Israel. Each time Balaam is urged to try again (with increased religious activity—more sacrifices—to try to make a difference), his vision of Israel becomes more glowing. When Balak eventually dismisses Balaam in anger, Balaam offers a fourth, unsolicited, oracle with a precise sting in its tail: disaster and death for Moab at the hands of Israel.

The other concern of the story is God's commitment to Israel, expressed in the divine resolve to bless Israel and make Israel prosper against its adversaries. The issue of power to curse and bless sets the dynamics of the story in motion at the outset (22:6) and forms the climax of Balaam's last solicited oracle (24:9). It is also the explicit issue that is addressed at the outset of the first two oracles that Balaam speaks. In the first oracle, Balaam tells of his being brought by Balak to curse Israel, and he instantly denies (with a rhetorical question) that he could curse one whom God has not cursed (23:7–8). When Balak insists on a second oracle, Balaam repeats the content of the first, only expressing it positively: "Behold, I received a command to bless; he has blessed, and I cannot revoke it" (23:20). It is this that is immediately preceded by the text we are interested in, that God "does not repent" (23:19). The sense of 23:19 in context is thus clarified. It is God's will to bless Israel, and God will not go back on that will nor be false to it. That this is the case, and that one needs to be able to see that this is the case, is the concern of the story as a whole.

In the wider pentateuchal context, the language of blessing and curse in the Balaam story resonates strongly with at least three other passages: Noah's pronouncement of a curse on Canaan, with a corresponding blessing of Yhwh the God of Shem (Gen 9:26); God's words to Abram that set in motion the story of Israel in the person of its ancestor (12:3a); and the climax of Isaac's blessing on Jacob at the expense of Esau (27:29). In general terms, the concern is with what subsequent theology would term God's "election" of Israel (a concept given terminological focus in Deuteronomy with the use of *bāḥar*). These texts all portray God's election of Israel as irrevocable and nonnegotiable (and also as a blessing of Israel at the expense of its neighbors; Canaan, Edom and Moab. Some of the paradoxes of this are drawn out by the deviousness of Jacob and the pathos of Esau in Genesis 27, and also by the portrayal of Israel as unfaithful and rebellious elsewhere in Numbers). It is one of the fundamental concerns of Israel's Scripture.

1 Samuel 15:29 within 1 Samuel 15

The story of 1 Samuel 15 has other, though not unrelated, concerns. If one takes the story as a whole (setting aside, for the moment, the problematic v. 29), it is a good example of a story illustrating the dynamics of divine "repentance," whereby bestowed gift or promised blessing is forfeited through wrong human attitude and action (as discussed above with reference to Jer 18:9–10).

The story is set in motion by Samuel's command to Saul to "put to the ban" (*ḥrm*) Amalek (vv. 1–3). This Saul carries out, but only in part, sparing Agag and the best of the animals (vv. 4–10). But it is part of the logic peculiar to *ḥrm* that partial fulfilment is not a possibility (cf. Joshua 7). Therefore Saul's action in sparing Agag and the animals, although amenable to positive rationalization (vv. 15, 20–21), in fact constitutes a sin of disobedience, as Saul himself comes to admit (vv. 22–24). It is for this reason that Yhwh "repents" of making Saul king. Verse 11 precisely spells out the relational, responsive dimension of Yhwh's "repentance" with regard to Saul's action (cf. vv. 23b and 26b, where the issue is formulated in terms of mutual "rejection," *mā'as*). The major part of the story tells of the dynamics of Samuel's encounter with Saul as the message of Yhwh is communicated.

The latter part of their encounter raises the issue as to whether Yhwh may "repent" of his "repentance" if Saul repents of his disobedience. This, however, is not seen as possible. Why not? One way of understanding this (setting aside, still, v. 29) would be to argue that Saul's confession of sin is not a genuine repentance. Saul's concern that Samuel should "honor" him publicly (v. 30) can readily be construed as self-seeking in a way that represents less than a genuine turning to God. Saul may be using correct religious language, but without the corresponding reality. If so, then the relational dynamics to enable a differing divine response remain lacking in Saul. But while this may be correct, it does not offer more than a partial explanation of the text.

It is at this point that we need to consider the meaning of v. 29. Insofar as commentators attempt to relate this denial of divine "repentance" to the clear affirmations of divine "repentance" elsewhere in the story (vv. 11 and 35; also in the parallel usage of "reject" [mā'as], vv. 23 and 26), they usually understand it as saying that the divine decision to reject Saul as king is nonnegotiable; so that, by implication, even if Saul did repent it would make no difference. As Robert Gordon puts it: "Too much can be made of the surface tension between the statements, in verses 11 and 29, concerning the possibility or impossibility of God's repenting. When God issues a decree that is plainly intended as irrevocable, as in the rejection of Saul, then says our text, there is no possibility of that decree being rescinded (cf. Nu. 23:19)."[7] This is certainly possible, and may be true in part. But it still leaves a little puzzling why the text of v. 29 should look so much like the formulation of a general principle about God, when a more simple formulation would presumably have sufficed for the purpose of saying that the decision about Saul was nonnegotiable—for example, "and in this matter YHWH will not repent" (ûbāzō't lō' yinnāḥēm YHWH).

There remains, however, a vital contextual clue to the meaning of v. 29 and it comes, unsurprisingly, in v. 28b. Samuel tells Saul not only that "YHWH has torn away the royal power over Israel from you today," but also that YHWH "will give it to someone else who is preferable to you." That person's identity is revealed to the reader within the very next story, when Samuel goes to anoint one of the sons of Jesse to be king (1 Sam 16:1–13). But the knowledge that David is the divinely chosen successor to Saul was already familiar to the narrator of 1 Samuel 15 who told the story thus. It is this—that God will give the kingship of Israel to David—that sets the context for v. 29 and explains why it is formulated as a general principle about God, that "God does not repent." That which is denied is not the responsive dynamics of divine "repentance" as consistently presupposed and expounded elsewhere in the story. Nor is the concern as such to deny that God could "repent of his repentance" in the particular case of Saul. Rather, the text specifies the positive commitment of God to make David king over Israel. It is this on which God will not go back, as though it were in any way an equivocal or deceptive undertaking such as humans commonly make.

---

7. R. P. Gordon, *1 & 2 Samuel* (Exeter: Paternoster, 1986) 146.

What is at stake in 1 Sam 15:29 is not, as in Num 23:19, God's election of Israel, but the other fundamental election within Israel's Scripture, the election of David. It is with reference to this that Samuel says that God does not "repent." As God's election of Israel is irrevocable, so is God's election of David. Hence the axiomatic statement with regard to each that God "does not repent."

Within the wider context of 1 Samuel, the choice of David to be king, and the rejection of Saul from that position, sets up a narrative dynamic similar to that formulated in the Genesis narratives, especially those of Cain and Abel and of Jacob and Esau. In all these stories one of the critical issues is how the person *not* chosen by God responds to the situation.[8] Despite the natural tendency to resentment, the challenge and possibility is to live well in the nonelect position: this is how YHWH depicts the situation to Cain (Gen 4:7). Cain fails the challenge, but Esau meets it most impressively (Gen 33:4).[9] The tragedy of Saul is in large part the tragedy of his inability to accept God's choice of David and live accordingly.

If, finally, we return to the issue of how "God does not repent" relates to "God repents," we find ourselves with one of the fundamental dynamics of Israel's Scripture as a whole, something perhaps more commonly expressed in terms of "election" and "covenant." On the one hand, God acts on God's own initiative, calling people with a call that is irrevocable precisely because it depends on God and not on the one called. On the other hand, the relationship thus initiated is a real one in which there is everything to be gained or lost according to how human beings live within that relationship with God. It depends on God, and it depends on human response. This is the dynamic tension at the heart of Israel's Scripture. It is a tension never to be "resolved," for it is definitional of what human life is and entails: a construal of humanity in relation to God that enlarges the scope and challenge and richness of what it means to be human.

Concluding Reflections

A few brief comments in conclusion. First, the study of this issue is, I think, a good example of the way in which theology and exegesis may fruitfully be combined. It is still sadly common to find it supposed that to bring theo-

---

8. I am indebted to the insights of J. D. Levenson, *The Death and Resurrection of the Beloved Son: The Transformation of Child Sacrifice in Judaism and Christianity* (New Haven and London: Yale Univ. Press, 1993), esp. chaps. 7–9.

9. The language of Esau's welcome to Jacob/Israel resonates with, and arguably was the model for, the depiction of the father's welcome to the prodigal son in Jesus' parable (Luke 15:20). For the Christian, there could be no higher recognition than this of the significance of Esau's act.

logical perspectives to bear on the biblical text, or to use the biblical text as a foundation for theology as a constructive discipline, somehow means that the interpreter submits the text to a "straitjacket of dogmatic control." Robert Carroll, for example, argues this way and cites 1 Samuel 15, with special reference to v. 29, as a prime example of "the unsuitability of the Bible for the creation of theological dogmas."[10] No doubt the biblical text is often misused by theologians. But the difficult questions of what enables the interpreter genuinely to understand the text and to use it constructively cannot be resolved by the weary dogma that biblical scholars must rescue the Bible from theologians.

Second, a responsible Christian use of Israel's Scripture as Christian Scripture must grapple with the difficult questions of precisely how the biblical portrayal of God may still be believed as true today. On the one hand, both of the basic concerns of this paper, the relational and responsive nature of God ("repentance") and the unswerving faithfulness of God to those he calls ("nonrepentance"), are fundamental to a Christian account of God. On the other hand, the particular forms in which Israel's witness is contextualized—its presupposition of Israel as a national entity over against Edom and Moab, its presupposition of the role of a particular royal dynasty—are problematic in various ways. Israel and its kings have long since disappeared into ancient history; and aspects of the morality and ideology of the biblical account are open to question from more than one perspective. The problems are manifold, and not least is the problem of accurately conceptualizing the questions. It is not, for example, a matter of timeless truths over against particular historical contingencies; rather, it is a question as to how a certain kind of understanding of God and humanity, which is only made possible through the specific history and witness of Israel, can be enduringly true through the constant transformations of human life and understanding—which requires, among other things, practices of faithful appropriation in every age. Nor, for the Christian, can the Old Testament account of God and Israel be considered as enduringly true apart from its being taken up in, and transformed by, the life, death, and resurrection of Jesus.

I conclude with three brief observations. First, the Old Testament as a whole contains painful wrestling with that faithful commitment of God, of which "God does not repent," when the circumstances of life seem most clearly to deny it. Psalm 89, in particular, wrestles with God's commitment to the house of David: A faithful and sovereign God (vv. 1–18 [MT 2–

---

10. R. P. Carroll, *Wolf in the Sheepfold: The Bible as a Problem for Christianity* (London: SCM, 1991) 41–43.

19]) has made promises to David (vv. 19–33 [MT 20–34]) of an utterly binding and irrevocable kind (vv. 34–37 [MT 35–38]), yet circumstances flatly differ from what God promised (vv. 38–45 [MT 39–46]), and the psalmist can only cast himself on God's inscrutable mercy (vv. 46–51 [MT 47–52]). In the Old Testament as a whole, there is no "easy" belief in God's election.

Second, although the language of divine "repenting" does not appear in the New Testament (with one exception), the relational and responsive nature of God does. In Jesus' teaching in Matthew's Gospel, forgiveness represents a mutuality of relationship between God and humanity; it is possible for the divine gift to be invalidated if it is not extended to others (Matt 6:14–15; 18:21–35). And Paul speaks of how presumption upon the goodness of God and lack of repentance transforms that goodness into wrath on the day of judgment (Rom 2:4–5); Paul's language of God's wrath (orgē) resonates strongly with the disaster (rāʿāh) that may be proclaimed, but also averted, in the Old Testament. His later discussion of the goodness and severity of God, which is inseparable from corresponding human responsiveness and so is variously encountered according to the response (Rom 11:19–23), is likewise using categories clearly recognizable from the Old Testament.

Third, Paul in Romans implicitly alludes to God's promises to David as fulfilled in Christ (Rom 1:3). Moreover, he explicitly discusses God's election of Israel and affirms, as strongly as any Old Testament writer, that the election of Israel is an irrevocable commitment on God's part (Romans 9–11; esp. 11:25–32). Indeed, the specific term he uses is that God's gifts and call are "not to be repented of" (ametamelētos), a term likely drawn from reflection upon Num 23:19 and/or 1 Sam 15:29.[11] However much the New Testament transforms the significance of the Old Testament, many of the fundamental contours and concerns of the New Testament remain profoundly those of Israel's historic Scripture.[12]

---

11. If Paul was reflecting on Num 23:19, it was not from the LXX, which does not use "repent" (metanoeō) and, indeed, changes the sense of the text. For the complex textual issues, see G. Dorival, ed., La Bible d'Alexandrie: Les Nombres (Paris: Cerf, 1994) 438–39.

12. I am grateful to my friends, Tony Gelston and Iain Provan, for their comments on a draft of this paper.

Part Three

God in the Prophets

– 9 –

Colonialism and the Vagaries of Scripture: Te Kooti in Canaan

(A Story of Bible and Dispossession in Aotearoa/New Zealand)

David M. Gunn*

And the LORD your God, he shall expel them from before you, and drive them from out of your sight; and ye shall possess their land, as the LORD your God hath promised unto you. (Josh 23:5, KJV)

So Joshua smote all the country...he left none remaining, but utterly destroyed all that breathed, as the LORD God of Israel commanded. (Josh 10:40, KJV)

And it came to pass, when Israel was strong, that they put the Canaanites to tribute, and did not utterly drive them out. (Judg 1:28, KJV)

Now these are the nations which the LORD left, to prove Israel by them...to teach them war. (Judg 3:1–2, KJV)

*   *   *

When a nation extends itself into other territories the chances are that it will there meet with other nationalities which it cannot destroy or completely drive out, even if it succeeds in conquering them. When this happens, it has a great and permanent difficulty to contend with. The subject or rival nationalities cannot be perfectly assimilated, and remain as a permanent cause of weakness and danger. It has been the fortune of England in extending itself to evade on the whole this danger.... [However] it is only in...the Australian colonies that the statement is true almost without qualification. The native Australian race is so low in the ethnological scale that it can never give the least trouble, but even here, since we reckon New Zealand in this group, we are to bear in mind that the Maori tribes occupy the Northern island

---

*I am greatly indebted to Michael Grimshaw, Knox College, Dunedin, for so generously providing the primary sources indicated with an asterisk.

127

in some force, much as in the last century the Highland Clans gave us trouble in the northern part of our own island, and the Maori is by no means a contemptible type of man. Nevertheless the whole number of Maories is not supposed to exceed forty thousand, and it is rapidly diminishing.[1]

✳   ✳   ✳

"The great threat to the Maori-European symbiosis," argues historian James Belich, speaking of that period in the mid-nineteenth century before the European zone of occupation in Aotearoa/New Zealand had come to predominate, "was less a material conflict of interest than a conflict of aspirations":

> A situation of parity with, or inferiority to, peoples like the Maori simply did not accord with British expectations. The British were not satisfied with part of the land, part of the economy, or part of the government. But the persistent stereotype of the fat and greedy settler has always been a scapegoat for less tangible factors. British expectations arose, less from individual greed, than from the racial and national attitudes that were part of the Victorian ethos.[2]

For many Europeans in that century (and since) it was in the natural order of things that the Maori should give way to the Europeans and their claims to the land, as the inferior gives way to the superior. This was the age of Darwin and "progress." Inasmuch as the Maori did at least selectively begin to adopt European (more particularly English) ways—in commerce and agriculture, in their rapid move to literacy, and in the willingness of many to think favorably of Christianity—the more they were liable to be viewed as "salvageable" for civilization. By contrast, resistance tended to confound those who believed that the indigenous race could learn to emulate European civilization and discover true religion (the position of many of the early missionaries), and to confirm those who had always viewed such a possibility with deep skepticism. White people quickly latched on to armed resistance and especially Maori "atrocities" involving the killing of civilians as "proof of [the Maori's] fundamentally unregenerate character."[3] As a newspaper editorial in 1863 put it:

> We have dealt with the natives of this country upon a principle radically wrong. We have conceded them rights and privileges which nature has refused to ratify.... We have pampered ignorance and misrule, and we now experience their hatred of intelligence and order. The bubble is burst. The

---

1. Sir John Seeley, *The Expansion of England* (Two Courses of Lectures; Boston: Little, Brown & Co., 1922) 55–56.
2. James Belich, *The New Zealand Wars and the Victorian Interpretation of Racial Conflict* (London and Auckland: Penguin, 1989; first published by Auckland Univ. Press, 1986) 304.
3. Ibid., 328.

Maori is now known to us as what he is, and not as missionaries and philan-thropists were willing to believe him. [In reality, the Maori is] a man ignorant and savage, loving darkness and anarchy, hating light and order; a man of fierce, and ungoverned passions, bloodthirsty, cruel, ungrateful, treacherous.[4]

*   *   *

Else if ye do in any wise go back, and cleave unto the remnant of these na-tions, even these that remain among you.... Know for a certainty that the LORD your God will no more drive out any of these nations from before you; but they shall be snares and traps unto you, and scourges in your sides, and thorns in your eyes, until ye perish from off this good land which the LORD your God hath given you. (Josh 23:12–13, KJV)

Thus saith the LORD of hosts, I remember that which Amalek did to Israel, how he laid wait for him in the way.... Now go and smite Amalek, and ut-terly destroy all that they have, and spare them not; but slay both man and woman, infant and suckling. (1 Sam 15:2–3, KJV)

My particular interest, in the present essay, lies in the place of the Bible in this ideology of Victorian colonialism. A perusal of documents relating to the European settlement of New Zealand suggests that the Bible was implicated in at least the following main ways.

First, the notion of the "chosen people"—ubiquitous in biblical texts—is ubiquitous in British (especially English) thought during the nineteenth cen-tury. It is, if you like, the English version of "manifest destiny." The term *destiny* crops up repeatedly, often in a specifically Christian understand-ing (behind which lies the Christian co-option of the biblical "people of Israel"), but not infrequently in more secular versions where "civilization" has largely taken the place of "Christianity" (which nevertheless usually sits alongside it), and the spirit of progress (often in the guise of providence) looks fair to supplant God. The promised land may be one particular land or it may be the many that it was the duty and destiny of the chosen Brit-ish race to populate and/or govern. Election, then, is one of the essential doctrines of British colonialism.

It is impossible to resolve these facts [viz., that the most numerous in the re-ligions of the empire are first, pagans; second, Muslims; third, Protestants; and fourth, Roman Catholics] without receiving a deep impression, that the moral state of England is of immeasurable importance to the whole human race. God has placed her in a position to advance or retard the highest inter-ests of our species, such as a nation never occupied before; such as involves a high and unappreciable trust.... Let it be the cherished hope of your heart, that, in ages to come, the people of other lands will refer to the English, not as the invaders who crushed their ancient dynasty, to introduce a foreign yoke,

---

4. *Southern Cross*, quoted by Belich, *New Zealand Wars*, 328.

but as the benefactors who, bringing the light of truth, cast a radiance on the path of their benighted fathers, by which they discovered first of all the way to God, and then to the arts, laws and institutions of civilization; to the inter-changes of friendship, and the endearments of home. (*Rev. W. Arthur, "The Extent and Moral Statistics of the British Empire," Exeter Lectures, 1845–46)

*   *   *

Thus saith God the LORD...I the LORD have called thee in righteousness, and will hold thine hand, and will keep thee, and give thee for a covenant of the people, for a light of the Gentiles; to open the blind eyes, to bring out the prisoners from the prison, and them that sit in darkness out of the prison house. (Isa 42:5–7, KJV)

Look unto me, and be ye saved, all the ends of the earth: for I am God, and there is none else. I have sworn by myself, the word is gone out of my mouth in righteousness, and shall not return, That unto me every knee shall bow, every tongue shall swear. (Isa 45:22–23, KJV)

The conviction of election sustained the settlers in the face of the hos-tility of the indigenous peoples. The following items were written in New Zealand during the land wars of the 1860s:

A divine mission was given to the colonial subjects of the Crown when New Zealand was given over to the sovereignty of Great Britain, a mission to mature and complete the civilization and Christianity of the native race, which, alas! has been of late years chequered with the renovated rise of hea-thenish maxims and customs. (*letter from "A Patriot," *Nelson Examiner,* March 6, 1861)

As to the sentimental side of the question—the right of a civilized race to colonize a barbarous country,—it is not worth disputing about. If necessary, it might be justified upon the very highest grounds. The fairest portions of the globe were not intended to remain for all time to come the hunting grounds of cannibals. It is the highest duty of a powerful nation to extend the blessings of civilization and Christianity to the utmost of its means. Our right to New Zealand is precisely what our right was to New Holland or to the continent of North America.[5]

The great civilizing peoples of the earth seem to have been deliberately chosen out and allowed to increase out of all proportion to their means of sustenance at home, for the very end that, driven abroad, they might carry civilization to all parts of the world in the train of Christianity....Our present war then is waged in the cause of civilization, and against, not Maoris, but barbarism.[6]

---

5. *New Zealand Herald,* March 31, 1864, 4, repr. from *Australia and New Zealand Gazette,* January 9, 1864.
6. *"Our Colonial Scheme," *Southern Monthly Magazine,* April 1864, 80.

The reverse side of destiny is the fate of those chosen not for a high and noble end but for doom. Providence, God's will, can raise some and crush others, and against that determination there is no recourse. In the hands of the faithful, this is powerful theology. There were no few Scottish Calvinists in New Zealand in the 1860s.

> What Noah did on his being made aware of his son's wickedness, flowed not from his paternal displeasure, but from the impulse of the Spirit of God, who is righteous in all ways. His providence shows, that parents not unfrequently are punished in the misery of their posterity; and from the subsequent history it will appear, how the Canaanites were terribly enslaved by the posterity of Shem and of Japhet, according to the tenor of Noah's curse.... Noah's curse was not causeless, and therefore it came. And it has descended from generation to generation; as no distance from the seat of Canaan's original settlement has hid the people of the curse from its operation, so no interval of time has weakened its power. The tribes of Africa appeared for ages to have escaped it. But when Japhet's posterity discovered and seized on the new world, they supplied themselves with servants from Africa, and the groans and oppression, the tears and the blood of Africa's sons, all proclaim that they own Ham for their father. To this day the slave trade is not suppressed, and the black population of both Americas, yet kept in degrading bondage, testifies to the same truth. Christians justly labour for their freedom, but till the curse remove, the expectation of success is vain. The origin of the original tribes of America, now so nearly exterminated, hangs in great doubt, but if we could trace them to Canaan, their fate would at once be accounted for.[7]

A second main area of biblical and colonial complicity concerns the land itself. Expressed in numerous contexts is some version—even if it be one that coyly denies its scriptural warrant—of the biblical passage in Gen 1:27, where God commands the humans to multiply, subdue the land, and make it fruitful. It is the unquestionable conviction of the colonizers that they have the fundamental right and, indeed, obligation to "improve" the land. The land to be taken is constantly judged to be wild and desolate, egregiously neglected by the native inhabitants. It is the God-given right of the British to take the land in order to fulfill the commandment and make the desert bloom:

> Though by virtue of our great Circumnavigator's discovery and surveys; though by virtue of that great unwritten law which declares that the earth is God's gift to man, and that a handful of savages shall nowhere lock

---

7. Reverend James Smith, "Canaan," in *Brown's Dictionary of the Holy Bible Corrected and Improved According to the Advanced State of Information at the Present Day* (1859) 176, 177–78. This book was carried from Scotland in 1862 by my great-grandfather, Farquhar MacDonald Gunn, on his journey to New Zealand.

up millions of acres of a wild garden wherein they pluck no fruit, a body
of hard-working, half-starved Englishmen had a *right* to plant their little
Settlements in New Zealand, and to *take* a portion of the immense unused
wilderness to the plough, yet they did not do this. (*Charles Hursthouse, *New
Zealand—the "Britain of the South,"* 2d ed., 1861)

We cannot hesitate for a moment to say that emigration is according to the
will of God. Given a world like this, with conveniences in every part for the
habitation of man, and one original pair appointed to be father and mother
of a race—a single centre and not many centres of human increase, and a
command such as we read in Genesis, "Be fruitful, and multiply, and replenish
the earth, and subdue it: and have dominion over the fish of the sea, and over
the fowl of the air, and over every living thing that moveth upon the earth"—
and emigration follows as a necessary consequence. (*Reverend J. Stoughton,
"Anglo-Saxon Colonies," Exeter Lectures, 1852–53)

[The author asks whether the trappings of empire—wharves, mills, ships,
mines, foundries, farms—are inconsistent with religion. He continues:] Quite
the contrary. We see in all this man pursuing his divinely appointed vocation,
and God's design in process of fulfilment. "Replenish the earth, and subdue
it, and have dominion over everything that moveth upon the earth." (*Reverend L. Wiseman, "Things Secular and Things Sacred," Exeter Lectures,
1855–56)

Why should immigrants who have come hither, and who will still come
hither, to cause the wastes to bloom and blossom, and give bread to their
fellow men to eat and to spare—why should such be "branded" as greedy,
grasping and overreaching, because church missionaries are sympathisers in
the land league [i.e., sympathetic to Maori land rights], and are opposed to
everything that does not square with their own idiosyncratical philanthropy?
(*Editorial: "False or True!" *Auckland Register,* May 5, 1860)

A third source of biblical inspiration for the colonial enterprise comes
with the image of the empty land. The Bible reiterates its "promised land"
or "Canaan" theme often without mentioning its corollary, namely, the
promise of dispossession for the indigenous inhabitants. Indeed, usage of
these "promised land" texts in nineteenth-century British Christianity suggests that commentators, preachers, and the instructors of youth were often
disposed to speak of the promise without reference to the violence of dispossession. Such rhetoric readily produces an empty land. With talk of land
as "wilderness," the elision of inhabitants is further facilitated, for Israel
in Canaan becomes superimposed upon Israel in the wilderness—Israel on
its way to Canaan—and the wilderness is, by popular account, uninhab-
ited. Land use is judged wholly by nineteenth-century European norms of
agricultural and industrial use, and by that measure a wilderness is clearly

empty. (This rhetoric served other European incursions powerfully, too, notably into the American West and later into Palestine.)

> It did seem an anomaly that in this wide world there should be, as Seeley puts it, "On the one side men without property, on the other side property waiting for men." The problem was how to provide outlets for the starving people, and open up waste lands for their possession and use.[8]

> Without protective institutions [i.e., British rule], such a country is also without all those things which are calculated to flourish under their protection. No arts or manufactures, or next to none—no general distribution of the people into trades or professions—no diffused appearance of regular industry—no commerce, domestic or foreign—no coin or other circulating medium;—these are a few of the more conspicuous deficiencies that must strike even the most ignorant observer of savage life, who have been accustomed to another condition of society. They will force themselves upon his attention, in fact, as he looks even upon the landscape around him. The country is nearly a wilderness,—all swamp or woodland, except a few scattered patches by the sea side, or along the courses of the rivers; the only cultivation to be seen is in the heart, or the immediate vicinity, of the villages; and these (how unlike the populous cities and towns of a civilized country, with their streets of palaces, and intermingled spires, and towers, and domes!) are merely small groups of hovels that dot the earth like so many mole-hills, each a shelter from the weather, only one remove from the caverns of the Troglodytes. Then there are no roads, those primary essentials of all improvement; and, it is needless to add, no artificial means of conveyance from one place to another. To make a journey of any length is an enterprize of labour and peril, which can only be accomplished by the union and co-operation of a band of travellers. There is not an inn throughout the land—nor a bridge—nor a direction-post—nor a milestone. The inhabitants, in fact, have not, in any sense of the word, taken possession of the country which they call their own; and they are merely a handfull of stragglers who wander about its outskirts.[9]

I was born in 1942 in a little country town called Te Awamutu ("The End of the River"). It lay in the upper Waikato district between the Mangapiko and Puniu rivers, at the border of the King Country. It was part of the land the British confiscated from the Maori—Waikato, Ngati Maniapoto, Ngati Ruru—after the British invaded the Waikato in the war of 1863–64. The British forces were for a time headquartered in the town. At nearby Paterangi, Rangiaowhia, Hairini Hill, Kihikihi, and (most famously) Orakau, desperate battles were fought. A few miles across the valley to the southwest, Kakepuku's indigo-blue volcanic cone rises up. The town

8. Reverend James Chisolm, *Fifty Years Syne: A Jubilee Memorial of the Presbyterian Church of Otago* (Dunedin: J. Wilkie & Co., 1898) 12.

9. Lillie George Craik [?], *The New Zealanders* (Library of Entertaining Knowledge; London: Charles Knight, 1830) 396–97.

itself sits in a valley plain, around it land that rolls gently, offering sheltered valleys, leisurely winding streams, dotted with small lakes. It was known years ago—I do not know if it still is—as "the old Maori garden lands," though after the confiscation the farms and groves that covered it were Pakeha cultivations. In the days before the war the population was wholly Maori apart from a few missionaries and their families and several traders and other "Pakeha-Maori." Communication with the lower Waikato and Waipa valleys was by canoe, a three-day journey. The first roads were pushed through by the military to facilitate the war.

In 1852 young Heywood Crispe made the canoe journey into the interior and years later related his story. The Maori at Rangiaowhia gave his party a royal welcome. After a good night's sleep he took in his surroundings:

> There was a line of whares [houses] erected on the crown of Rangiaowhia Hill, from which we could obtain a fine view of the surrounding country, and it had a grand appearance in our eyes. There was a long grove of large peach trees and very fine fruit on them. . . . One never sees such trees of peaches now. We, the Europeans, must be the cause by the importation of pests from other countries. A large portion of the ground round the hill was carrying a very good crop of wheat, for the Maoris believed in that as a crop, and they used to convert it into flour at the various flour-mills they had. It was of a very good quality, and some of the Waikato mills had a name for the flour they produced, a good deal of which was put on the Auckland market, being taken down the Waikato, via Waiuku and Onehunga. . . .
>
> The Maoris provided all their pakeha friends with a most excellent meal on the ground, and peaches galore, as well as horses to ride. We rode some distance round to view the county, the Maori flour-mills, and cultivation. There were a lot of good cattle and horses about, and the crops of wheat and patches of potatoes were particularly good, although no bonedust was used in those days.[10]

In later years, too, Mrs. Crispe, Heywood's widow, described life in the Upper Waikato as she saw it as a girl at school for two years in the Reverend John Morgan's mission school in Te Awamutu. The wheat fields were enclosed by hedges of hawthorn. The wheat grown and ground (in water-driven flour mills) by the Maori of the district was bagged and sent down by canoe to the white settlements for sale. The proceeds went to clothes, blankets, tea, sugar, and all kinds of European goods. James Cowan continues her reminiscences:

> In front of Mr Morgan's mission house at Te Awamutu there was a row of almond trees. These almonds—so seldom seen in a New Zealand orchard now [1922]—were widely distributed among the natives; hence the remarkably

---

10. James Cowan, *The Old Frontier. Te Awamutu: The Story of the Waipa Valley* (Te Awamutu, NZ: Waipa Post Printing and Pub. Co., 1922) 18–19.

large trees, up to about thirty feet in height, which grew on the old Maori cultivations at Orakau and elsewhere, and survived long after the land had been confiscated by the Crown and settled by white farmers.[11]

In 1859 Dr. Ferdinand von Hochstetter, an Austrian geologist, climbed Mount Kakepuku and from the summit viewed the valley of the Waipa:

> The beautiful, richly-cultivated country about Rangiaowhia and Otawhao lay spread out before us like a map. I counted ten small lakes and ponds scattered about the plains. The church steeples of three places were seen rising from among orchards and fields. Verily I could hardly realise that I was in the interior of New Zealand.[12]

This prosperous agricultural life of the Maori was destroyed by the war. The neatly arranged streets of thatched houses, shaded by groves of peach and apple trees, were abandoned. The inhabitants were driven off the land and settlers took their fields and orchards.

*   *   *

> I arrived at Te Awamutu at daybreak on the 21st [February 1864], and immediately pushed on to Rangiaowhia, which I found nearly deserted. The few natives who were in the place were completely taken by surprise, and, refusing to lay down their arms, fired on the Mounted Royal Artillery Forces and the Colonial Defence Force, whom I sent on in advance of the column. The natives were quickly dispersed, and the greater part escaped; but a few of them, taking shelter in a whare [house], made a desperate resistance, until the Forest Rangers and a company of the 65th Regiment surrounded the whare, which was set on fire, and the defenders either killed or taken prisoners.
>
> I regret to say that several casualties occurred on our side, and amongst them Col Nixon, commander of the Defence Force, who was severely wounded in endeavouring to enter the whare. Our loss was two killed and six wounded. About twelve natives were killed and twelve taken prisoner.
>
> I have detained 21 women and children who were found in the village. Immediately after the settlement was cleared I marched the troops back to Te Awamutu. (General Cameron's dispatch to Governor Grey; from Appendices to the Journals of the House of Representatives, 1864, E-3)[13]

> When it came to the time of the murder at Rangiaowhia, then I knew, for the first time, that this was a great war for New Zealand. Look also: Maori have been burned alive in their sleeping houses.... When the women were killed at the pa [fortified village] at Rangiriri, then, for the first time, the General advised that the women should be sent to live at places where there was no fighting. Then the pa at Paterangi was set aside as a place for fighting, and Rangiaowhia was left for the women and children. As soon as we

---

11. Ibid., 21.
12. Quoted by Cowan, ibid., 21–22.
13. Quoted from the novel by Heretaunga Pat Baker, *The Strongest God* (Whatamonga Bay, Queen Charlotte Sound, NZ: Cape Cately Ltd., 1990) 239.

arranged this, the war party of Bishop Selwyn and the General started to fight with the women and children. The women and children fell there.... It was the affair at Rangiaowhia that hardened the hearts of the people. The war was Rangiriri; a murder; Rangiaowhia; a murder.... (Wiremu Tamihana, chief of Ngati Haua, who lost several close relatives at Rangiaowhia; a document in English and Maori; from Appendices to Journals of the House of Representatives, 1864, G-5)[14]

The story of the Bible in the colonization of Aotearoa/New Zealand takes, however, some other turns, as I now relate.

The Bible, for many, was the hallmark of civilization (besides roads, milestones, and steeples). The missionaries brought it to the "benighted" and the "benighted" were apt students. Maori became a written language.

The language in which Maori [learned] to read and write was the Maori language. By the 1850s Maori had much higher rates of literacy than the European settlers, although because it was in Maori it had limited usefulness as the Pakeha society became more dominant.

For the Protestant missionary societies the Bible had ultimate significance as the textbook for life and faith. Great energy went into its translation, printing and distribution. By 1837 the complete New Testament was available in Maori. It was not until 1868 that the whole Bible was printed. The Bible had a profound effect on Maori. They learnt the Bible off by heart, they wove its message into their own beliefs in ways that did not always easily cohere with the missionaries' message. There was an unexpected impact.[15]

From the early days of European involvement in New Zealand most of the missionaries—in particular the (British) Church Missionary Society (CMS)—had opposed white settlement. Evangelicals, missionaries, and "humanitarians" were influential in making representations to the select Committee of the House of Commons, which reported in 1837 that "all past colonization had for non-European peoples been a calamity involving oppression or even extermination."[16] The CMS hoped to keep British interference in the country to a minimum in order to keep the country as a pristine preserve of the missionaries. The hope was for an eventual Christian Maori state. Thus, along with the likes of James Busby, British resident in 1833, and Captain William Hobson, R.N., sent to protect settlers in 1837, Dandeson Coates, the lay secretary of the CMS, proposed that the British government should recognize the "Native Authorities" and take the country under its "protection" with a view to controlling the ex-

---

14. Quoted by Baker, ibid., 239–40.
15. Allan Davidson, "The Interaction of Missionary and Colonial Christianity in Nineteenth Century New Zealand," *Studies in World Christianity* 2/2 (1995) 148.
16. Keith Sinclair, *A History of New Zealand* (4th rev. ed.; London and Auckland: Penguin, 1991) 63.

isting European settlers and contacts between Maori and settlers. Coates spoke against "the curse of colonization," and urged that further British settlement not be encouraged. "So long as New Zealand remained Maori territory, he thought that any Europeans could do little harm because they lived on sufferance, with no government to back them up and perhaps to oppress the Maoris in the event of trouble."[17] Most of the missionaries in the field agreed. In the end, however, this policy failed to carry the day, despite a significant measure of support in the Office of the Secretary of State for the Colonies. In 1839 settlement became (politically) inevitable.

The upshot of this struggle was a continuing uneasiness, if not at times an actual rift, between settlers and missionaries (as opposed to the settler churches). "[S]ympathy for the missionaries working among the Maori, let alone an interest in Maori Christianity, was very limited in settler society."[18] In the difference lay two visions of New Zealand society—a replica British society and a utopian Christian one. As war broke out the pressures on the missionaries, regarded as "soft" on the Maori, became intense. Few (T. F. Grace was one) managed to retain their alliance with their flock. One point of contention that arose in the bitter controversy brought on by the war concerned the Bible. Putting the Bible in the hands of the Maori, argued many settlers, was a dangerous thing. These "savages" could not be trusted to read it the right way:

> We do not deny the use or advantage of such monitors [i.e., missionaries to the Maori]; but when we find the natives taking up their teachings and describing us as Ahabs, and themselves as Naboths, we fear the effect of the seed they sow; and foresee a crop in which thistles are likely to gain the upper had, as much as in the deserted cultivations of Taranaki [where war waged]. They have encouraged ideas and expectations in the native mind, which have matured into a struggle for independence. (*Editorial in *Nelson Examiner,* January 26, 1861)

> Let the General Assembly send the Maoris a message to say "We wish to help you; but we will bring you to your senses if you resist Her Majesty's authority. We will give you the best assistance we can, and will teach you to do something more than misquote Scripture—to keep the Decalogue, which you have never done; to love your neighbour as yourselves; to give compensation when you do an injury." When they did this they might be called British subjects.[19]

> [The following writer, under the title of "Priestly Influence," is addressing the topic, What do the Maori get from the Bible? His barbs are directed at the missionaries—who have urged the Bible on the Maoris.] Two doctrines will,

---

17. Ibid., 63.
18. Davidson, "Interaction," 156.
19. *Mr. Wilson, *New Zealand Parliamentary Debates,* Want of Confidence Debate, July 3, 1861, 115–16.

no doubt, be to their taste—that of revenge; that of blood for blood in the Old Testament; that of equality in the New.... Far more intractable, therefore, are the Maories, than if they had never been converted. We do not say that their conversion was wrong; but it was a fatal gift if they are to live in permanent severance from the colonists. They will, from ignorance, transmute Christianity into a principle of antagonism. This is an element in future contests which has been altogether overlooked. The Maoris have set up a king; ere long they may have fanatical prophets among them, urging them, by examples from the Bible, to indiscriminate slaughter of their hated foes. (*The Taranaki Herald*, April 20, 1861; reprinted from the *New Zealand Examiner* [London])

Indeed, this last statement was to prove prescient, though whether the slaughter was any more or less indiscriminate than the killing of the inhabitants of Jericho or the massacre of the Amalekites is a moot point, as indeed is the question whether the prophets deserved to be compared to Samuel in terms of fanaticism. At any rate, the general point was well taken. The Bible was a subversive document.

A whole month, the month of October, 1868, was spent in finalizing his preparations. The recitation of passages of Scripture to stimulate the fire and enthusiasm of the raiders was part of the proceedings. One of these passages was from the Book of Joshua, chapter 23, verses 5 and 6, which reads as follows:

"And the Lord your God, he shall expel them from before you, and drive them from out of your sight; and ye shall possess their land, as the Lord your God hath promised unto you. Be ye therefore very courageous to keep and to do all that is written in the book of the law of Moses, that ye turn not aside therefrom to the right hand or to the left."

With a religious zeal such as that which characterizes the fiercest of crusaders or the administrators of the inquisition, the massacre was committed in the early hours of the morning of 10 November, 1868, four months after the landing from the schooner *Rifleman* at Whareongaonga. The position of the various settlers' residences was obtained, and the raiders divided into several attacking parties, each led by a man appointed by Te Kooti. Among those killed were some of the leaders of those who originally sent the prophet into exile. Thus the massacre served the double purpose of inflicting a blow upon the enemy, and of executing vengeance upon those who were responsible for sending a man into exile without even the semblance of a trial.

Among those killed were Major Biggs [who, with Captain Wilson, had presided over Te Kooti's deportation] and his wife and baby together with two servants and a half-caste girl; Captain Wilson and his wife, three of their four children, and a servant named Moran; two sheep-farmers named Dodd and Peppard; Lieutenant Walsh together with his wife and child; and many others, in all thirty-three Europeans and thirty-seven friendly natives.[20]

[I] returned to New Zealand to hear of a most lively massacre at Poverty Bay, perpetrated by three hundred Maori gentlemen, very well up in their Old Testaments and extremely practical in the use of the New (they made cartridges of them). (The Earl of Pembroke, from his introduction to the Australian edition of *Old New Zealand: A Tale of the Good Old Times*, by A Pakeha Maori, 1893, p. ix)

Te Kooti Arikirangi Te Turuki was born about 1830 and educated at a mission school near his home in the Turanga (Gisborne) area up the east coast of the North Island. "His name, Kooti, is a Maori version of Dandeson Coates, the lay secretary of the CMS after whom he was named."[21] It would seem that during the wars of the 1860s he was a *kupapa* (Maori forces in the service of the colonial government), employed as an ammunition carrier against the "Hauhaus," the fighting men of an indigenous religious movement called Pai Marire ("the Good and the Peaceful").

Prospects of peace, however, were shattered by the rise of the *Pai marire* religion or Hauhauism, a cult which mingled the worst elements of primitive religion with a debased form of Christianity. Its adherents made a rallying point for the implacable sections of the Maoris.[22]

In 1865 he was arrested, at the instigation of a chief friendly to the settlers, on a charge of spying for the enemy—a charge for which no good proof was forthcoming, so that he was released. With the suppression of the Pai Marire forces on the east coast, some of the captured "rebels" were allowed to go free. Others were deported to a penal settlement on the Chatham Islands, a desolate location 400 miles to the east of New Zealand. Te Kooti was rearrested and deported along with them. They were men, women, and children from several tribes, about three hundred in all. This was in early 1866. Te Kooti attempted to appeal to the superintendent at Napier. No answer was ever returned.

During his captivity Te Kooti fell into serious illness and despair. As Gabriel had appeared to Te Ua, the prophet of Pai Marire, so the Spirit of God spoke to Te Kooti:

When I became conscious my corrupt spirit and this sinful body became separated then the spirit of God raised me and said, Arise, God has sent me to bring you to life to make known His name to His people who are in captivity

---

20. William Greenwood, *The Upraised Hand or The Spiritual Significance of the Ringatu Faith* (Polynesian Society Memoire 21; Wellington, NZ: Polynesian Society, 1942) 25; cf. Hugh Ross, *Te Kooti Rikirangi: General and Prophet* (Auckland: Collins, 1966) 62ff.

21. Davidson, "Interaction," 151.

22. *The Cambridge History of the British Empire* (1933) 138.

in this place so that they may know that Jehovah drove them out into this place. (Te Kooti MS, February 21, 1868)[23]

Recovering, he began to read his Bible, especially the books of Joshua and Judges and some of the Psalms. He held religious services morning and evening. His fellow prisoners began to recite Psalms (Psalm 64 was a daily devotion—"Hear my voice O God in my prayer: preserve my life from the fear of the enemy...") and prayers that contained passages from Scripture.[24]

Te Kooti wrote a prayer:

O God, if our hearts arise from the land in which we now dwell as slaves, and repent and pray to Thee and confess our sins in Thy presence, then, O Jehovah, do Thou blot out the sins of Thy own people, who have sinned against Thee. Do not Thou, O God, cause us to be wholly destroyed. Wherefore it is that we glorify Thy Holy Name. (Translated by Bishop Colenso, *Fiat Justitia,* Napier, 1871)[25]

He made careful note of the Scripture[26] that said:

"Now go and smite Amalek, and utterly destroy all that they have, and spare them not; but slay both man and woman, infant and suckling, ox and sheep, camel and ass" (1 Sam 15:3, KJV).

So New Zealand was the homeland and the Chatham Islands the house of bondage. The Maori were the Israelites and their enemies the Canaanites or Amalekites. Te Kooti prophesied that soon an ark of salvation would appear and be their means of deliverance.[27] On June 30, 1868, a government schooner and a ketch arrived bringing provisions. With remarkably little bloodshed Te Kooti's followers overpowered the guards, seized the schooner, beached the ketch, took arms and supplies from the garrison, and sailed for home. After a stormy passage they arrived at Whareongaonga ten days later. They unloaded the ship and released the crew.

When the Europeans on the coast learned of the escaped prisoners' arrival, they sent a force to demand their surrender. Te Kooti refused but stressed that his intentions were peaceful—had his people not treated the garrison and the crew with consideration? He and his people then moved inland, heading from the alluvial coastal plains of Poverty Bay into the relative safety of the high country bordering the Urewera mountains and

---

23. Quoted in Ross, *Te Kooti,* 31; for other encounters with the spirit at this time, see ibid., 32–33. See also Bronwyn Elsmore, *Like Them That Dream: The Maori and the Old Testament* (Otumoeti, Tauranga, NZ: Tauranga Moana Press, 1985) 141.
24. Greenwood, *Upraised Hand,* 21; Ross, *Te Kooti,* 34.
25. Quoted in Elsmore, *Like Them That Dream,* 142.
26. See Elsmore, *Like Them That Dream,* 143.
27. Greenwood, *Upraised Hand,* 22.

Lake Waikaremoana. The colonial authorities refused to let him alone. Strong forces (of settlers and kupapa) were sent to intercept him, and there were several fierce engagements.[28] Te Kooti, wounded, made his escape, and his people fortified themselves in a mountain village. In November the fugitive turned into the hunter: abandoning his base at Puketapu, "he descended on the British and Maori settlements at Poverty Bay and destroyed them."[29]

The story of Te Kooti continues long beyond the attack on Poverty Bay.[30] Pursued from place to place, his people fought bravely for their independence. In the end they lost, and for many of them that meant their lives. When in early 1868 Te Kooti lost Ngatapa Pa to an overwhelming force of Pakeha and *kupapa,* he and others escaped down a precipice. Of some 500 people in the Pa, perhaps 300 or more were women, children, and Poverty Bay prisoners. About 135 women and children and 140 men were taken prisoner. "Some 120 of the male prisoners were then killed.... The men were collected and executed in batches 'after a few questions.' "[31] In 1872, with five men and one woman, Te Kooti made his way into the King Country, where he remained "still bitterly hated and feared by colonists and *kupapa,* and still with a price of £5,000 on his head, but securely protected by the King Movement. In 1883, he was finally pardoned as part of a government attempt to open up the King Country by peaceful means."[32] He died ten years later.

In Te Kooti's captivity on the Chatham Islands, the land of bondage, was born the Ringatu religion, a major spiritual force in Maori life up until the present day. The Ringatu, the Sign of the Upraised Hand, signified to Te Kooti, the prophet, not the power to ward off bullets (its meaning to Pai Marire) but an act of homage to God.

> Come my people enter thou into my chambers and shut thy doors about thee.
>   And none shall go out the door and will not suffer the destroyer to come into your houses and smite you.
>   I laid me down and slept, I awakened for the Lord sustained me. Now the Lord is that Spirit and where the spirit of the Lord is there is liberty.[33]

*   *   *

---

28. See Belich, *New Zealand Wars,* 216–26.
29. Ibid., 227 (see 227–34); Greenwood, *Upraised Hand,* 24–26.
30. See Belich, *New Zealand Wars,* 258–88; Greenwood, *Upraised Hand,* 27–28.
31. Belich, *New Zealand Wars,* 266.
32. Ibid., 286.
33. Panui 7, quoted by Wi Tarei, "A Church called Ringatu," in Elsmore, *Like Them That Dream,* 145.

The name of the woman taken in adultery was Herita.
The blind man whose eyes were anointed with clay was Tapaineho.
The fig tree that was cursed was Hiona.
Naboth's vineyard belonged to Tanupera.

(Te Kooti, 1868)[34]

*   *   *

"But when we find the natives taking up their teachings and describing us as Ahabs, and themselves as Naboths, we fear the effect of the seed they sow...."[35]

---

34. In Ross, *Te Kooti,* 33.

35. A postscript: A good many years ago, in Sheffield, after one of my first articles had appeared, a note of appreciation arrived from someone whose writing I much admired but whom I had not met. (Many readers of this volume, I suspect, will recognize the circumstance.) From those first few words of encouragement sprang a long and valued association. Thank you, Walter Brueggemann, longtime mentor and colleague.

– 10 –

"Who Is Blind But My Servant?" (Isaiah 42:19)

How Then Shall We Read Isaiah?

Ronald E. Clements

Of the many forms of writing and communication that constitute the human literary scene, that of biblical exegesis possesses several distinctive features. Prominent among these are features shared with other aspects of religious activity such as prayer and meditation, which are aimed at promoting an awareness of God, of the demands of religious obedience, and of the need to focus attention on the centrality of religious values. Because it takes a literary commentary form, however, biblical exegesis lays itself open to a rich variety of other levels of significance dependent on linguistic, textual, and verbal artistry. The readers of the Bible, therefore, and necessarily also the authors and readers of commentaries upon it, are presented with a wide range of reading strategies by which to interpret the text. It is in this regard that Walter Brueggemann's search to find a movement within a text that energizes it and makes it into a vehicle of faith and personal commitment has proved meaningful to a whole generation of scholars and Bible readers. In his words: "The text, is more than a text, it is a presentation of a way through to a world of faith."[1]

It is clear that the form and content of any text itself must provide the primary data for understanding what it is about and what it might mean to the contemporary reader. That a text is poetry rather than prose, as is the case with much recorded biblical prophecy, is a starting point. Beyond this, however, it is difficult to find similar writings to the four great "collections" of the Latter Prophets of the Hebrew Bible that can be used to provide suitable examples with which to compare them. That they are "anthologies" of prophetic sayings from various poet-authors would be meaningful if it

---

1. W. Brueggemann, "Unity and Dynamic in the Isaiah Tradition," *JSOT* 29 (1984) 91.

were certainly demonstrable that this is all that they are. That they emanate from four identifiable prophetic, or scribal, schools would provide a useful guideline for pinpointing their place of origin. Yet even this is not obviously the case and would, in any event, provide only a very meager guide as to how they should be interpreted. Overall it is the internal evidence provided by the text itself, coupled with the witness of later writers as to how these books of prophecies were being read, that give to us the most reliable pointers as to the kind of meaning we can expect to attach to them. However much we may succeed in classifying their literary forms and poetic quality, it is not until we recover the sense of authority that lent to them the power to transform whole communities and to generate within these communities hope and commitment that we regain a sense of their formative canonical role. In this sense their interpretation can never be complete.

Several factors have led to a fundamental shift of interest and perspective in the contemporary understanding of these books of the Latter Prophets. Foremost among these is the awareness that for two centuries Christian, and in related ways, Jewish, scholars believed that they were in possession of the necessary historical key by which these prophets of ancient Israel and Judah could be made meaningful. So the work and influence of Robert Lowth, J. G. Eichhorn, and J. G. Herder at the end of the eighteenth century appeared to establish a core of hermeneutical rules that provided the needful parameters for understanding biblical prophecy. The impact of these scholars has been profound, not least in sweeping aside virtually all the accrued weight of tradition that had built up, largely in Christian circles, about the messianic significance of biblical prophecy and its foretelling of fundamental aspects of the history of the Christian church.[2] Yet now, and with good reason, the limitations of this so-called Enlightenment view of biblical prophecy are increasingly becoming apparent, with a need to return to ask some fundamental questions as to what we are to make of the prophetic writings of the Hebrew Bible.

What is striking in the present is that the necessary abandonment of a single global hermeneutic concerning the nature of prophets and recorded prophecy has not been replaced by any single agreed alternative. Rather

---

2. The British background to these changes is well covered in the dissertation of Joanna Davson, "Critical and Conservative Treatments of Prophecy in Nineteenth-century Britain" (D. Phil., Oxford, 1991). The wider background is dealt with in E. S. Shaffer, *'Kubla Khan' and the Fall of Jerusalem: The Mythological School in Biblical Criticism and Secular Literature 1770–1880* (Cambridge: Cambridge Univ. Press, 1975); and Stephen Prickett, *Words and the Word: Language, Poetics and Biblical Interpretation* (Cambridge: Cambridge Univ. Press, 1986). The German developments from the mid-nineteenth century are covered in P. H. A. Neumann, *Das Prophetenverständnis in der Deutschsprachigen Forschung seit Heinrich Ewald* (Wege der Forschung 307; Darmstadt: Wissenschaftliche Buchgesellschaft, 1979).

we are presented with a plurality of reading strategies and insights that open fruitful and insightful possibilities, but that no longer command any comprehensive recognition of their appropriateness.

"Signs and Portents in Israel" (Isa 8:18)

The question of the unity of the book of Isaiah has understandably become a focus of attention because the critical division of the book into at least two literary units—the so-called First and Second Isaiahs—became something of a flagship for the historical-critical evaluation of the text.[3] My own essay on the subject of the book's unity appeared at a time when the reevaluation of earlier questions regarding it were being forced upon scholars as a result of a number of major observations.[4] Along with many others following similar lines this review pointed to the extensive use of allusion and citation between the separate parts of the book.[5] In general these studies have been strongly motivated by the need to take account of allusions and interconnections among the various parts in seeking an explanation for the origin of the book once the belief in a single authorship had been abandoned. The idea of "unity" emerged out of the recognition that belief in a single authorial unity was neither a necessary nor a plausible explanation why the book should be regarded as a literary whole. The questions that have drawn my particular attention have primarily been those of redaction history, directed toward asking how the book has come to be given its present shape in view of the overwhelming weight of evidence for the centuries-wide chronological spread of its contents. Can we now retrace this process?

In two important essays on this issue David Carr has rightly questioned what "unity" might mean in the light of these conclusions.[6] Once it is clear

---

3. The historical rise of this critical position in Christian circles is reviewed in Jean M. Vincent, *Studien zur literarischen Eigenart und zur geistigen Heimat von Jesaja, Kap. 40–55* (BBET 5; Frankfurt am Main: Peter Lang, 1977) 15–39.

4. R. E. Clements, "The Unity of the Book of Isaiah," *Int* 36 (1982) 117–29 (repr. in my *Old Testament Prophecy: From Oracles to Canon* [Louisville: Westminster/John Knox, 1996] 93–104).

5. Cf. esp. C. R. Seitz, "Isaiah 1–66: Making Sense of the Whole," in *Reading and Preaching the Book of Isaiah* (ed. C. R. Seitz; Philadelphia: Fortress Press, 1988) 105–26; Rolf Rendtorff, "The Book of Isaiah: A Complex Unity: Synchronic and Diachronic Reading," in *New Visions of Isaiah* (ed. Roy F. Melugin and Marvin A. Sweeney; JSOTSup 214; Sheffield: Sheffield Academic Press, 1996) 32–49; J. Vermeylen, "L'unité du livre d'Isaïe," in *The Book of Isaiah—Le livre d'Isaïe* (ed. J. Vermeylen; BETL 81; Leuven: Peeters, 1989) 11–53; and E. W. Conrad, *Reading Isaiah* (OBT; Minneapolis: Fortress Press, 1991).

6. D. Carr, "Reaching for Unity in Isaiah," *JSOT* 57 (1993) 61–80 (repr. in *The Prophets: A Sheffield Reader* [ed. P. R. Davies; Biblical Seminar 42; Sheffield: Sheffield Academic Press, 1996] 164–83); and "Reading Isaiah from Beginning (Isaiah 1) to End (Isaiah 65–66): Multiple Modern Possibilities," in *New Visions of Isaiah*, 188–218.

that the formation of the book of Isaiah was a process that was spread across a plurality of authors and extended over a minimum of three centuries, then it follows that any understanding of editorial intention must take full account of this plurality. One has to admit that the categories of "unity and diversity" have become almost too commonplace as descriptions for many unexplained incongruities and disjointed features of biblical literature to be very useful for hermeneutical purposes. Until we draw the boundary lines between the two more narrowly, the very inconclusiveness of such descriptions stands as a confession of frustration. Where is the unity and what does it mean in such a context? The phenomenon of literary allusion, even when applied on a grand scale, does not of itself provide a demonstrable basis of unity.[7] Citations and allusions by themselves may vary greatly in the degree of significance that is attached to them. They may be foundational, or they may be purely cosmetic.

We could be tempted to dismiss the search for any integrating unity altogether by simply treating the book of Isaiah as an anthology of prophecy in which we accord a more or less equal status to each of the separate oracles. This would recognize that each of them was addressed to a particular situation at a particular time. Their incorporation into the extant book need be regarded as no more than a literary procedure offering no specific interpretive guidelines for them. A Jerusalem provenance might then be sufficient to explain their common connectedness in a single scroll. Alternatively we could claim that they simply happen to belong to "the Isaiah tradition." But this claim rapidly shows itself to be a tautology, and the idea of literary unity is reduced to the level of a label of convenience. The degree of ideological connectedness between the various sayings becomes of so little significance that it ceases to have any worthwhile hermeneutical point. To a considerable extent this has been the approach adopted by many authors in respect of the material in Isaiah 56–66.[8] In these chapters, whether or not they are ascribed to a single identifiable "Third Isaiah," the connections with the earlier parts of the book are noted, but do little to rescue their hidden prophetic author(s) from obscurity. In such a circumscribed

---

7. The widespread use of allusion as a literary strategy, not least in the biblical writings, is reviewed in R. Alter, *The Pleasures of Reading in an Ideological Age* (New York: Simon and Schuster, 1989) 111–40.

8. Cf. P. A. Smith, *Rhetoric and Redaction in Trito-Isaiah: The Structure, Growth and Authorship of Isaiah 56–66* (VTSup 62; Leiden: Brill, 1995). In many respects chaps. 56–66 have proved themselves to be something of an Achilles heel for theories of the literary structure of the book of Isaiah. Belief that they once existed as an independent collection has never proved wholly convincing. At the same time simply combining them with chaps. 40–55 has also left many unanswered questions. Their place in the whole collection then raises further questions concerning the range and time of their incorporation into the whole and their possible links with chaps. 24–27.

approach to the claim for unity the "Isaiah tradition" is no more than a cover title. It is formal, literary, and devoid of any integrating ideology. Old themes and images have been put to new uses!

One may argue that this minimalist understanding of the book's unity is in line with the older claims that we must posit the existence of a circle of Isaianic "disciples" as a prophetic school that continued to develop and apply the original prophet's themes and ideas until centuries after his own time. Such a belief tells us too little to be of any use as a basis for understanding either the redaction or the controlling factors that shaped the later material. Who could, and who could not, gain membership of such a select circle? More fruitful has been the redaction-critical approach that points to a series of editorial literary "shapes" that were imposed on the preserved collection at major turning points in Judah's history. The possibility of a continued Jerusalem provenance for all of this activity must be taken very seriously, even for the seemingly "errant" contents of chapters 40–55, which have often been assumed to have a Babylonian provenance!

A positive approach toward resolving the formal and literary questions of the kind of unity that we can trace in the book is adopted by David Carr, Marvin Sweeney, and W. A. M. Beuken that there would appear to be identifiable structures and *inclusios* in it.[9] In particular the framing role of chapters 1 and 65–66 stands out as a prominent feature, indicating some overall "plan" for it. So also chapter 35 and the narratives of 36–39 serve to provide a fulcrum on which the book, in its final form, balances. Similarly the psalm of Isaiah 12 has been intended to mark a closure of the collection of (1)2–12. If it is regarded simply as an anthology of varied prophecies, then these structural characteristics appear as attempts to give it shape. They also impose a certain degree of ideological connection between the parts by marking major transitions and resumptions in a fashion reminiscent of certain musical structures. They introduce emphases and serve to distinguish between what is "past" and what prophecies point to events that belong to the category of "not yet." They help to make the reader aware of where he or she stands in the divine timescale and thereby establish priorities of importance between the confusing multiplicity of smaller units. Not everything within the book seems to stand on the same level, even though nothing falls out of the governing hermeneutic altogether, if we are to judge from the retention of material that is clearly

---

9. Carr, "Reaching for Unity"; cf. now esp. M. A. Sweeney, *Isaiah 1–39; with an Introduction to Prophetic Literature* (FOTL 16; Grand Rapids: Eerdmans, 1996) 31–62; W. A. M. Beuken, "The Main Theme of Trito-Isaiah: 'The Servants of YHWH,'" *JSOT* 47 (1990) 67–87; idem, "Servant and Herald of Good Tidings: Isaiah 61 as an Interpretation of Isaiah 40–55," in *Book of Isaiah*, ed. Vermeylen, 411–42.

marked as referring to past events. Yet even this past carries a certain typological significance as an anticipation of the future. Overall the question of the history-relatedness of the prophecies becomes a prominent issue, since the larger context of the literary form of the book serves to broaden and "dehistoricize" many of the individual sayings within it.

The book has many beginnings and endings—too many for it to be possible to set them all in a clear and certain chronological order. Nevertheless, so far as an overall structure is concerned, we cannot leave aside the strong impression that the three major units of the traditional, if now deeply suspected, critical division of it into 1–39, 40–55 and 56–66 correspond to some kind of ideological classification. The predominantly threatening tones of the first part stand in sharp contrast to the scarcely restrained assurances of the second. In turn these move on to a more measured inter-mixing of tone and character in the third part in which threat, admonition, and assurance all appear in relation to one another.

Whether we put this down to accident, to the skill of scribes and redac-tors, or simply to the inevitable shifts of mood and expectation that are to be found in any community facing political and social turmoil, these mood shifts create an almost Hegelian dialectical structure. The concluding inter-mixing of threat and promise, like the strident appeals for repentance in chapter 1, appear to result from a consciously designed effort at generaliz-ing in order to provide a basis for ongoing instruction and liturgical use. Accordingly, no threat or warning leaves the reader without hope; nor does any promise and assertion of coming deliverance stand without admoni-tory messages of the conditions under which such prizes are to be won. Once we have split the book into three parts the threats and the promises become more detached from each other. This may be wholly appropriate for a purely historical interpretation, focused on specific situations, but has obvious dangers for a balanced reading from a theological perspective. In a more timeless context it is arguable that even the great promises of chap-ters 40–55 need the measured constraints of 56–66 to pull them down to earth.[10]

Much of my own interest in the editorial structure of the prophetic writ-ings began by noting the patterns that are evident in the interweaving of threats and promises that lacked convincing explanation in the attempts to get back to the prophet's *ipsissima verba*.[11] Whatever the original prophet

---

10. Cf. my essay, "A Light to the Nations: A Central Theme of the Book of Isaiah," in *Forming Prophetic Literature: Essays on Isaiah and the Twelve in Honor of John D. W. Watts* (ed. James W. Watts and Paul R. House; JSOTSup 235; Sheffield: Sheffield Academic Press, 1996) 57–69.

11. Cf. my "Patterns in the Prophetic Canon," in *Canon and Authority* (ed. G. W. Coats

may or may not have said, it becomes evident to the reader that God gives no threats which leave no hope; nor yet does God give unconditional guarantees that are not tempered by admonitions and warnings. Whether this is due to the intended liturgical reading of the finished book or to the need to inject a theological balance within the preserved material is not clear. Thus little attention has been given to the possible reasons for the literary location of particular sayings and refrains. David Carr points out that, in any case, we know too little about the way in which prophetic writings were read in antiquity to draw any large-scale conclusions.[12] That any person was expected to read through the entire book at one sitting so as to observe its overall shape appears highly unlikely as a major reason for its final form.

The interest in the issue of the unity of the book of Isaiah leaves us without any clear overriding hermeneutical guideline as to how it was understood, or was intended to be understood, as a prophetic text. It shows itself ultimately to be a question not so much about literary form and reading strategy, but rather about prophecy and how it was understood as a means of transcendent, otherworldly communication. It is on this account that any understanding of the unity of Isaiah presses forward into becoming a series of questions about faith and its role in social transformation.

At a purely literary level it seems quite plausible that even the final form may be little more than an ultimate closing off of a prophetic scroll. This still left ample room for fresh prophecies in other collections and new creative interpretations in new writings, based on single citations and themes drawn from Isaiah.[13] Isaianic prophecy did not come to an end, nor lose significance, when the book reached its extant shape.

"Seal the Teaching Among My Disciples" (Isa 8:16)

In the case of the book of Isaiah the reader is in the unusual position of possessing stories about the prophet Isaiah and his interventions at a critical period in Judah's history (705–701 BCE) that give a dramatic and highly readable presentation of his activity (Isaiah 36–39).[14] In fact, in the case

---

and B. O. Long; Philadelphia: Fortress Press, 1977) 42–55 (repr. in my *Old Testament Prophecy*, 191–202).

12. Carr, "Reading Isaiah," 216–17.

13. Cf. my essay, "The Interpretation of Prophecy and the Origin of Apocalyptic," in *Bible, Church and World: Essays in Honour of D. S. Russell* (London: Baptist Historical Society, 1989) 28–35 (repr. in my *Old Testament Prophecy*, 182–88).

14. Cf. my *Isaiah and the Deliverance of Jerusalem* (JSOTSup 13; Sheffield: JSOT Press, 1980). Cf. further the essay by P. R. Ackroyd, "Isaiah 36–39: Structure and Function," in *Von Kanaan bis Kerala: Festschrift für J. P. M. van der Ploeg OP zur Vollendung des siebzigsten Lebensjahres am 4 Juli 1979* (ed. W. C. Delsman, et al.; AOAT 211; Kevelaer: Butzon &

of Amos, a brief narrative linking the prophet's declarations with a specific event reflecting the manner of their reception is also given (Amos 7:1–17). Later, in the case of Jeremiah, much more extensive narratives are preserved (Jeremiah 32–45) that tempt the unwary interpreter into believing that a form of biography may be possible that would give a readily intelligible context for understanding the prophet's words against the political crises of his own age.

Broader questions concerning the relationship between narratives and oracular poems in the prophetic writings cannot be dealt with here, except insofar as those concerning Isaiah have a bearing on their place in the book. A strong, but far from overwhelming, consensus has believed that the narratives concerning Isaiah did not originally belong within the book of Isaiah.[15] More disconcertingly still, the prophecies ascribed to Isaiah in the narratives do not fit comfortably with those that are ascribed to him in the earliest parts of the book that carries his name (chaps. 1–12; 28–32). The Isaiah of the narratives stands out as a person imbued with strikingly different beliefs and convictions from the Isaiah who challenged Hezekiah with prophecies contained in Isaiah 28–32. Yet the two presentations are not altogether unrelated, and significant contacts and interconnections can be, and have been, traced. There is no doubt at all that the authors of the narratives of Isaiah 36–39 were intending to establish a portrait of Isaiah and his message that aligned closely with the manner in which they had received and understood his words. This is surely how they wished him to be remembered.

All the indications, however, point conclusively to the recognition that the "Isaiah of the narratives" is a portrait fashioned approximately a century later than the time of the main sayings preserved in the earliest collections of his words. The key provided by the later date of the narratives simply highlights the problem of reaching certain conclusions as to which of the sayings contained in chapters 1–32 really originated with the eighth-century prophet. They have obviously been edited, augmented, and shaped to take account of events that took place after the prophet's own lifetime. Even a phrase or two added to an original oracle may make it appear rather differently from its bare original form. It is this fact that has drawn increas-

---

Bercker; Neukirchen-Vluyn: Neukirchener Verlag, 1982) 3–21 (repr. in P. R. Ackroyd, *Studies in the Religious Tradition of the Old Testament* [London: SCM, 1987] 105–20).

15. A full critique of the issue, with a conclusion differing from the usual consensus, is found in K. A. D. Smelik, "King Hezekiah Advocates True Prophecy: Remarks in Isaiah xxxvi and xxxvii/II Kings xviii and xix," in *Converting the Past: Studies in Ancient Israelite and Moabite Historiography* (OTS 28; Leiden: Brill, 1992) 93–128.

ing attention to the role of those most elusive figures who played a part in shaping the prophetic writings: the redactors.

The special relevance of the question of editorial redaction has arisen in connection with the problem of the Isaiah narratives precisely because there are good reasons for believing that the compilation of stories involving prophets and the editing of their sayings were related activities. One of the most productive researches into the literary formation of the book of Isaiah has been directly linked to the question of the "Isaiah" of the narratives. This concerns Hermann Barth's delineation of a "Josianic" phase of redaction of a collection of Isaiah's sayings in which the presumed Josianic context, with all its political implications, has a strong bearing on the manner in which the collection of older prophecies is presented.

All the many issues that arise from this cannot here be reconsidered. The point that touches directly on the question of a global hermeneutic for the prophetic writings is that, to a significant degree, such redactors may more truly be regarded as the "authors" of the books of prophecy than even the prophet himself. We do not know for sure whether the prophets themselves wrote down any of their sayings, although there are reasonable indications that they did. Yet even so, it is the redactors who have undertaken the task of shaping their sayings into books. John Barton has coined the phrase "the disappearing redactor" because the more fully we are able to ascribe the formation of collections of prophetic sayings to redactors, the more such figures emerge as the dominant authorial hands in creating a prophetic literature. What they thought the prophet meant is likely still to show through in the way his words have been recorded for later ages.

The point is easily overstated, since we need not exploit the problematic issues of "Who wrote what?" to the detriment of any one part of the complex process of book compilation where the prophets are concerned. The significant feature of speaking about redactors, rather than prophetic authors, is that we are entitled to regard the redactor as a scribe who put together a number of sayings and, in doing so, endeavored to harmonize them into a connected whole. Even when the prophets themselves were, or appeared to be, inconsistent in their threats and promises, the redactor is likely to have smoothed over the rough places. Moreover, it is reasonable to assume that it was such redactors who looked for a greater level of ideological consistency in the prophet's words than would have been the case among an open-air audience. Differences needed to be explained, even when full consistency was never expected.

A striking feature of the written Isaianic tradition is to be seen in the extraordinary way in which fundamental metaphors have been strained and reapplied in new contexts.[16] These show no interest whatever in the original applications, nor in limiting the range of new meanings that can be extracted from them. The allusion to the original saying was obviously felt to be important, yet the freedom to exploit its potential in wholly different directions was uninhibited by this. New wine could be preserved in old bottles, with no anxiety lest the bottle should burst!

E. W. Conrad has very positively suggested that the redactors are more truly the "authors" of the prophetic writings than we have supposed since we could not read the prophet at all apart from this redactional mediation.[17] Yet it becomes impossible, given the extent of the chronological spread of material that has been preserved in the book of Isaiah, to conclude that we are dealing with only one major layer of editorial structuring. In this regard the book of Isaiah differs greatly from the collections of Jeremiah and Ezekiel, where the work of redactional structuring and shaping appears far more homogeneous.

What has consistently provided the backbone of the conventional critical understanding of the book of Isaiah is that the apportionment of material among the pre-587, exilic, and early postexilic periods accords reasonably well with the major classes of editorial referencing that the book contains. What is different in the new criticism, though often more implicit in earlier critical studies than is usually recognized, is that these three categories of material are interwoven in a highly intricate way. They cannot simply be found in wholly separate "blocks" within the book. Literary location is no certain guide to time of origin! The consequence is that an awareness of the book's wholeness as a literary creation is important if we are not to be misled into premature and unwarranted assumptions about how it was put together. Questions of literary shape and structure do, therefore, have a bearing on major hermeneutical issues.

It is valuable at this point to take note of the work of both Hans Wildberger and Hermann Barth in seeking to set out their conclusions regarding the major layers of editorial presentation in the book in a manner that is easy to follow.[18] In this respect I should wish to affirm that, in spite of my

---

16. Cf. Kirsten Nielsen, *There is Hope for a Tree: The Tree as Metaphor in Isaiah* (JSOT-Sup 65; Sheffield: Sheffield Academic Press, 1989); R. E. Clements, "Patterns in the Prophetic Canon: Healing the Blind and the Lame," in *Canon, Theology and Old Testament Interpretation: Essays in Honor of Brevard S. Childs* (ed. G. M. Tucker, et al.; Philadelphia: Fortress Press, 1988) 189–200.

17. E. W. Conrad, "Prophet, Redactor, and Audience: Reforming the Notion of Isaiah's Formation," in *New Visions of Isaiah*, 308.

18. H. Wildberger, *Königsherrschaft Gottes. Jesaja 1–39*, part 2: *Die Nachfahren des Propheten und ihre Verkündigung: Der Text* (Kleine biblische Bibliothek; Neukirchen-Vluyn: Neukirchener Verlag, 1984); H. Barth, *Die Jesaja-Worte in der Josiazeit: Israel und Assur als Thema einer produktiven Neuinterpretation der Jesajaüberlieferung* (WMANT 48;

adherence to many aspects of Barth's uncovering of a "Josianic redaction," it has been increasingly the importance of his recognition of a post-587 level of editing in the Isaiah book that impresses itself upon me.[19] If we are seeking to find the most effective key with which to unlock the mystery of the bewildering shifts between threat and promise, and the partisan apportioning of blame on King Ahaz and praise for Hezekiah and Cyrus, it lies in the concern to contrast and explain the different fates of Jerusalem in 701 and 587 BCE. The fact of Jerusalem's desolation in 587 casts its shadow across the entire book of Isaiah as truly and as unmistakably as the shadow of the cross stretches across the three Synoptic Gospels of the New Testament. The events of that year lend color to everything that is recorded and remembered about what Isaiah said and did at the end of the eighth century. A knowledge of them determines the content and quality of the future that the reader of the book was looking forward to. Once this point is accepted, then it would appear that the idea of the book's "unity" does stand for something important. To divide it into two separate parts, as the classical concept of a "First" and "Second" Isaiah was wont to do, is to let drop the fact that knowledge of events of the sixth century holds both parts together. These events had witnessed the destruction of the temple of Jerusalem and the dethronement of the Davidic monarchy—events that subsequently affected forever the political shape of Israel.

In substantial measure the redactor is the first interpreter and a true disciple of the prophet. That there was more than one redactor and that the work of redaction serves as a kind of "proto-commentary" is an important guideline in our search for an understanding of the book of Isaiah as a whole. The claim by H. G. M. Williamson that the figure that earlier critics identified as the otherwise anonymous "Deutero-Isaiah" may well have been the redactor of the preserved collection of Isaiah's sayings, which he edited and to which he himself added, seeks to draw together the varied processes by which the primary shape of the Isaianic prophetic collection was brought into being.[20] It would appear to me, however, that its pursuit of an "economy of hypotheses" goes too far. It is no doubt true that a good poet may also have been a good scribe and a careful editor, but I personally doubt it very much. The lyrical assurances of the hymnic praise of God in Isaiah 40–55 have an independence and distinctive identity that

---

Neukirchen-Vluyn: Neukirchener Verlag, 1978); cf. also G. T. Sheppard, "The Anti-Assyrian Redaction and the Canonical Context of Isaiah 1–39," *JBL* 104 (1985) 193–216.

19. Barth, 285–94; cf. my essay, "The Prophecies of Isaiah and the Fall of Jerusalem in 587 B.C.," *VT* 30 (1980) 421–36.

20. H. G. M. Williamson, *The Book Called Isaiah: Deutero-Isaiah's Role in Composition and Redaction* (Oxford: Clarendon, 1994) 116ff.

leaves open the questions of how and when they were linked to an earlier collection of Isaiah's sayings.

Nevertheless, Williamson's hypothesis has the merit of drawing increased attention to the complementary nature of the prophecies contained in Isaiah 1–32 and those of Isaiah 40–55. It highlights also the important bridge-building function of the narratives of chapters 36–39 for the formation of the book as it now appears.

Good News for the Oppressed (Isa 61:1)

All of these considerations may well leave the present-day reader asking, "How then shall we read Isaiah?" Since the book of Isaiah was a work whose composition extended from the end of the eighth to the close of the fifth century BCE, we must take this unusual and complex process of book formation into our thinking when asking how we are to interpret it. Clearly it is not simply an agglomeration of prophetic oracles added with no regard for their interconnections and literary appropriateness. There are structures and attempts at establishing integrated layers of significance that clearly testify to levels of redaction carried out at major turning points in the history through which this prophetic literary tradition passed.

It is hard to find any convincing evidence that what we have come to describe as the final form of the text, the dating of which probably originated at the end the fifth century BCE, is anything more than the last of these levels of redactional attempts at unifying the preserved deposit and making it usable in some ongoing, and presumably liturgical, form. Even the valuable, and essentially convincing, claim that chapters 1 and 65–66 serve to provide an interrelated framework by which all the intervening passages are held together achieves this by laying down very broad guidelines. The call to repentance in the introduction matches the warnings and admonitions of the epilogue, showing that all the threats and all the promises that stand between them have a more or less timeless relevance. Prophecy has become "decontextualized" in the process of its literary fixation, thereby freeing the text from any unduly narrow application. It is not simply a collection of lessons from the past, nor merely a promise of a tomorrow that will be better than today. The sense of the uncertain and painful circumstances in which the reader of the hypothetical present can expect to be placed is never far away from the text.

It would seem, therefore, that it is mistaken to demand as the primary goal of exegesis the finding of such meaning as we sense to be appropriate to the final form of the text. To seek this to the neglect of the varied meanings that appear to have been attached to the collection at different stages during its formation is a needless limitation of expectation. To a very real extent, all the meanings have significance and relevance, even though they oscillate between warning and promise and appear to finish on a rather indeterminate note over such primary questions as the future role of the Davidic kingship. It would be improper to suppose that this openness and indeterminacy over so many of the basic issues including, besides that of the Davidic dynasty, what it means for Israel to become a "light to the nations"[21] and the role that Jerusalem and its temple will fulfill in a new world order is no more than the result of scribal uncertainty and confusion. Rather it must surely represent the way in which the Israelite and Judean communities became progressively more fully aware that history itself was a process of creative openness. God gives no unconditional guarantees! Even though a kind of paradigmatic fundamentalism appears in certain prophetic promises, these are never ultimate and unconditional. This is the case with the two-armed assertion by which the author of the Isaiah narratives explained why events would turn out favorably for Jerusalem when it was threatened by Sennacherib. God says through the prophet: "For I will defend this city to save it, for my own sake and for the sake of my servant David" (Isa 37:35). Such an uncompromising declaration inevitably called forth further reflection in the light of later events. Whether there was any truth at all in such a guide to God's providential purposes appears as the unspoken question that motivates every prophecy that follows after the events of 587 BCE.

We can plausibly claim that it is the setting out of sharply worded assertions such as this, each of them deeply embedded in the political and religious history of Israel as a people, that provides a foundation platform for the book of Isaiah. The building onto them of a massive structure of further prophecies in which these basic themes continually return—to be challenged or refuted, only to reappear later in modified form—explains the three-dimensional character of the book. To try to reduce it to two dimensions is to lose the spiritual vitality and creativity that this interior movement of ideas discloses to us. Yet this is what happens when we try to read it solely as a collection of oracles that must somehow be confined either within the forty years or so of Isaiah's actual prophetic activity or within the historical situation of the fifth century BCE, if not later, when the book was fixed in its present form.

It would seem that belief in the sovereign divine freedom to create and perform new things (Isa 43:19) within the historical process was central to the Israelite understanding of prophecy. This gives us the essential herme-

---

21. Cf. my essay, "A Light to the Nations."

neutical key toward understanding the editorial freedom with which new prophecies lend new directions and possibilities to earlier ones in the creation of the great prophetic books. The prophetic work of unmasking the intentions and purposes of God toward Israel and Jerusalem touches only the fringes of the divine garment of history. It is a complex and dangerous task. Nevertheless it is witness to a theological struggle against assigning all history to meaninglessness and absurdity.

All too often prophecy has been cited as a proof that belief in absolute divine sovereignty implies a form of historical determinism. Such in the end leads to a fatalistic view of the world and its history, negating all sense of human responsibility and participation in the divine creativity. It is meaninglessness of a different order since God both writes the script and directs the play, reducing the actors to little more than puppets. It cannot be too strongly urged that not only the book of Jonah but the biblical prophetic literature as a whole rejects such a fatalistic worldview. Far from prophecy declaring a future that is fixed and unalterable, the book of Isaiah, as the skilled redactor of chapter 1 painstakingly demonstrates, is first and foremost a call to repentance and a summons to return to the path of obedience. Instead of decrying and deriding the possibilities that are open to every human being, the message of prophecy becomes a call to energize and activate them:

> Cease to do evil,
>   learn to do good;
> seek justice,
>   rescue the oppressed,
> defend the orphan,
>   plead for the widow.
>   (Isa 1:16–17)

The sufferings and failures of the past have their lessons for the present as they had for the ancient reader. Nevertheless, the future is still to be grasped and the prophetic agenda remains much the same, with its still unfulfilled challenges and promises.

It is a pleasure to offer these reflections to a scholar whose consistency and unfailing enthusiasm to recover this ancient prophetic agenda of hope and commitment has served as a rich inspiration for a generation. His concern to combine critical honesty for the text with a deep faith in the divine purpose for humanity provides an ongoing model for the many-faceted task of biblical interpretation.

– 11 –

The Metaphor of the Rock in Biblical Theology

Samuel Terrien

For a long time, biblical theologians have sought to discover a central theme for both the Old Testament and the New.[1] Some have come to perceive that Holy Scripture presents not a single principle of thematic unification, but an unresolved tension between legal monotheism and divine vulnerability.

From Genesis to Revelation, God appears either as omnipotent or as compassionate, hence susceptible to pathos. Already four decades ago, one might dare to speak of "the failure of monotheism."[2] The debates of Moses with Yahweh, the prophets' awareness of God's suffering, and the Joban poet's hint at divine perplexity over creation[3] point to a discrepancy between a creedal catechism and a parturition of self-abasement. Sinai leads to Golgotha.

As Walter Brueggemann has put it, "Old Testament theology must be bipolar. It is not only about structure legitimacy but also about *the embrace of pain*."[4] He pertinently adds, "Embrace of pain opens the Old Testament to the future. It is this radical probe of a new way of relationship that runs toward the theology of the cross in the New Testament."[5]

---

1. S. Terrien, "The History of Interpretation of the Bible, III: Modern Period," *IB* (Nashville: Abingdon, 1952) 1:140–41; G. F. Hasel, "Biblical Theology, Then, Now, and Tomorrow," *HBT* 4 (1982) 61–93; B. S. Childs, *Biblical Theology of the Old and New Testaments: Theological Reflection on the Christian Bible* (Minneapolis: Fortress Press, 1992) 3–29.

2. S. Terrien, *Job, Poet of Existence* (Indianapolis: Bobbs-Merrill, 1957) 66–100.

3. S. Terrien, *The Iconography of Job Through the Centuries: Artists as Biblical Interpreters* (University Park: Pennsylvania State Univ. Press, 1996) 40–43.

4. W. Brueggemann, "A Shape for Old Testament Theology, II: Embrace of Pain," *CBQ* 47 (1985) 398; S. Terrien, *The Elusive Presence: Toward a New Biblical Theology* (San Francisco: Harper & Row, 1978) 138–60 (this is not a biblical theology; one or two critics overlooked or misinterpreted the subtitle).

5. Brueggemann, "Embrace of Pain," 399.

Does the metaphor of "the Rock" provide an accessory contribution to the study of biblical bipolarism?

I

Like other ethnic groups of the Mediterranean world, the early Hebrews endowed certain objects of nature, such as springs, trees, and especially rocks, with spiritual power and significance. Three words, *sela'*, *ṣûr*, and *'eben*, quite synonymous, designate the stone, rough hewn or smoothly polished, originally a cliff, a crag, a boulder, or a pebble. These terms occur more than a hundred times in the entire Old Testament. On account of their natural qualities of solidity, they become figuratively symbols of endurance, protection, security, or firmness. Two of them appear as metaphoric names for Yahweh on account of his faithfulness (at least forty-five times). The psalmists especially speak of God as "the Rock" or "my Rock."

The stone or the rock may also receive a double meaning, not only of firmness but also of hardness (Ezek 11:19; 36:26) and obstinacy (Jer 5:3). The metaphoric meaning of foundation stone, cornerstone, or capstone may also be that of a rock of devastation and emptiness (2 Kgs 21:13; Isa 34:11; Amos 7:7–8). It may connote a state of terror (for one "petrified with fear"; Exod 15:16; 1 Sam 25:37). The cornerstone, which completes a construction, may also be a rock of stumbling (Isa 8:13–15; cf. 28:16–17).[6]

II

Several critics maintain that all the oracles of Isa 28:1–29 represent a post-exilic collection of miscellaneous poems, most of which contain an Isaianic core. It is frequently said that the central oracle on the stone in Zion (vv. 16–19) dates from the Persian period, that it refers to the rebuilding of the Jerusalem temple by Zerubbabel and to the post-exilic community, possibly with a polemical intent directed against the Samaritan cultus in Shechem or at Mount Gerizim.[7] The various poems gathered in Isaiah 28 are collected not only on account of the familiar tag words or mnemonic expressions—in this instance, "scoffers," "drunkards," "flood," and the like—but also spectacularly because every one of the poems deals with the theological motif of the temple, either at Shechem or in Jerusalem.

Furthermore, the oracles of promise that are now integrated within the oracles of warning and judgment are all concerned with eschatological

---

6. H. Wildberger, *Jesaja 28–39* (BKAT 10/3; Neukirchen-Vluyn: Neukirchener Verlag, 1982) 1069–70.

7. See O. Kaiser, *Isaiah 13–39* (trans. R. A. Wilson; OTL; Philadelphia: Westminster, 1974) 237–38.

times, not with the proximate future in the this-worldly economy of history. It is this lack of accurate understanding that probably led some critics to propose a postexilic date. No philological, stylistic, or form-critical argument prevents the attribution of these oracles of judgment as well as of promise to Isaiah, the prophet of the eighth century BCE.

These oracles come from the early part of Isaiah's ministry, either soon after his inaugural vision in 742 or during the Syro-Ephraimitic war in 735–734 under the threat of Tiglath-pileser III. Moreover, Isaiah was not a theologian of cultic presence.[8] The seraphic song in Isa 6:3 accurately signals the prophet's attack against the cultic restrictiveness inherent in the *theologoumenon* of glory. "The whole earth," sing the seraphim, "is filled with his glory." In the *Sanctus*, Yahweh's glory is no longer confined to the shrine (as in 1 Kgs 8:11). Isaiah explodes the spatial notion of divine presence.[9] The traditions of Exodus, Deuteronomy, and Kings relate the motif of *kābôd* to the privileged caste serving clerical enclosures; and this motif, in spite of Isaiah, persists in Ezekiel, who was probably the son of a Jerusalem priest. The explosion of that spatial restrictiveness is parallel to the prophetic notion of the holy, which Isaiah may well have received from his masters, Amos and Hosea. It stresses moral behavior in secular life rather than ritual deeds in a sacred place: "The holy God shall be manifested as holy by righteous behavior" (Isa 5:16).

The whole sequence of theological thinking encompassed in chapter 28 is quite clear. An oracle of woe (28:1–4), when Ephraim is threatened but not yet destroyed, menaces: "the proud crown of drunkards of Ephraim and the fading flower of the beauty of its splendor." The term *ʿăṭeret-malkām* refers typically to shrine idols (2 Sam 12:30), to the Jerusalem temple (Jer 13:18; Ezek 16:12; cf. 21:31), or to Jerusalem and Samaria (Ezek 23:42). In a similar way, *ṣĕbî tipʾeret* especially describes the Jerusalem sanctuary (Ps 96:6) or the heavenly temple (Isa 64:11 [MT 10]). A partially identical terminology, with key words skillfully interchanged through an elegant chiasmus, is employed in the second oracle (vv. 5–6), where a dynamic transfer will take place, not during the historical era of earthly existence but at the end of time, "in that day," a *terminus technicus* of the eschatological speech (*bayyôm hahûʾ*). The transfer moves from Yahweh of hosts, who is himself "the crown of glory" (*ʿăṭeret ṣĕbî*) and "the

---

8. E. Jacob recognizes the universal character of divine presence and ascribes to the royal dynasty more importance than to the temple. See "La pierre angulaire d'Esaïe 28.16 et ses échos néotestamentaires," *RHPR* 75 (1995) 5.

9. J. G. Gammie, *Holiness in Israel* (OBT; Minneapolis: Fortress Press, 1989) 79; J. J. Schmitt, *Isaiah and His Interpreters* (New York: Paulist, 1986) 39–127.

diadem of beauty," to "the remnant of his people." The remnant becomes a link between the two worlds and the two eras.

The attack on the intoxicated priests and prophets (cultic diviners), who reel, stagger, and stumble in their vomit (vv. 7–8), evokes once again the context of the temple by excoriating its clergy. A satire is directed against the same group of personnel, who either utter magical litanies or deride the prophet's ecstatic utterances (*ṣaw lāṣāw, qaw lāqāw*, etc.; vv. 11–13).

There follows an oracle of judgment against the rulers of Jerusalem, who boast about their covenant with death and their agreement with Sheol (vv. 14–15). The oracle of promise on the laying of the stone in Zion comes now climactically (vv. 16–17). The final threat indubitably implies the failure of a response from the religious leaders of Jerusalem to the preceding oracle and concludes with a divine decree of destruction (vv. 18–22).

III

It was in such a tightly woven context that the first-century CE readers understood the oracle on laying the stone in Zion. It concerns an eschatological temple. Zion, to be sure, is still to be viewed as a geographical center, just as in the probably Isaianic oracle of Isaiah 2 (=Micah 4). But it is a new Zion, a new earth, at the end of time, "in the last days" (Isa 2:2). Such a temple will be erected by the Lord. In other words, it shall not be built by human hands. It is not a temple designed for this earthly era but a sublimated temple, the heavenly place duplicated on earth—a re-created earth, a new earth, in an otherworldly economy of nature and history.

Isaiah must have known that, from its inception, the temple of Solomon was a semipagan institution, the very symbol of a syncretism that had spoiled the religion of Moses in the wilderness and in the land of promise. The myth of Zion was at best an ambiguous inheritance from West Semitic cults. The significance of Zion as the cosmic mountain, the world center, and thus the navel of the earth, has often been pointed out.[10] But its woeful consequences for the religion of Judah and early Judaism have not always been followed through.[11] Repeated reforms—those of Asa, Je-

---

10. S. Terrien, "The Omphalos Myth and Hebrew Religion," *VT* 20 (1970) 315–18.
11. Ibid., 337–38; D. Bodi, "Jerusalem and Babylon as the Navel of the Earth," in *The Book of Ezekiel and the Poem of Erra* (OBO 104; Fribourg: Universitätsverlag; Göttingen: Vandenhoeck & Ruprecht, 1991) 219–30; S. Talmon, "The 'Navel of the Earth' and Comparative Method," in *Scripture in History and Theology: Essays in Honor of J. Coert Rylaarsdam* (ed. A. L. Merrill and T. W. Overholt; PTMS; Pittsburgh: Pickwick, 1977) 243–68; idem, "The 'Comparative Method' in Biblical Interpretation—Principles and Problems," in *Congress Volume: Göttingen, 1977* (VTSup 29; Leiden: Brill, 1978) 320–56, esp. 348–49; S. D. Sterling, "Navel of the Earth," *IDBSup* (1976) 621–23. Cf. R. L. Cohn, "Jerusalem: The Senses of a Center," *JAARSup* F 44 (1978)

hoshaphat, Hezekiah, and Josiah—failed to eradicate from the temple the rites that the pagan sacrality of its site continued to attract—namely, the adoration of the earth-goddess, ophiolatry, heliolatry, and practices of male homosexuality probably connected with methods for mystical divination. The ambiguity of Zion is to be found in the belief, amply documented by Jewish folklore in New Testament times, that the Rock on which the temple was erected constituted the meeting point not only between heaven and earth but also between earth and Sheol.[12] Later on, the Rock of Zion became known as the *'eben šĕtîyāh*.[13]

One is now in a position to appreciate the atmosphere of awe, at once of fascination and of terror, against which Isaiah delivered the oracle of 28:16–19. He boldly demythologized a prehistoric belief inherited from the Canaanites and tenaciously adapted to Yahwism.

No more of that nonsense, said the prophet. In the days to come, the cosmic capstone on which Yahweh himself builds his own temple will be a tested stone, indeed the foundation stone that will keep the myth of Sheol and Death from corrupting his people. This cosmic Rock will be the final act of Yahweh, the conclusion to the *Opus Dei*, the climax of the grand opera of history. It will produce a faithful remnant and enable those who rely upon Yahweh alone to survive without hesitation, wavering, or compromise. "He who has faith will not waver" (Isa 28:16).

IV

Notice the context of the Isaianic oracle: the rulers of Jerusalem have made a covenant with Death (*môt*), an agreement with Sheol. The prophet did not necessarily allude to the political alliances that Ahaz[14] or Hezekiah may have negotiated with Judah's neighbors and especially with Egypt. The words imply far more than diplomatic and military entanglements. They point to the deep-seated attractiveness of the chthonic female powers for

12. H. Schmidt, *Der heilige Fels in Jerusalem: Eine archäologische und religionsgeschicht-liche Studie* (Tübingen: Mohr, 1933) 61–62, 97–99. The cosmic character of the Zion Rock has already been pointed out by Joachim Jeremias, *Golgotha* (*Angelos* Beihefte 1; 1926) 264–80; idem, *Golgotha und der heilige Fels* (*Angelos* Beihefte 2; 1926) 74–77; cf. idem, *ZNW* 29 (1930) 264–69. See also Wildberger, *Jesaja 28–39*, 1065–66.

13. N. Rhodokanakis, "Omphalos und Ewen Setiia," *Wörter und Sachen* 5 (1913) 198–99; and the rabbinical texts gathered in R. Patai, *Man and Temple in Ancient Jewish Myth and Ritual* (2d ed.; New York: Ktav, 1967) 56–58, 94–95.

14. See J. Lindblom, "Der Eckstein in Jes. 28,16," in *Interpretationes ad Vetus Testamentum pertinentes Sigmundo Mowinckel Septuagenario Missae* (2 vols.; Oslo: Land og Kirke, 1955) 1:123–25. O. Kaiser proposes the time of Hezekiah and interprets the covenant with death as referring to "some mystery rituals on immortality" (*Isaiah 13–19*, 252); R. E. Clements finds this view "very unlikely" but does not offer a cogent alternative (*Isaiah 1–39* [NCB; Grand Rapids: Eerdmans, 1980] 229).

those whose faith in Yahweh wavered and who sought instant security and certainty in the performance of sacred deeds inherited from the prehistoric recesses of the human psyche. Prophetic faith calls for that inner attitude of total attachment to the God of Moses, who has power over the forces of nature and is never to be confused with them. Here, as elsewhere, Isaiah showed that faith is a dynamic orientation providing solidarity, stability, and endurance for those who rely exclusively on the will of Yahweh. In the dialogue between Isaiah and King Ahaz, during the Syro-Ephraimite war, wordplay makes this meaning entirely clear: "If you will not have faith, surely you will not endure and survive (*'im lō' ta'ămînû kî lō' tē'ăminû;* 7:9).[15]

Faith produces courage and fearlessness, but not recklessness. It engenders the ability not to hesitate, not to change one's attitude from hope to despair—in other words, not to stumble. "He who has faith shall not waver." Nevertheless, the quietude counseled by Isaiah (7:4) has nothing to do with "quietism,"[16] since it implies alertness to danger and steadfastness in stepping forward. The use of *'mn,* from which *'ĕmûnāh,* "faith," derives, conjures up the risk of falling into the precipice, even when the straight path is followed. It includes at once fascination with the void and the capability of resisting its downward pull. Faith always stands in the context of the fear of nonbeing.

The affinities of Isa 28:16–17 with 7:9 are made more evident when one notices that the context in both poems refers to the very real phantasm of Sheol. For, in 7:11, the prophet taunts King Ahaz to ask for a sign: "Let it be as deep as Sheol or as high as Heaven." One can scarcely avoid the conclusion that in 28:16–17 the same contextual proximity between faith and Sheol is not coincidental. Faith is a reality that implies the peril of Sheol. Cosmic Rock becomes for the prophet an effective metaphor destined to convey the theological truth par excellence: Yahweh will act, and the expectation of the *Opus Dei* is what enables a remnant to survive.

Isaiah never espoused the shallow, pseudomagical dogma of the inviolability of Jerusalem. To be sure, the Zion tradition had formed him in his early years. Indeed, he may well have been at first an official in the sanctuary, a temple diviner. But his vision of Yahweh shattered his professional

---

15. R. Smend, "Zur Geschichte von האמין," in *Hebräische Wortforschung: Festschrift zum 80. Geburtstag von Walter Baumgartner* (VTSup 16; Leiden: Brill, 1967) 284–86, *et passim;* D. A. Cress, "Isaiah 7:9 and Propositional Accounts of the Nature of Religious Faith," *Studia Biblica 1978* (ed. E. A. Livingstone; JSOTSup 11; Sheffield: JSOT Press, 1979) 111–17; H.-J. Hermisson and E. Lohse, *Faith* (trans. D. W. Stott; Biblical Encounter Series; Nashville: Abingdon, 1981) 74, 81.

16. Cf. C. Keller, "Das quietische Element in der Botschaft des Jesajas," *TZ* 11 (1955) 81–89.

conventionalism. He then moved into the most stringent opposition against cultic rites that had been corrupted into magical manipulation.

No hasty conclusions should be drawn concerning the prophet's attitude during the siege of 701 BCE.[17] The work of H. Barth demonstrates that the prose accounts of Isaiah's comforting words to Hezekiah represent the interpretation of a later generation.[18] In effect, the oracle of promise in Isa 28:16 is strictly conditional. It forms an integral part of a threat. The word of indictment makes the word of hope highly ambiguous: Where is the source of faith?

The opening formula, "Thus says the Lord Yahweh," is form-critically indicative of the oracle of judgment. The new edifice will not be, on this earth, a guarantee of security—as Judaism in postexilic times came to believe—but, on the contrary, a metaphor of divine salvation and of human transformation in the new time, the eschaton. The stone that Yahweh will lay in Zion may still be described in the language of the cultic architectural style of the ancient Near East, but the expression *'eben bōḥan* (v. 16b) evinces several overtones. It suggests "a tested and reliable stone"; it provides "a testing" for human faith; it echoes derisively the practice of Egyptians, who erect some of their temples on and around the *bōḥan,* stone, the meaning of which is uncertain,[19] but it possibly refers to the cosmic rock of ancient Near Eastern mythology. Nurtured in the Yahwistic tradition, Isaiah was entirely aware of the notion of "testing," with its painful and salutary connotations.[20]

The architectural image continues in 28:17 with the ideology of civil rights as a builder's plumb line, and of social justice as a carpenter's level.[21] The word *qāw,* however, means a "surveyor's measure" rather than a

17. B. S. Childs, *Isaiah and the Assyrian Crisis* (SBT 2/3; London: SCM, 1967) 68–69.

18. H. Barth, *Die Jesaja-Worte in der Josiazeit* (WMANT 48; Neukirchen-Vluyn: Neukirchener Verlag, 1977); cf. R. E. Clements, *Isaiah and the Deliverance of Jerusalem* (JSOTSup 13; Sheffield: JSOT Press, 1980) 72–74.

19. L. Köhler, "Zwei Fachwörter der Bausprache in Jesaja 28:16," *TZ* 3 (1947) 392–95; cf. Lindblom, "Der Eckstein," 123–24.

20. Pss 7:9 (MT 10); 11:4–5; 17:3; 26:2; 66:10; 139:23; Zech 13:9. See J. Vermeylen, *Du prophète Isaïe à l'apocalyptique* (Ebib; Paris: Gabalda, 1977) 394; H. Wildberger, *Jesaja 28–39,* 1076–77. Clements correctly states, "The very rock of their foundation . . . would become a rock of 'testing'" (*Isaiah 1–39,* 229); cf. Isa 8:14–15, in which the metaphor, used of God, turned into a warning of judgment.

21. K. Galling, "Serubbabel und der Wiederaufbau des Tempels in Jerusalem," in *Verbannung und Heimkehr: Beiträge zur Geschichte und Theologie Israels im 6. und 5. Jahrhundert. Von Chr. Wilhelm Rudolph zum 70. Geburtstage gebracht. Festschrift W. Rudolph* (ed. A. Kuschke; Tübingen: Mohr, 1961) 72–73; Kaiser, *Isaiah 13–39,* 254–55. The translation of W. H. Irwin (*Isaiah 28–33: Translation with Philological Notes* [BibOr 30; Rome: Pontifical Biblical Institute, 1977] 32), who sees in *hamma'amin* (28:16) not "he who had faith" but "the Master Builder," is conjectural based on the noun *'amon* in Prov 8:29 but is not justified by the *Hiphil* use of the verb *'mn*. See also Wildberger, *Jesaja 28–39,* 1069–70.

plumb line (Isa 44:13; Jer 31:29 *Qere;* Jub 38:5), and the *mišqōlet* is a scale for weighing rather than a level (2 Kgs 21:13). Hence, the rhetoric of the oracle broadens itself from v. 16 to v. 17 with an emphasis on communal growth in solidarity. The promise never softens the rigor of the eschatological judgment.[22] Just as Isaiah's conversation with Ahaz during the Syro-Ephraimite war brings together the themes of faith and salvation with those of unfaith and destruction (as shown by the ambiguity of the name Immanuel in 7:14 and 8:8), so also the motif of faith (which binds 28:16 with 7:9) relates the theme of the eschatological capstone in 28:18 with that of the rock of offense,[23] the stumbling stone of 8:14.

The rock, which at the end of time will be laid in the Zion of a new earth by Yahweh himself, will be a temple "not made by human hands." It represents not the foundation of human faith but the reality of a divine presence in the midst of a new humanity.[24]

V

At the dawn of the Christian movement, the Qumran sectarians were inspired by the ideology of the Rock; but, unlike Isaiah, they identified it with their community, not with the cosmic act of God. The *Damascus Document* describes the community as a house erected by God within the people of Israel, a "secure" house, such as had never been before then.[25] In the *Hymns,* the imagery of the Rock (*sela'*) appears to relate to the concern for the secret brotherhood (*sôd*).[26] The symbolism of the "tested" stone recalls

---

22. Isa 1:27; see Vermeylen, *Du prophète Isaïe,* 394–95; cf. R. F. Melugin, "The Conventional and the Creative in Isaiah's Judgment Oracles," *CBQ* 36 (1974) 301–11.

23. As G. von Rad put it: "by a tremendous paradox, it is on this very God who has hidden his face from the house of Israel that Isaiah sets his hope. What confidence in the face of the absence of faith! But the surprise is rather that the message actually brought faith forth, even if only within a very narrow circle" (*Old Testament Theology* [trans. D. M. G. Stalker; 2 vols.; New York: Harper & Row, 1962–65] 2:41).

24. Contra E. J. Kissane, *The Book of Isaiah* (repr. Dublin: Browne and Nolan, 1960) 307; S. Mowinckel, *He That Cometh* (trans. G. W. Anderson; New York and Nashville: Abingdon, 1954) 134–35; G. Fohrer, *Das Buch Jesaja* (3 vols.; Zürcherbibelkommentare; Stuttgart: Zwingli, 1960–64) 2:59.

25. CD 3:19–20; see A. Jaubert, "La communauté sanctuaire," in *La notion d'alliance dans le judaïsme aux environs de l'ère chrétienne* (Patristica Sorbonensia; Paris: Seuil, 1963) 152–63.

26. 1QH 7:8–9; see J. Ringger, "Das Felsenwort: Zur Sinndeutung von Mt 16,18, vor allem im Lichte der Symbolgeschichte," in *Begegnung der Christen Studien: Studien evangelischer und katholischer Theologie* (ed. M. Roesle and O. Cullmann; Stuttgart: Evangelisches Verlagswerk, 1960) 285–91; G. Klinzing, "Die Gemeinde als Tempel," in *Die Umdeutung des Kultus in der Qumrangemeinde und im Neuen Testament* (SUNT 7; Göttingen: Vandenhoeck & Ruprecht, 1971) 50–93, 205–7. Cf. É. Puech, "La pierre de Sion et l'autel des holocaustes d'après un manuscrit hébreu de la grotte 4 (4Q522)," *RB* 99 (1992) 676–96.

the Isaianic oracle of 28:16 with its *'eben bōḥan*,[27] interpreted in a social and eschatological sense. As in Isaiah's proclamation on laying stone, the context significantly alludes to safety in the face of turmoil "at the time of Judgment."[28] Those who will enter the fortified city will not stumble.

VI

The Qumran interpretation of Isaiah 28 may have constituted a link between the eighth-century prophet and the Matthean pericope. Whatever, the meaning of the "rock" in Matt 16:18, temple and underworld are related.[29][30] Both Jeremiah and Jesus shared a highly offensive, indeed a completely blasphemous, attitude toward the temple.[31] Moreover, Jeremiah played a role in the Hanukkah tradition (2 Macc 2:1–8).

The motif of the temple permeating the section of Matthew 12–13 finds its climactic manifestation in the foundation of the eschatological community, the new temple. The verb *oikodomein* ("to build, to erect") was not only used in Matt 16:18 but also appeared as the prominent metaphor in early Christian literature whenever the eschatological community as the new temple was described or evoked.[32]

Jesus as the foundation stone of the new community is a capital theme of the entire New Testament.[33] When the author of Ephesians enlarges upon

27. 1QH 6:25–26; see Lindblom, "Der Eckstein," 129–30; O. Betz, "Felsenmann und Felsengemeinde (Eine Parallel zu Mt 16₁7–19 in den Qumranpsalmen)," *ZNW* 48 (1957) 49–77.

28. 1QH 7:23–29.

29. H. Schmidt, *Der heilige Fels*, 100–102; cf. E. Burrows, "Some Cosmological Patterns in Babylonian Religion," in *The Labyrinth* (ed. S. H. Hooke; London: Oxford Univ. Press, 1935) 57–59; cf. also P. Dreyfus, "La primauté de Pierre à la lumière de la théologie biblique de reste d'Israël," *ISTINA* 2 (1955) 338–46: B. Lindars, *The New Testament Apologetic* (Philadelphia: Westminster, 1961) 180–81; J. Dupont, "La révélation du Fils de Dieu en faveur de Pierre (Mt 16:17) et de Paul (Gal 1:16)," *RSR* 2 (1964) 415; J. Kahman, "Die Verheissung an Petrus: Mt. XVI, 18–19 im Zusammenhang des Matthäusevangeliums," in *L'évangile selon Matthieu: rédaction et théologie* (ed. M. Didier; BETL 29; Gembloux: Duculot, 1971) 267–68.

30. J. Carmignac, "Pourquoi Jérémie est-il mentionné en Matthieu 16:14?" in *Tradition und Glaube: Das frühe Christentum in seiner Umwelt* (ed. G. Jeremias, et al.; Göttingen: Vandenhoeck & Ruprecht, 1971) 283–85.

31. M. D. Goulder, *Midrash and Lection in Matthew* (London: SPCK, 1974) 388.

32. If the transfiguration corresponded to the Feast of Tabernacles (note Peter's exclamation, "Let us make here three booths!"), Tishri 15 was the date of Sukkot, and the date for Peter's confession "six days previously" (Mark 9:2) would consequently fall upon the eve of Tishri 10, or Yom Kippur, the Day of Atonement. That was the day when the high priest penetrated alone beyond the veil, entered the holy of holies, and faced the cosmic rock. Thus the gospel tradition brought together all the motifs of Isaiah 28: the old temple, the new temple, Sheol, faith. Cf. Burrows, "Some Cosmological Patterns."

33. P. Vielhauer, "Oikodome: Das Bild vom Bau in der christlichen Literatur vom Neuen Testament bis Clemens Alexandrinus," in *Oikodome: Aufsätze zum Neuen Testament* (ed. G. Klein; Theologische Bücherei 65; Munich: Kaiser, 1979) 5–6; P. Hoffmann, "Der Petrus-Primat im Matthäus-Evangelium," in *Das Matthäus-Evangelium* (ed. J. Lange; Darmstadt:

this motif and associates "the apostles and the prophets" as the *themelion* ("basement"), he does not propose that they are substitutes for, or even successors to, Christ Jesus, who himself remains the *akrogōniaios,* "foundation stone" (Eph 2:20).[34] It is no accident that this word happens to be the LXX choice for the translation of the *pinnat yiqrat mûsād* in Isa 28:16. The architectural term "cornerstone" refers to the element of permanence and of numinous inception by which an edifice is begun.[35] In the case of the temple of Zion this stone is the cosmic Rock, not the keystone at the top of the monument but the lock of the underworld, the capstone of Sheol in late Jewish and early Christian times, the granite "plug" that closes Hades.[36]

VII

In the balance of Isa 28:18, the reference to Sheol and its gates has for centuries tried the ingenuity of its commentators. If, indeed, Matt 16:18 is an embryonic midrash on Isa 28:16, one should expect the association of themes between the cosmic Rock, on which the eschatological community as the new temple will be founded, and the horrors of death and Sheol. As we have seen, the oracle of Isaiah is embedded within the context of oracles of judgment, which deal precisely with the same motifs. In Matthew the use of the verb *katischuein,* traditionally rendered "to prevail," constitutes a major difficulty. Is it appropriate to say that the gates of Hades shall not "prevail" against the community?[37] In the traditional translation, which repeats Jerome's rendering, "et portae inferi non praevalebunt aedversus eam," the gates have not remained a passive and immobile tool of closure, but have become an active weapon for offensive warfare.

The LXX may reflect a phonetic misunderstanding of the original Hebrew, since it apparently read *šō'ărê šĕ'ôl,* "the gatekeepers of Sheol."

Wissenschaftliche Buchgesellschaft, 1980) 422–23. The "stone" as a messianic symbol appears also in the rabbinical literature. See H.-L. Strack and P. Billerbeck, *Kommentar zum Neuen Testament aus Talmud und Midrasch,* vol. 2 (Munich: Beck, 1922) 877.

34. Rom 15:20; 1 Cor 3:9–17; Eph 2:22; cf. M.-A. Chevallier, "La construction de la communauté sur le fondement de Christ (1 Cor 3,5–17)," in *Paolo a una chiesa divisa (1 Cor 1–4)* (ed. L. de Lorenzi; Rome: Abbazia de S. Paolo fuori le mura, 1980) 109–29.

35. R. J. McKelvey, *The New Temple and the Church in the New Testament* (Oxford Theological Monographs; Oxford: Oxford Univ. Press, 1969) 193–94.

36. The words for "rock" and "stone" became interchangeable. See J. Betz, "Christus – Petra –Petrus," in *Kirche und Überlieferung* (ed. J. Betz and H. Fries; Freiburg: Herder, 1960) 15, nn. 50, 51.

37. Commentators have traditionally circumvented the difficulty by assuming that "the gates of Hades" designated personified powers of evil. It is true that "the gates" came to mean "the palace" (Dan 2:49; Est 2:19); but is it legitimate to conclude from this observation that "only one more step was needed to treat" the gates of Hades as the personified power of death? (M.-J. Lagrange, *L'évangile selon Saint Matthieu* [Ebib; Paris: Gabalda, 1928] 325–26).

Such an error may have already occurred in the reading of various Old Testament uses of the expression *ša'ărê šĕ'ôl*, (Isa 38:10), *ša'ărê-māwet* (Job 38:17a; Pss 9:13 [MT 14]; 107:18), and even *ša'ărê ṣalmāwet* (Job 38:17b).[38] The question remains: Why should the gatekeepers of the underworld become offensive warriors fighting against the church?[39]

The sentence might refer to the water of the cosmic Deep or the Abyss (*tĕhôm*), a constantly recurring threat to the dry surface of the earth. When, according to rabbinic lore, David dug the perpendicular shaft on Mount Zion for his preliminary work on the site of the temple that Solomon was later to erect, the water of the Tehom arose and threatened to submerge the whole earth. Under the counsel of Ahithophel, David cast down into the hole a shard on which the ineffable name had been inscribed, and he sang the fifteen Songs of Ascent. Thereupon the Deep subsided sixteen thousand cubits, and finally settled down at one thousand cubits under Mount Zion.[40] The fear of the abysmal waters is graphically expressed several times in these legends, for which the Rock of Zion is less the foundation of the temple than the capstone, which presses down the cosmic flood.

If such beliefs were attested in a period earlier than the second or third century CE, one might use them to explain the aggressive sense of the verb "prevail." But the meaning of the phrase in Matt 16:18 would still be strange, if not entirely reversed, since the function of the gates would be to prevail not against the eschatological community but against the cosmic flood emerging from the underworld.

Furthermore, Sheol or Hades remains definitely distinct from Tehom, not only in the Hebrew Bible but also in the Apocrypha, the Pseudepigrapha, the Qumran texts, and the whole New Testament. The psalmist's expostulation, "From the depths of the earth thou wilt bring me up again" (Ps 71:20, RSV), does not constitute an exception to the Old Testament distinction between Tehom and the Deep, since it uses the plural *tĕhōmôt* to designate not the Abyss but the lower parts of Sheol, or Abaddon.

That Matt 16:18 refers to the gates of death and not to the mouth of Tiamat, the jaws of the Dragon, or the cosmic flood is consistent not only with the Old Testament usage but also with a similar expression in a more

---

38. R. Eppel, "L'interprétation de Mt 16,18b," in *Aux sources de la tradition chrétienne: Mélanges offerts à M. Maurice Goguel à l'association de son soixante-dixième anniversaire* (ed. O. Cullmann; Bibliothèque théologique; Neuchâtel and Paris: Delachaux et Niestlé, 1950) 71–73.

39. The same objection applies to those who view "the gates" as a metaphoric expression for "the government of Hades," comparable to the designation of the administration of the Turkish Empire in Constantinople as "La Sublime Porte."

40. b. Sukk. 53a–b; b. Mak. 11a; cf. Patai, *Man and Temple*, 56.

recent past (*Pss Sol.* 16:2; Wis 16:13).[41] The association of Hades with "a serpent," subsequently called "Dragon" (*drakon*), appeared only at a later time (*3 Bar.* 4:2).

If Matt 16:18 reflects an early, Aramaic stage of the tradition that may go back, beyond the primitive Jerusalem community, to the sayings of Jesus himself, the Semitic verb, translated by *kataschyein,* may well have been one that meant not "to overpower in combat," as in Gen 32:25 and 28, where Jacob was said to have "prevailed" over the angel at the Jabbok, but any one of fifteen other verbs that meant "to maintain a steady and immobile strength."[42] The LXX used the verb *katischyein* about one hundred and five times (not counting three additional occurrences in Aquila, Symmachus, and Theodotion) to translate as many as sixteen different Hebrew verbs, several of which, like *gbr, ḥzq,* or *kbd,* meant "to be strong, immovable," "to stand firm," "to be heavy," "to be inflexible." The point is that in Matt 16:18 the gates of Hades are passive, inactive doors, which will not resist the community if its members want to enter Hades.

The expression "the gates of Hades" goes back to the Sumerian, Akkadian, and Hittite mythologies.[43] The Hittite Myth of the "Disappearance of Telipinu" told how "the porter opened the seven gateways.... What goes in never comes out, because it perishes there."[44] The Sumerian Inanna or the Akkadian Ishtar descends to the sojourn of the dead. At each of the Seven Gates of the Netherworld she is compelled to leave an ornament or a piece of clothing behind her. Eventually she arrives at her destination below, completely naked.[45] The expression "the gates of death" found its way

---

41. The Qumran hymnist distinguished between Tehom, which "echoed his groaning," and the gates of death, near which he had apparently come (1QH 6:24). The allusion is in the nature of a poetic metaphor and does not justify the interpretation of "the gates of Hades" in Matt 16:18 as a designation of "Satan's might." Contra O. Betz, "Felsenmann und Felsengemeinde," 70, 76–77; J. Jeremias, "πύλη," *TDNT* 6 (1968) 927; cf. M. Wilcox, "Peter and the Rock: A Fresh Look at Matthew 16:17–19," *NTS* 22 (1975) 80.

42. Neither K. Beyer in his *Semitische Syntax im Neuen Testament* (SUNT 1; Göttingen: Vandenhoeck & Ruprecht, 1962) nor M. Black in his *Aramaic Approach to the Gospels and Acts* (3d ed.; Oxford: Clarendon, 1967) mentions Matt 16:18 as a Semitism. The fact that *katischyein* in the LXX is sometimes constructed with a genitive rather than with an accusative does not justify the interpretation "to vanquish" instead of "to be strong" or "to resist" (contra J. Jeremias, *TDNT* 6 [1968] 927).

43. See A. S. Kapelrud, "The Gates of Hell and the Guardian Angels of Paradise," *JPOS* 70 (1950) 151–56.

44. C. Kühne, "Hittite Texts: The Myth of the Disappearance of Telipinu," in *Near Eastern Religious Texts Relating to the Old Testament* (ed. W. Beyerlin, et al.; trans. J. Bowden; OTL; Philadelphia: Westminster, 1978) 164.

45. E. A. Speiser, "Akkadian Myths and Epics," in *ANET,* 106–7. A parallel form of the myth was common in the Mediterranean world during the Hellenistic and Roman times. See W. F. J. Knight, *Cumean Gates: A Reference of the Sixth Aeneid to the Initiation Pattern* (Oxford: Blackwell, 1936) 54–56; idem, *Elysion: On Ancient Greek and Roman Beliefs Concerning a Life after Death* (London: Rider, 1970) 98, 131–36.

into the religious life of ancient Israel. Typically, the psalmist who addresses Yahweh as "thou who liftest me up from the gates of death" (Ps 9:13, RSV) immediately adds "that I may recount all thy praises, that in the gates of the daughter of Zion I may rejoice in thy deliverance" (v. 14, RSV). The parallelism between the gates of death and the gates of the temple cannot be missed.

In Matt 16:18, however, the overtones of meaning appear to be different from what was implied by the psalmist. They recall, rather, the ancient oriental mythologies of a voluntary descent into the netherworld.

VIII

The ancient and traditional function of the gates of Sheol is to remain shut and to keep away those who wish to pass through them, unless the proper ritual for entry has been performed. Might it be, therefore, that the Matthean phrase referred not to the church as it developed historically on earth, but to the eschatological *qāhāl*, *qehillāh*, or *kĕnîštāh*, the transitory company of the followers of Jesus, who were, so to speak, the forerunners of the kingdom of God? Their Master was about to build an *ekklēsia*, not the church of a later age but the tiny company of those who trusted him.[46] Unlike the faithful of the Isaianic oracle, who in the eschatological time shall not waver, the disciples of Jesus are a sorry lot. Jesus, or the evangelist, had no illusion about them. The *ekklēsia* is not endowed with an eternal stability, an unconquerable permanence, that ability to sustain the temptation of death.

On the contrary, according to this exegesis, Jesus warns his disciples and implies the fragility of their faith. They will be tempted to court death. They will be possessed by the *thanatos* drive. They may yield to the temptation of forcing their way into Sheol. And the gates of Hades will not remain shut. They will not prevent the *ekklēsia* from entering the realm of nonbeing. The *ekklēsia* is as fragile as the faith of its members.[47]

The ambiguities of faith, central to the teachings of Isaiah and Jesus, are further emphasized in all the Gospels by the theme of Peter's characteristic

---

46. It is unfortunate that the word *ekklēsia* in Matt 16:18 is translated by "church," since the early Christians were accustomed to reading in the LXX (about 100 instances) or in the Targum the meaning of "congregation," or "company."

47. See J. Kahmann, "Simon als Fels und Petrus als Satan," a section in his chapter, "Die Verheissung an Petrus: Mt. XVI, 18–19 im Zusammenhang des Matthäusevangeliums," in *L'évangile selon Matthieu*, 261–64; J. D. Kingsbury, "The Figure of Peter in Matthew's Gospel as a Theological Problem," *JBL* 98 (1979) 72; E. Dinkler, "Peter's Confession and the Satan Saying: The Problem of Jesus' Messiahship," in *The Future of Our Religious Past: Essay in Honour of Rudolf Bultmann* (ed. J. M. Robinson; New York: Harper & Row, 1971) 173–75.

weakness. It is to be noted that while Matthew adds to Mark and Luke the sayings on the rock and the *ekklēsia,* he does not omit the sequel to the words spoken at the synoptical site (the vicinity of Caesarea Philippi). This sequel portrays Peter as the instrument of Satan and a rock of scandal (v. 23).[48]

If Matt 16:18 is an embryonic midrash on Isa 28:16, it follows that the cosmic Rock, now the rhetorical vehicle of the presence of God on earth in the historical person of Jesus, cannot in any way be identified with Peter, the paradigm of the ambiguity of faith. The heavenly aspect of Peter's revelation in v. 17 is neutralized by the charge that he minds the things of humans rather than the things of God (v. 23b). There is no certainty concerning the interpretation of *kepā'.*[49]

The traditional identification of Peter with the foundation stone of the church as a promise of permanence completely disregards the influence of the Isaianic cosmic Rock on the Matthean saying. It ignores the Matthean context of Peter as Satan's mouthpiece. It contradicts the unanimous testimony of the other New Testament writers who favor the image of the rock as a description of Christ Jesus. Above all, it is incompatible with the famous disquisition on the "living stone," which, in the first letter ascribed to Peter (2:6), develops on the basis of the LXX the quotation of Isa 28:16, together with Ps 118:22 and Isa 8:14–15 (cf. Rom 9:33). What a coincidence! Is it that the author of this document, whether Peter himself or Sylvanus or another member of the Petrine circles, was consciously polemi-

---

48. It is possible that the theme of the descent into Hades reflected a polemic against initiation rituals practiced by some mystery cults or against the techniques of magicians who claimed that they could enter the underworld. For a different interpretation of "the gates," see W. Bousset, *Kyrios Christos: A History of the Belief in Christ from the Beginnings of Christianity to Irenaeus* (trans. J. E. Steely; Nashville: Abingdon, 1970) 65. Bousset suggested that Matt 16:18b reflects the myth of the descent into Hades, which Hellenistic Christianity associated with the three days spent by Jesus in the grave. "The company of the righteous who have fallen asleep also belongs to the *ecclesia triumphans.* The gates of Hades are open and they no longer hinder passage to freedom." The trouble with this view is that in the Matthean *logion* the gates are not open. Cf. other forms of the myth in Matt 27:51; Acts 2:24; 1 Pet 3:19; 4:6; Rev 1:18; *Gos. Pet.* 10:41; etc. In a somewhat similar vein, L. E. Sullivan, S.J., observed that in Matt 16:18 it is the *ekklēsia* that forces the gates open; but he saw in Sheol "the citadel of Satan" rather than the land of the dead and therefore concluded that the church will ultimately be victorious over the powers of evil ("The Gates of Hell [Mt. 16:18]," *TS* 10 [1949] 62).

49. H. Clavier, "Πετρος και πετρα," in *Neutestamentliche Studien für Rudolph Bultmann* (ed. W. Eltester; Berlin: Töpelmann, 1954) 94–109; J. A. Fitzmyer, S.J., "Aramaic *Kepha* and Peter's Name," in *Text and Interpretation: Studies in the New Testament Presented to Matthew Black* (ed. E. Best and R. Wilson; Cambridge: Cambridge Univ. Press, 1979) 121, 132; cf. P. Lampe, "Das Spiel mit dem Petrus-Namen—Matt. XVI.18," *NTS* 25 (1979) 242–45; cf. G. Strecker, *Der Weg der Gerechtigkeit: Untersuchung zur Theologie des Matthaeus* (FRLANT 82; Göttingen: Vandenhoeck & Ruprecht, 1962) 198; Kingsbury, "Figure of Peter," 67–69; A. Stock, "Is Matthew's Presentation of Peter Ironic?" *BTB* 17 (1987) 64–69.

cizing against a Petrine-primacy interpretation of the Aramaic *logion* by the Matthean redactor?

In this "perspective of incongruity," the notion of faith promoted by Isaiah and Jesus includes the weakness of humankind and the greatness of God. It does not open the way to the sin of idolatry—idolatry of Israel, of Zion, and of the church. It reflects both the good news of salvation and the prophetic warning of judgment.

*   *   *

The identification of Peter and the rock on which the church was to be built has never been the view of the New Testament writers (outside Matthew), and this was by no means the opinion that prevailed among the church fathers, of either East or West. Diversity of opinions continued throughout the Middle Ages. The debate intensified in modern times,[50] and it remains inconclusive. Far from being exhausted, the special problem of Peter and the rock contains a still wide-open mine of possibilities.[51]

The bipolar tension between the God of retribution and the God of compassion, or between structure legitimation and embrace of pain, which will construct a truly biblical theology, appears in the metaphor of the rock, both in the Isaiah oracles and in the Matthean tradition. A truly biblical theology is needed as a springboard toward the formulation of Christian faith and its translation into cogent beliefs for every generation of history. Its importance is particularly urgent today, when a cultural revolution rapidly alters the worldwide conditions of humanity.

---

50. J. A. Burgess, *A History of the Exegesis of Matthew 16:17–19 from 1781 to 1965* (Ann Arbor: Edwards, 1976) 5–30 *et passim*.

51. F. W. Beare, *The Gospel According to Matthew* (San Francisco: Harper & Row, 1981) 353–56; D. R. A. Hare, *Matthew* (Interpretation; Louisville: Westminster/John Knox, 1993) 190–92; J. E. Powell, *The Evolution of the Gospel: A Commentary on the First Gospel, with Translation and Introductory Essay* (New Haven: Yale Univ. Press, 1994) 145–46; cf. U. Luz, *The Theology of the Gospel of Matthew* (trans. J. B. Robinson; New Testament Theology; Cambridge: Cambridge Univ. Press, 1995) 96–97.

– 12 –

The Tears of God and Divine Character in Jeremiah 2–9

Kathleen M. O'Connor

The character of God in the book of Jeremiah is multiple and unstable. Images and metaphors about the deity tumble over and contradict each other in a poetics of divine proliferation and profusion. This multiplicity appears to undermine any consistent characterization or portrayal of the divine and creates by linguistic abundance a language of a God who is multiple and many faceted.

For historical-critical interpreters, Jeremiah's proliferation of theological language was the logical consequence of the book's complex process of composition. Understood as an amalgamation of disparate literary pieces, the book inevitably portrayed God in a variety of ways. Inconsistencies in divine portrayal resulted from the mixing of sources, genres, and traditions in an unruly process.[1] But as Jack Miles has cogently observed, such an approach conveniently overlooks the fact that God is the speaker throughout. "Seemingly contradictory messages all come from the same divine source."[2]

Recently, a variety of literary studies of Jeremiah have begun to challenge views of the book as an unreadable amalgamation. Brueggemann, Biddle, Liwak, Diamond and O'Connor, and Stulman, among others, have begun to locate synchronic coherence in the book, irrespective of historical origins of materials.[3] Diamond and O'Connor find a loose narrative unity in 2:1–4:2 that emerges from the metaphor of Yhwh's broken marriages with

---

1. For summaries of the discussion, see Siegfried Herrmann, *Jeremia* (BKAT 12: Neukirchen-Vluyn: Neukirchener Verlag, 1986); and William McKane, *Jeremiah*, vol. 1 (ICC; Edinburgh: T. & T. Clark, 1986) xv–lcii.

2. Jack Miles, *God: A Biography* (New York: Knopf, 1995) 195.

3. Walter Brueggemann, "The Baruch Connection: Reflections on Jeremiah 43:1–7," *JBL* 113 (1994) 405–20; Mark Biddle, *Polyphony and Symphony in Prophetic Literature: Rereading Jeremiah 7–20* (Macon, Ga.: Mercer Univ. Press, 1996); A. R. P. Diamond and Kathleen M. O'Connor, "Unfaithful Passions: Coding Women Coding Men in Jeremiah 2–3 (4:2)," *BI* 4 (1996) 288–310; Rüdiger Liwak, *Der Prophet und die Geschichte: Eine literar-historische Untersuchung zum Jeremiabuch* (BWANT 121; Stuttgart: Kohlhammer,

Israel and Judah. Mark Biddle locates a "polyphony" of voices in Jeremiah 7–20, created by the juxtaposition of speakers that include Yhwh, the prophet, personified Jerusalem, and the people. Rather than progressing in linear argument, the book resembles a musical composition in which voices speak, fade, reappear, overlap, and grow quiet. Although Biddle does not study metaphorical groupings of material, poetic cycles in chapters 2–9 gain further unity from the presence of organizing metaphors and images.

Three poetic cycles or metaphorical groupings follow the introductory call narrative (Jeremiah 1): the broken marriage, or more accurately, the broken family metaphor (2:1–4:2), the mythic battle (4:3–6:30; 7:1–8:3), and the weeping (8:18–9:22). After 4:2, the marriage/family metaphor recedes but does not disappear. It remains in the background as divine discourse on the mythic battle moves to the foreground (4:6–6:30).[4] In chapters 8–10, both marriage and mythic battle are decentered and language of weeping becomes prominent (8:18–9:23). This essay studies divine characterization in the poetic cycles of Jeremiah 2–9, giving particular attention to the weeping God in 8:18–9:2. Divine depiction varies greatly among these poetic cycles.

Timothy Beal shows the instability of the divine character in Micah 1 in part by intertextual readings with other passages.[5] That Yhwh is not unified, not one, but a destabilized character is evident within the poetic cycles of the book of Jeremiah itself. Three characterizations of the deity emerge from this study that are difficult to ascribe to the same speaking subject. In Jer 2:1–4:2, Yahweh is the divine husband, angry, jealous, petty, and abusive. In 4:5–6:30, Yahweh is the military general, the fiendish but troubled initiator of the mythic battle and destroyer of creation. In 8:22–9:3, Yahweh is a weeping God who grieves unceasingly over the destruction of the people. In all three depictions, Yahweh's behavior responds to the poetic presence of the female persona as symbolic representation of the unfaithful people.

Divine Husband (2:1–4:2)

As divine husband, Yhwh appears as a brokenhearted and abandoned spouse, dumbstruck and enraged by the collapse of a relationship in which

---

1987); Louis Stulman, "Insiders and Outsiders in the Book of Jeremiah: Shifts in Symbolic Arrangement," *JSOT* 66 (1995) 65–85.

4. The prose temple sermon serves as a parenthetical comment on the battle, in which insiders rather than the foe from the north threaten Jerusalem's destruction. See Stulman, "Insiders and Outsiders."

5. Timothy K. Beal, "The System and the Speaking Subject in the Hebrew Bible," *BI* 2 (1994) 171–89.

he thinks he has done everything possible to make the marriage flourish.[6] In that material he rails at his unfaithful wife with a rhetoric of shaming in accusatory, blaming terms, and he finally casts her aside once and for all.

Jeremiah 2:1–4:2 combines previously separate materials to create a metaphorical and narrative drama of the broken family told almost entirely as a divine monologue. YHWH's speech alternates in addressing male Israel (2:4–16; 2:26–32; 3:14–18) and female Judah/Zion (2:17–25; 2:33–3:5; 3:12–13). This alternation of addressee between the male and female personae contributes to the identification of the two literary representations as one entity, and in 2:1–3 and 3:19–20 YHWH explicitly equates the two as one people. YHWH accuses male Israel and female Judah/Zion of similar offenses. Both turn away from him to other lovers or deities. YHWH uses the same rhetorical devices of direct address, rhetorical questions, and quotation of their speech to interrogate and accuse each of them. These poetic devices further identify the male and female personae with one another.

One function of the female persona is to present her infidelity in the most shameful, sexual, intimate terms possible in a nearly unthinkable betrayal of her spouse. A second function of the female is to symbolize or encode the whole nation. The metaphor uses a female to shame male Israel.

Across this material, YHWH portrays himself as a fully sympathetic figure, wronged by treacherous adulterers who have forsaken him and "loved strangers" (2:25). Divine discourse is a one-sided harangue and dominates not only the poetry itself but also the speech of the others whom YHWH quotes simply to accuse them with their own words. YHWH focuses on his own pain and betrayal (2:4–16) and on his astonishment that he could be treated so badly by someone for whom he had done so much (2:4–8, 21, 31–32). The husband's pride is hurt, and the husband is publicly shamed (3:1). In 3:1–5 he divorces her, and their relationship is over.

For ancient readers this husband would be a figure of sympathy. He has been doubly unfortunate in his choice of wives, for in 3:6–10 YHWH reveals that he had a previous wife who also betrayed him. Modern readers, by contrast, might get suspicious of this husband and his dominating ways, and wonder if there are other stories hidden in this metaphor, if the wives could speak.[7] But they do not.

Because the first wife appears in retrospect to have been less faithless

---

6. Arguments by Diamond and O'Connor, "Unfaithful Passions," form the basis for study of the divine husband.

7. For feminist critiques of the metaphor see Diamond and O'Connor, "Unfaithful Passions"; Renita J. Weems, *Battered Love: Marriage, Sex, and Violence in the Hebrew Prophets* (OBT; Minneapolis: Fortress Press, 1995); and Tikva Frymer-Kensky, *In the Wake of the Goddesses: Women, Culture and the Biblical Transformation of Pagan Myth* (New York: Fawcett Columbine, 1992).

than the second, YHWH sends Jeremiah to win her back. But she does not reply to the invitation (3:12–13). Only the children of this broken family, to whom the husband/father makes glowing promises and from whom he does not demands repentance (3:14–18), only they do repent and return to him (3:21–25). The children signify and encode the implied readers in exile who are invited to return and who are provided here with a model of liturgical repentance.

The broken family metaphor describes symbolically the history of YHWH's relationship with Israel and Judah. The narrative thread of the marriages, divorces, invitations to return, and the acceptance, not by the wives but by the children, constructs a version of the nation's past, present, and hoped-for future. It explains the nation's fall as deserved punishment for idolatry; it appeals to the exiles to repent in the present, and it gives hope for a restored future.

The highly emotional language of the divine husband, his nostalgia, anger, and jealousy, all create a character in search of exoneration from blame, one who cannot be charged with injustice or capriciousness, for clearly his wives deserve what they get. In the ancient world, such a character would gain the empathy of readers, presumed to be male, by bringing them to the side of the betrayed husband. But the metaphor tricks them, for they discover that they are the wanton, treacherous female, doubly shamed by being identified as a woman and as a whore.

Architect of War

In 4:5–6:30 (and less abundantly 8:4–10:27) a military metaphor replaces the domestic one, and a rhetoric of terror overtakes the rhetoric of shaming. Leo Perdue has recognized the cohesiveness of these poems in their blending of creation traditions with the mythic battle of the foe from the north.[8] Perdue places all the poetry in 4:5–6:30 under the rubric of mythic battle and includes much of the poetry in 8:4–10:27 as well. Interest in historical origins of individual poems and the generic grouping of the poetry in chapters 2–25 as "accusations against Judah and Jerusalem" has in the past obscured the predominance of battle language.[9]

Symbolically, the mythic battle constructs a *post facto* reflection on the nation's collapse as a military, political, and theological upheaval that destroyed a world. The highly dramatic poetry in which the mythic foe from

---

8. Leo G. Perdue, *The Collapse of History: Reconstructing Old Testament Theology* (OBT; Minneapolis: Fortress Press, 1994) 141–46.
9. Robert P. Carroll, *Jeremiah* (OTL; Philadelphia: Westminster, 1986), is a notable exception.

the north attacks daughter Zion brings readers into a time and space out-side history that interprets history. The battle's poetic enactment discloses divine ordination of Jerusalem's destruction, its inevitability and totality, and the rightness of the divine decision to destroy. Yahweh remains the principal, although not sole, speaker,[10] and a female, identified here as daughter Zion, appears as the object of attack.

The literary unity of this poetic cycle is neither narrative nor sequential, in contrast to the episodic drama of the broken family (2:1–4:2). Rather the military poetry repeatedly announces the battle's approach (4:5–22; 5:14–17; 6:1–12, 16–26; 8:14–17; 9:17–26 [MT 16–25]), describes its sta-tus as cosmic event (4:23–28), and provides reasons why YHWH cannot avoid executing the divine plan of attack and destruction (5:1–13, 20–31; 6:13–16, 27–30; 8:4–13; 9:4–9 [MT 3–8]). Poems of battle create the con-stant and noisy backdrop against which YHWH ruminates about sending the foe from the north and expresses his efforts to avoid the disaster. The impressionistic depiction of war across these chapters evokes the chaos of battle and creates high drama by the inequity between attackers and at-tacked. The poetry discloses a divine character who threatens, oversees, and engineers war in fearsome ways, even as he is at war within the divine self about doing it.

The battle poems use metonymy to create by details of sight and sound the feelings of terror at the approach of the army about to attack and de-stroy Jerusalem. Trumpet and standard (4:5–6, 19, 21; 6:1, 17) signify the mustering of troops and their preparation for attack. Sounds of horseman and archer (4:29), voices of enemies planing the siege (6:4), noise of an approaching cavalry "like the roaring of the sea" (6:23), the snorting and neighing of horses (8:16)—all conjure up warfare, make it vividly present in the imagination, and create terror by the invocation of its nearness.

The initiator, designer, and director of battle is YHWH himself. In this rhetoric of fear, divine agency is paramount: "for I am bringing evil from the north and a great destruction" (4:6). The evil from the north is a lion, a destroyer of nations who has set out purposefully "to make your land a waste" (4:7). The coming of the enemy is due to the "fierce anger of YHWH" (4:8). "I am going to bring disaster on this people" (5:19a).

The mythic power of the enemy, either the foe from the north or YHWH himself, is clear from his supraterrestrial approach. "He comes like clouds, with chariots like the whirlwind, his horses swifter than eagles" (4:13). The enemy's might is not human, but incomparable and terrifying. It is a "great

---

10. The people (5:8, 19), Jeremiah (4:10, 19, 23–26a; 5:4–5, 10–11; 6:26), the enemies (6:4–5), and female Jerusalem/Zion speak (4:20b, 31).

nation" with bow and javelin, cruel and without mercy; their "sound is like the roaring of the sea"; they come on horse, "equipped as a warrior for battle" (6:22–23).

Not until 20:4–6 is the foe from the north historicized and Jerusalem's attacker revealed to be Babylon. Although critics have sought to find an historical enemy behind the foe, Childs and Perdue are surely correct in seeing its mythic nature.[11] To do so is to see the poetry's power. The foe is superhuman, sent by God, and described in hyperbolic, transcendent terms. They are "an enduring nation," "from far away," "their quiver is like an open tomb," all of them are mighty warriors who will eat, eat, eat, the population, the animals, and the fruit of the land itself (5:15–17). This is the language of terror.

In contrast to the monstrous power of the foe from the north is the weakness and vulnerability of the one attacked. The object of invasion is daughter Zion (4:14–20, 29–31; 5:7–11; 6:2–23; 10:19–24). In the book of Jeremiah, gendered language constructs not only the broken family metaphor but also the mythic battle, for it is against a woman that Yahweh amasses the invading army. Jerusalem's personification as female is a conventional gender designation of cities in antiquity, but within the symbolic world of the mythic battle, daughter Zion's gender heightens the unequal possession of power and resources among the opponents.[12] The one is demonic, possessed of might, weaponry, and an army that surpasses human experience and requires supraterrestrial language to be described; it is opposed not only to the merely human but to a female whom ancients agreed needed protection. She is defenseless as the foe approaches. She laments the destruction of her tents (4:19–20; 10:19–20), panics before the attack (4:19), and faints before killers (5:31).

Daughter Zion's portrayal in the battle cycle is consistent with the characterization of Yahweh's wife Judah/Jerusalem in 2:1–4:2, although there she is unnamed and untitled. Daughter Zion is rebellious (4:17) and faithless (5:10–11). She behaves like a whore (4:30), and her inhabitants do not "know" Yʜᴡʜ (4:22). To avert disaster, she is to wash herself clean, but the besiegers are already at hand (4:14–17). Yahweh turns to her directly and accuses her of bringing doom upon herself (4:18). In the battle cycle, however, language of broken intimacy is conspicuously absent. Yʜᴡʜ

11. Brevard S. Childs, "The Enemy from the North and the Chaos Tradition," *JBL* 78 (1959) 187–98; Perdue, *Collapse of History*.

12. D. Bourguet, *Des métaphores de Jérémie* (Ebib 9; Paris: Gabalda, 1987) 117. See F. W. Dobbs-Allsopp, *Weep, O Daughter of Zion: A Study of the City-Lament Genre in the Hebrew Bible* (BibOr 44; Rome: Pontifical Biblical Institute, 1993); Julie Galambusch, *Jerusalem in the Book of Ezekiel: The City as Yahweh's Wife* (SBLDS 130; Atlanta: Scholars Press, 1992).

speaks to her with disgust (6:8) and only briefly recalls her past loveliness (6:2). Daughter Zion's personification as female, whatever its ancient roots, here underscores the extreme inequity between the city and the mythic forces unleashed against her by YHWH. What drives the divine warrior is not an attack to suppress a bellicose bully or an arrogant aggressor but the desire to avenge himself and to punish an impotent weakling.

But YHWH wavers in his resolve. He hesitates and questions. To avoid invasion, he sends Jeremiah to play Diogenes or Abraham, to run up and down the streets of Jerusalem in search of one righteous inhabitant so that he may pardon Jerusalem (5:1–6). But no righteous ones can be found, since they all behave as YHWH's wife who "broke the yoke" and "burst the bonds" (5:6; cf. 2:20). Using second-person singular forms, YHWH then plaintively asks daughter Zion, "How can I pardon you?... Shall I not punish them for these things?" (5:7–9, 29). It is as if the divine warrior has weighed the options and decided that he cannot pardon, forgive, or turn back the advancing foe. It is not within his character to ignore her crimes.

The onslaught of the mythic army will cause cosmic upheaval and the "uncreation" of the earth (4:23–28). At first glance, the poem of uncreation appears to change the subject from the mythic battle. The poem depicts, instead, the cosmic effects of the war as a total, world-destroying onslaught that will leave a bombed-out place of chaos.

The poem contains two voices, Jeremiah's in 4:23–26 and YHWH's in vv. 27–28. Jeremiah witnesses the reversal of creation, step by step, in a cosmic upheaval. The land returns to *tōhû wābōhû* ("waste and void"). Light is extinguished in the heavens, mountains and hills quake, and the earth is emptied of all its inhabitants. The land returns to desert and cities lie in ruins before YHWH's fierce anger (4:23–26). Massive and total annihilation, the grieving of the earth, and the darkening of the heavens occur because of the divine word, purpose, and unrelenting resolution. The mythic battle destroys the cosmos as Judah knew it. And the one who designs, executes, and presides over this demolition is the Creator himself.

In the cycle of the mythic battle poems, YHWH is the military general who prefers not to go to war, who seeks other courses of action, but is ultimately driven to it. He has the resolve, the power, and the furious rage that enable him to complete his purpose. He is the Creator who disassembles creation. At his disposal is an army of unsurpassed power and cruelty whom he calls for and sends against the woman, daughter Zion. The divine character disclosed here is not inconsistent with the divine husband in 2:1–4:2, but the tenderness and brokenheartedness of the family drama is completely absent. Instead, this deity is a killer—a hesitant one, but a killer nonetheless. He determines that Zion's character is irredeemably flawed so destruction must follow. The warrior's rage and resolution emotionally separates him from daughter Zion, and she is doomed.

The poetry of the mythic battle is not randomly placed in the book, nor is the characterization of the divine as warrior arbitrary. The battle poems could not appear before the divine husband casts off his recalcitrant wife. If the book began with the mythic battle cycle, YHWH's summoning of the foe from the north and his decision to destroy the nation would characterize him as a capricious destroyer, a cold, distant, killer and uncreator. The book would comprise an attack on YHWH, a protest against his cruelty, rather than a theodicy that seeks to win readers to YHWH's side and defend him as a wronged lover and husband from charges of capriciousness in the national tragedy.

The Weeping God (8:18–9:22 [MT 21])

In sharp discontinuity with the God who executes war and the God who casts off his unfaithful spouse is the God who weeps (8:18–9:22 [MT 21]). In this cluster of poems about weeping, YHWH weeps (8:18–9:1 [MT 2]) and orchestrates the weeping of others (9:10–11, 17–22 [MT 9–10, 16–21]). These poems function as dramatic response to the ineluctable coming of the mythic battle (8:15–16). Since death has come up to the windows (9:21 [MT 20]), since the enemy cannot be turned back, there is nothing to do now but mourn, shed tears, and grieve the nation's death publicly and privately.

That divine laments are prominent in the book has long been recognized, but interpreters have usually assigned the tears in 8:18–9:3 (MT 2) to Jeremiah.[13] Indeed, speakers, demarcation of units, and meaning of these verses find no consensus among interpreters.

8:18–9:3 (MT 2)

8:18	My cheerfulness is gone, grief is upon me, my heart is sick.
8:19	Listen [*hinnēh*], the cry of the daughter of my people from far and wide in the land: Is YHWH not in Zion? Is her king not in her? Why have they provoked me to anger with images and with their foreign idols?
8:20	"The harvest has past, the summer is ended, and we are not saved."

---

13. Both J. J. M. Roberts ("The Motif of the Weeping God in Jeremiah and Its Background in the Lament Tradition of the Ancient Near East," *Old Testament Essays* 5 [1992] 361–74) and Biddle (*Polyphony*, 30) have made similar claims.

8:21   For the crushing of the daughter of my people I am
       crushed, and I grow leaden in spirit,
        and dismay has seized me.

8:22   Is there no balm in Gilead?
       Is there no physician there?
       Why then has the health of the daughter of my people
        not been restored?

9:1 (MT 8:23) O that my head were waters and my eyes a fountain
       of tears,
       that I might weep day and night for the slain of the
        daughter of my people.

9:2 (MT 1) O that I had in the wilderness a traveler's lodging place
       that I might leave my people and go away from them!
       For they are all adulterers, a band of traitors.

9:3 (MT 2) They bend their tongues like bows:
       they have grown strong in the land for falsehood and not
        for truth;
       for they proceed from evil to evil and do not know me,
        says YHWH.

Particularly disputed is the principal speaker in 8:18–9:3 (MT 2). Who is
the "I," and who grieves over "the daughter of my people" (8:19, 21, 22;
9:1 [MT 8:23])? A sampling of commentators reveals vast disagreement.
Carroll assigns these verses to personified Jerusalem, whereas Condamin
attributes them to the people, and Craigie, et al., and Clements make
Jeremiah the speaker.[14] Holladay finds three voices in the poem and limits divine speech to v. 19b and v. 22a.[15] Even Fretheim, who has written
beautifully about the suffering of God, assigns these lines to Jeremiah as
the embodiment of divine pain.[16]

By contrast, Brueggemann's observation that divine pathos structures
the poem gains specificity from a number of speech markers that indicate
that YHWH is the poem's principal speaker.[17] At the end of the poem the
speech formula, *ně'um* YHWH ("says YHWH," 9:3 [MT 2]), ascribes preceding verses to Yahweh. The only possible speaker of the rhetorical question,

14. Carroll, *Jeremiah*, 255; A. Condamin, *Le Livre de Jérémie* (Ebib; Paris: Gabalda, 1920)
84; Peter Craigie, Page Kelley, and J. F. Drinkard, *Jeremiah 1–25* (WBC 26; Dallas: Word,
1991) 136; Ronald E. Clements, *Jeremiah* (Interpretation; Atlanta: John Knox, 1988) 59.

15. William L. Holladay, *Jeremiah* (2 vols.; Hermeneia; Philadelphia: Fortress Press, 1986–
89) 1:288–89.

16. Terence E. Fretheim, *The Suffering of God: An Old Testament Perspective* (OBT; Philadelphia: Fortress Press, 1987) 135, though later (161) he proposes that vv. 18–19 might be
divine speech.

17. Walter Brueggemann, *To Pluck Up, to Tear Down: A Commentary on the Book of
Jeremiah 1–25* (International Theological Commentary; Grand Rapids: Eerdmans, 1988) 88.

"Why have they provoked me to anger...with their images and foreign idols?" (8:19d), is Yhwh. Yhwh frequently uses the rhetorical device of direct quotation of the accused in 2:1–4:2, as may be the case in 8:19bc and possibly 8:20.[18] Typically, Yhwh is the speaker of the phrase "my people," which appears in 8:18, 19, 21, 22; 9:1, 2 (MT 8:23; 9:1) (cf. 2:11, 13, 32; 6:14, 30; 8:7, 11; 9:7; 15:7; 18:15; 23:22; but less clearly 6:26; 14:17). Biddle adds to this list of divine speech markers the observation that 9:1 (MT 8:23) resembles Yhwh's statement in 14:17–18.[19] In addition, extrabiblical evidence indicates that a weeping deity is not an anomaly in the ancient world. J. J. M. Roberts provides a long list of weeping gods and goddesses in Mesopotamia who shed tears over the destruction of their cities as does Yhwh over the "crushing of the daughter of my people [Zion]" (8:21).[20] With the clear exception of 8:20 and 8:19bc,[21] (indented above in the translation) Yhwh is the poem's principal speaker. Yhwh is the one who weeps.

The poem is a monologue of divine grief, interrupted by speech of "the daughter of my people" or her inhabitants. She is personified Jerusalem—that is, daughter Zion—in the poems of the mythic battle, and Yhwh's divorced wife in 2:1–3:5. The literary structure of the poem is not rigidly symmetrical, but it does contain repeated patterns. There are two first-person statements of divine grief (8:18, 21), two sets of three rhetorical questions[22] (8:19b–d, 22), a first-person plural statement of terror and despair, two syntactically parallel divine wishes (9:1, 2 [MT 8:23; 9:1])—all culminating in the reason for Yhwh's behavior in this poem (9:2b–3 [MT 1b–2]).

In Yhwh's opening expressive burst of pain, first-person verbs spiral downward in the direction of despair.[23] His cheerfulness disappears, grief descends upon him, and sickness invades the heart of God (8:18). With urgency (hinnēh), Yhwh announces the sound of a female voice, literally, "the sound of a cry for help [qôl šaw'at] of the daughter of my people" (8:19a). The two questions that follow may contain the content of the daughter's cry, expressed either in her own voice or as Yhwh's quotation of her speech. "Is Yhwh not in Zion? Is her king not in her?" (8:19b–c). The

---

18. See Diamond and O'Connor, "Unfaithful Passions."

19. Biddle, Polyphony, 30.

20. Roberts, "Motif of the Weeping God."

21. In 8:20 a first-person plural pronoun wa'ănaḥnû and the verb nôšā'nû indicate a corporate voice, and in 8:19b–c Yhwh is referred to in the third person.

22. See Walter Brueggemann, "Jeremiah's Use of Rhetorical Questions," JBL 92 (1973) 358–74.

23. See Holladay, Jeremiah, 1:287–88; and McKane, Jeremiah, 194, on translation problems.

import of the daughter's questions is not clear. The questions may express her arrogant confidence[24] that YHWH is in Zion and she must therefore be safe. But YHWH heard a cry for help, not of confidence. Viewed this way, her cry probes divine abandonment of the city. YHWH is not in Zion but has departed, and she is in mortal peril.

The third question is YHWH's, and it poses a countercharge to the daughter's questions. "Why have they provoked me to anger with... their idols?" (8:19d). He has not abandoned the inhabitants of Zion; they have abandoned him for other loyalties and provoked his righteous anger just like his wife Judah/Jerusalem (2:1–4:2) and daughter Zion (4:5–6:30). The city's inhabitants respond to YHWH's question in seeming desperation. Time is up, and "we are not saved" (8:20). Something awful is happening, presumably the invasion, and YHWH does not act.

Using language reminiscent of clinical depression, YHWH trades anger for sinking despair in the poem's second statement of grief. "For the crushing of the daughter of my people, I am crushed, I grow leaden in spirit, horror has seized me" (8:21). First-person verbs identify YHWH with daughter Zion. As she is broken (*šeber*), he is broken (*hošbārtî*). His spirit grows leaden (*qādartî*), horror seizes him (*heḥĕziqātnî*). His life dims; he is wounded by her wounds and seized by feelings that overwhelm him. In a remarkable poetic turn, the distance between YHWH and the daughter has dissolved. YHWH participates in and is emotionally intertwined with the miseries that afflict her.

With three further rhetorical questions, constructed like the previous three (8:19b–d, *'ên... 'ên... maddûa'*), YHWH declares his amazement that her crushing, her woundedness, goes untended. "Is there no balm in Gilead? Is there no healer there? Why is the daughter of my people not healed?" (8:22). Yahweh inquires sympathetically about her health and wholeness. His questions reveal inner helplessness, desperation, and sorrow. That YHWH is the inflicter of wounds, the warrior who orders and designs the attack on her (8:16–17), and the husband who casts her off does not appear within the world of this poem. Instead YHWH weeps with her.

Divine sorrow leads to two wishes (9:1, 2 [MT 8:23; 9:1]). YHWH is so immersed in daughter Zion's pain, the boundaries between them have become so permeable, that his first wish is to weep forever. With glorious hyperbole he wants to becomes tears on her account. "O that my head were waters and my eyes a fountain of tears, that I might weep day and night for the slain of the daughter of my people" (9:1 [MT 8:23]). The weeping God,

---

24. Holladay, *Jeremiah*, 1:293.

with a head turned to waters, eyes become a fountain, desires to go on a crying jag for days and nights over daughter Zion and her dead. So much sorrow overtakes God that an endless river of tears is required to express it.

YHWH's second wish (9:2 [MT 1]) is syntactically parallel to the first.[25] Both wishes begin with the idiomatic expression *mî-yittĕnēnî* (literally "who will give me," I translate as "O that"). What YHWH yearns for now is escape. He wants to run from the sorrow and to abandon the cause of tears. "O that I had in the wilderness a traveler's lodging place that I might abandon my people and go away from them" (9:2 [MT 1]). The deeply troubled deity wants to return to the wilderness where his relationship with his bride flourished (2:1–3). Two verbs emphasize the leaving: *'āzab* is a verb of separation, of forsaking, and of abandoning; *hālak* is a verb of action, of motion, of walking out. YHWH's two wishes express profound inner disturbance.

The poem's conclusion provides the reasons for the tears of God and God's desire to escape to the wilderness (9:2b–3). In terms that summarize the sins of the faithless wife (2:1–4:2), YHWH declares them all adulterers, traitors, liars, and evildoers who "do not know me" (9:3 [MT 2]).

Within the imaginative confines of this poem, betrayal does not lead to violence, warfare, or vengeance. It brings out, instead, divine empathy, vulnerability, and profound sorrow. Grief overtakes anger, sympathy replaces fury. In Brueggemann's language in another context, the tears of God portray a divine character who "enters hurt." In 9:10–11 (MT 11–12) and 16–22 (MT 17–23) YHWH invites the earth and the whole people to weep with him.

The rhetorical function of the weeping poems at this juncture of the book is to mark the tragedy, to lament it, and to dwell on the loss of a world that once existed in Jerusalem and Judah, but that is no more. But as divine characterization, the tears of God convey something more.

A Semiotics of Divine Tears

The resistance of biblical scholarship to poetic characterization of God as a weeping deity may be because such a deity appears too vulnerable, powerless, and embodied—or perhaps insufficiently macho—to accord with the jealous husband and angry warrior from the book's earlier poetry. Recognition of the divine identity of the weeping in Jer 8:18–9:3 (MT 2) is, however, theologically crucial. To recognize that YHWH speaks and weeps

---

25. Arguing against J. A. Thompson, *The Book of Jeremiah* (NICOT; Grand Rapids: Eerdmans, 1980).

in this poem is to see a temporary but massive turning in the book.[26] God's tears recall the brokenhearted husband, but rather than keeping Yʜwʜ at a distance as does the drama of the divorce of his wife (2:1–3:25), these poems unite Yʜwʜ with the personified Zion (8:18–9:1 [MT 2]) and the people in their weeping (9:16–21 [MT 17–22]). God's tears mean that there may be a balm in Gilead; healing may be possible because God draws near, abandons fury, leaves aside honor, and joins in the people's suffering.

Tears heal because they bring people together in suffering, and reveal them to one another in their vulnerability. In the words of C. S. Song, tears "stir all living souls."[27] In Song's parable of political theology on the building of the great wall of China, only the tears of Lady Ming have strength enough to cause the wall's collapse and to reveal the bones of the oppressed who built it. Tears are a political language that opposes the language of power. In Jeremiah, God's tears are more powerful even than the armies under divine command because, for a poetic moment at least, God, people, and cosmos articulate a common suffering and God changes sides.

Professor Brueggemann has written profoundly on the imagery and rhetoric of pain in the Old Testament in general and in Jeremiah in particular. He notes that Jeremiah "brings the tradition of lament to intense personal speech."[28] But the theme of weeping, the river of tears that runs through the book, though related to lamentation, stands outside the tradition of protest inherent in lament. Punishment, rage, and resistance are missing from it. When the mourning women, Jeremiah, the earth, and forlorn Rachel weep, their weeping signifies the imminence and inevitability of the destruction and the recognition of profound, irrevocable loss. But the poetry of divine weeping connotes something more. The tears of God are part of the imaginative literary enterprise that ruptures theological language. The book's lead character breaks from his role as dominating prideful male, cruel architect of war, and for a brief poetic interlude embodies and participates in the pain of the people.

The tears of God offer an alternative interpretation of the suffering of the exiles. Divine tears put aside punishment, eschew questions of causality, and characterize God in radically different terms from much of the rest of the book. This is a God who is fluid, unstable, changing, and active, and whose external relations to the humans parallel the same dynamics.[29]

---

26. I am grateful to Columbia Theological Seminary graduate Mark Gray for several ideas expressed here.

27. C. S. Song, *The Tears of Lady Meng: A Parable of the People's Political Theology* (Risk 11; Geneva: World Council of Churches, 1981) 38–45.

28. Walter Brueggemann, "A Shape for Old Testament Theology, II: Embrace of Pain," *CBQ* 47 (1985) 404.

29. Serene Jones, "This God Which Is Not One: Irigaray and Barth on the Divine,"

Language of divine tears offsets language of the divine punisher and wrath-ful judge, for it posits God's vulnerability to the conditions of the other. It provides a glimpse of another kind of deity: an unpredictable, unknown, and uncontainable being with a fluid inner life who expresses it in biologi-cal, material tears. Tears are the mighty act of a God who, in this poem, is deeply relational, infinitely active, and "radically multiple."[30] Divine tears suggest a deity who vacates sovereignty and hierarchical transcendence, at least temporarily, and relates in vulnerability to the other, "the daughter of my people." The incommensurable other is not so by excessive, tran-scendent might but by a woundedness, a sorrow, a lack. The God of tears interrupts theological discourse and offers a glimpse of relationship without violence. Without such disjunction in the divine character, healing would not be possible.

---

in *Transfigurations: Theology and the French Feminists* (ed. C. W. Maggie Kim, et al.; Minneapolis: Fortress Press, 1993) 109–41.

30. Ibid., 132.

– 13 –

Alas for the Day!

The "Day of the LORD" in the Book of the Twelve

Rolf Rendtorff

I

One of the most fascinating practices of "canonical" reading of biblical texts is to follow the advice of biblical authors or editors in reading those texts as a unity that are obviously composed of parts and elements of quite different and even divergent character. Years ago Bible scholars started this kind of reading with the Pentateuch, later continued with the book of Isaiah, the Psalter, and now also the Book of the Twelve.[1] The first time the Twelve Prophets are mentioned at all they are quoted as *one* book. It was Ben Sira who praised them as those who "comforted" or "healed" Jacob and "helped" or even "saved" him by a "faith full of hope"(Sir 49:10).[2] About whom is Ben Sira speaking? About Amos? But did he not preach judgment and doom? Even Hosea, Micah, and others, did they not preach much more about disaster and divine punishment than about hope and salvation?

From Ben Sira's quotation we learn that according to his view the comforting tone was the dominating element in this collection of prophetical sayings and writings. But is it possible to read everything in these writings from one particular point of view? This brings us to a central point of reading those complex "books" like the Twelve.[3] How shall we handle the

---

1. These developments can easily be traced in the programs and unit formations of the Society of Biblical Studies during the years. For the Psalter see also W. Brueggemann, "Bounded by Obedience and Praise: The Psalms as Canon," *JSOT* 50 (1991) 63–92. For the Book of the Twelve, see also my article: "How to Read the Book of the Twelve as a Theological Unity," in *SBL Seminar Papers*(Atlanta: Scholars Press, 1997).

2. LXX reads "comforted," MT "healed," translated according to *Dictionary of Classical Hebrew,* vol. 3 (ed. David J. A. Clines; Sheffield: Sheffield Academic Press, 1996) 238.

3. In the following I will use the term *book* almost exclusively for the Book of the Twelve, while the individual collections of prophetical sayings will be named "collections" or "writings."

obviously different and even contradicting utterances in those collections? With regard to the Twelve we are still at the beginning and in a stage of experiments, so to speak.[4]

One of the important observations is the use of certain key words through different writings within the Book of the Twelve that give a certain structure to the composition as a whole or to parts of it. In this article I will concentrate on one specific topic that appears in a remarkable culmination in the Book of the Twelve: the "day of the Lord." I think that this will also fit in the framework of this volume honoring Walter Brueggemann, because the question whether and how God is "above the fray" or "in the fray" will always be present.[5]

II

Amos usually is deemed to be the first to use the term *yôm yhwh* (Amos 5:18, 20).[6] But the reader will realize that Amos does not use a hitherto unknown term; on the contrary, he is opposing an obviously common understanding of this particular day among his audience: "Why do you want the day of the Lord?" Amos's listeners know about this day, and they desire it to come. But what about the reader? Does he or she know as well? Yes, of course, from the previous use of this term in the writing of Joel. Therefore, in order to understand Amos we have to read Joel first.

One could call the Joel collection the "book of the day of the Lord." But what does this expression mean in the context of this book? And how could that be related to Amos? Obviously for Joel and his audience the day of the Lord is a terrible experience. It refers to a disastrous plague of locusts that destroys the bare necessaries of life. There are great lamentations

---

4. The most recent attempts to read the Twelve as one book still show very divergent methodological approaches. I mention a few of them: P. R. House, *The Unity of the Book of the Twelve* (Bible and Literature Series 27; Sheffield: Almond, 1990); T. Collins, *The Mantle of Elijah: The Redaction Criticism of the Prophetical Books* (Biblical Seminar 20; Sheffield: JSOT Press, 1993) chap. 3; R. C. Van Leeuwen, "Scribal Wisdom and Theodicy in the Book of the Twelve," in *In Search of Wisdom: Essays in Memory of John G. Gammie* (ed. L. G. Perdue; Louisville: Westminster/John Knox, 1993) 31–49; J. D. Nogalski, *Literary Precursors to the Book of the Twelve* (BZAW 217; Berlin: de Gruyter, 1993); idem, *Redactional Processes in the Book of the Twelve* (BZAW 218; Berlin: de Gruyter, 1993); R. J. Coggins, "The Minor Prophets—One Book or Twelve?" in *Crossing the Boundaries: Essays in Biblical Interpretation in Honour of Michael D. Goulder* (Biblical Interpretation Series 8; ed. S. E. Porter; Leiden: Brill, 1994) 57–68; A. Schart, "Die Entstehung des Zwölfprophetenbuchs: Neubearbeitungen von Amos im Rahmen schriftenübergreifender Redaktionsprozesse" (Habilitationsschrift, Philipps-Universität Marburg, 1995).

5. I will take up certain observations from the literature quoted without mentioning it in detail.

6. For general information on the topic of the Day of the Lord see *ABD* (Garden City, N.Y.: Doubleday, 1992) 2:79–85. To the literature I want to add H. P. Müller, *Ursprünge und Strukturen alttestamentlicher Eschatologie* (BZAW 109; Berlin: de Gruyter, 1969) 69–85.

throughout the whole country, and finally the assembly is summoned for a holy fast (Joel 1:2–14). At this point the outcry is heard: "Alas for the day!" (v. 15). What a day! Then the day is called by its name: "the day of the LORD." But was it already the day of the LORD that had happened? "The day of the LORD is near." Does it mean that this day is still near to come? "It shall come like havoc from Shaddai" (*yābô'*)—it shall come as an even more terrible destruction. The destruction is called a *šōd*, and it will come from *šadday*. This is a shocking wordplay: The destruction will come from the Almighty. But notwithstanding the shocking wording, this is an exact definition of the day of the LORD: a mighty, even terrible event, including destructive elements, coming from the divine sphere. For those who experience its coming near, the question is what to do. Will there be any chance to survive? This includes the questions of whether this event is directed toward a certain country or group of humans and whether those who experience its coming will have a chance to escape.

At this point we have to turn briefly to Isaiah 13. There exactly the same wording appears: "The day of the LORD is near; it shall come like havoc from Shaddai" (v. 6). But this time the situation is completely different. This chapter is a great oracle against Babylon, and it is quite clear that the LORD Sebaoth (v. 4) himself is going to fight against Babylon in order to destroy it (v. 19). The day of the LORD is characterized as "cruel, with wrath and fierce anger" (v. 9). So it shows a quite different face from that described in Joel 1, which says nothing about wrath and anger. In particular, it is not Israel that is attacked, but Israel's archenemy, Babylon.

But back to Joel: even here the situation changes. The horn is blown, the alarm is sounded (Joel 2:1). The locusts seem to have changed into something that looks like an army of human warriors, riding horses and chariots, using weapons and climbing walls (vv. 4–9). And behold, the LORD himself "roars aloud at the head of his army" (v. 11). At this moment it becomes clear again: This is the day of the LORD; it is great—and most terrible! This time, almost as in Isaiah 13, the day of the LORD shows a face of war, and the LORD himself is at the head of the army. The prophet cries: "Who can endure it?"

The answer comes from God himself: "Yet even now, turn back to me [*šubû 'āday*] with all your hearts" (v. 12). Here the basic difference between the situation in Joel and in Isaiah 13 becomes evident. For Israel, the day of the LORD is not an inescapable fate. They have the chance to turn, to repent—even now! God himself calls them to do so, and the prophet adds the basic reason why there will be a chance, quoting one of the most fundamental confessions of God's grace and mercy, one that Moses was the first to hear through God's own voice: "For he is gracious and merciful, slow to anger and abounding in kindness" (Joel 2:13; cf. Exod 34:6). Even now when the day of the LORD is near there is a chance to turn and to endure the disaster.

The prophet knows that there is no guarantee that God himself will turn away (*yāšûb*) from his plans; there can only be a fearful hope: *mî yôdēaʿ* "Who knows?" If God really will, it would be an event of fundamental relevance, because God will have to do what according to his own words in other contexts he never would do: relent, change his mind (*niḥām*, Joel 2:14; cf. Num 23:19; 1 Sam 15:29). The prophet did include this aspect of God's hoped-for behavior already in the quotation from the Sinai tradition by adding the phrase *wĕniḥām ʿal-hārāʿāh*, "and renouncing punishment" (Joel 2:13), which is not found in Exodus 34.[7]

The reaction is prompt. The horn is blown again, this time not for war but to sanctify a fast (Joel 2:15). The people assemble and the priests pray: "Spare your people, O LORD!" (vv. 16–17). And God hears the prayer. Again he behaves like a human, getting jealous and having compassion upon his people (v. 18). He gives them back what they had lost, makes the country fruitful, and assures them of peace and joy (vv. 19–26). For the people, this is not only the end of the disaster but more than that: "You shall know that I am in the midst of Israel, and that I am the LORD, your God, and there is no other" (v. 27). This is an unusually extended version of the "recognition formula." The LORD, the only god, is in the midst of Israel, in his temple on Zion, from where the horn has been blown (2:1, 15).

One might think that now the threatening by the day of the LORD with its dangerous features will be over and Israel can live in quiet peace with God dwelling in their midst. But there will be a new phase of events. These "will happen after that" (*wĕhāyāh ʾaḥărê-kēn*, 2:28 [MT 3:1]). This is a very unusual expression. Many times it is said in narrative contexts that something *happened* (*wayĕhî*) "after that," just to express a normal progress in time and events (e.g., 2 Sam 2:1; 8:1; 10:1; 13:1). But that something *will happen* (*wĕhāyāh*) "after that" is said in the Hebrew Bible only here in Joel 2:28 (MT 3:1). So the question arises: After what?[8] The answer cannot come out of the immediate context, where the "children of Zion" (2:23 [MT 3:2]) are peacefully living with God in their midst. The events that are announced to come are going far beyond that. Again the day of the LORD will be coming, and again it will be "great and terrible" (2:31 [MT 3:4]). But certain things will happen "before" (*lipnê*) it comes.

---

7. For a more detailed explication see J. Jeremias, *Die Reue Gottes: Aspekte alttestamentlicher Gottesvorstellung* (Biblische Studien 65; Neukirchen-Vluyn: Neukirchener Verlag, 1975) 1975.

8. This text is quoted in Acts 2:17: *kai estai en tais eschatais hēmerais*.

Thus there will be a time "after that" (whatever that means) and at the same moment "before," namely, before the coming of the day of the LORD. It will be a time "in between," so to speak.

In this time the whole of humanity, "all flesh," will be included in God's actions. God will pour out his Spirit on them so that they will behave like prophets (*nibbě'û*) and will have dreams and see visions (Joel 2:28–29 [MT 3:1–2]). It will be like a fulfillment of Moses' desire "that all the LORD's people were prophets, and that the LORD would put his spirit on them" (Num 11:29, NRSV). But even more than that: Not only "the LORD's people" but "all flesh" will be the recipients of the divine Spirit, even the slaves, male and female. All boundaries will be torn down, national as well as social. This is what will happen "in between." But the life under the guidance of the divine Spirit will not last long before the coming of the day of the LORD will be foreboded by spectacular portents in the sky and on earth: blood and fire and pillars of smoke, the sun darkening and the moon turning into blood (2:30–31 [MT 3:3–4]). These will once more be signs of the day of the LORD similar to the earlier ones when the LORD himself came at the head of his army (2:10–11).

Again a question arises: Who will escape from the danger that is coming through the day of the LORD? In particular, what will happen to those who have received the Spirit that God has poured on them, making them like prophets? This is what will happen (*wěhāyāh*): "Everyone who calls on the name of the LORD shall escape" (2:32 [MT 3:5]). According to the context this can only mean that those from "all flesh" who have received the divine Spirit are called to invoke the name of the LORD and be saved. This will just be a small number of people, those who escaped (*pělêṭāh*), a remnant. These survivors will be those "whom the LORD calls." This expresses a very important interrelation between "to call on [*qārā'*] the name of the LORD" and the LORD's "calling" (*qārā'*) the survivors, the latter appearing as a kind of divine reaction to the invocation. All this will happen on Mount Zion and in Jerusalem. If I understand this passage correctly, it announces the existence of a very limited group of survivors after the day of the LORD: a group that will comprise not only Israelites but all those who, under the impact of the divine Spirit, will call on him in the days of need and whom he will call into the group of survivors.[9]

Yet this truly eschatological vision is not the last word in the collection of sayings under the name of Joel. Another chapter begins, this time with the much more common formula "In those days" (*bayyāmîm hāhēmmāh*),

---

9. Many commentators try to avoid such an interpretation. Even the NJPS says in a footnote to the last words of 3:5: "Meaning of Heb. uncertain." But why?

expanded by "in that time" (*bā'ēt hahî*; 3:1 [MT 4:1]). We are back in history, and the roles are clearly defined. On the one side there are the nations (*gôyim*) in a global sense, with some specifications in vv. 4–8 and 19; on the other side there is Israel (v. 2) or Judah (mostly mentioned together with Jerusalem, vv. 1, 6, 8, etc.), which is called "my people and my heritage" (*naḥălātî*) (v. 2). The day of the Lord will affect only the nations; but Israel is indirectly involved because the day of the Lord will come as a judgment upon the nations owing to their misdeeds against Israel. God's actions begin as a trial against the nations (v. 2), turning into a war (v. 9), which finally takes on the features of the day of the Lord (v. 14): darkening of sun, moon, and stars (v. 15), and the Lord roaring from Zion (v. 16).

But suddenly the representation of the events breaks off, turning into a message: "The Lord is a refuge for his people, a shelter for the children of Israel" (v. 16b). The immediately following recognition formula (v. 17) shows that this is the actual focal point of the whole chapter. God's final judgment of the nations will leave Israel, and in particular Jerusalem, untouched. More than that: Israel shall know that the Lord himself dwells on Zion (cf. v. 21), and that not only Zion—the mount on which the temple stands—but all of Jerusalem will be holy. It is the second time in Joel that this formula concludes a chapter (cf. 2:27); it gives the whole collection its stamp.

It is not a balanced doctrine of the day of the Lord that we find in the Joel writings. The day of the Lord can be disguised as a terrible attack of locusts; but when it becomes obvious that God himself is acting in these events it turns into a great cycle of liturgical lament, repentance, and finally divine forgiveness and restitution (Joel 1–2). Here the day of the Lord is a transaction between God and his people. But there is also the distinctively different idea of the day of the Lord as a divine judgment against Israel's enemies. Here Israel stands aside, accepting the final affirmation of Zion's and Jerusalem's holiness and safety (chap. 3 [MT 4]). In a third concept the day of the Lord is a much more "eschatological" event accompanied by thoroughgoing changes in human behavior and leaving only a remnant of believers on Mount Zion and in Jerusalem (2:28–32 [MT 3:1–5]). There is not a clear-cut sequence among these concepts in the Joel writings. Rather, these writings look at the day of the Lord from different angles. But one message is important: as far as Israel itself is concerned, the only way to survive is to repent and to call the name of the Lord.

III

Returning to Amos, what idea of the day of the Lord may his contemporaries have had? In Amos 5:18, one finds the only mention in the Hebrew

Bible that the people *desire* the day of the LORD. It is usually said that they fear it, tremble, and are seized with panic. Why do these people desire the coming of the day of the LORD? Of course, they must think that it will not be directed against Israel but against other people—namely, Israel's enemies. At the beginning of his sayings, Amos had announced a divine judgment coming against a number of nations (Amos 1:3–2:3). This might have been taken by his audience as an announcement of a day of the LORD according to a concept similar to that of Joel 3 (MT 4). But the reader knows that Amos had also announced divine judgment against Judah and Israel (Amos 2:4–16), so that it would be rather a day of the LORD directed against Israel according to a concept similar to that of Joel 1–2.

Immediately before 5:18 Amos sharply criticized the social and legal behavior of his audience (5:7–12) and called the present time an "evil time" (*'ēt rā'āh*, v. 13). He called his audience to turn around, to do the opposite of what they have done before: "Seek good and not evil.... Hate evil and love good, and establish justice in the gate," and he added: "Perhaps [*'ûlay*] the LORD, the God of hosts, will be gracious to the remnant of Joseph" (vv. 14–15). This *'ûlay* comes close to the *mî yôdēa'* ("Who knows?") in Joel 2:14. Amos then began to describe a situation of wailing and mourning culminating in the words: "Then I pass through your midst, says the LORD" (vv. 16–17). All these are signs of God's coming for judgment and punishment of his people. Therefore, if this really is the day of the LORD, it would obviously be directed against Israel, and the only chance to escape would be to turn away from evil and repent.

Whatever traditions about the day of the LORD that Amos and his contemporaries might have had in detail, the basic structures are obviously similar to those unfolded in Joel. The readers coming from Joel are provided with certain ideas that will give them associations while reading Amos. Consequently, the passage on the day of the LORD will be much less isolated within Amos than some commentators claim.

IV

The theme of the day of the LORD continues. It is the main topic of the short Obadiah writings. One gets the impression that the Amos writings have been framed by the two smaller writings, Joel and Obadiah in particular (neither of which is dated), because of their common topic: the day of the LORD.[10] In Obadiah the concept is close to that in Joel 3 (MT 4). The day of the LORD is directed against one of Israel's closest enemies:

10. See Schart, "Die Rahmung der Amosschrift durch Joel und Obadja," chap. 8 in "Entstehung."

Edom. By calling it "Esau" (seven times!) both the closeness and the enmity are emphasized. The LORD comes to punish Edom/Esau because of all his misdeeds against his brother Jacob/Judah. But when the day of the LORD is explicitly mentioned, it is directed "against all nations" (*'al-kol-haggôyim*, Obad 15). This again corresponds to Joel 3 (MT 4) where the nations in toto are the enemy against whom the day of the LORD is directed. In Obad 16 all the nations will have to drink the cup, which was previously mentioned in Jer 25:15–29, where it is named "the cup of the wine of wrath."

In contrast to Edom and the nations, on Mount Zion there will be those who escaped (*pĕlêṭāh*), a remnant (Obad 17). This corresponds with Joel 2:32 (MT 3:5). But there is one remarkable difference: In Joel the remnant consists of the believers, those who called on the name of the LORD and whom he himself calls. The name of Israel or any corresponding name is not mentioned and nothing is said about the relation of the remnant to the rest of the nations—if there will be any. In Obadiah it is the house of Jacob, also called the house of Joseph, who shall possess those who formerly possessed them and who shall be the fire and the flame to burn them and consume them; and there will be no remnant from the house of Esau (v. 18). Up to the end Israel is ruling over its enemies and even judging them from Mount Zion (v. 21).[11]

The whole tone in Obadiah is different from Joel. The element of enmity and the vision of ruling over the enemy for centuries is dominant. But it is finally said that God will be there on Mount Zion, as in Joel (2:27; 3:21 [MT 4:21]): "The kingdom shall be the LORD's." This makes clear that the ultimate rulership is with God, not with humans. In addition, because the Obadiah writings are included in the Book of the Twelve, one cannot read Obadiah without hearing Amos's critical question: "Why do you want the day of the LORD?" And reading about the remnant on Zion one will remember what is said in Joel 2:32 (MT 3:5) about the remnant of believers called by God himself. This takes the edge off Obadiah's sayings that they would have when read on their own.[12]

V

The framing of Amos by Joel and Obadiah forms a group of writings referring to the day of the LORD near the end of the Northern Kingdom. Joel

---

11. It is not quite clear who are the *mošî'îm* in v. 21.

12. In the context of the Book of the Twelve Jonah might be understood as a critical reaction to Obadiah, showing that even a great enemy of Israel like Nineveh could repent and be saved.

and Obadiah, of course, speak about Judah and Jerusalem; but Amos is the only one of the three whose sayings are dated, so that, in the structure of the Book of the Twelve, this group of texts is to be read in that chronological context. This is important because the next mention of the day of the LORD appears near the end of Judah in the dated writings of Zephaniah. This collection of prophetical sayings again, like Joel, could be called a "book of the day of the LORD."

Zephaniah has his own terminology. Alongside of the term *yôm yhwh* (1:7, 14; 2:2, 3) he uses the expanded terms *yôm 'ebrat yhwh* (1:18) and *yôm 'ap-yhwh* (2:2, 3), "the day of the LORD's wrath," or other terms describing the terrifying character of that day (in 1:15–16 he uses a whole series of these). He calls it *yôm zebaḥ yhwh* (1:8), "the day of the LORD's sacrifice," or simply says *bayyôm hahû'*, "on that day" (1:9, 10). In the later parts of the Zephaniah writings these terms do not appear. In 3:8 God calls the day when he will arise as an accuser *yôm qûmî*, "the day of my arising." Finally, the term *bayyôm hahû'* appears twice in a totally different sense (3:11, 16), speaking about a time when, for Israel, all disaster will have gone.

Zephaniah speaks of a great disaster that will come upon the whole world, by which God will sweep away everything, humans and animals (1:2–3). But then the judgment concentrates on Judah and Jerusalem, particularly on those who are carrying out foreign worship of Baal, of the host of heaven, and of Malcam (vv. 4–6). For those "the day of the LORD is near" (v. 7). It will be directed against those who are responsible for all that in one or another capacity (vv. 8–11) and who got fat and rich and forgot the LORD (vv. 12–13). Again: "The day of the LORD is near" (v. 14), and nothing will save them (vv. 15–18).

This is the first time in the Book of the Twelve that particular reasons are given why the day of the LORD will come upon Israel. It is the worship of foreign gods that provoked God's wrath so that he now will set out to judge and to punish his people and, in particular, those responsible for the false worship. But now the prophet calls them to gather before the day of the LORD's wrath will come upon them and to seek the LORD (2:1–3). Here the prophet turns from the cultic field to that of righteousness: "Seek righteousness, seek humility!" The right worship and the doing of righteousness are closely linked to each other because they are different sides of the one right service of God. Therefore the prophet expresses the hope: "Perhaps you will find shelter on the day of the LORD's wrath." These wordings are close to Amos 5:14–15: "Seek" (Zephaniah: *baqqĕšû*; Amos: *diršû*), and than the hopeful *'ûlay* looking forward to a gracious divine reaction.

But there is no immediate answer. The prophet speaks about God's judgment upon other peoples: the Philistines, Moab, Ammon, the Cushites, and Assyria/Nineveh (2:4–15). In this passage the term "day of the Lᴏʀᴅ" (or related terms) does not appear. Then the prophet turns again toward Jerusalem and its leading groups (3:1–7). Finally, God himself calls to wait for the "day" when he will arise as accuser: *yôm qûmî* (v. 8). Will this waiting now lead to an answer?

God arises. He will pour out his indignation upon the nations and will send the fire of his passion over all the earth (3:8b). But then he will change everything. First he will give the nations pure lips so that they will call on the name of the Lᴏʀᴅ (v. 9). This is reminiscent of Joel 2:32 (MT 3:5): "everyone who calls on the name of the Lᴏʀᴅ shall be saved." This will be the result of God's pouring out his spirit on "all flesh." Now in Zephaniah, God himself will enable the nations to call on his name. So they are saved by God's own action.

On that day (*bayyôm hahû'*) (3:11) Israel must no longer be ashamed because of its former deeds. The reason is that God will also change Israel. He will remove from its midst those who might arouse God's anger by their haughtiness (v. 11), and he will leave there a poor, humble folk. Again it is the "name of the Lᴏʀᴅ" in which they will find refuge (v. 12). They are called "the remnant of Israel," and they will behave according to God's delight (v. 13). All will be joy and exultation (vv. 14–19), and finally God will gather them and bring them home (v. 20).

Thus in the course of Zephaniah's writings, the situation has fundamentally changed from the threatening announcement of the approaching day of the Lᴏʀᴅ to the vision of a joyful future for Zion with the Lᴏʀᴅ, the king of Israel (v. 15) and the saving hero (v. 17) in their midst. According to the chronological structure of the Book of the Twelve these are the last words before the destruction of Jerusalem and the temple on Mount Zion. The next verse speaks about Darius, the king of Persia (Hag 1:1). These words, therefore, at the same time form the end of the second section of the Book of the Twelve. Looking back from here we will see that even the first section, chronologically speaking, ends with a vision of a peaceful and joyful future for Israel (Mic 7:11–20).

VI

The last chapter of the Book of the Twelve[13] speaks again of the day of the Lᴏʀᴅ. The full title *yôm yhwh* is mentioned only at the very end (Mal 4:5 [MT 3:23]) where the day is called again "the great and terrible day of the

---

13. In the Hebrew Bible, Malachi 3 is the last chapter, including as it does chap. 4 in the English Bible.

LORD." But that day is announced already at the beginning of this chapter. God will send his messenger, "but who can endure the day of his coming?" (3:1–2). This is reminiscent of the first appearance of the day of the LORD in the Book of the Twelve where the same question has been asked (Joel 2:11). It seems to be a kind of *inclusio:* The question "Who can endure?" is always present when the day of the LORD is near.

This time the day of the LORD will first be an internal scrutiny within Israel, a refinement and judgment with regard to cultic and social behavior (Mal 3:2b–5). But then God will write in a book (the names of) those who fear him and value his name, and "on the day that I am preparing" they will be his special possession (*sĕgullāh*) (vv. 16–17). Again the reverence for the name of the LORD plays an important role, as it did previously in Joel 2:32 (MT 3:5) and Zeph 3:9, 12. Finally, the day will come "burning like an oven" and will burn all the evildoers like straw (Mal 4:1 [MT 3:19]). In Obad 18 the house of Esau was the straw and the house of Jacob the flame, but now in Malachi it is an internal discrimination: the evildoers will burn like straw, while for those who revere the name of the LORD the sun of righteousness shall rise (4:2 [MT 3:20]); and they shall tread the wicked under their feet (4:3 [MT 3:21]).

The last verses of Malachi (4:4–6 [MT 3:22–24]) are at the same time the last paragraph of the entire section of the Hebrew Scriptures known as the *Nebi'im* ("Prophets"). Here the day of the LORD appears in a remarkable context. Mentioning of Moses at the end of the collection of prophetical writings alongside Elijah obviously has the function of connecting the first two main parts of the canon of the Hebrew Bible, Torah and *Nebi'im*, to each other.[14] The second coming of Elijah will happen "before the day of the LORD comes." This wording is reminiscent of Joel 2:31–32 (MT 3:4–5). But what is the meaning of the last verse: God "will turn the hearts of parents to their children and the hearts of children to their parents" (Mal 4:6 [MT 3:24])? It means that he will bring reconciliation among those who, according to the discussion in the Malachi writings, are split in several respects. This is necessary in order to avoid the eschatological judgment. Again this reminds one of Joel, where it is said that those who call on the name of the LORD shall escape. The parallelism is obvious: certain fundamental elements of behavior in the face of God are essential in order to be blessed with eschatological salvation.

*   *   *

---

14. See J. Blenkinsopp, *Prophecy and Canon: A Contribution to the Study of Jewish Origins* (Notre Dame: Univ. of Notre Dame Press, 1977) 120–23.

This little essay does not pretend to be a full study of the structure of the Book of the Twelve nor even of the great topic of the day of the LORD. Yet I felt that it might be an appropriate expression of appreciation and friendship to Walter Brueggemann. He always likes to struggle with those texts in our deeply venerated Hebrew Bible that are not to be read too smoothly, but challenge us to get through their rough exterior to reach the message they had for their contemporaries, and have for us today.

– 14 –

Divine Incongruities
in the Book of Jonah

Phyllis Trible

Walter Brueggemann finds an unresolvable tension pervading Israel's testimonies about God. Alongside the dominant testimony of faithful sovereignty and sovereign fidelity runs the countertestimony of ambiguity,
unreliability, and negativity. For readers to choose one of these witnesses
in disregard of the other falsifies the biblical record and misunderstands the
vibrant dialectic of faith. That dialectic presents God as *"A character who
has a profound disjunction at the core of the Subject's life."*[1]

According to Brueggemann, the validity of his thesis comes through
the reading of texts, one after another. To honor his claim (and to test
it) this essay explores divine incongruities in the book of Jonah. Among
the reasons for selecting the text are happy memories of graduate school
where Professor Brueggemann and I were classmates. As students of James
Muilenburg, we shared the experience of writing dissertations, he on
Deuteronomy and I on Jonah.

Introduction

Structured in two scenes of corresponding length (chaps. 1–2 and chaps. 3–
4), the book of Jonah exhibits symmetry in vocabulary, motifs, and the
order of events.[2] Both scenes open with the word of YHWH to Jonah,
and both close with interaction between YHWH and Jonah. Both depict
groups of non-Israelites confronting disaster. Both use natural occurrences

---

1. This quotation and the accompanying description appear in Walter Brueggemann, *Theology of the Old Testament: Testimony, Dispute, Advocacy* (Minneapolis: Fortress Press,
1997) 268. For a literary reading that achieves a characterization of God similar to Brueggemann's theological reading, see Jack Miles, *God: A Biography* (New York: Knopf, 1995).

2. For a full discussion of the design and structure of Jonah, see Phyllis Trible, *Rhetorical
Criticism: Context, Method, and the Book of Jonah* (Minneapolis: Fortress Press, 1994) 107–
225.

and creatures of nature to advance the plot. Within the impressive symmetry, asymmetry flourishes through incompatible theologies and competing points of view. The mix renders impossible facile summaries about the meaning of the story.[3]

Scene One

God of the Commanding Word

The beginning of the Jonah narrative (1:1–2) models a conventional situation. God commands; the human creature resists. As YHWH once called Moses, Elijah, and Jeremiah, so the deity calls Jonah. The standard prophetic formula, "the word of YHWH," prefaces the specific imperative, "Arise, go to Nineveh...."[4] Like his predecessors, Jonah shrinks from obeying.

Yet the particularity of Jonah's resistance diverges from the conventional. When YHWH ordered Moses to go to Pharaoh, Moses stood his ground and argued (Exod 3:10–4:17). When YHWH questioned Elijah on Mount Horeb, Elijah stood his ground and complained (1 Kgs 19:1–18). When YHWH appointed Jeremiah a prophet to the nations, Jeremiah stood his ground and protested (Jer 1:4–10). By contrast, Jonah neither stands his ground nor speaks. Instead, he arises to flee to Tarshish from the presence of YHWH (1:3). He goes first to Joppa where he boards a ship, pays its (!) fare, and sets out on the journey that will take him away. Rather than talk, Jonah travels. In changing the script for human resistance to the divine command, he invites an unconventional response.

God of the Violent Act

YHWH pursues Jonah not with a commanding word but with a violent act. The deity hurls (*ṭwl*) a great wind (1:4). It results in a mighty storm upon the sea, a threatened ship about to splinter, and frightened sailors crying to their gods (1:4–5). The fury of YHWH toward disobedient and taciturn Jonah lashes out indiscriminately to terrify his environment. An unconventional response overpowers an unconventional situation.

Attributing the violence of the storm to divine punishment, the sailors seek to appease the sea-god with sacrifices (1:5). All the wares on the ship they hurl (*ṭwl*) into the sea. Meanwhile, Jonah has withdrawn through

---

3. The following exposition draws upon earlier research. See esp. Phyllis Trible, "The Book of Jonah: Introduction, Commentary, and Reflections," in *NIB* (Nashville: Abingdon, 1996) 7:461–529; ibid., "A Tempest in a Text: Ecological Soundings in the Book of Jonah," *Theology Digest*.

4. On the unconventional use of the formula, see Trible, *NIB*, 7:124–25.

sleep in the womblike recesses below deck. The wrath of YHWH has not reached its target, but it has caused the innocent to suffer. So the captain of the ship arouses Jonah, beseeching him to call upon his god for deliverance. Although ignorant of the cause of the storm, the captain seeks a theological solution. "Perhaps the god will show us favor so that we do not perish" (1:6).[5]

The proposed solution recognizes the sovereign freedom of Jonah's God. Words of entreaty cannot manipulate or coerce this deity, though they do offer the "perhaps" of faith. But the storm continues, whereupon the sailors cast lots to identify the culprit among them (1:7–8). When the lot falls on Jonah, they ply him with questions. For the first time he speaks. What the commands of YHWH and of the captain have not achieved, the questions of the sailors elicit: a verbal reply from Jonah.

Besides giving his Hebrew identity and reporting his fear, Jonah makes a theological statement. He identifies YHWH as "God of the heavens...the one who made the sea and the dry land" (1:9). "God of the heavens" indicates transcendent power; "the one who made the sea and the dry land," imminent power. Together these phrases depict YHWH as god of the cosmos. The positive portrayal fits well a biblical theology of creation. Jonah's theology echoes the soaring affirmation, "When God created the heavens and the earth" (Gen 1:1), and the resounding elaboration, "You stretch out the heavens like a tent...you set the earth on its foundations...yonder is the sea, great and wide" (Ps 104:2, 5, 25). As in much of Scripture, so for Jonah, sovereignty and creatorship characterize YHWH.

Although Jonah's declaration belongs to the dominant testimony of faith, its context hints at the countertestimony. YHWH, "God of the heavens who made the sea and the dry land," is YHWH who "has hurled a great wind to the sea" (1:3). Jonah's description witnesses to creative power; the narrator's report, to destructive power. In the activity of YHWH ambiguity resides.

As the sailors come to understand the crisis, their fear grows (cf. 1:10 with 1:5) and their plight intensifies. They ponder what to do with Jonah (1:11–13). With a seeming altruism that masks his persistent motive to flee from YHWH, he proposes that they hurl (*ṭwl*) him overboard. The verb "hurl," which propelled the wind of YHWH on the sea and the wares of the sailors into the sea, Jonah now uses self-referentially to get himself into the sea. For calming the storm, he offers a theology of human sacrifice. Yet the sailors waiver. They try escape rather than appeasement. Rowing furiously to return to dry land, they are unsuccessful. The sea rages with

---

5. Unless noted otherwise, all the biblical translations are my own.

increasing ferocity. The sailors then pray to the aggrieved and angry God of Jonah. Asking that they not perish, they affirm the freedom of YHWH to do as the deity pleases (1:14). They recognize that this sovereign God has power to save and to destroy.

The answer to the sailors' prayer follows their expelling Jonah to the sea. Without reference to YHWH or to the divine wind, the storyteller reports the outcome. The sea ceases from its raging (1:15). Unaffected by inanimate wares, it responds to the sacrifice of Jonah. In turn, the sailors worship YHWH. As they perform cultic acts, their fear transfers from the storm (1:5, 10) to the deity who perpetrated and eliminated it. They worship the God of the violent act, the God to whom they made a human sacrifice so as to be spared a destruction they did not deserve. In pursuing its own purpose, divine wrath has manipulated nature, objects, and people. The presence of YHWH is menacing power even when it saves. Thereby the dominant and the countertestimonies of Israel merge.

God of the Continuing Pursuit

Leaving the sailors behind, the story follows YHWH and Jonah. "YHWH appoints a great fish to swallow Jonah" (1:17 [MT 2:1]). Like the first divine act of hurling a great wind, the second uses nature to pursue Jonah. Unlike the wind, however, the fish is not itself violent. Whether it plays a benign or malignant role remains a moot issue. It rescues Jonah from drowning but does not deliver him from the presence of YHWH. From Jonah's perspective drowning would be his salvation. The fish thwarts his flight. In appointing the fish, YHWH the oppressor saves and YHWH the savior oppresses. The divine act mirrors ambiguity.

As mediator between YHWH and Jonah, the fish performs two contrasting actions, to swallow (*bālaʿ*) and to vomit (*qîʾ*). Both actions carry negative meanings in the Old Testament. By the work of YHWH at the Exodus, the earth "swallowed" the enemies of Israel (Exod 15:12). By the work of YHWH in the wilderness, the earth "swallowed" those who revolted against Moses; they went down alive into Sheol as they perished from the assembly (Num 16:30, 32, 34). So by the work of YHWH, the fish swallows Jonah. He descends alive into its belly. With reference to the verb "vomit," the book of Proverbs declares that to eat the bread of the stingy is like a hair in the throat; "you will vomit up the little you have eaten" (Prov 23:6–8, NRSV). Another proverb says that if you overindulge in the eating of honey, "you will vomit it" (Prov 25:16, NRSV). So the fish to whom YHWH speaks vomits Jonah. If the verb "swallow" suggests that the fish is a hostile environment for Jonah, the verb "vomit" suggests that Jonah is a hostile substance for the fish. But neither the fish nor Jonah makes the decisions. They belong to the God of the continuing pursuit.

While in the belly of the fish, Jonah prays a psalm.[6] Although it accents deliverance (2:2, 6, 9 [MT 3, 7, 10]), it does not minimize distress. Jonah claims that Yʜwʜ cast him into the deep, indeed into the womb (*beṭen*) of Sheol (2:2–3 [MT 3–4]). The waves and billows of Yʜwʜ passed over him; weeds wrapped around his head; he was driven out from the sight of Yʜwʜ; and his life was ebbing away (2:6–7 [MT 7–8]). Jonah then claims that his cries to Yʜwʜ reversed the situation (2:2, 6, 7 [MT 3, 7, 8]). Yʜwʜ, who took him to the brink of death, brought up his life from the grave. To this God he renders thanks (2:9 [MT 10]).

The psalm contains both the dominant and the countertestimony of Israel. Yʜwʜ is the faithful sovereign who delivers the distressed from danger. Yʜwʜ is the perpetrator of the danger who sends the distressed to Sheol. Jonah prays in thanksgiving to the God from whose presence he seeks to flee, to the God who has fed him to a fish, and to the God who relentlessly pursues him. Dissonances within the psalm and dissonances between the psalm and the surrounding narrative exacerbate the theological tensions of the story.

Altogether, scene one of Jonah exploits these tensions. Yʜwʜ, God of the heavens who made the sea and the dry land, exercises crushing power. It begins with the commanding word (*dābār*) to Jonah and ends with the declarative speech (*'āmar*) to the fish. Bending nature to the divine will, the deity stalks disobedient Jonah and in that pursuit endangers the lives of innocent sailors. Divine sovereignty and divine freedom spell vengeance, vindictiveness, and violence. Divine sovereignty and divine freedom also spell deliverance. The sea ceases from raging; the sailors do not perish; Jonah does not drown. Conflicting portraits of Yʜwʜ emerge. The creator vies with the destroyer, the punisher with the rescuer. Brueggemann rightly discerns "a profound disjunction at the core of the Subject's life." As coercive savior, this Subject now returns Jonah to dry land, there to confront him again.

Scene Two

God of the Commanding Word

Like scene one, scene two begins with Yʜwʜ's commanding word to Jonah, "Arise, go to Nineveh . . . " (3:1–2). This time Yʜwʜ prevails; divine power

---

6. For the psalm as an addition to the story that is yet integral to the final form, see Trible, "The Book of Jonah: Introduction, Commentary, and Reflections," 464–65.

overwhelms human disobedience. Yet unlike Moses, Elijah, and Jeremiah, Jonah still does not talk to God. Instead, the storyteller reports that he obeys the call. He goes to Nineveh "according to the word of YHWH" (3:3). Thereupon YHWH recedes for a time as the narrative turns to Nineveh.

God of the Repentant Act

Entering the great city, Jonah calls, "Yet forty days and Nineveh will be overturned" (3:4). The words abound in unstable properties. "Nineveh" as definitive subject precedes an ambiguous verb (*hpk*). It holds the opposite meanings of destruction and deliverance.[7] In addition, the grammatical form *nehpāket* may be passive or reflexive. Nineveh will be overturned or will overturn itself.[8] Jonah himself neither interprets the sense of the verb nor specifies the agent of the overturning. Moreover, he neither prefaces nor concludes his words with a standard prophetic formula such as "thus says YHWH" or "oracle of YHWH." Nowhere in the story has YHWH given Jonah these exact words to speak. Is the prophecy, then, true or false? Is it the word of YHWH? As YHWH never spoke to the sailors, so God never speaks to the Ninevites.

Yet the Ninevites hear the words of Jonah as an authentic and ominous message from God. They believe God and they initiate change (3:5). "From the greatest to the least" they fast and clothe themselves in sackcloth, the traditional garb of mourning and repentance. Like the sailors, the Ninevites are god-oriented; unlike the sailors, they are not innocent. When their response reaches the king of Nineveh, he emulates it and then asserts his authority through a decree calling for repentance. Extending to the animals, the decree acknowledges the evil and violence of the city and so its imminent destruction (3:6–9). Like the captain of the ship facing disaster, the king of Nineveh nonetheless sounds a cautious note of hope. He appeals to the perchance of faith.[9] "Who knows, God may repent... and we will not perish" (3:9). Both leaders base hope on the theological premise of sovereign freedom. The God who has power to destroy may also save.

New to the story, the theology of repentance sets up a correlation, neither inevitable nor necessary, between human and divine turning. What the Ninevites do may effect (but does not determine) what God does. The theology works on a quid pro quo basis, an equal exchange between the city and the deity. Mutuality and reciprocity eliminate evil to yield salvation.

---

7. For the predominant meaning "destruction," see, e.g., Gen 19:21, 25, 29; Deut 29:22; Jer 20:16; Lam 4:6; for the meaning "deliverance," see, e.g., Deut 23:5; Jer 31:13; Ps 66:6.

8. See Jack M. Sasson, *Jonah* (AB 24B; New York: Doubleday, 1990) 233–37.

9. On the perchance of faith, see Martin Buber, *The Prophetic Faith* (trans. C. Wilton-Davis; New York: Harper & Row, 1960) 104–5.

And so it comes to pass. The Ninevites turn from evil; God turns from evil (3:10). God never punishes Nineveh for its violence; divine repentance supersedes retribution.

The theme of divine repentance, present in Jonah through the vocabulary of *nḥm* and *šûb*, cuts across the dominant and the countertestimonies of Israel. First, within even a single text the theme receives contradictory treatment. It is affirmed and denied. God repents; God does not repent (1 Sam 15:11, 29, 35; cf. Num 23:19). Second, among a variety of texts the theme works for weal and for woe. The repentance of God may bring disaster (e.g., Gen 6:6, 7); the repentance may avert disaster (e.g., Exod 32:14; Amos 7:3, 6).

As witnessed in Jonah 3:10 (and later in 4:2), the theme of divine repentance bears a positive message. God repents of evil toward Nineveh and does not do it. Yet that repentance carries disturbing irony, particularly in juxtaposition to the theology of violence that characterizes scene one. There innocent sailors experienced the life-threatening fury of Yhwh; here guilty Ninevites experience the redemptive power of God. How can Yhwh move so easily to the destruction of the innocent? How can God move so easily to the salvation of the guilty? If the character of the deity comes across as faithful, it is also unreliable—and certainly unpredictable.

God of the Persuading Word

The challenge to Yhwh. The repentance of God angers Jonah. He lashes out in a prayer that explains why at the beginning he arose to flee to Tarshish (4:1–3). The explanation lies in the ancient confession that God is "merciful and gracious, slow to anger, abounding in steadfast love and repenting of evil."[10] These qualities belong to Israel's dominant testimony about Yhwh. Although some versions add that God punishes the guilty (cf. Exod 34:6–7), this one does not. Jonah depicts Yhwh as solely merciful, even though the terrifying behavior of Yhwh in scene one suggests otherwise. But here Jonah uses the positive version to justify himself and to account for the salvation of Nineveh. He does not question the authenticity of Nineveh's repentance; what bothers him is Yhwh's merciful response.

In reciting the confession Jonah expands the meaning of repentance beyond reciprocity. Rather than being just a corollary to Nineveh's repentance, God's repentance parallels God's mercy. It exceeds a quid pro quo formula. Though different, the categories of repentance and mercy work well together in chapters 3 and 4 of the story. But they stand in bold con-

---

10. Cf., e.g., Exod 34:6–7; Num 14:18; Deut 4:31; Pss 86:5; 103:8; 111:4; 112:4; 145:8; Nah 1:2–3; Joel 2:13; Neh 9:17, 31; 2 Chr 30:9.

trast to the categories of retribution and violence that characterize chapters 1 and 2. Strikingly, Jonah never complains about the latter theologies, only about the former. He is angry about the repentance and the mercy of YHWH but not about the retribution and the violence. After reciting the ancient confession of divine attributes as a complaint, Jonah asks YHWH to take his life.

The reply complicates further the depiction of God. YHWH, who has thus far spoken to Jonah only with the commanding word (1:2; 3:2), reemerges with a different kind of rhetoric that suggests a different mode of relating. "Is it good for you to be angry?" asks YHWH (4:4). The interrogative mode supplants the imperative; the commanding God becomes the questioning God. But the rhetorical maneuver appears not to work. As Jonah once fled from the command of YHWH, so now he leaves town without answering the question (4:5). YHWH then pursues him through a series of appointments that use nature to reassert divine power.

Divine appointments. A plant appointed by YHWH grows up over Jonah "to shade his head, to deliver him from his evil" (4:6).[11] Although he delights in the plant, his "evil" as anger remains (cf. 4:1 and 4:9). The delight itself is short-lived. With the coming of dawn, a divinely appointed worm attacks the plant. It withers (4:7). YHWH uses nature to assault nature. How Jonah responds to this development is not reported here. A gap opens in the narrative sequence; it presages the ending of the story (cf. 4:10).

In Hebrew the sound of the verb "wither" (*wayyîbāš*) echoes the sound of the noun "dry land" (*hayyabbāšāh*) to evoke association with the fish episode (2:10 [MT 11]). Like the fish of the sea, the worm of the earth is God's instrument. By mediating between YHWH and Jonah, the fish put distance between the deity and the man. By mediating between God and the plant, the worm shields the deity from directly perpetrating botanical death. Unlike the fish whose role was ambivalent, both devouring and saving, the worm has only a negative function. It kills. Yet this destructive act belongs to YHWH's purpose of saving Jonah from his anger.

The divine use of nature continues with the appointment of a sultry east wind. Reminiscent of the great wind that YHWH hurled to the sea, it accompanies the rising of the sun. As the worm attacked (*nākāh*) the plant, so the sun attacks (*nākāh*) Jonah's head (4:8). As the plant withered, so now Jonah faints and asks to die.

In scene one YHWH pursues Jonah at sea with wind, storm, and fish; in

---

11. The phrase "to deliver him from his evil [*rāʿāh*]" picks up on the report in 4:1, which reads literally, "It was evil [*wayyēraʿ*] to Jonah a great evil [*rāʿāh*]," a description of his anger. To understand the word *rāʿah* in 4:6 as "discomfort" (so NRSV) is to miss the connection and to minimize the meaning.

scene two YHWH pursues him on land with plant, worm, wind, and sun. In both settings the deity garners the vast resources of the created order to bear on this one man. The Creator uses nature indiscriminately for weal and for woe. Unlike Jonah, nature has no power to resist. The sovereign God of the heavens who made the sea and the dry land controls it all. To bring Jonah around, YHWH spares nothing in the entire cosmos. This depiction of God is as chilling as it is comforting.

At the conclusion of the divine appointments, as Jonah suffers from the demise of the plant, he reiterates his wish to die (4:8; cf. 4:3). God continues to question him. Having earlier interpreted the death wish as the expression of anger (4:4), the deity returns to the subject, this time with a specific focus. "Is it good it angers you about the plant?" (4:9). Unlike his first reaction to a divine question (cf. 4:5), Jonah does not exit. He stands his ground and answers the question. "It is good it angers me unto death" (4:8). In giving a defiant response, Jonah joins Moses, Elijah, and Jeremiah, who stood their ground and talked back to God. His last words thus open a dialogue.

A new premise. YHWH continues with a declarative sentence that gives new information. It fills the gap that appeared in the narrative sequence after the worm killed the plant (4:7). There the response of Jonah was not recorded. Here YHWH declares, "You, you pitied the plant..." (4:10). The response contrasts with Jonah's self-referential reactions to the appointments of the plant and the wind. Shaded by the plant, he delighted in it; buffeted by the wind and beaten by the sun, he sought death. But between these self-serving reactions, when the plant withered, he showed pity for it apart from the effect of the withering upon him. Thereby Jonah acknowledged the intrinsic rather than the utilitarian value of the plant (which YHWH did not). The withholding of his response until now introduces yet another theological turn in the narrative.[12] This crucial information, supplied by YHWH in a declarative sentence, becomes the premise for a third divine question.

Central to the declarative sentence and to the interrogative is the verb *ḥûs.* It signifies the attitude or emotion of sympathy expressed in gracious action toward another.[13] At places in the Bible the verb appears with the noun "eye" (*'ayin*) to convey the image of overflowing tears on behalf of an

---

12. On the technique of delayed information, see Trible, *Rhetorical Criticism*, 206, 222, 234. Cf. Jonah 1:10 and 4:2–3.

13. For discussion and biblical references, see S. Wagner, *"ḥûs,"* in *Theological Dictionary of the Old Testament* (ed. G. Johannes Botterweck and Helmer Ringgren; trans. David E. Green; Grand Rapids: Eerdmans, 1980) 4:271–77. Note that negative expressions of *ḥûs* (not showing pity) signify violence, disaster, and destruction (e.g., Deut 7:16; 19:21; 25:12; Jer 13:13; 21:7).

object (e.g., Ezek 20:17; cf. 16:5). The range of positive meanings includes compassion, benevolence, and mercy. Appearing for the first time in the book of Jonah, *ḥûs* signals something new about Jonah and about YHWH.

A new question. The new theology builds on analogy. "You, you pitied the plant.... And I, shall not I pity Nineveh the great city?" (4:10–11). YHWH does not argue from sovereign power, mighty acts, or inscrutable mysteries. Nor does YHWH argue from divine mercy as presented in the confession Jonah just quoted. Instead, YHWH develops the argument through natural rather than revealed theology. It moves from the human response to nature to the divine response to urbanity, from Jonah's pity for the plant to YHWH's pity for Nineveh.

The argument by analogy carries dissimilarities. Although Jonah pitied the plant, he had no power over it. He could neither stop its withering nor restore its life. Moreover, his pity came after the plant's destruction. By contrast, YHWH had total power, not only over the plant but over Nineveh and its outcome. Divine pity thus prevented the city's destruction. If Jonah's *ḥûs* argues for YHWH's *ḥûs*, YHWH's *ḥûs* exceeds Jonah's *ḥûs* (*qal waḥomer*).[14] The imprecise analogy thus moves the story to another level of theological discourse.

Dissonant theologies. The appearance of the verb *ḥûs* only in 4:10–11 signals a theology different from, though not opposed to, divine repentance (*nḥm*, *šûb* in 3:10) and divine mercy (*ḥannûn wĕraḥûm ʾerek ʾappayîm wĕrab-ḥesed wĕniḥām ʿal-hārāʿah* in 4:2). YHWH pities Nineveh not because it repents and YHWH is then full of mercy or not because YHWH is full of mercy and the city then repents but because YHWH (following the lead of Jonah regarding the plant) pities the city. Scene two of the story yields then two theologies of grace: the mercy linked to repentance and the pity independent of repentance. In 4:10–11, the vocabulary and the argument by analogy yield the second understanding.

Both theologies raise disturbing issues. In the first case, the immediate repentance of God, after the swift repentance of the Ninevites, appears facile and unfair.[15] Is there to be no punishment of Nineveh? Jonah knows the answer to the question, and it angers him. With Nineveh's repentance of evil, there is to be no retribution (and certainly no vengeance) but rather the prompt mercy of YHWH, who repents of evil. This answer Jonah finds in the dominant testimony of Israel, the confession about divine mercy (4:2–3).

---

14. On an argument that moves from the small to the great, see L. Jacobs, "The *Qal Va-ḥomer* Argument in the Old Testament," *BSOAS* 35 (1972) 221–27; also Sasson, *Jonah*, 307–8.

15. Many scholars formulate this problem as the tension between justice (espoused by Jonah) and mercy (espoused by Yhwh). For an evaluation, see Trible, *NIB* 7:483–85.

In the second case, the pity of YHWH for Nineveh, which is not linked to repentance (human or divine), appears unstable and capricious. The pity is predicated on the ad hoc situation of Jonah and the withered plant and thus on an ad hominem argument with an unreliable subject. As argued by YHWH, the pity suggests a sovereignty and freedom that is independent of Israel's dominant testimony about God. The suggestion borders on the unpredictable and the arbitrary. And if on this occasion the arbitrary is compassionate, what guarantee does YHWH give that on another occasion it will not be destructive?[16] In the theology of pity lurks the countertestimony of Israel.

Not unlike scene one, scene two holds theological tensions. The unconditional threat to do evil to Nineveh vies with God's repentance of evil after Nineveh's repentance. The God who threatens is the God who saves. Yet the God who saves also destroys. The divine ambivalence surfaces in relation to nature. For the Creator, its utilitarian value supersedes its intrinsic value. Although Jonah pitied the plant, YHWH does not. Through a killer worm, the Maker of the dry land (cf. 1:9) causes vegetation to wither.

At the end of the story, YHWH's relationship to Jonah and Nineveh hints further at unresolved tensions in the character of God. Are the divine appointments manipulative or didactic? Are the divine questions coercive or persuasive? Is the divine pity capricious or compassionate? In each instance the countertestimony of Israel contends with the dominant testimony. Ambiguity, unreliability, and negativity meet faithful sovereignty and sovereign fidelity.

Conclusion

The book of Jonah teems with divine incongruities. Both scenes testify to a transcendent God who is deeply in the fray: the God who commands, questions, and argues; who creates and destroys, acts and withdraws, threatens and spares. Within this single text, sovereignty, freedom, retribution, vindictiveness, violence, repentance, mercy, and pity sound the disjunctions that Brueggemann perceives at the core of Israel's God. The dialectic of these disjunctions yields the terror and the hope of the story.[17]

---

16. Cf. Alan Cooper, "In Praise of Divine Caprice: The Significance of the Book of Jonah," in *Among the Prophets: Language, Image and Structure in the Prophetic Writings* (ed. Philip Davies and David J. A. Clines (Sheffield: *JSOT*, 1993) 144–63.

17. For homiletical reflections on divine disjunctions and the dialectic of faith, see Walter Brueggemann, "Holy One in Your Midst," *The Living Pulpit* (January–March 1997) 44–45.

Part Four

God in the Writings

– 15 –

Prayer and Divine Action

Patrick D. Miller

No issue seems to set the question of God and what can be claimed about the activity of God more sharply than prayer.[1] In one of the more significant theological attempts to give clarity and intelligibility to the notion of "act of God," Gordon Kaufman ends up acknowledging that the resulting doctrine of providence

> is more austere than the pietistic views often found in Christian circles. God's subordinate acts here are governed largely by his overarching purposes and ultimate objectives, not simply by the immediate needs or the prayerful pleas of his children. This is no God who "walks with me and talks with me" in close interpersonal communion, giving his full attention to my complaints, miraculously extracting me from difficulties into which I have gotten myself by invading nature and history with *ad hoc* rescue operations from on high.... [W]e should hardly expect that he can or will bend his cosmic activity much to meet our private and peculiar needs or wishes.[2]

Kaufman's conception of God's activity as a master act consisting of subordinate acts aimed toward a goal that determines and guides all the activity has many resonances with the biblical picture of the God who acts.[3] Indeed,

---

1. I am indebted to members of the Theology and Science Consultation at the Center of Theological Inquiry in Princeton, under whose auspices an earlier draft of this essay was prepared, for their helpful criticism.

2. Gordon Kaufman, "On the Meaning of 'Act of God,'" in *God the Problem* (Cambridge: Harvard Univ. Press, 1972) 146–47. This essay, written in 1964, was one of the first attempts to respond to Langdon Gilkey's famous essay, "Cosmology, Ontology, and the Travail of Biblical Language" JR 41 (1961) 194–205, criticizing the formulations of contemporary biblical theology on the activity of God and calling for an ontology of God's acting that would lend credibility to a theological appropriation of the biblical language (repr. in *God's Activity in the World: The Contemporary Problem* [American Academy of Religion Studies in Religion 31; ed. Owen C. Thomas; Chico, Calif.: Scholars Press, 1983] 29–43).

3. The word *picture* is used with a high degree of intentionality. All of the biblical language about the activity of God, language that is carried by various images and many active verbs, is thoroughly metaphorical. That such metaphorical language truly has to do with the reality to which it points without being literally identical to that reality is something that the contemporary discussion on metaphor has made abundantly clear. Nor can one deal with the biblical text theologically without recognizing the place and role of its "images."

it may turn out to have more resonance with Scripture and its depiction of reality than it does with the evolutionary and scientific view of reality that Kaufman was seeking to accommodate. At least, some of the contemporary thinking about theology in the light of science seems to work out of a less mechanistic and more open view of time, events, and the universe than appears to lie behind Kaufman's depiction of the "interconnected web of events."[4] Furthermore, one notices that the more "pietistic" views as set forth by Kaufman are dismissed without much of a hearing. That such views have a deep rootage in Scripture suggests the need for more attention to them than he attempted in his analysis.

In this essay I will not attempt to effect an accommodation of the sort that Kaufman attempted. I will, however, suggest some dimensions of the view of prayer and providence that one uncovers in Scripture. I want to make several claims and elaborate on each one of them. The claims, while distinct, nevertheless have some logic and coherence to them that should become evident in the discussion.[5]

1. *The active involvement of God in the human situation is evoked by cries to God, by prayers for help.*

Christian theology has given much emphasis to the prominence of sin and disobedience at the beginning of the biblical story. Less attention is paid to the fact that the story of God's involvement in human affairs also begins in pain and oppression. For the first human word that is addressed to God in that whole story, without prior address by the deity, is an inarticulate cry of the innocent victim of a brother's murderous rage: "What have you done? Listen; your brother's blood is crying out to me from the ground" (Gen 4:10). That cry going up to God suggests what the rest of the biblical story confirms, namely, that the divine-human relation is rooted in the experience of human pain. The conversation with God is characteristically initiated from the human end as a cry for help on the part of the oppressed or the sufferer. God is drawn into the fray by the prayers of those in trouble.

Two dimensions of the anthropomorphic imagery for God come into play at this point. One is the notion of God *listening,* of God hearing sounds. The other is the image of God *dwelling in the heavens* and surrounded by a host of semidivine and angelic beings (see below). Neither of these images is susceptible to literalizing. Both of them are central to the

---

4. E.g., Robert Russell, "Does the 'God Who Acts' Really Act? New Approaches to Divine Action in the Light of Science," *TToday* 54 (1997) 43–65.

5. For several of these claims, a more extended development may be found in my *They Cried to the Lord: The Form and Theology of Biblical Prayer* (Minneapolis: Fortress Press, 1994).

biblical depiction of God and God's activity. The biblical story as manifest in many particular texts claims that the "ears" of God are attuned to the cries of the innocent and the oppressed. Indeed, the biblical story is *charted* by these cries and what happens when they reach the ears of God. In the story of the destruction of Sodom and Gomorrah, the Lord says: "How great is the *outcry* against Sodom and Gomorrah and how very grave their sin! I must go down and see whether they have done altogether according to the outcry that has come to me; and if not, I will know" (Gen 18:20–21, NRSV). The cry of the victims of Sodom and Gomorrah, a cry whose content may be constructed from the many laments of the Bible, has gone up to heaven and been heard by God. To shift the metaphor a bit, the divine "antenna" are attuned to this particular wavelength. Such a cry triggers an effect; it elicits a divine response: "I must go down and see...." The judgment on Sodom and Gomorrah arises not out of some continuing divine perusal of things on earth—a notion that has biblical rootage (Zech 4:10)—but out of God's hearing the prayer for help of the suffering ones in those cities.[6]

The biblical story of redemption begins in the exodus with these words:

> After a long time the king of Egypt died. The Israelites groaned under their slavery, and cried out. Out of the slavery their cry for help rose up to God. God heard their groaning, and God remembered his covenant with Abraham, Isaac, and Jacob. God looked upon the Israelites, and God took notice of them. (Exod 2:23–24, NRSV)

Then in the Lord's words to Moses, God confirms that the revelation of the divine power over the tyrannical power of Egypt rises out of the cry of human pain, the affliction of Israel: "I have observed the misery of my people who are in Egypt; I have heard their cry on account of their taskmasters" (Exod 3:7). Again and again in the period of the judges, when Israel had suffered under the oppressive hand of a foreign ruler, they *cried out* to the Lord and the Lord delivered them. In the legal codes of ancient Israel, the cry of the afflicted widow or orphan or one economically oppressed was "institutionalized" as a part of the mechanism of redress by structuring in the Lord's listening and responding to that cry (Exod 22:21–27). The Psalms give words to these cries for help. Psalm 34, a song of thanksgiving with a didactic character, sets this movement from human cry to divine response as paradigmatic for the divine-human relation:

> This poor soul cried, and was heard by the LORD,
>   and was saved from every trouble.

---

6. On the various terms for crying out to God and their character as petitions or prayers for help, see Richard N. Boyce, *The Cry to God in the Old Testament* (SBLDS 103; Atlanta: Scholars Press, 1988).

The eyes of the LORD are on the righteous [or innocent],
and his ears are open to their cry.

When the righteous cry for help, the LORD hears,
and rescues them from all their troubles.
(Ps 34:6, 15, 17, NRSV)

The reality of human hurt and its power to evoke a divine response are not simply items in the story. Neither human existence in its very nature nor the nature and reality of God can be understood apart from the dynamic of the cry of human hurt and the compassionate hearing of God. The joining of those two at the very center of the biblical story is found in the figure of Jesus dying on the cross, who, in his agony, "cried with a loud voice,... 'My God, my God, why have you forsaken me?' " (Matt 27:46, NRSV).

Here, therefore, is a theology from below, an understanding of God's active involvement in the human situation as something that is not manifest simply in the broad sweep of things but is evoked by what is going on and is responsive to that. In all these texts, the intervention of heaven seems very much tied to what is happening on earth and particularly to the cries for help of suffering people. The pervasiveness of this theme in the biblical text suggests that any notions of divine power and activity developed in relation to Scripture will need to incorporate this understanding. It holds in tension the particularity of every incident of cry heard and the constancy of the structure of hearing cries, that is, the clear indication that God is "bent" in a particular way, that the "machinery" of divine activity includes at its center a responsiveness to human hurt voiced in prayers for help. The particular interventions of God's activity are consistent with and a reflection of the structure of reality reflected in the biblical story.

2. *Petitionary prayer is fundamentally an act of **persuasion**, seeking to lure or coax God into responding to the cry for help.*

In its terminology, its assumptions about God, and its structural character, the prayer for help in Scripture functions as much as anything else to lay out a case that will catch the attention, the "ears," of God, and thus elicit a response that in some fashion will change things. The two primary technical terms for prayer are *tĕpillāh* and *tĕḥinnāh*. In their particular meanings they provide a significant clue to what goes on in prayer. The former, *tĕpillāh*, comes from a verb meaning to estimate or assess, and, in the form it takes to express the act of praying, to seek an assessment, to lay out a case or make a case for God's assessment. The latter term, *tĕḥinnāh*, comes from a verbal form that has to do with asking or seeking for oneself grace, mercy, or favor. Together, these terms identify the bases of prayer: the laying out of a case for God's assessment in order to evoke mercy and favor. The deity is thus understood to be open to the situation as presented and leaning toward a gracious response, and prayer is defined in its terminology as the enterprise that seeks to persuade the deity toward such gracious reaction to the plight that has been presented.

Various reasons for God acting are signaled in different ways in prayer. They may have to do with the character or nature of God, so that God's help is sought "for his name's sake" (e.g., Ps 23:3) or "for your steadfast love" (e.g., Pss 6:4 [MT 5]; 31:16 [MT 17]). A clear example of this is offered by the prayer of Moses in Num 14:17–19 (NRSV):

> And now, therefore, let the power of the LORD be great in the way that you promised when you spoke, saying, "The LORD is slow to anger, and abounding in steadfast love, forgiving iniquity and transgression, but by no means clearing the guilty, visiting the iniquity of the parents upon the children to the third and the fourth generation." Forgive the iniquity of this people according to the greatness of your steadfast love, just as you have pardoned this people, from Egypt even until now.

Moses draws upon one of the ancient and classic confessional statements about God as the basis of his appeal, seeking to effect a manifestation of that steadfast love that has long been recognized as characteristic of the Lord of Israel.

Some aspect of the situation of the petitioner may be a reason why God should act. Thus the psalmist cries out, "Hear a just cause, O LORD; attend to my cry," and then lays out the case by protesting his innocence and describing the terrible things that are being done to him (Psalm 17). Such prayers assume a relationship between the deity and the petitioner so that part of the reason for God's acting is because of that relationship. This is why there is such frequent reference to "my God" in the prayers, though that relationship may be spelled out much more extensively as a part of the motivational rhetoric, as, for example, in Ps 22:9–10 (NRSV):

> Yet it was you who took me from the womb;
>   you kept me safe on my mother's breast.
> On you I was cast from my birth,
>   and since my mother bore me you have been my God.

Furthermore, the appeal may carry implicit and direct indication that the reputation of God is at stake in the situation of the petitioner. That is indicated, for example, in the argument that God should act "for your/his name's sake." This is particularly evident in those communal laments that are the voice of an oppressed people seeking God's help. In Psalm 79, the people appeal to God to "deliver us, and forgive our sins, for your name's sake" (v. 9); then go on to ask why the nations should say, "Where is their

God" (vv. 10a); and finally at the end of the prayer plead with God to turn back against their tormenters "the taunts with which they taunted you" (v. 12). In all of these expressions, the nation is suggesting that God's fate is somehow tied to their own fate. So Moses in the prayer quoted above from Numbers 14 says to the Lord:

> Now if you kill this people all at one time, then the nations who have heard about you will say, "It is because the LORD was not able to bring this people into the land he swore to give them that he has slaughtered them in the wilderness." (vv. 15–16, NRSV)

The texts cited above are all instances in which the petitioner lays out a case to get the attention of the deity and to provide grounds for the appeal. At one point that may be primarily rooted in the nature and character of God; in another case it may be the plight of the petitioner that is so bad that a righteous and merciful God cannot help but come to deliver. At still other points God is pushed and prodded to help in order to preserve the Lord's own place in the world.

Every part of the structure of the prayer for help participates in this act of persuasion and coaxing. When the psalmist laments his or her condition, the description of the plight contained therein and the distress of the petitioner are intended to evoke a sympathetic response from the deity. So also words of address—"O LORD," "my God," and the like—as well as the many expressions of confidence and trust—such as, "You are my God" or "I trust in you"—claim the relationship between God and petitioner as grounds for God to act. When the psalmist protests his or her innocence, a fairly common feature of psalm prayers, it is in order to make the case so that a just judge will rule in his or her favor. The frequently occurring vow of praise is explicitly designed to motivate the deity as the praying one promises to enter the sanctuary with offerings of thanksgiving when the prayer has been answered.

In this understanding of prayer as a powerful and complex act of persuasion seeking to lure God into positive involvement in the situation in a way not evident at the moment of the prayer, there is a clear assumption that God can be moved and persuaded to act in a situation so that it is changed for good. Against a notion of an impassible God, the Scriptures paint a picture of God as one who acts significantly in the light of an assessment of the situation, an assessment to which human prayer contributes much.

It is critical at this point to recognize that what has just been described does not, as might seem at first glance, evoke the image of a capricious God, who in un-Godlike behavior is manipulated by the pleas of human beings. Here the nature of the arguments becomes a very important factor.

The appeals are always made toward the direction of God's already intended action. That is, motivating clauses that urge divine action "for your name's sake" or "for your steadfast love" seek an involvement by God that is consistent with the way that God is and with the way that God has chosen to act. The particular moment of suffering and distress is presented as an opportunity that, when clearly heard and assessed, will be seen to fit the circumstances appropriate to divine activity. This is not simply a prayer that God's will be done. The one praying seeks quite specific help, seeks deliverance and relief. But precisely because all the urging is grounded in an understanding of God's way and what it is that God is doing in the world, the prayer is in fact a plea that God's will be done.[7] The God who is just and compassionate, abounding in steadfast love, righteous and attentive to the weak and the helpless, is called upon to be that way in the immediate situation. Thus prayer is consistent with God's will and purpose for the world—large and small—as it seeks something that is wholly consistent with the divine nature. The modes of persuasion and urging seek to open up the faithfulness of God. That is why God makes God's self subject to persuasion, to the case that prayer makes. If this sounds as though human prayer is in some fashion part of the "mechanism," of the "apparatus," of divine activity in the universe, that is just the point; and the next claim will make that even clearer.[8]

3. *Within the Old Testament, intercession is primarily made by the leaders seeking to evoke a change of heart in the intent of God to judge a sinful people. Such intercession is expected by God and incorporated into the divine activity.*

Intercession, understood as the prayer of one or more on behalf of another party, was not the primary mode of prayer in ancient Israel. Where such prayers occur, their primary focus is the threat or reality of judgment, and their aim is to avert God's judgment. Examples of these are numerous, from the prayers of Abraham (Genesis 18 and 20:17–18) to the frequent intercessions of Moses on behalf of the people (e.g., Num 14:13–19), to the prophetic intercessions appealing to God to avert the judgment that the Lord has announced (e.g., Amos 7:1–6). Such intercession seems to have been a role or responsibility that belonged to the prophetic vocation.[9] While

---

7. The Lord's Prayer, as it builds into the life of the community a regular prayer for the doing of God's will, continues the trajectory that is opened up by this mode of praying in the biblical story.

8. For a more extended elaboration of the understanding of prayer as persuasion, see Patrick D. Miller, "Prayer as Persuasion: The Rhetoric and Intention of Prayer," *Word and World* 13 (1993) 356–62.

9. See Samuel A. Balentine, "The Prophet as Intercessor: A Reassessment," *JBL* 103 (1984) 161–73, and the bibliography in n. 2 of that article.

not every prophet is so depicted, and on occasion other individuals engage in prayer to God in behalf of another person or the larger community, such prayers "on behalf of" are so fully identified with the prophetic function that when Abraham prays to God to heal King Abimelech, the king is told by the Lord to approach Abraham because "he is a prophet, and he will pray for you and you shall live" (Gen 20:7, 17). Indeed, this is the only occasion in which Abraham is so described. The prophet is identified as intercessor again in the book of Jeremiah. Several times, the Lord tells Jeremiah not to intercede for the people even though no such intention has even been indicated by the prophet (Jer 7:16; 11:14; 14:11). On one such occasion, the Lord says: "Though Moses and Samuel stood before me, yet my heart would not turn toward this people" (Jer 15:1).

Two things are particularly noteworthy about this prophetic intercession:

a. The Lord *expects* the intercession of the prophets and *takes it into account* in whatever action is taken. To put it another way, the responsive action of God to the human situation depends on the intercessory prayer of the prophet.

Several texts attest that God is not simply open to prayer at this point but *depends upon such prayer to affect and effect God's actions*. The instances in Jeremiah where the Lord forbids Jeremiah to intercede suggest this indirectly. That is, there is no reason why the prophet should withhold intercession unless it is going to have some effect on the Lord's response to the people. If it is simply a matter of ignoring the intercession or saying no to it, then there is no point in restraining the prophet. Only in one instance is there some intimation that God can ignore the intercession of the prophet. That is the passage already cited from Jer 15:1, which indicates that there would be no divine change of mind even if Samuel and Moses interceded. That text simply highlights how far things have deteriorated in the covenantal life of Judah. Intercession may have been effective up to this point, but now the situation is past all possible redemption. It is not unlike the vision reports of Amos 7, where the prophet intercedes twice effectively, but things are so bad that in the final two vision reports, there is not even an attempt at intercession.

Yet further indication of the capacity of intercessory prayer to shape divine action is suggested by the conversation in Exod 32:7–12 between God and Moses in reaction to the making of the golden calf by the people. Just before Moses' plea on behalf of the people, the Lord says to him: "I have seen this people, how stiff-necked they are. *Now let me alone*, so that my wrath may burn hot against them and I may consume them" (vv. 9–10; cf. Deut 9:14). In other words, the deity, as in the case of Jeremiah, puts off

Moses so as not to be affected by the prayer of Moses for the people. The burning wrath of the Lord can only come to expression if it is not derailed by the prayer of God's prophet. But of course derailment is exactly what happens. Moses prays, and the narrative reports: "And the LORD changed his mind about the disaster that he planned to bring on his people" (Exod 32:14, NRSV). Prayer thus interferes with the impetus for judgment.

Furthermore, the divine rebuff, "let me alone," actually serves indirectly to invite the response of intercession. The deity could simply act, but this word to Moses is itself an indication that Moses' prayerful involvement can and will affect things. "[J]ust as God involved Abraham in the 'consultation' prior to the judgment of Sodom and Gomorrah, ..., so here God pauses and makes the divine will 'vulnerable' to human challenge."[10] That the prayer of intercession can and does change the mind of God or move God to act differently than once intended is clear in the biblical story. But this prayerful intervention is not an intrusion on the divine rule, as Kaufman, for example, seems to characterize it. Rather it is "an integral part of the way God's sovereignty in history is exercised ... God not only allows human intercession, God invites it and builds it into the decision-making processes of the heavenly council in ways we can never fathom."[11] Moses does not so much argue *against* God as participate in the ongoing argument *within* God.[12]

That God's purposive activity builds into itself the intercessory act is most clearly indicated by two texts from the book of Ezekiel. In a condemnation of the "senseless prophets who follow their own spirit," the Lord tells Ezekiel to prophesy against them saying, "You have not gone up into the breaches, or repaired a wall for the house of Israel, so that it might stand in battle on the day of the LORD" (Ezek 13:5, NRSV). The significance of this indictment is clear only when one sets it against Ezek 22:30-31 (NRSV):

> And I sought for anyone among them who would repair the wall and stand in the breach before me on behalf of the land, so that I would not destroy it; but I found no one. Therefore I have poured out my indignation upon them; I have consumed them with the fire of my wrath; I have returned their conduct upon their heads, says the Lord GOD.

Consistent with the texts discussed above, the Lord expects, even requires, the intercessory prayer of "his servants, the prophets" to push the divine act in a particular direction. Thus Samuel says on one occasion: "[F]ar be

---

10. Christopher Wright, *Deuteronomy* (New International Biblical Commentary; Peabody, Mass.: Hendrickson, 1996) 139.
11. Ibid., 140.
12. Ibid.

it from me that I should sin against the LORD by ceasing to pray for you" (1 Sam 12:23, NRSV). Moses' prayers of intercession described above are spoken of in Psalm 106 in a way similar to the words of the Lord about prophetic intercession in Ezekiel:

> Therefore he said he would destroy them—
>   had not Moses, his chosen one,
> stood in the breach before him,
>   to turn away his wrath from destroying them.
> (Ps 106:23, NRSV)

The imagery of the wall and the breach comes into play in a different but related way elsewhere in the prophets and serves to connect the *intercessory* involvement in the divine activity with what has been said above about the *persuading* involvement in God's activity:

> If you remove the yoke from among you,
>   the pointing of the finger, the speaking of evil,
> if you offer your food to the hungry
>   and satisfy the needs of the afflicted,
> then your light shall rise in the darkness
>   and your gloom be like the noonday.
> The LORD will guide you continually,
>   and satisfy your needs in parched places,
>   and make your bones strong;
> and you shall be like a watered garden,
>   like a spring of water,
>   whose waters never fail.
> Your ancient ruins shall be rebuilt;
>   you shall raise up the foundations of many generations;
> you shall be called the *repairer of the breach*,
>   the restorer of streets to live in. (Isa 58:9b–12, NRSV)[13]

The work of justice and compassion in the human community is an activity that is comparable to intercession for the sinful community. In both cases, a human activity corresponds to the nature and activity of God. In the case of prophetic intercession, the relation of this to the divine purpose is made explicit. One may infer, however, that those other prophetic words and deeds that enhance a just, merciful, and compassionate society also participate in and effect God's will for human life.

There is, therefore, an openness on God's part, an expectation that the intercession will have an impact, an invitation to shape the future. Such praying may seem audacious. Indeed, if one reads a number of the prayers

---

13. The connection of this text to the Ezekiel texts that speak about the wall and the breach was suggested to me in an unpublished paper by Christoph Schroeder, " 'Standing in the Breach': Divine Wrath and the Human Representative According to a Biblical Metaphor."

of Moses, for example, one finds them very pushy. But that seems to be just what the deity expects of the prophetic intercessors, that they will really make the case that appeals to the heart of God and effects a merciful response.

b. When the biblical story tells of a "change of mind" on the part of the deity in response to prayer, it is always the intercessory prayer of the prophetic figure and always has to do with a reversal of God's intention to punish the people in judgment. There is a common tendency to see *all* prayer as somehow "interfering" or "intervening" in God's purposive activity. That is not quite the picture that comes from the Scriptures. In that context, one presumes that the case presented by the petitioner who is in trouble, oppressed, sick, or suffering in some fashion will have its effect on the deity because God is "bent" in that direction. Where the change of mind takes place is in relation to the purpose of God to punish or judge those who have sinned, broken covenant, and the like, and in response to the prophetic intercession. In other words, the one "violation" of the divine intention that can be identified, and indeed with some frequency, is in regard to judgment. The will of God to judge is thus always open to a transcending appeal to the divine will to mercy and compassion, a manifestation again of God's being bent toward mercy, compassion, and forgiveness. It is no accident that several of the references to a possible change of mind on the part of the deity make direct allusion to the confessional formula of Exod 34:6–7: "The LORD, the LORD, a God merciful and gracious, slow to anger, and abounding in steadfast love and faithfulness...."[14] The change of mind, therefore, is indeed a deeper consistency, or, to use the biblical language, *faithfulness* to the way God is and does.

4. *The prayers of Scripture consistently expect and receive a response from God in a word that has a particular character to it and in help that transforms the situation, redeeming the one(s) in trouble. Such help may be perceived to a more or less degree as miraculous.*

Whatever the modern problem of unanswered prayer may be, that is not the norm in Scripture. There are many prayers of whose outcome there is no record—most of the Psalms, for example. Whether these prayers were prayed once or often, one cannot tell if they were always perceived or felt as answered.[15] But where there is some indication of what happens after

---

14. Num 14:13–19; Joel 2:12–14; Jonah 3:2; cf. 3:9–10.

15. In one or two cases (e.g., Psalm 88), there is little sense of expectation or confidence on the part of the petitioner that God will help. This psalm is a powerful complaint against God because of the suffering that places the psalmist "like those who have no help, like those forsaken among the dead." Precisely because of the regular expectation that God will respond,

prayers are uttered, especially in prose texts, most of the time there is a response from God that works positively on behalf of the praying one. Many texts suggest that the one who prayed for help expected a response from the deity, and the typical response is discernible in several places. It was what has come to be called an *oracle of salvation*. However it was received, possibly through a priest in the sanctuary, it was a divine assurance, "Do not fear." This assurance was addressed to the petitioner in highly personal terms, usually calling the recipient of the oracle by name. That fundamental assurance, which may vary with and be simply the word *Peace*, is grounded, then, in two kinds of basic claims made by the deity. One type of claim reasserts *the reality of the relationship*, for example, "I am your God" or "I am with you." The other indicates an *intention to help*, for example, "I will help you" or "I will support you." In some instances, both claims may be present.

These two types of claims—one the confirmation of the relationship (the continuing presence of God with the petitioner) and the other the promise of help in the distress—identify what seems to matter in the expectation of the petitioner and do, in fact, ease or remove the fear. They effect a transformation in the situation that is regularly understood as God's answer to prayer. That change and deliverance are effected in no small measure through the very deliverance of the oracle. That is, the word of God that assures the suffering petitioner of God's presence in the situation of trouble is itself transformative. The divine activity is present in the mediated speech. Even before there is a visible change in the external circumstances, transformation may happen by the divine word of assurance, the promise of the companioning presence of God.[16]

Such a claim, evident constantly in the prayers of the Old Testament, is also fundamental to the Christology of the New Testament. The category of "word" in relation to Jesus Christ and the reality of incarnation are not simply revelatory category and revelatory reality. The presence of God in Jesus Christ is the transforming word in the human situation that indicates the continuing activity of God to be with human beings in their distress and to overcome that distress. That is why the New Testament takes Psalm 22, one of the most anguished cries for help of all the Old Testament prayers, and turns it into the hermeneutical key to the passion, to the suffering and

---

the prayer that hears no response is from beginning to end an assault on God as the one who lies behind whatever is going on in the life of the sufferer. There is no letting God off the hook.

16. The story of Hannah's prayer and Eli's response in 1 Samuel 1 is a paradigmatic instance of this "process." She moves from depression, crying, despair, and inability to eat to a changed countenance, a transformation of the self, when the word of the priest comes as an oracle of salvation.

death of Jesus Christ. It is in the divine presence with suffering humanity that one finds a fundamental clue to the character of God's activity in
the world.

But it is not only in the word of the oracle that God acts in response
to the prayer. The petitioner often experiences a deliverance from the fear,
threat, or trouble that he or she has confronted. Thus Jacob ("greatly afraid
and distressed," Gen 32:7), prays a prayer for help on the night before he is
to meet Esau (vv. 9–12). Later, after the encounter is safely over, he builds
an altar "to the God who answered me in the day of my distress and has
been with me wherever I have gone" (35:3).

God acts to help in numerous ways. So people are healed, children are
born, the dead are resuscitated, plague destroys armies, people's lives are
preserved in the face of death, and natural events occur in ways that help
those who pray. The matter of historicity with regard to any of the accounts of the outcome of prayer is not verifiable, and some of the narratives
are obviously legends or stories that invite no questions of facticity. But
apart from questions of facticity, the modes of divine help are of varying
sorts. Some partake of the miraculous—as viewed from any perspective,
including from within the story itself (sudden appearance of fire on an altar and water from a rock or the opening of blind eyes)—while others are
natural or historical occurrences that may be understood or perceived as
miraculous precisely because they are consequent to the prayer for help
and consistent with the petition uttered by those who pray. Healing, which
may or may not be accompanied by human therapeutic activity (e.g., 2 Kgs
20:7), the birth of children, military victory, and the like can be understood as ordinary events; but they also can and are perceived as the activity
of God responding to prayers and petitions for help.[17]

Such help may be manifest in more extended ways and conjoined with
the activity of human agents, as in Eliezer's search for a wife for Isaac (Genesis 24). David's overcoming of the counsel of Ahithophel in his conflict
with Absalom is the result of prayer and a savvy subterfuge. This is reported as undertaken at the command of the Lord but is just what one
would expect from a militarily shrewd David (2 Samuel 15–17). The classic example of such a response to prayer through God's involvement in the

---

17. On one occasion when I felt, with a firm and still standing conviction, that God had
acted in response to my urgent prayer, the help that was given was not a miraculous activity
of any obvious sort, not even a matter of some kind of healing, but the moving of the heart
and will of another person. No one else would probably have thought to view the sequence
of events as God's acting and being responsive to the event and to my petition, and I may
be entirely wrong in that assessment. But it is still persuasive to me as an intelligible analysis
of what happened forty years ago. Consistent with the point made in the previous claim, the
petition was for a movement toward a more just dealing in a racial matter.

processes of history is the return of the Israelites from captivity in Babylon as a result of the edict of the Persian king Cyrus. Both Lamentations and Isaiah 40–55 are full of the prayers of the people in distress over the destruction of Jerusalem and Judah and their exile far from home. The latter text also contains oracles of salvation announcing God's presence and God's help, a presence and help that are manifest in the work of Cyrus, the Lord's "anointed" (Isa 45:1). The prophet claims that the return of Israel from exile reveals the glory of God before all flesh (40:5). The event is fully public and recorded in the historical annals of a contemporary people, accessible to examination and study; but it is also announced beforehand and effected by agents of the Lord who do not even acknowledge the Lord's rule (Cyrus and his forces).

The christological confirmation of this word that represents God's active involvement in nature and history to help those who cry out in prayer is the resurrection. As Psalm 22 functioned to connect the prayer for help with the suffering and death of Jesus, so that same psalm testifies to a response from God and an ever flowing stream of praise for the deliverance of God, the praise of the low and the mighty, of the rich and the poor, of those long dead and those not yet born. The final verses function paradigmatically for all the prayers for help and proleptically for the Christ-event when they declare:

> Posterity will serve him;
>   future generations will be told about the Lord,
> and proclaim his deliverance to a people yet unborn,
>   saying that he has done it. (Ps 22:30–31, NRSV)

5. Trust in God is a dimension of the context of prayer and also part of the transforming act.

The starting point for thinking about this claim can be the brief sentence in the Letter of James: "The prayer of faith will save the sick" (5:14). That sentence seems simplistic, especially when one is aware of many prayers for the sick that have not produced evident healing. But there is something to this simple statement, something that is not contradicted by recognition of facts in conflict with the claim of the epistle. For the sentence serves to identify the dimension of trust that works in the act of prayer and in the act of transformation. Central to the lament prayers of Scripture is a stance of faith and trust that is articulated in many ways in the prayer itself. Petitionary prayer is—despite all its complaining, all the radical questioning of the hiddenness of God, and the experience of God-forsakenness that can come boiling to the surface in the prayer—a confident act, an expectant word. The petitioner prays between fear and trust. But the prayer has a form, and part of that form is an expression of confidence and an expectation of God's response.[18]

Such trust, however, is not only what is brought to the act of prayer; it is what is taken from the response. The stance of faith and trust taken by the one who hears or receives the oracle of salvation is itself part of the transformative process. One of the classic Old Testament texts states this as follows:

> Those who wait for the LORD shall renew their strength,
>   they shall mount up with wings like eagles,
> they shall run and not be weary,
>   they shall walk and not be faint. (Isa 40:31, NRSV)

The waiting is an expectancy, a hoping, not simply a passive waiting around. It is an attitude that truly does expect to experience God's delivering help; but the expectancy itself effects a movement of transformation, signaled here in the language of "renewing" strength, an action that is like putting on a new suit of clothes. One recalls Hannah's transformed countenance on hearing the word from the priest even though nothing had happened to change her physical condition of barrenness (1 Samuel 1).

Thus the activity of God encompasses not only the work of political liberation and restoration (so the context of Isaiah 40) or making the barren fertile (so Hannah). It also incorporates the positioning of those who pray. The attitude of confidence and trust serves in some fashion to break open the situation. Even as the intercession of the prophet joins with the will of God to mercy and compassion, so the expectation of the one who prays that God will be present in power joins with that presence and power to effect a renewal that is a dimension of what God is doing in the world. The Letter to James continues in its words about praying for the sick: "the prayer of the righteous is powerful and effective" (James 5:16).

6. *The Bible speaks of God's providential activity under the rubric of blessing and knows a continual provision of the matrix of nature and history in which "the world and those therein" may exist. It also knows a veiled but real providential activity to preserve and enhance human life. The absence of prayer in the Joseph story is an important clue.*

Sustaining the world and human life within the world is what Scripture calls "blessing." It is a way of speaking of God's provision of the continuity of life, seasons of the year, cycles of the soil's production, daily food on the table, the birth of children. With reference to the deity, such provision is expressed in God's blessing. Thus the work of creation concludes with the

---

18. Cf. Walter Brueggemann, "The Formfulness of Grief," in W. Brueggemann, *The Psalms and the Life of Faith* (ed. P. D. Miller; Minneapolis: Fortress Press, 1995) 84–97.

word of blessing on the human pair that set in process a matrix of existence in which human life continues in interface with the world God made (Gen 1:28–30). At the conclusion of the story of the flood, the Lord lifts the curse on the ground and vows a blessing that seedtime and harvest, cold and heat, summer and winter, day and night shall not cease as long as the earth endures (8:21–22).[19] And the creation blessing of Genesis 1 is reiterated to the new human community that begins with Noah's sons (9:1–7).

With reference to prayer and petition, such provision for life is sought in the benediction or prayer of blessing. Preeminent here is the Aaronic benediction, which is prayed by the priests whenever the people leave the presence of God in the sanctuary as the prayer for God's blessing on every aspect of life in the days that lie ahead (Num 6:22–27). This prayer never changes, for the blessing of God is fundamentally unchanging, though it may be manifest in various ways. So also at the birth of children, at the leave-taking on a journey, at the end of life, in the ordinary give-and-take of daily affairs, and at similar kinds of regularities of human life, blessings are uttered, prayer-wishes for God's continuing beneficent care and sustenance of life, God's direction and protection against the vicissitudes of human existence.

In one of the more extended biblical narratives, the Joseph story (Genesis 37–50), there is a veiled but real providential activity to preserve and enhance human life. It is neither accidental nor insignificant that through all the trials and oppressions Joseph endures, no prayer of his is recorded in the story. While from any perspective that reads the story in relation to human experience Joseph is a victim in trouble, instead of praying for help he interprets the human situation and identifies his own suffering as part of the purpose of God. He perceives his role in the story not as oppressed sufferer but as the means of God's provision for life. He articulates this perception twice at climactic points in the story:

> God sent me before you to preserve for you a remnant on earth, and to keep alive for you many survivors. So it was not you who sent me here, but God....I will provide for you. (Gen 45:7–8a, 11a, NRSV)

> *You* intended to do harm to me; *God* intended it for good, in order to preserve a numerous people, as he is doing today. So do not fear; I will provide for you and your little ones. (Gen 50:20–21a)

---

19. This does not exclude the possibility that human acts can so undo the earth ecologically that it no longer "endures," so that the fundamental conditions for God's blessing are altered. See Rolf Rendtorff, " 'Where Were You When I Laid the Foundation of the Earth?' Creation and Salvation History," in *Canon and Theology: Overtures to an Old Testament Theology* (trans. M. Kohl; OBT; Minneapolis: Fortress Press, 1993) 112.

The relation of the two clauses in Gen 50:20 regarding the intention of the brothers and the intention of God is left mysteriously undescribed. There is no conjunction to clue the reader in on how these two things, the brothers' harm and God's good, are connected to each other. Both statements speak truthfully about reality, but how they can both be true is left unexplained. There is something profoundly mysterious about this juxtaposition that resists any explanation about God working *through* the brother's evil, or *over against* their intent to harm, or *in spite* of their evil. The brother's harm has happened; so also has God's intention for good in the same events. Joseph is not the sufferer who prays for help but the interpreter and the agent of God's provision.

7. *God's **inscrutable work** is asserted indirectly in the dialogues of the book of Job as the questions in the human cry for help are met with questions from the divine side rather than with words and deeds of deliverance. Yet such inscrutability, also echoed in Ecclesiastes, is set in the book of Job within a framework that is consistent with the rest of the biblical story.*

The dialogues of the book of Job are themselves filled with laments or prayers for help uttered by Job. They pose not simply the question of suffering, but the deeper question that is always implicit in the "Why?" of the laments. That is the question of the reality of God, or the question of the presence and power of God. In this instance, the response God makes to the laments of Job is not the oracle of salvation. It is instead a series of questions thrown back at Job asserting the creative power of God and the impossibility of a Job, one of the creatures, comprehending the work of God (Job 38–41). Their intention seems to be to declare the sharp differentiation of Creator and creature, of the divine world and the human world, to claim both the godness of God, which is not subject to rational analysis and perception (not even of the kind that is manifest in an essay such as this) and the humanity of the creature, who is part of the world God made and relates to but is beyond.[20]

Here, therefore, in the midst of the biblical story, petitionary prayer gets another kind of answer. It is an encounter with the deity and a sharp coming up against the limits of human existence and the transcendence of God. But the response to prayer here is also a response to theology in any form. For the questions of God in Job become questions back to the theologian

---

20. The use of a spatial metaphor implicit in the word *beyond* must not be literalized any more than any of the biblical language and imagery. It is, like all metaphor, a pointer. For possible ways of working theologically with the notion of "beyond" and "limit" in thinking about divine transcendence, see Kaufman, "Transcendence without Mythology," in *God the Problem*, 41–71.

who would take God into the dock and seek to discern what God is doing in the world. The book thus presses a radical critique of the theological enterprise but does it at the most vulnerable point: the prayer of the sufferer. The implications for more rational, dispassionate, even scientific inquiry, however, are not to be missed. One might set the issue propositionally: the elaboration of the biblical story's discernment of God's activity in response to prayer is to Job's encounter with the transcendence and inscrutability of God's work as the theological and scientific analysis of God's action in the world is to the humility and modesty of theology's claims to understand that action. There is a sense in which theology stands before God as both a discerning Joseph and a creaturely Job, interpreting God's work and knowing it does not know.

Yet even this unknowing voice is set finally in a context consistent with the larger thrust of the biblical story and its presentation of the prayer of the sufferer. The significant discrepancy between the prologue (Job 1–2) and epilogue (42:7–17) and the dialogues that they frame leads many readers to ignore the prologue and epilogue as harmonizing additions to straighten out the theology of the dialogues. That reading is dubious in terms of the growth of the book but even more so as a view of the interpretive significance of the framework. The framework does not so much correct and negate the dialogues as place them in the context of the more knowing story that is in the rest of Scripture. The dialogues of Job, which tell us of another kind of experience and a different kind of encounter with God than is present in much of the rest of the Old Testament, have their say. But they are not allowed to negate the picture of the compassionate and just Lord of Israel, who speaks and acts in response to prayer in ways consistent with the divine nature and helpful to the human creature. So the epilogue depicts the response of God not only to Job's laments but also to his intercession in behalf of the friends. An indissoluble bond between the epilogue and the dialogues and an unavoidable tension are created by the words of the Lord to the friends of Job who speak with him in the dialogues: "My wrath is kindled against you and against your two friends; for you have not spoken of me what is right, as my servant Job has.... I will accept his prayer not to deal with you according to your folly..." (Job 42:7b, 8b). The stance of Job in the dialogues is correct, but the God who speaks at the end is not finally lost in mystery and remains faithful to the purposes and ways that have been identified in the mainstream of the story. That tension is difficult for the human creature to maintain, but Scripture suggests we try to do so.

8. *The dominant language of prayer in the form of a cry for help that arises out of the pain of suffering and oppression, however responded to*

in the story, carries with it an implicit claim that there is a moral ground to the universe.

The goodness of creation and the goodness of God are not options in this world but fundamental assumptions. Nor must one forget that the questioning that goes on, as Job so clearly indicates, is a two-way street. When Abel's blood cries out from the ground, God asks a question of Cain: "Where is your brother Abel?" (Gen 4:9). Human oppression raises not only human questions. It evokes divine questions that are as paradigmatic as those of the prayers for help. All the questions—whether those of the psalmist, Jeremiah, Hannah, Job, an oppressed Israel, or Abel's inarticulate cry—are questions that ask for a moral accountability to the universe.

In the mythopoeic Psalm 82, all the gods of the nations are condemned to death by the Lord of Israel because of their failure to carry out justice for the weak and the poor, as well as those laws that affirm God's compassionate hearing of the widow, the orphan, and the poor. This psalm testifies unequivocally that the *reality of God* is tied to moral accountabilities and asserts that the sovereignty of God is power in behalf of justice and compassion. All the questions and challenges of the individual and community laments in the Bible arise out of this conviction. The book of Job joins in this testimony and reminds us that sometimes such moral accountability is beyond our ken even if we believe it is true. As one lament that never finds its way beyond the questions, Psalm 88 gives voice to those moments when even the affirmation is not possible.

9. *The imagery of the God who hears in heaven the cries for help and judges and decrees in the divine council is a way of distinguishing between the world in all its particularity and the God who rules and acts for the world and in the world.*

No image from Scripture is less subject to literalizing than the image of God enthroned in the heavens and surrounded by a coterie of semidivine beings who, in concert with the deity, determine and decree what happens in the universe.[21] Psalm 82 is set in such a context. Precisely because it cannot be literalized but also because of its centrality to the biblical understanding of the activity of God, the divine council has a particular

---

21. Among the more substantial treatments of this image or theme are E. Theodore Mullen Jr., *The Divine Council in Canaanite and Early Hebrew Literature* (HSM, 24; Chico, Calif.: Scholars Press, 1980); and Lowell K. Handy, *Among the Host of Heaven: The Syro-Palestinian Pantheon as Bureaucracy* (Winona Lake, Ind.: Eisenbrauns, 1994). The ancient Near Eastern background to this imagery has been worked out in various essays by Thorkild Jacobsen in *Toward the Image of Tammuz and Other Essays on Mesopotamian History and Culture* (ed. William L. Moran; Cambridge: Harvard Univ. Press, 1970); and esp. chap. 3 of his *Treasures of Darkness: A History of Mesopotamian Religion* (New Haven: Yale Univ. Press, 1976), entitled "Third Millennium Metaphors. The Gods as Rulers: The Cosmos as Polity," 75–91.

theological significance.[22] This imagery, which comes to play in various and significant ways in the biblical story and is most familiar in the form of the heavenly vision, has several functions:

a. The divine council is the locus of the rule of God. It is the principal symbolic form by which the sovereign work of God is set forth.[23] The decrees and words of God go forth from heaven, from the deliberations of the divine assembly. The imagery is from start to finish political, the primary way of depicting the divine governance of the world. Nowhere is that more clear than in the phenomenon of prophecy, the agency of divine government in ancient Israel. The prophet functions as messenger of the divine decree from the divine council.[24] There is some tendency within theology to think of the divine act as a single and momentary thing and then seek to discern how one may comprehend intelligibly the connections to events before and after in the understanding of divine governance reflected in the image of the council, such events, while often depicted as single, are tied into ongoing rule, decision, decree, and agential action. They are therefore complex, but the complexity is not confined to the nexus of an event in relation to other events.

b. The image of the heavenly court distinguishes the rule and activity of God from the nexus of nature, culture, and history without separating that activity from the world. The modes of action familiar to us, the processes we propose to account for God's involvement in the world, even the rationality that human minds bring to thinking about this, are not themselves part of God.[25] The distinctions between God and human life, between God and the world, are not distinctions that can be understood simply within the human experience of nature and culture. Whatever the modes of God's impingement upon the universe, they may not be reduced simply to things discernible within the universe. Heaven and earth are both God's creation; but they are not the same.[26] The customary picture of the three-storied uni-

---

22. On the broad-ranging significance of the imagery of the divine council, see my "Cosmology and World Order in the Old Testament: The Divine Council as Cosmic-Political Symbol," *HBT* 9 (1987) 53–78.

23. See my "Sovereignty of God," in *The Hermeneutical Quest: Essays in Honor of James Luther Mays on His Sixty-Fifth Birthday* (ed. Donald G. Miller; Allison Park, Pa.: Pickwick, 1986) 129–44.

24. See, e.g., 1 Kgs 22:19–23; Jer 23:18–22. Cf. James F. Ross, "The Prophet as Yahweh's Messenger," in *Prophecy in Israel* (ed. D. L. Petersen; IRT; Philadelphia: Fortress Press, 1987) 112–21.

25. In a study of the first eleven chapters of Genesis, I have tried to show that the distinction between the divine world and the human world is one of the central themes of that formative part of Scripture. See *Genesis 1–11: Studies in Theme and Structure* (JSOTSup 8; Sheffield: JSOT Press, 1978).

26. The connection and the separation of heaven and earth vis-à-vis God is indicated in various texts. In the dedicatory prayer for the temple, for example, Solomon prays that God

verse, dismissed by much of theology when Bultmann called attention to it, is a misreading of the text. There is a layered universe indeed, but these layers are not qualitatively the same. Heaven is the realm of God and the *fons et origo* of the divine activity, however that activity may impinge upon the world. Thus whatever analyses we may give to the divine activity, corresponding in different ways to our notions of scientific rationality, they are penultimate in their significance and truthfulness. No earthly perspective comprehends the heavenly rule.

c. The domain of the divine activity is cosmic in scope. While much of the perspective of Scripture is on the human story, the divine council assumes a cosmic and universal frame of reference. Thus the biblical understanding of the rule of God is always large. Whatever particular manifestations it may take in response to human prayer, sin, and the like cannot be separated from the divine rule encompassing the whole of the universe.

d. The complexity of the divine activity is not simply in the acting process but has its starting point in God. Michael Welker has spoken about this imagery as a "hypercomplex reality":

> If we remain within this world of political images, successful, uncontested procurement of power and loyalty is aptly expressed by the picture of the king on his throne surrounded by his court. To be sure, we have here a simple, monocentric image, oriented upon hierarchically divided, stratified societies. But this image, which one can regard as an early, elementary form of "political theology," already possesses great conceptual power. As will be shown, this image makes it possible simultaneously to think about God's singular and plural presence of power or about different manners of God's determinate and indeterminate presence. Moreover, this image makes it possible to imagine the plural presence of God's power concentrated, packed together, as it were, around God's throne.[27]

in heaven hear the prayers of the people when they pray toward "this place," that is, toward the temple. One of the primary biblical depictions of the involvement of God on earth even as God is distinguished and totally separate from earth is found in the claim that God dwells in the temple enthroned on the ark but also dwells enthroned in heaven:

> But will God indeed dwell on the earth? Even the heaven and the highest heaven cannot contain you, much less this house that I have built! Regard your servant's prayer and his plea, O LORD my God, heeding the cry and the prayer that your servant prays to you today; that your eyes may be open night and day toward this house, the place of which you said, "My name shall be there," that you may heed the prayer that your servant prays toward this place. Hear the plea of your servant and of your people Israel when they pray toward this place; O hear in heaven your dwelling place; heed and forgive. (1 Kgs 8:27-30, NRSV)

In this connection, see Michael Welker's discussion of creation as heaven and earth in *Schöpfung und Wirklichkeit* (Neukirchener Beiträge zur systemalischen Theologie 13; Neukirchen-Vluyn: Neukirchener Verlag, 1995) 56-68.

27. Michael Welker, "Angels in the Biblical Traditions: An Impressive Logic and the Imposing Problem of Their Hypercomplex Reality," *TToday* 51 (1994) 375-76. [This essay appears in German as a chapter in *Schöpfung und Wirklichkeit*, 69-88].

Thus God's acting is relational, perhaps subject less to an ontology than to a sociology or a systems analysis. It is part of a system that moves from a complex source (the divine council) to a complex reality (the world). Epistemology focuses then upon the spoken word, upon oracle, announcement, and divine instruction.[28]

Even that questioning of the divine activity best represented in the book of Job has its setting in the council (Job 1), another indication that the framework of the book cannot be ignored because of one's preference for the dialogues. With only the dialogues in view, most readers tend to see the issue of suffering and the questions about God raised by the book as anthropologically grounded, arising out of human experience. The opening chapter that indicates this issue is raised *in the divine world,* precisely where divine governance, order, and the matters of righteousness, justice, and compassion have their starting point. The theodicy question, as one discerns it in this book, is not raised from below but from above, in the context of the divine governance and the procedures by which the divine council maintains a righteous order in nature and history.

One should not close this discussion without noting that what has been said above about the complexity of God and the locus of divine governance and divine activity in the heavenly council has its analogue, if not its direct consequence, in the Christian affirmation of the Trinity.[29] The divine action in the world is manifest in varied ways and out of a divinity that is complex and manifoldly manifest. It is particularized and localized but also nonrestrained and pervasive.[30] The pairing of Son and Spirit is important precisely because the one gives concreteness, particularity, and definitive location, while the other, which is indeed the Spirit of Christ, resists definitive location even as it is manifest in particular ways. The fixity of the person is joined with the mobility, elusiveness, power, and invisibility of the spirit-wind to speak about the work of God in the world. Christology tells us of the nature and character of God's activity in the world; the Spirit opens up that activity in specific spheres of life, such as justice in the life of the nations, the sanctification of the church and its missionary impulse, and the public responsibility of leaders.[31]

---

28. See Nicholas Wolterstorff, *Divine Discourse: Philosophical Reflections on the Claim That God Speaks* (Cambridge: Cambridge Univ. Press, 1995).

29. On the trinitarian character and context of Christian prayer, see Miller, *They Cried to the Lord,* 314–21.

30. On the fixed and spatial location of the divine presence in Jesus of Nazareth, see Karl Barth, *Church Dogmatics,* II/1 (trans. T. H. L. Parker, et al.; Edinburgh: T. & T. Clark, 1957) 481–82.

31. On the work of the spirit, see esp. Michael Welker, *God the Spirit* (trans. John F. Hoffmeyer; Minneapolis: Fortress Press, 1994).

– 16 –

The Complaint Against God

Claus Westermann

(Translated by Armin Siedlecki)

The title for this volume, *God in the Fray,* focuses on unresolved theological tension in the Bible. In my study of the Old Testament I have found that this tension is particularly evident in the complaint against God, a form of speech attested throughout the entire Hebrew Bible.[1] We perceive it in the voice of the sufferers who cannot understand why their God, who had bestowed so many favors on them, has become their enemy and has abandoned and forgotten them. This voice is clearly audible in many parts of the Old Testament, and the large body of texts reflecting a complaint against God offers the most valuable clues to what is involved in this tension and inconsistency in God's actions.

The Historical Development of the Complaint Against God

The "complaint against God"[2] is one of three components that constitute the genre of lament in the Old Testament, along with the lament over personal (or communal) suffering and the complaint against the enemy. The history of this genre in biblical literature is primarily characterized by changes in the relationship of these three components to each other. Its development proceeds in three distinct phases: the early period, where it appears in narratives, the lament as a constitutive element of the Psalms (as a lament of the people or a lament of the individual), and the laments of the later, postexilic period. These three phases provide evidence for the distinctive development of the complaint against God.

---

1. Cf. my *Praise and Lament in the Psalms* (trans. K. Crim and R. N. Soulen; Atlanta: John Knox, 1981).

2. Translator's note: The term *Gott-Klage* covers a relatively broad semantic field in German, denoting a complaint against God, as well as a lament before God—or even a (legal) charge against God. Following the translation of Crim and Soulen, I render it here as "complaint against God." Nevertheless, the other nuances of this term should also be kept in mind.

The Complaint Against God in the Early Period

The three-part structure of the lament reflects an anthropological outlook in which human existence cannot be understood in isolation from the community in which it is situated, or apart from its relationship to God—using modern terminology: theology, psychology, and sociology are not yet separate domains. The language of suffering pertains to the whole human being. The lament of the early period is entirely constituted by the complaint against God, while the other two components are merely implied. It appears generally in the form of a question and always refers to a specific situation. It often poses the question "Why?" since the speaker does not understand God's actions.

> Gen 25:22 Rebekah: "If it is this way, why do I live?"[3]
>
> 27:46 "If Jacob marries . . . why should I live?"

Likewise, the lament of the mediator:

> Judg 15:18 Samson: "You have granted this great victory through me, and now, am I to die of thirst?"
>
> 6:13 Gideon: "If Yahweh is with us, why has all this happened to us?"
>
> 21:3 People: "Yahweh, God of Israel, why has such misfortune come upon Israel that today one of its tribes should be missing?"

Samson accuses Yahweh of being inconsistent, pointing out the contradiction in God's actions. The same is true in the complaints of Moses:

> Exod 5:22 LORD, why have you mistreated this people?
>
> Num 11:11 Why have you treated your servant so badly?

In the early period, human speech is still closely focused on God, as people accuse God directly, unable to understand his actions. Their discourse still lacks reflection.

The Complaint Against God in Jeremiah

> Jer 4:10 Ah Lord Yahweh, you have utterly deceived this people!
>
> 15:10–20 Seized by your hand I sat alone
> for you had filled me with anger!
> You have become to me like a deceitful brook,
> like water on which one cannot rely!
>
> 20:7–11 For the word of Yahweh has become to me
> a reproach and derision all day long!

---

3. All biblical quotations are directly adapted from the author's own translation in conjunction with the translator's reading of the MT and the NRSV.

20:14	Cursed is the day on which I was born!
20:18	Why did I come forth from my mother's womb, to see toil and sorrow, and to spend my days in disgrace!

In the complaints of the early period as well as in Jeremiah's relatively late complaints about suffering and desperation, it is particularly noteworthy that God does not give an answer and that life is portrayed as meaningless from the moment of birth (cf. Gen 15:22; Jer 22:18). The complaints question the very meaning of life, which could only have a purpose if God offered a reply. These direct questions, which accuse God of being inconsistent, resurface later in the postexilic period (cf. below, e.g., 2 Esd 8:14: "If then you should destroy with a light word what has been fashioned with such great labor, to what purpose was it made at all?").

The Complaint Against God in the Psalms

I have discussed in detail the complaint against God in the Psalms in a number of other studies. In the Psalms the lament is presented in its three constitutive components as a prayer to God. The complaint against God is more frequent and more severe in the laments of the people than in the lament of the individual, where it sometimes occurs only formulaically or is posed as a negative petition: "Do not abandon me!" But it is an essential element of the Psalms, as is particularly evident in Psalms 13 and 22. In a passionate accusation, the petitioner in Psalm 22 demands to know why God has abandoned him, why his supplications to God receive no answer. The psalm presents a poignant paradox with its contrast between the address "my God" and the subsequent charge. For the petitioner there is no one besides God, he is still his God, for he still calls out to him.

The Complaint Against God in Lamentations

The complaint against God appears particularly in those places in the Old Testament where human beings can no longer understand the suffering that has come upon them. This is as true for the suffering of the individual as for the suffering of the people as a whole. At no other time was the experience of suffering so shocking as in the collapse of the state and the destruction of Jerusalem. This is reflected in the book of Lamentations in a most stirring and poignant way. Most of its verses have God as their subject and are complaints against God. Here we find the most important statement about the work of God: God himself has brought about this collapse. The complaint against God expresses what was inconceivable as the sufferers pour out their hearts before God, always posing the same question in different ways: Why? Why? But since they confess their own guilt at the same time, the why remains within the realm of the human-divine relationship, which is explored in all five songs from different angles.

> Lam 1:1, 12c–15. This is a list of the types of suffering that Yahweh inflicted on his people: "He sent fire, he spread a net, he broke my strength." It was Yahweh who caused the military collapse and the fall of Jerusalem. Nonetheless, the list is framed by a confession of guilt: "Yahweh is just."

> Lam 2:1–9, 17, 21. The central idea is that God in his wrath has brought about the fall and has destroyed the land, the cities, the houses, and the temple; he has overthrown the country's leadership and has put an end to the temple service. God has fought against his people like an enemy would. God the helper did not help. Why? His anger has been ignited. Should it continue to burn forever?

> Lam 3:1–17. This is a complaint against God within a lament of an individual, unconnected with the other laments. Only 3:42b–45 is a complaint within a lament of the people further intensified through the use of the second person: "You have not forgiven; you have wrapped yourself in a cloud, so that no prayer could pass through. You have pursued us and killed us without pity. You have made us like filth and rubbish in the midst of the peoples."

> Lam 4:11. "Yahweh has spent his wrath, poured out the heat of his anger; kindled a fire in Zion that consumed its foundations." This statement is followed by a confession of guilt in v. 13.

> Lam 5:20, 22. "Why have you forever forgotten us, abandoned us for so long? Have you rejected us completely, are you so enraged over us?" The last question is posed in near desperation. Nevertheless, the fact that it is posed at all shows that the questioner recognizes the possibility of change in God's actions.

In Lamentations, the traditional lament over the dead becomes a complaint concerning suffering. God has wrapped himself in anger, but is nonetheless acknowledged. In their complaints, the sufferers continue to hold on to the one who has afflicted them. They continue to hope for mercy. It is highly significant that there is no attempt anywhere in Lamentations to request restoration. All that is asked for is God's return. God continues to be remembered, and the memory is kept alive in the complaints. They are placed before God in the hope that God's compassion will be aroused.

The New Testament offers a distant parallel to Lamentations when Jesus weeps over Jerusalem (Matt 23:37–38). When suffering takes on such horrific forms as in the Holocaust, the accusing question is posed to God once again. This is evident in the prayers and laments of that time, such as those preserved from the Warsaw ghetto.

The Complaint Against God in Job

The speeches of Job are all dominated by the complaint against God, which frames the dialogues (Job 4–27) with chapters 3 and 31. It is already suggested in Job's cursing of the day of his birth (Job 3), which picks up and intensifies a central theme of complaint of the early period: "If it is this way, why do I live?" Chapters 6–7 show that the complaint against God is at the very center of Job's accusation. Allusions to the struggle against chaos and demonic elements heighten the charge that God has become Job's enemy (cf. Job 9). Chapter 10 is completely governed by the question why: "Why do you reject the work of your hands?" This paradox is further developed in 10:8–17, where the praise of the Creator sounds ironically close to an accusation. In chapters 12–14 and 23–27 Job challenges God to a legal dispute. The charge concludes in 14:20: "You do violence to human beings and destroy them!" In the fourth and fifth speeches (Job 16–17, 19) the complaint against the enemy is applied to God. Chapters 29–31 mark the final accusation: God has become Job's enemy, a fiendish demon (30:18–25).

The book of Job can be read as a fugue with the complaint against God as its main theme. In face of his friends, who represent the doctrine of retribution, Job continues to hold on to God, even as he brings forth his charge against him. In desperation he turns to God with passionate accusations. The text gives expression to a desperate faithfulness in a God whom Job can no longer understand.

The Complaint of God

There are instances in which even God himself complains as one lamenting over his creation.

Isa 1:2–3   Children have I reared and raised,
            and they have rebelled against me!

Jer 8:4–7   Why is this people turning away,
            turning away continually!

In both cases the complaint is followed by a reference to domestic animals who act appropriately in contradistinction to their human counterparts.

Despite the burning anger, God's compassion for the suffering is not diminished.

Hos. 6:4   What shall I do with you, Ephraim?
           What shall I do with you, Judah?

Here the proclamation of judgment has become a sympathetic lament,[4] and God's anger and compassion stand in surprising proximity to each other. Only the most extreme boundary situations call for such an expression. The author does not intend to say anything about God himself, but speaks rather about God's relationship to his people in such extreme situations: God laments the destruction of his possession, which he has to deliver into the hands of its enemies.

Distinctive Features of the Complaint Against God

The complaint against God as a distinct form of discourse is found throughout the entire Old Testament. Its historical development is marked by numerous changes. It is based on the idea that the individual has been created as a finite being. The suffering associated with death constitutes one of humanity's limitations and is reflected in the language of lament. The complaint against God is one of three components within the genre of lament, since the divine-human relationship arises out of the human condition of being created by God. In the early period the lament is entirely a complaint against God; in the later period the complaint splits away from the form of prayer and continues alongside it. Humanity is created in such a way as to be exposed to pain and is therefore threatened by suffering. The experience of suffering finds an expression in the lament, in which human beings must be able to pour out their hearts (cf. Ps 102:1). In the complaint against God, the sufferers cling to the one who causes suffering, as God is the only one who can turn aside their suffering.

In the early prose laments, the complaint against God articulates a contradiction unintelligible to the sufferer. In Judg 15:18 Samson accuses Yahweh of being inconsistent, pointing out the contrast between Yahweh's past and present actions: "Why do you act this way now, if you have acted differently before?" The why is at the core of the complaint against God throughout the entire Old Testament. The one who laments can no longer understand God. This is true even for those whom God has enlisted for his service. "Why have you wrapped yourself in a cloud, so that no prayer can pass through to you?" (Lam 3:44). This complaint expresses the ambivalence with which the sufferers perceive God: God was like this—now he is like that. He is no longer the same God whom they used to know, who was familiar to them. They perceive a discrepancy within God.

Still, this discrepancy is not a contradiction within God's being. Those

---

4. Cf. H. W. Wolff, *Hosea* (trans. G. Stansell; Hermeneia; Philadelphia: Fortress Press, 1974) 119.

suffering are concerned with events, with a contrast in action, with Yahweh's work. They do not try to analyze the discrepancy; rather, they say how it affects them. Thus the complaints are not statements but petitions and dialogic speech. They are accusations of God, not condemnations. They are appeals in order to bring about change. This difference is of fundamental significance for Old Testament theology: there are no observations about God himself or about the nature of God contained in these accusations. Rather, the complaints must be understood within their concrete context, constituted by specific conditions of suffering and despair over God. They are not objective declarations. The complaints say nothing about the essence or character of God. It is impossible to speak about God's "character"; indeed, the notion of "character" is unique to human existence and cannot be applied to the divine. God cannot be confined to a specific category, and the complaint specifically avoids this. The complaints against God are specific appeals put forth by those who are suffering. Thus the question asked by Moses in Exod 5:22, "LORD, why have you mistreated this people?" is not a judgment of God, nor a pronouncement about the nature of God. It expresses rather that the people, afflicted by pain, cannot understand Yahweh's actions at that particular moment.

In order to understand these texts it is important to note that the individual may call out in despair, "God, why have you forsaken me?" but not once does the caller say, "so I shall forsake you too, I shall also turn away from you." The sufferers continue to cling to God, whom they no longer understand. Their despair can almost exhaust their patience: "My feet had almost stumbled" (Ps 73:2); or "Have you rejected us completely?" (Lam 5:22). But they can go no further than this; accusation never turns to condemnation.

The Protestant reformers speak about the "hidden God," *deus absconditus*. The prophecies of Deutero-Isaiah give a slightly different expression to this idea: Isa 45:15, "You are a God who hides himself," *'ēl mistattēr*. The idea that God hides himself is not based on an intrinsic quality of God; rather, it is a possibility of divine action experienced by the one who laments in his own suffering.

Considering the abundance and diversity of these texts, it is surprising that none of them attempts to explain this experience on the basis of a characteristic of God or of a change in God's being in order to rationalize human suffering. All these passages agree that the sufferers are encountering something about God which they cannot comprehend and that they have reached the limits of their own intellectual capacity. The sense of awe before the majesty of God prevents any attempt of rationalization. This sense of awe is well expressed in the parable of the miners in Job 28:20–23:

Where is wisdom found, and where is the place of understanding?
It is hidden from the eyes of all living, concealed even from the birds of the sky.
Abaddon and Death say, "We have heard a rumor of it with our ears."
God knows the way to it, and he knows its place.

There are situations in which the reasons for God's actions are not accessible to human beings, just as they are incomprehensible to the sufferers who present their grief before God and who know that their understanding is finite. In their distress, they do not attempt to explain God's unfathomable ways; they merely want God to turn toward them once again. They all agree on one point: If God has hidden himself behind a cloud, they shall not seek to penetrate this cloud.

There is yet another constituent characteristic of the complaint against God. The question "Why?" is most pronounced in the early period, where it functions as an accusation. The element of accusation then fades gradually into the background, only to return full force around the time of the great disaster (the Babylonian exile), as in the laments of Jeremiah, in the book of Lamentations, and in the drama of Job. Human beings remain fundamentally the same; in severe cases of suffering they must pour out their hearts before God. In many cases the complaints of the later period are identical to those found in earlier texts: nothing has effectively changed.

The Later Period

In the later period, the complaint breaks away from the genre of prayer. Prayers without laments exist alongside independent complaints which exhibit strong similarities to those of the early period.

> 1 Macc 2:7   Alas! Why was I born,
>   to see the ruin of my people,
>   the ruin of the holy city!

Chapter 8 of the Psalms of Solomon represents a complaint in the form of a description rather than in the form of prayer.

> 2 Bar. Apoc. 11:4   Oh Lord, how could you have tolerated this!

> 2 Esd 3:8   They did ungodly things before you,
>   but you did not hinder them.

In fact, all of 2 Esdras 3 is a complaint against God.

> 2 Esd 5:28   But now, O Lord, why have you handed over the one to
>   the many?

In contrast to this, there is no complaint in the prayer of 2 Esdras 8:20–36.

Conclusions

Israel's experience of God's silence, an experience of the people as well as of the individual, is well expressed in two great works composed in the later period, the book of Job and 2 Esdras, along with the book of Lamentations on which they draw. In all three the complaint constitutes the central core, and in all three the complaint is in contrast with the way the sufferers continue to cling to God, whom they can no longer understand. They may not have received an answer to their questions, but their merciful God continues his work, as he had done in the past. Thus the angel in 2 Esdras 4:11 responds: "But you, mortal, how could you comprehend the eternal?"

In the end one wonders why the question "Why?"—the question posed by sufferers at the moment when their pain becomes unbearable—persists from the earliest texts through the later writings without any attempt to seek an answer within the nature of God. One of the many examples may at least suggest a solution.

Ps 22:1–3 [MT 2–4]   My God, my God, why have you forsaken me?
                     Why are you far from my rescue, from the words
                           of my groaning?
                     My God, I call by day, but you do not answer,
                     by night, but I find no rest.
                     But you are holy,
                     enthroned on the praise of Israel.

The complaint against God continues, but v. 3 (MT 4) is somewhat surprising in that it appears out of context and is not easy to explain. The interjection "but" marks a contrast to the accusation; however, the expression "but you . . ." (*waw* adversative) pertaining to God is highly significant in the Old Testament. The verse is explicable only on the premise that praise and lament are interdependent forms in the Hebrew Bible. It is an example of the polar thinking so characteristic of Old Testament theology. The one could not exist without the other. Praise and lament in their reciprocal representations dominate the Psalter as a whole: one has only to think of the many psalms in which lament turns into praise. The enthronement of God on the praise of Israel, the celebration of God's majesty, continues even when the individual or the people cry out in despair and no longer understand God. Like the complaint, the praise of God is a form of action situated in time. God's holiness operates in the persistence of the interaction between God and humanity despite everything that happens.

– 17 –

Quarter Days Gone

Job 24 and the Absence of God

David J. A. Clines

From medieval times in England, there have been in the calendar four "Quarter Days": Lady Day, Midsummer, Michaelmas, and Christmas. These are the days when accounts have to be settled, days when magistrates paid their visits to outlying parts in order to determine outstanding cases and suits. There is a principle of justice enshrined in this institution: debts and unresolved conflicts must not be allowed to linger on. However complex the case, however difficult to settle the debt, a reckoning has to be made and publicly recorded; for it is one of the oldest legal principles of this country that justice delayed is injustice. Among the provisions that the barons wrested from the extortionate and unjust King John in the Magna Carta (1215 CE), a safeguard for gentry like themselves and hungry peasants alike, was the promise that "To none will we sell, or deny, or delay right or justice." These "days of assize"[1] ensure openness, assurance, and timeliness of justice—justice not sold, not denied, not delayed.

Job's complaint is that God holds no such assizes, but allows wrongs to continue unchecked and never brings offenders to book. God's failure to provide regular days for judgment has two harmful outcomes: it dismays the pious who suffer oppression, and it serves to encourage wrongdoers in their belief that they will never be called to account. As an absentee governor of the world of humans, standing aloof above the fray of human affairs, God is charged by Job with irresponsibility and cosmic mismanagement. With quarter days gone and the absence of God advertised, scoundrels can prosper and God's own fecklessness can never come to trial.

Walter Brueggemann, our most intellectually engaged Old Testament theologian, has been pondering over the tension in the Old Testament be-

---

1. The phrase used by the author here may be unfamiliar to American readers. It refers to periodic court sessions held in England (and described in this paragraph). The author uses the phrase to translate Job 24:1. Ed.

tween what he calls its "contractual theology," which views God as judge and upholder of social and ideological structures, and the "embrace of pain," which is the affirmation of the experience of those who suffer, from quotidian human ills but notably also from the absence of justice.[2] In this paper, I should like to acknowledge the fruitfulness and force of his analysis by reading Job 24 again with his bipolar vision.

But whose voice shall I use for my exposition? Is it to be that of the Job who speaks in chapters 23–24? Or is to be that of the narrator, who agrees with Job but ignores most of what he says? Or is to be that of the author, who has crafted the characters and the rhetoric of Job and of the narrator, ensuring that, despite the narrative resolution of the plot there is no ultimate resolution of the intellectual issue of the book, each of the positions proffered by the book lingering in the reader's mind? Or is it be my own readerly response? I feel I shall have to take it in turns.

Turn 1: A Present Fray, and an Absent God (Job)

Job wants a God who is master of his universe, a God who embodies fairness and justice, a God who executes exact retribution. Most of his life Job has known such a God, and he himself has been one of the living examples of the truth of the doctrine of exact retribution. For he, the godliest man of his day, fearing God and eschewing evil, has also been the wealthiest of the Easterners. But in recent days he has become, willy-nilly and by force of his circumstances, a convert to the opposite opinion. Now he has come to believe that there is no correlation between piety and prosperity, and that the God he had always seen as the upholder of justice is indifferent to his creatures, if not positively malign to the best of them, such as himself.

That at least is what he says. But what he also still believes is that this God is a rational being with a conscience, who could in principle be brought to acknowledge the error of his ways, if only it were possible to hale him to a courtroom and argue the matter out with him.

And that has been the movement of the book of Job, up to his speech in chapters 23–24. Long ago, in the bitterness of his undeserved suffering, he imagined a lawsuit with God, his tormentor, in which he could declare his innocence and have it publicly recognized (9:3–4). But along with the imagination of such a lawsuit came the realization that such a debate was futile, for, as he said, "Who can arraign him?" (9:19). If God were to ac-

---

2. Walter Brueggemann, "A Shape for Old Testament Theology, I: Structure Legitimation," *CBQ* 47 (1985) 28–46; "A Shape for Old Testament Theology, II: Embrace of Pain," *CBQ* 47 (1985) 395–415.

cede to the challenge, if he were to take the initiative in the dispute, Job knows all to well that no one could answer God once in a thousand times; "Who ever argued with him and succeeded?" (9:4). If Job himself were to take the initiative and if God were to respond to him, he could still never be sure that God was really listening to him (9:14–16). The whole idea of God being compelled into a court as if he were some human being (9:32) is nonsense.

Yet once the idea of a legal disputation has been given life by Job's words, it comes to take on a reality of its own. So in his next speech, even though he realizes that the case is a hopeless one (13:15), the desire for confrontation with God has seized hold of him: "It is to the Almighty that I would speak; it is with God that I crave to enter into dispute" (13:3). By the time of the subsequent speech, the idea has taken on yet more definite contours: here he claims that he already has a "witness" stationed in heaven—which is to say, his "cry" that is his "spokesman" in God's presence (17:19–20). In the next speech that cry has become his "champion" that will plead his cause, even if Job himself should die before his case is heard. That of course is not the way Job would like things to turn out; that scenario would be very much a second best. For what Job most desires is to confront God in person, "to see him for myself" (19:27), to gain God's personal acknowledgment of his innocence.

But nothing happens. The speech of chapter 21 makes no allusion to the idea of a lawsuit with God, and we might be tempted to imagine that Job is now content to let his heavenly champion prosecute his cause—after his death, that is to say. But not so. The moment the speech of chapters 23–24 opens, we find that Job has remained intent upon carrying his case forward. The image of the witness or champion that might prosecute his cause after his death has dropped away, and the desire, already expressed in chapter 19, for a face-to-face encounter with God has overwhelmed everything. Since God is evidently not going to make any move toward Job, Job has come to realize that if anything is to happen, it is for him to search God out, to find the way to his dwelling, to beard the lion in his lair (23:3).

The quest for personal vindication from God is, of course, not a new idea for Job. In a way, he has been set upon it ever since the four messengers arrived on that fateful day. He has been seeking God east, west, north, and south (23:8–9). But, like every other of his plans for vindication from the deity, like every other conceptualization of the conflict between reality and dogma, it is a hopeless quest. Not only can God not be found, it is pointless to bring to the bar of rational judgment a being who acts solely on whim and impulse. "Whatever he desires, he does" (23:13)—that is the key to the truth about God. This is not some cry of faith in praise of divine freedom and unfettered omnipotence; it is a bitter and hopeless conclusion that the moral governor of the universe is a giant Id, unaccountable and un-arraignable. All that can be said of him with any certainty is that whatever he has planned he will carry out (23:14), for he pleases none but himself.

There are two directions Job can now move in, and he takes them both. One, a more subjective one, is to retreat further into himself and experience again his feelings of terror and hopelessness before the mean-inglessness of the moral universe. The other, a more intellectual one, is to project his own experience upon the world of humans generally and to ask what his own experience signifies for religion and theology; to ask also whether his own experience coheres with that of other humans of his own kind.

In 23:15–17 he makes the first move, and from our experience of the dying fall in so many of Job's speeches we might well think that with the line "I am annihilated by darkness, and thick darkness covers my face" (23:17) he has relapsed into the hopelessness of his first monologue (chap. 3). But he has not, for the second half of the speech opens with a rousing challenge, "Why are days of assize not kept by the Almighty?" (24:1), and a wonderful and terrifying arraignment of the God of justice unfolds. Job is no prophet, and the kaleidoscope of images of how the poor are victimized by the powerful in society does not serve as a cry for sympathy for the poor, not even as a condemnation of the oppressors. Rather, it is the gravamen of his charge against God that not only he, Job, the in-nocent man, is suffering unjustly at the hands of an angry God, but that the weakest of humanity generally are the victims of God's refusal to bring oppressors to book.

The point of chapter 24 is that Job is not the only sufferer from God's abdication of responsibility for the world's moral governance. His theme hitherto in this speech has been the impossibility of wringing justice for himself from an inaccessible God, but now he turns to the broader truth: there are others also who desperately need justice. In his previous speech (chap. 21) he had argued from the prosperity of the wicked ("How often is the lamp of the wicked snuffed out?" v. 17) that the doctrine of retribution for wrongdoing is false. Though he does not say so explicitly, in that speech he has been effectively arguing that the prosperity of the wicked proves that God has abandoned governing the world in justice. Here in chapter 24 that conclusion is extensively illustrated by the effects of human wickedness on the poor. The wicked can dispossess others of their livelihoods with impunity; there is no retribution for them, and there is no justice for the dispossessed any more than there is for Job.

Let us be specific. What exactly is this human fray that Job so wishes God would be involved in? What is it that calls forth his opening question:

> Why are days of assize[3] not kept by the Almighty?
> Why do those who know him not see his judgment days?
>
> (24:1)

This is not a question seeking a reply, but a complaint that there is no system of regular recompense for the pious any more than for wrongdoers. "Those who know him," who recognize him and his rights, are dismayed that they never see sinners where they deserve to be—in the hands of an angry God. But what, from the perspective of Job and his like-minded friends, is the wickedness they would like to see brought to trial? In this context it is, interestingly enough, not religious indifference, not illicit worship, not personal immorality; it is exclusively social oppression, in the interests of maximizing the wealth of those already rich.

> [2] The wicked[4] remove boundary stones,
>   they carry off flocks and pasture them as their own.
> [3] They drive away the donkey of the fatherless,
>   and take the widow's bull as a pledge.
> [4] They force the needy off the road,[5]
>   and the poor of the land are utterly driven into hiding.[6]
>
> (24:2–4)

And who are the perpetrators of these crimes against the poor? Not furtive thieves, not marginal people. Burglars do not get up in the middle of the night and move a neighbor's boundary stone. Removers of landmarks believe they are within their rights in so doing, and may in fact have the law

---

3. The Hebrew term *ʿittîm* is literally "times," but in the context obviously "times for judgment" (NIV, NJPS), or "sessions of set justice" (Moffatt).

4. The Hebrew lacks an explicit subject, and the first half of the line is unusually short. It makes little difference whether we understand some such subject as "the wicked" or follow LXX, with its explicit subject *asebeis* ("the impious"), and restore *rĕšāʿîm* ("the wicked") to the text; so E. Dhorme, *A Commentary on the Book of Job* (trans. H. Knight; London: Nelson, 1967; French original, Paris: Gabalda, 1926) 354; and Gustav Hölscher, *Das Buch Hiob* (HAT I/7; 2d ed.; Tübingen: Mohr-Siebeck, 1952; original edition, 1937) 58.

5. This is probably not a general statement of how the wicked rob the needy of their rights, as in Amos 5:12, where they "turn aside" (*nṭh*; Hiphil, as here) the poor in the gate. For "in the gate," that is, at the place where justice is dispensed (or denied), is not the same as "from the road." What we have here is rather the idea that the wicked, adding insult to injury, arrogantly or violently thrust the poor off the public path, where anyone has a right to walk.

6. Why "hiding?" It is for safety's sake (as *ḥbʾ* also suggests in Job 5:21; cf. Gen 31:27 and Amos 9:3), as if to say that their very presence in society is a standing inducement to their oppressors to fasten upon them. It may also be a sign of self-effacement, as if they had internalized the scorn of their oppressors for them and had come to feel themselves unworthy members of society (like the young men who in ceremonious respect for the grandee Job "hide" [29:8; also *ḥbʾ*] from him when he takes his seat in the gate of the city).

on their side. When landmarks are moved there is at least a tacit approval by the community. In this depiction of the human fray in which Job wishes God would intervene, then, we do not meet with professional thieves or brigands who make their living from theft, for such people might do better robbing from the rich than from the poor. And they do not make off with what they have stolen, for landmarks have little resale value, and the flocks these wicked people have stolen they pasture under the noses of their victims. So they are people of the same community as the poor. They have the wealth to lend money at pledge, and they have the power and authority to remove landmarks. They must be the chieftains and ruling class—in a word, Job's kind of people.

And what are the effects of their social wickedness upon their victims?

> [5] Like onagers of the wilderness
>   they go out to their work,
>   foraging for provisions,[7]
>   and the desert yields them food for their children.
> [6] They reap in a field that is not their own,[8]
>   and glean in the vineyard of the wicked.
> [7] They pass the night naked, without clothing;
>   they have no covering against the cold.
> [8] They are drenched by the mountain rain,
>   and for lack of shelter take refuge among the rocks.
> [9] The wicked snatch the fatherless child from the breast,
>   and seize the child of the poor as a pledge.
> [10] And the poor go about naked and unclothed,
>   starving even as they carry the sheaves.
> [11] Among the olive rows of the wicked they press oil;
>   they tread the wine presses, but suffer thirst.
> [12] From the towns comes the groan of the dying,
>   and the souls of the wounded cry out for help.
>   But God charges no one with wrong.[9] (24:5–12)

---

7. It is not "prey" (RSV), as if they were themselves animals. The term *ṭrp* can be used of food for humans (Ps 111:5; Prov 31:15; Mal 3:10).

8. Reading *bĕlîlô* ("his fodder") as *bĕlî lô* ("not theirs"); so Ferdinand Hitzig, *Das Buch Hiob übersetzt und ausgelegt* (Leipzig and Heidelberg: C. F. Winter, 1874) 181, following the ancient versions; Robert Gordis, *The Book of Job: Commentary, New Translation, and Special Notes* (New York: Jewish Theological Seminary of America, 1978) 254, 265; and L. Alonso Schökel and L. Sicre Díaz, *Job, comentario teológico y literario* (Nueva Biblia Española; Madrid: Cristiandad, 1983) 349; cf. GNB, "They have to harvest fields they don't own." Compare the idioms *bĕlî-māh* ("nothingness," literally "not anything," 26:7), *bĕ'ereṣ lō' lāhem* ("in a land that is not theirs," Gen 15:13), *rîb lō'-lô* ("a dispute that is not his," Prov 26:17), and *miškānôt lō'-lô* ("dwellings that are not his," Hab 1:6).

9. Literally "God does not set wrong/folly," implying either "he does not impute wrong *to them* [the wicked]" (supplying *bām*, "to them"; cf. 4:18) or "does not set it to his heart" (supplying *'el-libbô*, "to his heart," or *'al-libbô*, "upon his heart"). Cf. NIV, "God charges no one with wrongdoing"; and Norman C. Habel, *The Book of Job: A Commentary* (OTL; Philadel-

Job's purpose here, we should notice, is not to bewail the lot of the oppressed or to urge that some action should be taken on their behalf. He is not even principally concerned to charge society at large with cruelty or their oppressors with injustice. The sufferings of the poor are not depicted for the sake of the poor but for the sake of Job's theological program: their abandonment to misery is the evidence he needs to show that God has forsaken the moral government of the universe.

Then who exactly are the poor? Here they are essentially those who have lost, along with the man of the household (for they are widows and fatherless), the possessions they once had: flocks and ass and bull and land protected by boundary stones (vv. 2–3). They are, in other words, Job himself, on a small scale; they are the recently impoverished, not the long-term poor. They have not, of course, like Job, been thrown into poverty by the raids of Sabeans and Chaldeans (1:14, 17), but through the operation of the loan system that has obliged them to put up their possessions as pledges (vv. 3, 9). Despite the privations they suffer, they are evidently working for a wage. They would not be carrying sheaves, pressing oil, and treading the winepresses if they were not earning something; and, callous as it may sound, it must be in their interest to be hard at work in agriculture and industry; otherwise, why would they be there?

It is not much of a life. Their chief priority has to lie in finding food for themselves and their families. When they "go out to their work," it is not to some creative or rewarding labor; their one concern is to seek enough food for survival. All they can find, so it is said, is the produce of the steppe, plants and roots, which are properly the food of animals. Because they have no land of their own they are forced to seek their food in the wasteland, the home of the onager—metaphorically speaking, that is. For how can those foraging for provisions in the desert be at the same time reapers in the field and gleaners in the vineyard (v. 6) and be engaged in various agricultural processes (vv. 10–11)? Obviously they cannot. What Job is telling us is that to earn a living as a farm laborer is as laborious, unrewarding, and soul-destroying as scavenging for roots in the steppe.

And where is the *wrong* in that?—not just the misery but the social evil that God should be correcting by a system of assize days? It is not primarily that people are robbed of their cattle and their land, but that they are dispossessed by members of their own community, who enjoy the regard of society and are not ostracized by them.

---

phia: Westminster, 1985) 352: "Eloah seems to consider nothing wrong." The emendation of *tiplāh* ("folly/wrongdoing") to *těpillāh* ("prayer")—as does the RSV, "yet God pays no attention to their prayer"—misses the point. It is not that God ignores the cries of the oppressed, but that he ignores the crimes of the wicked, as the headline verse (v. 1) has indicated.

In v. 9, the social injustice that God does not prevent is that of taking children as pledges. It is not so much that enslavement for debt is regarded as a social evil, nor even that children should have to work as debt slaves, but that the poor, who have no property but their children, have taken from them even that which they have.

In vv. 10–12, it is the alienation of the workers from their production, as Marx would call it, that is the social evil. Though the poor spend their days working on the land, they have no ownership of the grain, olive oil, and wine they are producing, but are starving in the midst of plenty. To some extent, this has to be rhetoric rather than social reportage, for it is hardly in the interests of any landowner to starve his laborers so that they become too weak to carry out their physical work. The real injustice is the socially approved practice of denying workers, especially farmworkers, a realistic living wage.

The real *wrong* in Job's eyes, however, is not the social evil, but God's indifference to it. The matter of his complaint could easily be turned to social critique; Isa 58:7 expresses such a prophetic challenge to the presence of the hungry and the naked in the community. But Job's point is different: he is not urging that society should change its ways but that God should change his. This is the way the world is, says Job, and the real injustice is that God does nothing about it, neither avenging the oppressed nor punishing their oppressors. The nub of the matter is that "God charges no one with wrong" (v. 12).

And the wrong is self-evident. In the following verses (vv. 13–17), Job's point is that the subjects of his critique, the wealthy landowners like himself, the pillars of his society, are no better than murderers and adulterers and thieves. Relying on social custom and law for their legitimation, they would be horrified at being classed with lawbreakers. But Job calls them fellows of those who flagrantly breach the law: they are "among" those shady characters who are "rebels against the light" (v. 13):

> [13] They are among those[10] who are rebels against the light;
> > they do not know its ways
> > and they do not frequent its paths.
> [14] The murderer rises at daybreak
> > to kill the poor and needy;[11]
> [15] The eyes of the adulterer watch for the twilight,
> > thinking, "No one will see me then";
> > and he masks his face.

---

10. Many erroneously ignore the *bet;* thus RSV, "There are those who...."

11. Why would anyone want to murder the poor and needy? It is not that the murderer leaves his bed in order to look for poor people to kill, but rather that anyone whose life is brought to an end by violence is an oppressed person, and thus one of the poor and needy.

> ¹⁴ᶜ At night the thief prowls;¹²
> ¹⁶   in the dark he breaks into houses.
>   By day they shut themselves in,
>   for they do not know the light.
> ¹⁷ To all of them, morning is the darkness of death;
>   for they make friends with the terrors of death's shadow.
>   (24:13–17)

Job's complaint against God is not that he does not call murderers and adulterers and thieves to account; he does not need to do that, for society already has its sanctions against the "light-shy" (as the German term has it). Job's criticism of God and his absence from days of assize is that he does not carry out the judgments that he alone is responsible for: determining that social injustice, even when it is according to law, is an evil, and punishing those who, because they are in power in society, can take advantage of its unjust system.

Job's experience is then a microcosm of the experience of humans caught up "in the fray" of the pain of human experience. God for his part stands above the fray, or perhaps, if the worst is to be believed, is somehow responsible for the fray, refusing to act against evil when he can and should, and even actively encouraging wrongdoers and persecuting the innocent. Any theologian, of his own day or of ours, who would advise Job to embrace the pain would get the sharp edge of his tongue. In Job's book, pain is not for embracing but for eradicating, and any God worth the name would bend his energies to that task.

Turn 2: The Old Order Is Unshaken (Narrator)

The voice of the narrator in the book of Job is singular and clear. Throughout the book it is heard from time to time, reporting at every chapter opening the participation of each of the characters in the dialogue, though

---

12. The Hebrew is literally "and at night let him be like a thief." If the colon is left in its place, at the end of v. 14, and it is still the murderer who is in view, it is banal to say that he is like a thief (as NRSV; cf. GNB, "At dawn the murderer gets up and goes out to kill the poor, and at night he steals"). So many move this colon to prefix v. 16a, making the burglar follow the adulterer; thus, e.g., Dhorme, *Job*, 363; Hölscher, *Hiob*, 60; Marvin Pope, *Job* (AB 15; 3d ed.; Garden City, N.Y.: Doubleday, 1973) 178; John E. Hartley, *The Book of Job* (NICOT; Grand Rapids: Eerdmans, 1988) 349; and both NEB and NAB. There remain difficulties, however: the jussive *yehi*, "let him be," and (if we have now moved on to the image of the thief) the *kaph* (how can a thief be *like* a thief?). Adalbert Merx, *Das Gedicht von Hiob* (Jena: Mauke [Hermann Dufft], 1871) 132, offered a simple and persuasive emendation to *yĕhallēk gannāb*, "the thief goes about/roams." His emendation is followed by Samuel Rolles Driver and George Buchanan Gray, *A Critical and Exegetical Commentary on the Book of Job* (ICC; Edinburgh: T. & T. Clark, 1921) 169; Dhorme, *Job*, 363; Hölscher, *Hiob*, 59; A. de Wilde, *Das Buch Hiob eingeleitet, übersetzt und erläutert* (OTS 22; Leiden; Brill, 1981) 258; among others. It is also adopted by the NEB and JB.

without a hint of comment or evaluation (except in the case of Elihu in chap. 33). But in prologue and epilogue that narratorial voice takes total control, bending the minds of its narratees to its conception of what the tale of Job shall be about, and of what indeed, despite the persiflage of the dialogues, it has really been about. On what the interlocutors have to say the narrator has nothing to tell, for his business lies elsewhere: it is to show what actually is the case, in all the years that stretch *ante quem* and *post quem* this little blip in the life story of the man Job. And what is actually the case, in a nutshell, is that the world is governed according to the strictest of moral laws, that the principle of retribution is unshaken by the strange case of Job's temporary misfortune. The narrator is nothing if not a exponent of the "common theology," contractual and structure legitimating.

It all began with the first *waw* consecutives of the book, in 1:2–3. There Job was said to be a perfect man "and" there were born to him the perfect family, of seven sons and three daughters, "and" his flocks—which is to say, his wealth—became enormous, "and" he became the greatest of all the sons of the East. This is no mere temporal sequence; this is the sequence of logic, of the way things ought to be. (Someone should invent a grammatical term for it, the *waw theologiae contractualis,* or the *waw retributionis.*) That is the way the narrative ends as well: the excellent man, who never sins and so never needs to be forgiven but is himself an intercessor on behalf of his erring friends (42:9–10), is rewarded for his piety. Yahweh blesses the latter end of Job more than his beginning and gives him twice as much as he had at the start (42:12, 10). The principle of retribution rules. For the narrator, there is no ambiguity about the moral order: the old order is not only unshaken by the case of Job, it is if anything reaffirmed.

So Job's misgivings with the outworking of divine governance, not to say his vituperation against God, are marginalized by the narrator. It is the outcome of the story that is the key, not Job's protestations. The only time the narrator can be said to comment on what Job has said is when he reports Yahweh's speech about Job as having "spoken of me what is right" (42:7). What that sentence can mean is very hard to say, since Yahweh can hardly be accepting Job's charges against him as malign and careless. But if Yahweh means that Job has rightly regarded him as responsible for all that happens in the world, and as rational enough to be appealed to for justice, that would fit very well with the narrator's theological position. For the narrator, nothing else that Job has said carries any lasting significance, only his adherence to the contractual theology.

One other crucial aspect to the narrator's view of Job is that throughout the book Job is under a vast illusion about his suffering. He never knows what the narrator knows, and what we readers know too: his suffering has nothing to do with the laws of retribution, but has its unique cause in a private dispute between God and the Satan. It is not because he is wicked, or deemed to be wicked, that he is suffering, but precisely because he is good and innocent and better than any other human. The reality of Job's suffering is indeed, prima facie, an argument against the doctrine of retribution, but the case is so unique that no inferences can be drawn from it. As far as the narrator is concerned, the story of Job—which is to say, his story from birth to death, not the incidental story of his suffering—is a magnificent exemplification of the contractual theology.

Turn 3: *Quod Scripsi, Scripsi* (Author)

Unlike the narrator's voice, the voice of the author is hugely ambiguous and subtle. In default of other indications, we normally suppose that the narrator represents the position of the author; the storyteller who speaks within the book is often unself-consciously identical with the author who composes the book. But it is not so with the book of Job. The author cannot possibly be one with his narrator, for example, in marginalizing the importance of the dialogues; for otherwise why would he have written them at such length and with such evident passion? Nor could the divine speeches of chapters 38–41, in which the author has invested such energy and creativity, fail to play a part in the narrator's summation of the story in chapter 42 if the narrator spoke for the author.

So what is the author up to? Or, if we would prefer not to speak of author's intentions (though the author assuredly had intentions), what is the work as a whole saying? Walter Brueggemann has already alluded to the kind of distinction I am drawing here:

> [T]he protesting posture of Job still stays with the normal presuppositions of the common theology of deed and consequence. However, the poem as such (as distinct from the character of Job in the poem) is intended to move out of those presuppositions.[13]

I am assuming that by "the poem as such" he means the book of Job as a whole, and by "intended" he means "intended by the author"—unless perhaps he is thinking anthropomorphically of the work itself having an intention. It is all the same for the present purpose. I cannot but agree that the work moves away from the presuppositions of the "common theology"— but only at the same time as it reinforces them. It wants to say (and here I too am speaking anthropomorphically) that the laws of retribution prevail, *and* that they do not always prevail, *and* that there are perspectives from

---

13. Brueggemann, "Embrace of Pain," 405.

which the laws of retribution are neither here nor there. The author and the book do not offer a resolution of the logical conflicts they create; there is no way of stating their "position" other than that they have no position. *Quod scripsi, scripsi* ("What I have written, I have written") is the only answer we can glean from the author when we inquire after his intentions.

The book's effect, when it is single-mindedly considered as the sum of its parts, can only be to engage the reader in the conversation it engenders. Deeply deconstructive, it enables the undermining of all the positions it espouses. As far as the issue of chapter 24 is concerned, the book of Job wants to persuade us that God does not hold assize days, and at the same time that of course he does, and at the same time that whether or not he does is beside the point. In a technical sense, we can allow that the conclusion of the book, which is a victory for the rule of law in the governance of the universe, overwhelms Job's complaint, "Why does the Almighty not hold days of assize?" But in terms of the effect of the book, it is Job's complaint (not just at this point but everywhere) that wins the day and lingers with the readers. Even when we have borne in upon us that Job is in the wrong in virtually everything he says—in that he is arguing from the false premise that his suffering is punishment—we still want to cheer Job on, to lend him our consent to protest at the injustices in human existence, to call God to account. If Job is refuted, by the divine speeches or by the outcome of the narrative itself, he is refuted in such a different voice that Job's savagery remains undiluted. Heinrich Heine called the book of Job "the Song of Songs of skepticism" for its seductiveness, its powerful entrancement of the reader to share its vision of the world. Who has the nerve to dispute Job's vision? *Can* God be charmed or inveigled by humans into answering their prayers—even if they are prayers for justice long delayed? *Does* God indeed rule the world, or does the evidence of oppression and misery all around us not show up the governor of the universe as feckless and unjust?

The author who wrote this book—wrote this book this way—has to be to some degree responsible (has he not?) for the effects the book has on its readers. Readers will read the book whatever way they choose, of course, and those of a difficult and deconstructive disposition will inevitably find it more ambiguous and multiplex than those who expect of it a clear solution to a plain problem. Nevertheless, it must be a rare reader who does not find Job to be the hero of the book and discover their sympathies engaged with him even beyond the rational deserts of his case; and it is also, I suggest, a rare reader who cannot be brought to admit—even if she or he did not recognize it at first—that chapter 42 represents the triumph of the retributive principle. The book as a whole leaves us with this tension between "common theology" and "the embrace of pain" unaddressed and unresolved.

Whether it is "intended to move out of" the presuppositions of the common theology, as Brueggemann puts it, is more than I can say; but it is at least intended to counterpoise those presuppositions with irreconcilable alternatives.

Turn 4: Beyond In/Above the Fray? (Reader)

Of course, whatever I surmise about the impact of the book of Job on its readers, there is only one reader I can truly speak for. And what this reader asks—when all is said and done over the matter of assize days gone, of the absence of God—is: What is it that Job really wants of God? What does he imagine happening on these famous days of assize? Why does he think that management of the universe is essentially a matter of settling accounts? Why does he seem so constrained to think in absolute and binary terms, about riches and poverty, about the righteous and the wicked, about the presence and absence of God? So long as Job is permitted to construct the discourse about God and divine rule, or about ethics, his position may seem well nigh unassailable, and certainly very engaging. But does not even the hero Job need to be read against the grain, to have his underlying assumptions questioned and even perhaps unmade?

I find three key assumptions and principles in Job's theology, and I make bold to offer my own reflections on them.

1. What Job wants, as a theologian of the "common" tendency, is to have the wicked judged and punished by God. That is the only way he knows of dealing with human wickedness. The ideas of the repentance, reform, forgiveness, understanding, or education of wrongdoers do not occur to him. This is a very sad position to find oneself in. It has to be called a moral bankruptcy if one has no resources for dealing with wrong except punishment, and it is a deep insult to any God worth the name to imagine that he has to be shut up to this petty principle of tit for tat.

2. Job draws a hard-and-fast distinction between the wicked and the righteous, according to which a person is ranged definitively in one camp or the other. This position has to be recognized as an instance of moral immaturity. It is the morality of the school playground, of the Western B movie, to divide everyone into goodies and baddies. What of the good ruler who is sometimes selfish and careless, whose neglect can amount to cruelty but whose conscience can soon be pricked? What of the bad widow, whose ill temper and self-righteousness make her a torment to family and neighbors alike, but who suffers real poverty and perpetual frustration of her hopes?

3. Job believes that the rectification of social injustice is God's responsibility. But why should he think that? By what right does he displace the

responsibility for equity and justice among humans from society to God? If there are rich and poor in a community, and if that is an injustice, to appeal to God to do something about it is to absolve humans of responsibility, of the rich to care for the functioning of the whole community that sustains their wealth and of the poor to unite in action against a system from which they are suffering. Job is very concerned about those who remove the landmarks of the widows' property, for example, but to put the problem on God's doorstep is to evade the issue. God actually has fewer resources for dealing with the problem than do humans: to be sure, he can bring the life of the landowner to an untimely end, but he cannot restructure the system of loans or institute social welfare programs or rebuild a sense of family solidarity or produce a social system in which women are not dependent on men for their livelihood and so do not need special support when their partners die. Religion becomes the opiate of the people when it is used to sidestep issues of social justice; and Job, for all the passion of his speech and the bravery of his resistance to traditional dogma, is an enemy of the people so long as he insists on making God's business everything that needs amendment in the world.

Job's complaint against God in his speech of chapters 23–24 has been twofold: that he cannot win from God a declaration of his innocence, and that God himself has given up on governing his world. I hear Job, and he evokes enormous sympathy. But if I allow myself the privilege of stepping outside the ideology of the text, I am bound to reply to him in some such terms as these.

1. However uncomfortable it is for Job in his particular society to be suffering and poor, he is on a fruitless search if he thinks that God is going to do anything about it. If his society believes that prosperity and health are signs of divine approval and certificates of moral integrity, the society is laboring under a vast illusion, and the best thing God can do is to let lots of excellent people suffer dreadfully until the dogma withers away of its own accord. Job himself had better not be "restored," for that will only mean further support for the illusion. If Job does get his health and wealth back, it will mean that God is complicit in the illusion society has wrapped itself in.

2. As for Job's second complaint, about quarter days gone and the absence of God, I reply that there are more ways of managing an enterprise than being an accountant. Job wants God to hold days of assize, days in which bills can be settled, fines can be levied, punishments meted out. This is all accounting after the event, and it is very different from managing. A good manager will be at least as concerned with developing a vision for the enterprise, a sense of identity and worth for the workers, good

personal interrelationships, and cooperative management structures. The manager whose eye is constantly on the bottom line is a monster. If Job is to be allowed in this book to construct for the world's management the discourse according to which God is going to be assessed, God will need to watch out.

The book of Job is a danger for theology, for the very questionable ideology that Job represents comes bundled with a charming, or rather, well-nigh irresistible, portrait of the character Job himself. This is where the divine speeches of chapters 38–41 become more important and less tangential than they seem. For by not responding to Job or addressing any of the issues he raises, they implicitly refuse his discourse and its terms. Though Job and the friends are at one with the narrator in affirming the "common theology," the voice from the whirlwind, which neither affirms nor denies it, is the sound of a different discourse.

According to the discourse of the whirlwind, it is not a matter of whether God is above the fray of human affairs or involved in it, it is not a matter of whether he embraces human pain and is moved by it, or of whether his dealings with his creatures are just. Such questions, so central to Job's self-understanding and well-being, so influential in the history of theological thought, are not interesting questions at all, according to the character God in the divine speeches. There *is* a universal order, which God upholds ever since he instituted it at creation; but its principles are not balance and equity and retribution and equivalence. Its principles are more strategic than that. It majors on intimacy, on sustenance, on variety.

In this discourse, God knows his universe intimately. He knows how broad the earth is (38:18), the directions to the dwellings of light and darkness (38:19), the system of the stars (38:33), the birth cycle of mountain goats (39:1–3). He implants migratory instincts into birds (39:26) and maternal fecklessness into ostriches (39:16–17). This God is very wise, and he has a lot on his mind. He loves the detail, and even when he is talking big picture, he only ever works with examples.

In this discourse, sustenance and nurture are key objectives of the universal order. Whether it is the physical universe or the animal world, the divine intimacy is directed to sustaining life. Creation is not just a past event for this worldview; every day the morning has to be remade by its creator, calling up the dawn, grasping the fringes of the earth, shaking the Dog Star from its place, bringing up the horizon in relief as clay under a seal till everything stands out like folds in a cloak and the light of the Dog Star is dimmed as the stars of the Navigator's line go out one by one (38:12–15, NEB, adapted). In this worldview, the God of all the earth is counting the months of each wild animal mother's pregnancy (39:2), imbuing wild horses with their strength (39:19), training hawks in flight (39:26), providing fresh meat for the young of eagles in their rocky fast-nesses (39:27–30) and for young lions in their lairs (38:39–40), directing the raven to its quarry when its fledglings croak for lack of food (38:41, NEB, adapted).

In this discourse, the world is other and hugely various. It lives for it-self, and if anything is instrumental, if anything serves a purpose other than itself, that is coincidental. The purposes of the universal structure are infinitely multiple, each of its elements with its own quiddity and its own mission—whether it is the sea, the clouds, light, darkness, rain, stars, mountain goat, ostrich, warhorse, or eagle. Like Gerard Manley Hop-kins's "Pied Beauty," this vision evokes "Glory to God for dappled things / For skies of couple-colour as a brindled cow.... Landscape plotted and pieced—fold, fallow, and plough; / And all trades, their gear and tackle and trim."

Where is the space in such a discourse for distinctions like "above"/"in"? Or binary oppositions like "fixity"/"flexibility" or "rule"/"freedom" or even "contractual theology"/"embrace of pain"? The fact is, this is a discourse without abstracts, without oppositions, without propositions, without generalizations. It works with images and maximizes impact and affect. It has little time for clarity or logic. It is not the language of the *Summa* or the *Institutes,* or even of Deuteronomy or the Joban dialogues.

There is nothing about humans in the divine speeches, of course, nothing about ethics or justice or days of assize. That is talk for accountants; God's task is to be CEO of the global enterprise. The divine speeches are his mis-sion statement, his vision, the corporate thinking. The human is only one division of the global economy, and its specific problems cannot be given top priority. Let Job adopt the CEO's vision, learn a new discourse, and his problems will resolve themselves. Says Job thereupon, "I recognize that you are Manager of the Totality [*kol tûkāl*], and that none of your strate-gies will lack implementation [*lō'-yibbāṣēr mimměkā mězimmāh*]. I had not been trained in the appropriate discourse ['*ēṣāh bělî dā'at*], and spoke be-yond my competence [*niplā'ôt mimmennî*]. Now that I have been apprised of your vision ['*ênî rā'ātěkā*], I am internalizing it ['*em'as;* from *m's* as a byform of *mss,* 'melt'], and I feel more integrated into the company ethos [*niḥamtî*], though still awaiting reinstatement after my present low-ranking situation ['*al-'āpār wā'ēper*]" (42:2–6).

That is no solution to the problem of social injustice, of course. While the voice from the whirlwind does not actually say, "Don't bother me with the accounting," it plainly refuses to take responsibility for the issue that is vexing Job. And that—though Job does not know it, nor yet the author of the book—is probably how it is best dealt with. The suffering of the poor is a human problem, created by humans and soluble, if it is soluble at all, by humans. To collapse the social problem into a theological one, to make it God's problem, is, however traditional a theological move it may be, an abdication of responsibility. Divine days of assize should not be handling the business of tribunals of human rights and duties.

– 18 –

"What Are Human Beings, That You Make So Much of Them?"

Divine Disclosure from the Whirlwind: "Look at Behemoth"

Samuel E. Balentine

In his search for a new shape for Old Testament theology, Walter Brueggemann has argued that serious attention must be given to Israel's restless practice of lament, for herein lies "a fresh hunch" about God. In his words, "The hunch is that this God does not want to be an unchallenged structure, but one who can be frontally addressed."[1] A central thesis in Brueggemann's proposal is that lament forces both God and Israel to recalculate the possibilities and the requirements of covenant relationship. It draws God into the fray of human pain and trouble, and as a result God must *do* or *be* something new. In the process Israel learns that obedience is more than "docile submissiveness" it is also "bold protest."[2]

As evidence of Israel's courage and persistence in lament, Brueggemann points specifically to a "countertradition" of approaching God that is represented by Moses, the lament psalms, Jeremiah, and Job.[3] What is most striking about these examples is that in the case of Job, the practice of lament seems to have failed. Here, the single most sustained and harsh lamentation in the Hebrew Bible is coupled to a divine response from the whirlwind that is conventionally interpreted as an unequivocal rebuke of Job. Job dares to address God frontally, so this line of interpretation goes, and he pays a heavy price for his recklessness. With the force of hurricane-

---

1. W. Brueggemann, "A Shape for Old Testament Theology, II: Embrace of Pain," *CBQ* 47 (1985) 401.
2. Ibid.
3. Ibid., 402–6.

like winds, God denies Job's approach and drives him into silence and submission.[4]

With this essay I wish to express my deep appreciation for Brueggemann's passionate insistence that Israel's lament traditions be accorded their rightful place in the theology of the Old Testament. As one small witness to the influence of Brueggemann's own daring and imaginative reconstrual of Israel's faith traditions, I propose here to reconsider the revelation that Job receives from the whirlwind. I suggest that God's speech may be interpreted not as a rebuke or a denial of Job, but rather as a radical summons to a new understanding of what it means for humankind to be created in the image of God. In this view, it is not silence and submission that God requires; it is steadfast lament and relentless opposition to injustice and innocent suffering, wherever it appears. In this view of the divine speeches, God regards Job not as an aberration within the created order that is to be corrected or eliminated. He is rather a supreme model for humankind that God is committed to nurture and sustain. /

The emergence of this model in Job may be traced through three stages: (1) the debate within the dialogues about what it means, in Job's world, to be created in the image of God; (2) the importance of the revelation concerning Behemoth and Leviathan in addressing this debate; and (3) Job's final response to God's revelation.

Primordial Questions: "What Are Human Beings, That You Make So Much of Them?"

The prologue to the book of Job envisions "the land of Uz" as the setting for a drama that returns imaginatively to the beginnings of creation.[5] Job's

---

4. Brueggemann does not offer extended discussion of the divine speeches in Job in his programmatic essay for Old Testament theology, but his proposal suggests some sympathy with the conventional understanding noted above. He observes, for example, that while Israel's laments had the power to evoke from God a new posture of relationship, they did not always do so. On some occasions, as in Job, the lament is "rejected" or "disregarded" (Brueggemann, "Embrace of Pain," 404, 405).

5. A number of verbal and thematic parallels sustain the connection between Job 1–2 and Genesis 1–3, of which the following may be singled out. (1) "The land of Uz" orients the story towards the east (cf. Job 1:3), the putative locus for the Garden of Eden (Gen 2:8), thus marking the location where humankind was first prepared for the revelation of God's cosmic design. (2) As the hero of the story, Job is portrayed as a second Adam. His full family and his contingent of servants and possessions (Job 1:2–3) suggest his exemplary fulfillment of the creational commission to "be fruitful and multiply" and to have "dominion" over the created order (Gen 1:28). (3) The story of Job 1–2 is enacted through six scenes alternately set in heaven and earth (1:1–5; 1:6–12; 1:13–22; 2:1–7a; 2:7b–10; 2:11–13). A seventh scene is introduced with Job's curse (Job 3), which serves as the preface to the poetic dialogues. The structuring of this grand drama in seven scenes recalls the heptadic patterning of the creation story in Genesis 1. On these and other connections see S. Meir, "Job I–II: A Reflection

world is idyllic, a perfect recapitulation of primordial Eden. Everything is in place for life that is in complete harmony with God's cosmic design. But then Job's paradise is shattered, and his story of what it means to live in accordance with God's design for creation takes a radical turn. The loss of his wealth and his possessions, the unjust death of his children, and the affliction of horrible physical suffering suggest that the forces of the cosmos, heaven and earth, have been unleashed against this servant of God.[6] Still more unsettling is the report that Job's world has been undone "for no reason" (2:3: *ḥinnām;* cf. 1:9), other than that God has been "provoked" (*swt*) by the satan.

How will Job respond to *this* world of brokenness and loss, where the harmony of creation's design yields to unexpected and unwarranted assault? The prologue wants to insist that Job blesses (*brk*), not curses, God (1:21). But as commentators have noted, the semantics of blessing in Job are unclear. Despite all efforts to resolve the ambiguity, the reader is left with no certain criteria for deciding whether Job blesses or curses God, or offers some other response that moves between these two poles.[7]

The ambiguity of Job's response to God in the prologue is suspended once the poetic dialogues begin. After seven days of quiet suffering in this now afflicted world, Job breaks the silence of pain with words of curse, not blessing (3:1–10), words of lament, not praise (3:11–26). With a series of seven curses against the day (vv. 3a, 4–5) and the night (vv. 6–9) Job speaks a "countercosmic incantation" that parodies the language of Genesis 1.[8] He calls in effect for a negation of creation and a reversal of its orders. The lament in vv. 11–26 tracks Job's steady deterioration, through the repetition of the question "Why?" (vv. 11, 12, 20), into a bitterness of soul marked by rage and agony (v. 26: *rōgez*). These opening words signal that suffering like Job's calls the whole of creation into question and with

---

of Genesis I–III," *VT* 39 (1989) 183–93. On creation imagery generally in Job, see L. G. Perdue, *Wisdom in Revolt: Metaphorical Theology in the Book of Job* (JSOTSup 112; Sheffield: Almond Press, 1991); idem, *Wisdom and Creation: The Theology of Wisdom Literature* (Nashville: Abingdon, 1994) 123–92.

6. In Job 1:13–22 the agents of the calamities that befall Job are described as alternately from earth and heaven (vv. 13–15: Sabeans; v. 16: "fire of God"; v. 17: Babylonians; vv. 18–19: a "great wind" (*rûaḥ gĕdôlāh;* cf. Gen 1:2).

7. The uncertainty derives from the fact that in the prologue the word *bārak* seems to convey its normal meaning "bless" in 1:10, 21, but in 1:5, 11, and 2:5, 9 it seems to have an opposite meaning, "curse, blaspheme." Cf. T. Linafelt, "The Undecidability of ברך in the Prologue to Job and Beyond," *BI* 4 (1996) 154–72.

8. Note esp. the work of L. G. Perdue, "Job's Assault on Creation," *HAR* 10 (1987) 295–315; "Metaphorical Theology in the Book of Job: Theological Anthropology in the First Cycle of Job's Speeches (Job 3; 6–7; 9–10)," in *The Book of Job* (ed. W. A. M. Beuken; Leuven: Univ. Press, 1994) 142–48; *Wisdom in Revolt,* 91–110; *Wisdom and Creation,* 131–37. On the countercosmic incantation see M. Fishbane, "Jeremiah IV 23–26 and Job III 3–13: A Recovered Use of the Creation Pattern," *VT* 21 (1971) 153.

it the Creator who is responsible for its design. Job's questions will reverberate throughout the rest of the dialogues and will set the agenda for the friends' responses. Whatever answers are proposed, Job will insist that they must have meaning not only in the paradisiacal world of Eden/Uz, but also in the world of innocent sufferers who sit among the ashes.

The ensuing dialogues address a variety of issues and questions, but for the purpose of this essay, none is more important than the primordial question about what it means—in Job's world—for humanity to be created in the image of God. The exploration of this question begins in Job 7:17–21, where Job's critical scrutiny of a traditional vision of humankind subverts praise into a doxology of sarcasm.[9]

The model for Job's doxology is Ps 8:3–5 (MT 4–6).[10] For the psalmist the hierarchy of the created order, which exalts humankind as a near equal to God (as in Genesis 1), witnesses to God's wondrous attention and beneficence. In God's design mere humans are elevated to royal status and given dominion and responsibility for God's creation. In the world of the psalmist such a design is occasion for astonished praise: "What are frail mortals ['ĕnôš], that you should be mindful of them, human beings, that you should take notice of them?" In the world of Job, however, these words are laden with vexed ambiguity. They evoke astonishment, but not praise: "What *are* human beings ['ĕnôš]?" that God should expend such effort to "examine" (*pqd*) them and "test" (*bḥn*) them so relentlessly (Job 7:18). Job's perspective from the ashes indicates that the status of the human being before God is that of a powerless victim, not a royal steward. Through the lens of innocent suffering he concludes that humans are creatures targeted for destruction, not for special care and exaltation.

It is the nature of the dialogues that virtually no assertion or reflection goes unchallenged. Job's critique of the theology of Psalm 8 is no exception. Of the friends, it is Eliphaz who repeatedly takes up the question of what it means to be a human being before God (cf. Job 4:17–19; 15:7–16; 22:1–11). Especially pertinent is the speech in 15:7–16 in which Eliphaz responds to Job specifically by returning to the psalmist's question, this time with a

---

9. Cf. Perdue (*Wisdom in Revolt*, 153–56), who describes Job's speech in 13:13–25 as a "doxology of terror." In this speech Perdue observes that hymnic praise is subverted into a doxology to God's destructive power.

10. On the rhetorical links and differences between Job 7 and Psalm 8, see esp. M. Fishbane, *Biblical Interpretation in Ancient Israel* (Oxford: Clarendon, 1985) 285–86; idem, "The Book of Job and Inner-biblical Discourse," in *The Voice from the Whirlwind: Interpreting the Book of Job* (ed. L. G. Perdue and W. C. Gilpin; Nashville: Abingdon, 1992) 87–90; P. E. Dion, "Formulaic Language in the Book of Job: International Background and Ironical Distortions," *SR* 16 (1987) 187–93.

strategic shift of focus: "What are mortals [*ĕnôš*], that they can be clean [*yizkeh*]?" (v. 14).[11]

On the surface the argument by Eliphaz is a simple one: human beings are sinful. They cannot claim to approach God in innocence, as Job repeatedly insists he is doing (9:15, 20–21; 10:15; 12:4), because they are inevitably flawed and imperfect reflections of the Creator (cf. 4:17–21). To insist otherwise is a foolish and risky breach of the boundary established by God between the divine and the human. Eliphaz warns Job that he stands on the verge of violating this boundary by invoking an old creation tradition about "the firstborn [*ri'yšôn*] of the human race" (15:7).[12] Does Job dare to imagine that he was present at creation, privileged by birth and by status to participate in the decisions of the divine council (v. 8)?

It is interesting, however, that as part of the argument against Job's misplaced hubris, Eliphaz challenges him with a question: "Were you brought forth before the hills?" (v. 7). The question is a quotation of Prov 8:25, where it is used with reference to the origins and vocation of personified Wisdom.[13] The context for the verse is Prov 8:22–31, a hymn in which Wisdom exults in being the "first" (v. 22: *rē'šît*) of God's creative acts. The hymn carries no suggestion of hubris, no indication that primal Wisdom should be regarded as a figure for rebuke or condemnation. Instead, Wisdom celebrates its role as the firstborn child who works as a cocreator beside Yhwh, the divine parent and master architect of the cosmos (vv. 27–29). Indeed, the parent Creator and the begotten cocreator are intimately linked by their mutual delight in one another (vv. 30–31). Joyfully partnered with God in the work of creation, Wisdom invites all who will to take up the life it models: "happy are those who keep my ways.... For whoever finds me finds life" (vv. 32, 33).

Eliphaz clearly intends his question about the "firstborn" to be a rebuke of Job for misunderstanding his proper place in the hierarchy of creation. But in the tradition from which he draws in order to challenge

---

11. Cf. Fishbane, "Book of Job and Inner-biblical Discourse," 93.

12. Rooted in ancient Near Eastern mythology, the figure of "the primal human" was used to speak of the origins of kingship. The assumption of the myth is that the king, as the first human created by the gods, was present at creation and participated in the divine decisions that ordered the cosmos. In biblical texts some vestige of the myth may be detected in Genesis 3–11 and in Ezekiel 28, where it takes on a negative connotation in association with the temptation of humans to rebel against divine rule and to arrogate to themselves divine authority and wisdom. On the significance of this myth for Job, see esp. Perdue, *Wisdom in Revolt*, 165–70.

13. The myth about the primal human is no doubt older than both Proverbs and Job. On the question of the relative datings of Proverbs and Job, a good case can be made that the direction of literary dependence is from the former to the latter; cf. D. J. A. Clines, *Job 1–20* (WBC 17; Dallas: Word, 1989) 350.

Job, there is a latent ambiguity. Is it *misguided hubris* or *radical faith* to believe that human beings are created in the image of God and are thereby specially prepared for delightful communion and shared partnership with the deity? Eliphaz asserts the former, but the evidence he cites ironically invites consideration of the latter. Between Eliphaz and Job, therefore, the debate about the theology of Psalm 8 produces no clear affirmation. The primordial question of human identity and vocation remains contested and unresolved.

In the broken world of Job, where innocent suffering calls every faith assertion into question, what are human beings to be and to do? The question is addressed by other speakers in a variety of ways throughout the dialogues, but without resolution, and the drama therefore reaches an important juncture with the divine speeches in Job 38–41. It is highly suggestive, I believe, that the exploration of Psalm 8 and of the image of the firstborn that has so concerned Job and Eliphaz reappears in God's speech about Behemoth and Leviathan.

Divine Disclosure: "Look at Behemoth"

The whirlwind speeches provide God's "answer" to Job; but as Carol Newsom has aptly observed, they are fraught with "irreducible ambiguities" that invite and perhaps require more than one interpretation.[14] In what follows I do not pretend or necessarily desire to resolve these ambiguities. I do wish to suggest, however, that certain clues in the text invite new ways of thinking about how this theophany, in both form and substance, serves to unite God and Job in perhaps the most daring and revealing exploration of what it means to be created "in the image of God" that is found in the Hebrew Bible.[15] Four discernments inform my own "fresh hunches" about what God is revealing to Job.

---

14. C. Newsom, "The Book of Job," in *NIB* (Nashville: Abingdon, 1996) 4:595. Newsom observes, rightly in my judgment, that the polyvalence of the divine speeches is more than a problem to be resolved. It is an invitation to each reader to wrestle imaginatively with the meaning of divine disclosure. "The elusiveness of the divine speeches requires the reader to assume a more active role in making meaning than does a text in which the 'message' is simple and transparent" (596).

15. Interpretive efforts often emphasize the apparent incongruity between the *medium* for the divine response, theophany, and the *message* that the theophany conveys. Theophanies mark a special revelation that brings God into more intimate relationship with human beings than is ordinarily evident or possible. Yet God's appearance to Job seems designed to rebuke him and to deny his search for intimacy with the one he would embrace. See, e.g., J. L. Crenshaw ("When Form and Content Clash: The Theology of Job 38:1–40:5," in *Creation in the Biblical Traditions* [ed. J. J. Collins and R. J. Clifford; CBQMS 24; Washington: Catholic Biblical Association of America, 1993], 70–84): "If anything, the portrayal of deity in the speeches increases the distance between human beings and their maker. This distancing takes place, paradoxically, despite a literary form that emphasizes incredible closeness. Here form

(1.) Both the structure and the content of Job 38–41 recall the heptadic vision of creation presented in Genesis 1. At the outset, therefore, the reader may know that the divine speeches will return the Joban drama to the prologue and to the primordial questions that have been raised in the land of Eden/Uz. God's "answer" begins with a vision of the cosmic boundaries of creation (38:4–18: earth, sea, heaven, underworld), followed by six strophes describing the meteorological phenomena that are assigned places within creation's domain (38:19–38).[16] A seventh component in this vision is the discourse on the animal world, comprising initially five groups of paired animals (38:39–39:30) and subsequently, after Job's initial response, one additional pair that receives special attention: Behemoth (40:15–24) and Leviathan (41:1–34 [MT 40:25–41:26]).

This review of creation's design—boundaries, objects, and animals— corresponds in part to the sequence in Genesis 1. There is, of course, one often noted exception: the creation of human beings is not presented.[17] This omission is typically interpreted as a strategic subversion of the assumption that humanity occupies a special place of importance in creation's design.[18] Without discounting this view altogether, I suggest that the text also invites consideration of other perspectives. One may understand that Job is a special creature who is *addressed* by God and not simply one of many creatures who can be *listed* in the divine catalog.[19] Further, within the sequence of the speeches Behemoth and Leviathan, the sixth and last pair of creatures, recall the creation of humankind on the sixth day as the crown of God's cosmic design. Perhaps God not only addresses humanity, through Job, but also provides a particular model for humanity, in Behemoth and Leviathan, of what it means to occupy this privileged position within creation.

2. God's review of creation's design serves primarily to confront and challenge Job, not to condemn or silence him. A number of clues buttress this observation. Job is challenged to gird up his loins like a *geber* (38:3;

---

and content clash, with the latter gaining supremacy. Must 'the greater glory of God' always require a belittling of human beings?" (84).

16. Creation imagery in Job 38–41 is commonly recognized. For this particular literary analysis, see esp. Perdue, *Wisdom in Revolt*, 204–12; idem, *Wisdom and Creation*, 168–72.

17. On the differences between creation's design in Job and in other traditions see R. Albertz, *Weltschöpfung und Menschenschöpfung: Untersucht bei Deuterojesaja, Hiob und die Psalmen* (Calwer theologische Monographien 3; Stuttgart: Calwer, 1974) 140–46.

18. E.g., R. Gordis, *The Book of God and Man* (Chicago: Univ. of Chicago Press, 1965) 118. The comment of J. L. Crenshaw states the position clearly: "The absence of any reference to humans in the entire speech is calculated to teach Job the valuable lesson that the universe can survive without him" (*Old Testament Wisdom: An Introduction* [Atlanta: John Knox, 1981] 110).

19. Cf. J. G. Janzen, *Job* (Interpretation; Atlanta: John Knox, 1985) 229.

40:7), that is, like a "mighty man" or "warrior" who is preparing for combat. It is often assumed that the image is used negatively with reference to Job, that God either mocks him as a "pretend warrior" or summons him to a battle in which he will certainly be defeated.[20] But the image may just as well be understood positively, as a summons to make the right preparation for a valiant encounter that God intends and desires (cf. Jer 1:17).[21]

Further, V. Kubina has shown that there is a form-critical connection between the interrogatory style of the divine speeches and prophetic trial speeches. She calls particular attention to trial speeches in Second Isaiah, which function to challenge false understandings about God.[22] It is worth noting that the function of such speeches in Second Isaiah is not only to counter misunderstandings of God, but also to summon forth fresh articulations of faith from weary and despairing exiles.[23] Such parallels suggest that God also questions Job not only to correct him but also to elicit affirmations that may generate new possibilities in the midst of a broken world.

It is not only the manner in which Job is addressed or the form of his divine interrogation that indicates he is being summoned for a positive encounter with God. The very substance of the created order teaches Job that God designs creation not to silence and subdue all opposition, but to protect it and nurture it as a proper and necessary component in God's master plan. In his opening curse, Job looked inward and found inexplicable suffering to be the unbearable center of his world. In Job 38 God counters with a panoramic vision that affirms creation is teeming with life and vitality.[24] Some of these life forces, like the animals described in 38:39–39:30, are wild and undomesticated. Outside their designated boundaries they may be harmful to human life. Yet God provides for them (38:39–41) and sustains them in their wild, potentially threatening freedom (39:5–12). Other life forces, by God's design, fulfill their appointed

---

20. E.g., S. Terrien, "The Yahweh Speeches and Job's Response," *Review and Expositor* 58 (1971) 507.

21. Cf. Janzen, *Job*, 232–33.

22. V. Kubina, *Die Gottesreden im Buche Hiob* (Freiburger theologische Studien 115; Freiburg: Herder, 1979) 131–43. See further H. Rowold, "Yahweh's Challenge to Rival: The Form and Function of the Yahweh-Speech in Job 38–39," *CBQ* 47 (1985) 207–9.

23. In the opening disputation of Isa 40:12–31, for example, a series of rhetorical questions resembling those in Job 38–41 climaxes with a ringing affirmation of the Creator's promised empowerment of the weak and the helpless (see esp. vv. 27–31). Such connections between Second Isaiah and Job are often noted. See, e.g., P. D. Hanson, *Isaiah 40–66* (Interpretation; Louisville: Westminster/John Knox, 1995) 26–32.

24. R. Alter has convincingly argued that God's speech in Job 38 constitutes "a brilliantly pointed reversal, in structure, image, and theme," of Job's opening curse. In his view, God's poetry, that is, God's "imagination of the world," transcends the limitations of creaturely modes of perception (*The Art of Biblical Poetry* [New York: Basic Books, 1985] 96–110).

roles by aggressively challenging the boundaries God imposes on them. The "proud waves" of the sea (*yām*), traditional symbols of primordial chaos, constantly threaten destruction. Yet God attends them with parental care, wrapping them in "swaddling bands" that both restrain and protect them (38:8–11).[25] Through this review of creation, Job is invited to understand that God intends not to eliminate or banish forces of opposition and challenge but to preserve and direct them, because they are vital elements in the architecture of life.

God's initial review of creation's design ends with a challenge to Job (40:2).[26] S. Mitchell has captured the sense of the divine query nicely: "Has God's accuser resigned? Has my critic swallowed his tongue?"[27] Job's initial response in 40:3–5 seems to answer with an unqualified yes. He places his hand over his mouth in an act of deference that may indicate either contempt or shame.[28] In either case he responds with silence, not with a fresh articulation of faith. Some commentators take Job's silence to be the pathetic but normative response that God intends from those who risk confronting the Creator of the world as Job has done.[29] But with the initiation of the second speech from God, both Job and his readers learn that God desires not silence but something more.

3. God's design for humankind's role in creation attains clarity when viewed through the lens of Psalm 8. Once more God summons Job to prepare as a *geber* for an encounter with divinity (Job 40:7). The subject of this second encounter is the "governance" (40:8: *mišpāṭ*) of the world that

---

25. Note further that the verb in Job 38:8a, usually translated "shut in" (e.g., NRSV, NIV, NAB), is *swk*, literally "hedged in." The same verb occurs in Job 1:10 and 3:23. In the prologue the reference is to God's protective hedging in of Job against the afflictions that may beset life. In chap. 3 the reference comes in the form of Job's complaint that God has hedged him in in negative ways that obstruct his discernment of life's meaning. The ambivalence in the imagery conveyed by these occurrences of the term echoes in Job 38. As Alter observes, "What results is a virtual oxymoron, expressing a paradoxical feeling that God's creation involves a necessary holding in check of destructive forces and a sustaining of those same forces because they are also forces of life" (ibid., 100).

26. In a most discerning way Janzen has called attention to the parallels between the divine response to Job and that given to Jeremiah in Jer 12:5. Of the latter he suggests that "The point of this divine response is not to put the prophet down with an impossible question, but to express surprise over the quickness with which the prophet succumbs to discouragement and disillusionment and to challenge the prophet to a deeper loyalty and vocational endurance" (*Job*, 242). With Janzen, I suggest that God's question to Job represents a similar challenge to struggle on toward greater vocational clarity.

27. S. Mitchell, *The Book of Job* (New York: HarperCollins, 1992) 84.

28. On Job's gesture as an image of shame, see C. Muenchow, "Dust and Ashes in Job 42:6," *JBL* 108 (1989) 608.

29. See, e.g., the conclusion of J. T. Wilcox: "if we assume, as I do, that the theophany is normative, then we must conclude that the book as whole is profoundly skeptical, agnostic; its message is largely a counsel of silence" (*The Bitterness of Job: A Philosophical Reading* [Ann Arbor: Univ. of Michigan Press, 1994] 122).

God has designed.[30] Divine governance is signified through images of power
(v. 9: the "arm" [*zĕrôaʿ*] and the "voice" [*qôl*]) and glory (v. 10: "glory
and splendor" [*hôd wĕhādār*]). These images are usually understood to
convey God's rebuke or denial of Job's presumptuous criticisms of divine
governance. According to this interpretation, God's rule is undergirded by
sovereign power and majesty that cannot be equalled by Job. Hence Job's
charge that God has denied his justice (19:7) and perverted the process
through which his justice can be sought (9:32) is more than mere ignorance.
It is an impertinent assault on the very nature and character of God.

Although the element of rebuke may be present in Job 40:7–14, there
are hints that this is not God's only purpose in addressing Job. The divine
challenge is couched in terms that invite Job to offer more than a simple
concession that God alone has responsibility for the governance of the cosmos. A clue is found in the expression "glory and splendor" (v. 10). The
phrase *hôd wĕhādār* is used in the Hebrew Bible primarily, but not exclusively, with reference to God. Four of the six occurrences are ascriptions
of praise offered to God (Pss 96:6 [par. 1 Chr 16:27]; 104:1; 111:3), but
two are used with reference to human beings. In Ps 21:6 (cf. Ps 45:3 [MT
4]) the phrase describes the blessings that God peculiarly bestows upon the
king. In Job 40:10 God summons Job, like a king, to put on the regalia of
"glory and splendor."[31] The recognition that the endowment with "glory
and splendor" is shared in Hebrew Scripture, albeit unequally, by a triad of
persons—God, king, and Job—invites one to consider that God is not simply rebuking Job for arrogating to himself that which he can never attain.
Instead, God may be understood as summoning Job to a royal responsibility
that represents the apex of his vocational calling to image God.[32]

God's speech invites Job to consider his royal responsibilities for governance by subtly calling once more for further exploration of the vision
of humankind that is affirmed in Psalm 8. In Job 7:17–21 Job reflected
on the psalmist's question "What are human beings?" and proceeded to
move outside the affirmations of the psalm to construct an answer from
his own experience that envisioned the human creature as little more than
a target for divine destruction. Eliphaz returned to the psalmist's question
(Job 15:7–16), but in response to Job he too moved outside the psalm's as-

---

30. On the dual connotations of *mišpāṭ* as both a forensic act, i.e. "judging," and an ad-
ministrative procedure, i.e. "governance," see S. Scholnick, "The Meaning of *Mišpāṭ* in the
Book of Job," *JBL* 101 (1982) 522–23.

31. On the royal imagery that is used with reference to Job in 40:10–13, see Janzen, *Job*,
243–44.

32. Note, e.g., that the collocation in Job 40:10, "*clothe* yourself [*tilbāš*] with glory and
splendor," occurs also in Ps 104:1, but with reference to God: "You [God] are *clothed*
[*lābāštā*] with glory and splendor."

sertions to construct an answer. What are human beings? They are sinful, flawed creatures who may claim special status for themselves only if they are willing to violate God's established boundaries between the divine and the human. God's speech in 40:7–14 puts the psalmist's question once more to Job, this time more specifically framed in terms of Job's capacity to govern: "Have you an arm *like God* [*kā'ēl*]? Can you thunder with a voice *like his* [*kāmōhû*]?" Whereas both Job and Eliphaz moved outside the psalm to construct their answers to the question about human identity, God's speech stays inside the claims of the psalm to issue Job a directive: "Deck yourself with majesty and dignity; clothe yourself with glory and splendor [*hôd wĕhādār*]." The latter part of this directive is only a slight variation of the affirmation that is celebrated in Ps 8:5 (MT 6): "You have made them a little lower than God, and crowned them with glory and honor [*kābôd wĕhādār*]."

This subtle echo of Psalm 8 suggests that God summons Job to dispense with all manufactured answers to the question about human identity and vocation. He is to return to the psalmist's vision of humankind, a vision that is anchored in the primordial design of creation. He is challenged to take up the role that God has specially created for the human being. He is to participate in the governance of the world with a "glory and splendor" that is only a little lower than God's. Such a mandate, however, serves only to invite a further question. What does it mean to participate in the governance of the world with power and glory that is only slightly less than God's?

4. Behemoth and Leviathan are models for Job. Behemoth and Leviathan represent the sixth and final pair of animals that God asks Job to consider. The "poetic logic" of the divine speeches indicates that these two creatures signify the climax of God's revelation to Job.[33] In terms of Johannes Hempel's discernment of what is at stake in the book of Job, the presentation of Behemoth and Leviathan brings the search for the "last truth about God" to the point of ultimate disclosure.[34]

There is substantial support for the general understanding that Behemoth and Leviathan signify the primordial forces of chaos that God defeats to ensure the stability of creation. In this interpretation of Job 40:15–41:34 (MT 26), Job is destined to learn that he, like these mythical opponents,

---

33. Alter has noted that with the presentation of Behemoth and Leviathan, the "poetic logic" of the divine speeches arrives at the climax of the "movement from literal to figurative, from verisimilar to hyperbolic, from general assertion to focused concrete image" (*The Art of Biblical Poetry*, 107).

34. J. Hempel, "The Contents of the Literature," in *Record and Revelation* (ed. H. W. Robinson; Oxford: Clarendon, 1938) 73.

cannot challenge God and survive.[35] It would clearly be unwarranted to argue that there are no grounds for this interpretation. I suggest, however, that here, as throughout the book of Job, the text contains subtle clues that permit a more nuanced understanding.

Unlike the previous animals, Behemoth is introduced with affirmations, not questions (40:15–24). Job is not asked to do anything or to make any response. He is instructed simply to look, listen, and learn.[36] When he looks at this creature Job sees one whom God has made "just as I made you" (v. 15: *'ăšer-'āśîtî 'immāk*; literally "whom I made along with you"). This is the only direct reference to the creation of humans in the divine speeches, thus suggesting that Behemoth represents the one true analogue for humankind that God has placed in the created order.[37] I suggest that Job is invited to understand this particular creature as modeling for him three characteristics that may clarify his own identity and vocation in relation to God.[38]

First, Behemoth is a creature with extraordinary strength and power (40:16–18). With bones like "tubes of bronze" and limbs like "bars of iron," Behemoth is fortified to withstand almost any force that may be brought against it. Its strength, however, resides not merely in its ability to protect itself against life-threatening forces. It also has the sexual potency to generate new life out of its own resources.[39] In short, Behemoth is a creature that is peculiarly endowed for sustaining and generating life.

---

35. On the ancient Near Eastern mythical traditions concerning Behemoth and Leviathan as applied to Job, see O. Keel, *Jahwes Entgegnung an Ijob* (FRLANT 121; Göttingen: Vandenhoeck & Ruprecht, 1978) 127–58; Kubina, *Gottesreden*, 68–75.

36. N. C. Habel, *The Book of Job* (OTL; Philadelphia: Westminster, 1985) 538.

37. The mythical imagery that informs the presentation of Behemoth and Leviathan may contribute an additional perspective on this point. Newsom observes that traditional interpretations have mistakenly focused on whether these two creatures should be viewed as literal animals (e.g., the hippopotamus and the crocodile) or as mythical monsters. She suggests that they are better understood as liminal creatures whose characteristics place them somewhere between mere animals and extraordinary, supernatural creatures ("Book of Job," 615). They are in this respect, I suggest, particularly well suited as models that invite exploration of what it means for human beings to be created "in the image of God," i.e., as mortal creatures who are nevertheless "a little lower than God" (Ps 8:5 [MT 6]).

38. J. G. Gammie has also interpreted Behemoth and Leviathan as positive models for Job, and I am indebted to him for some of the insights developed here, although I make the case along somewhat different lines. Gammie suggests that Behemoth and Leviathan are caricatures of Job and as such serve both to rebuke him and to instruct and console him. I am not persuaded that the element of rebuke, which has traditionally been so emphasized, is as prominent as Gammie assumes. See "Behemoth and Leviathan: On the Didactic and Theological Significance of Job 40:15–41:26," in *Israelite Wisdom: Theological and Literary Essays in Honor of Samuel Terrien* (ed. J. G. Gammie, et al.; Missoula, Mont.: Scholars Press, 1978) 217–31.

39. It is likely that the description of Behemoth's "tail" (*zānāb*) as "stiff like a cedar" (40:17) is a euphemistic expression for an erection of the penis; see, e.g., Habel, *Job*, 565–66. On the importance of the rhetoric of sexual potency in the Behemoth speech, see Alter, *The Art of Biblical Poetry*, 108.

Second, Behemoth is described as the "first [rē'šît] of the great acts of God" (v. 19). The word rē'šît recalls not only the creation narrative in Genesis 1 (v. 1: běrē'šît), which presents God's purposive design for the cosmos, but also the description of Wisdom in Prov 8:22, who celebrates its role as a cocreator that God called forth at the beginning (rē'šît) of the master plan for creation. It should be noted that Eliphaz had rebuked Job for daring to imagine that he could compare himself with the "firstborn [ri'yšôn] of the human race (Job 15:7), thereby claiming for himself a special royal status as a near equal to God. God's description of Behemoth as the "first" of creation's works, however, presents a model of royalty that invites from Job the very self-understanding that Eliphaz would deny. Behemoth is a king in its own domain: the mountains bring forth tribute; the wild animals play as contented subjects of the realm; nature itself serves its sovereign ruler (Job 40:20–22).[40] If Job were to respond to Eliphaz with what God has shown him in this comparison with Behemoth, he might be expected to counter by saying, "Yes, indeed, I *am* like the primal creature who is a near equal to God; I *am* summoned forth and endowed with royal prerogatives and responsibilities."

Third, Behemoth is distinguished among the creatures by the way it responds to aggression and violence. If the river rages against it, it does not flee in fear. If the Jordan should burst forth against it, it trusts (yibṭaḥ) in its own resources (Job 40:23). The picture is of one who may be subject to attack, perhaps even by God (cf. vv. 19b, 24), but who nevertheless responds with confident resistance.[41]

It is striking that in this review of Behemoth's distinctive characteristics, this great animal is held up as worthy of praise. If elsewhere Behemoth is portrayed as an opponent of God that must be eliminated or defeated, in the divine speeches something else is indicated. Here God commends Behemoth to Job as an object lesson in what it means to stand before one's maker with exceptional strength, proud prerogatives, and fierce trust. The lesson for Job would seem to be that those who dare to imitate Behemoth may come nearer to realizing God's primordial design for creaturely existence than by following any other model in all of creation.

The presentation of Leviathan (41:1–34 [MT 40:25–41:26]) may also be understood to offer Job a positive role model. A figure clearly associated with the mythical sea monster, Leviathan is depicted here also as a mortal creature who may teach Job something about his own existence.[42] Unlike the Behemoth pericope, the Leviathan poem includes a number of

---

40. Cf. Perdue, *Wisdom in Revolt*, 222–23; idem, *Wisdom and Creation*, 177.
41. Cf. Gammie, "Behemoth and Leviathan," 220.
42. Ibid., 222–25.

rhetorical questions that clearly serve to challenge Job in a manner similar to the interrogations of the first divine speech.[43] The latter half of the poem (41:18–34 [MT 41:10–26]), however, uses declarative sentences to describe positively the distinctive features of Leviathan. Here, as elsewhere in the divine speeches, the rhetoric seems designed primarily not to rebuke and belittle Job but to elicit from him some new and positive articulation of faith that is uniquely informed by his consideration of Leviathan. I suggest that Leviathan models for Job three characteristics that may instruct him in the formulation of a new response to God.

First, Leviathan, like Behemoth, possesses extraordinary strength and power (41:12–32 [MT 41:4–24]). On earth Leviathan is a "creature without fear," a king (*melek*) without peer in its own realm (41:33–34 [MT 41:25–26]).[44] As a royal figure, Leviathan's relation to God is described somewhat ambiguously. Textual uncertainties in 41:10–12 (MT 41:2–4) permit different interpretations. Even so, the main interpretive options yield, in different ways, a common construal of Leviathan's special status in the hierarchy of creation. *Only God* can confront and control Leviathan; or vice versa, *only Leviathan* dares to "stand before" the One who has such demonstrably superior power.[45] Such a description portrays Leviathan as a near equal to God, hence as a figure that invites reflection once more on the theology of Psalm 8. Indeed, in the psalm as in this poem, the creature who

---

43. A series of questions introduced by the interrogative *he* in 41:1–9 (MT 40:25–41:1), ask generally, "Can you, Job, capture Leviathan?" The expected answer is "No, of course not." The questions with the interrogative pronoun *mî* ("who?") in 41:10–14 (MT 41:2–6) ask generally, "If you, Job, cannot confront and control this beast, who can?" The logic of the question is that Job should answer, "Only you, God, can control Leviathan."

44. The phrase normally translated "on earth" in 41:33 (MT 41:25) is ʿal-ʿāpār, literally "on dust." Gammie has noted that elsewhere in the book Job is prominently positioned "on the dust" (2:8; 30:19; 42:6). He cites this common rhetoric in support of the argument that Leviathan is presented as a mortal creature, like Job, and thus can serve as a "didactic image" for him ("Behemoth and Leviathan," 224).

The word translated "creature" in Job 41:33 (MT 41:25), heʿāśû, is difficult. As it stands the word may be taken as an archaic form of the *Qal* passive participle, hence "the one made," i.e., "creature"; cf. R. Gordis, *The Book of Job: Commentary, New Translation, Special Studies* (New York: Jewish Theological Seminary of America, 1978) 490. A similar translation may be derived from an alternative spelling, heʿāśûy, which is found in some Hebrew manuscripts. Perdue has noted, however, that if the Masoretic pointing is changed slightly to hāʿōśô, the reading would parallel 40:19, "the one who made him." The sense of the verse would then be that God, who made Leviathan, has no fear of this creature. Perdue rejects this option as unlikely (*Wisdom in Revolt*, 231).

45. The Leningrad text of 41:2b–3 [ET 41:10b–11] is first-person speech, "Who can stand before *me* (lĕpānay)? Who will confront *me* (hiqdîmanî)?" The emphasis of the speech would be on the incomparability of God, i.e., "Who can contend with *God*?" In some Hebrew manuscripts the speech is third person, thus "Who can stand before *him* (lĕpānāyw)?" In this reading the emphasis would be on the incomparability of Leviathan, i.e., "Who can contend with *Leviathan*?"

enjoys such close proximity to the divine is the object of God's admiration and praise (cf. vv. 18–24 [MT 10–15]).[46]

Second, the poem affirms that Leviathan's extraordinary power is especially evident in what comes forth from its mouth. Two images in the poem are instructive: one that emphasizes what does not come forth from Leviathan's mouth; the other, that does. In 41:3–4 (MT 40:27–28) Leviathan is described as a creature that will not be subdued into docile service. In the unlikely event that this creature should ever be captured and forced into domestication, it would not even then make a "covenant" (bĕrît) with its master that required it to plead for mercy or to speak "soft words." That which more typically comes from the mouth of Leviathan is vividly described in 41:18–21 (MT 10–13). The rhetoric emphasizes fire and light, smoke and flames, phenomena that are identified with the strong and compelling appearance of divinity.[47] Leviathan, like mythic divine beings, *and* like YHWH (cf. Pss 18:8–14 [MT 9–15]; 29:7), announces its presence with an awesome fierceness that commands attention and defies coercion. If what does and does not come forth from the mouth of Leviathan is intended to instruct Job, then the lesson commends strong words, not soft or gentle ones, speech that commands recognition, not disregard.[48]

Finally, the description of Leviathan's power and presence culminates with an affirmation of its royal dominion. Leviathan, like Behemoth, is king (*melek*) in its own domain (41:34 [MT 26]). Behemoth's royalty derives from its status as the "first" of God's works, the one to whom all creation offers respectful tribute (40:19–22). Leviathan's royalty is conveyed with images of governance: Leviathan "looks on everyone who is haughty [kol-gāboāh yir'eh] (41:34[26])." In this respect also Leviathan presents to Job a model for the very challenge that God has extended to him. In 40:7–14 God's speech returned to the rhetoric of Psalm 8 and summoned Job to put on the regalia of "glory and splendor" (v. 10). The success of Job's kingship would be evident if he could "look on all who are proud" (40:11: rĕ'eh kol-gē'eh) and deal with them justly. Now, in this final acclamation of Leviathan as king, God offers Job a worthy example of how to enact the very assignment he has been given.[49]

---

46. On the hymnic style of these verses, see Perdue, *Wisdom and Revolt*, 230–32.

47. Alter suggests that this imagery may be linked to the cosmic imagery of light in the first divine speech (Job 38), which serves rhetorically to counter Job's opening curse of creation (*Art of Biblical Poetry*, 109–10).

48. Cf. Gammie ("Behemoth and Leviathan," 223, 225), who also notes that what comes forth from Leviathan's mouth is a major emphasis in the poem. He suggests that the poet uses this emphasis both to caricature Job's verbal defenses and at the same time to affirm his protests.

49. Newsom ("Book of Job," 625) has noted that the conclusion of the Leviathan poem, 41:34 (MT 26), forms an *inclusio* with 40:11b.

To summarize, I have suggested that the divine speeches are intended to challenge Job, but not to condemn or silence him. What is desired is a fresh articulation of faith, in Brueggemann's terms, a "fresh hunch" about God. After the review of creation's design in the first speech, Job appears to have concluded that there is no significant place or role for suffering humanity in the world that God has crafted. Job responds with silence. But a second divine speech then follows, indicating that Job's initial response has somehow to be extended or enlarged before the divine-human encounter can be complete. God invites consideration of special representatives of the animal world, Behemoth and Leviathan, two figures of power, pride, and dominion, that are celebrated as near equals of God. They may be subject to confrontation and assault, but they will not relinquish their identity nor abandon their creaturely responsibilities. God has power sufficient to combat and to control them, but God does not eliminate them or deny them a meaningful role among the vital life forces in creation's design. The logic of the second speech from the whirlwind is that Behemoth and Leviathan reveal something important about God's design for creaturely existence that belongs in Job's understanding.

Job's Final Response: "Now My Eye Sees You"

Job's final response in 42:6 has generally been interpreted as a confession of sin for having wrongly attacked the justice of God. This understanding has been preserved and nurtured by a host of prominent Bible translations, of which the NRSV is but one contemporary example: "therefore I despise myself, and repent in dust and ashes." This rendering of Job's words affirms that God always holds supreme power over frail and flawed humans. Before such a God as this, human discourse is necessarily limited and submissive. Following the counsel of Eliphaz, the proper role for humankind is simply to "agree with God, and be at peace" (Job 22:21).[50] However ingrained in our consciousness this traditional view of Job's response has become, it can scarcely be regarded as a new or fresh articulation of faith.

Modern commentators now regularly acknowledge and grapple with the intractable ambiguities encoded in Job's last words. No less than five different translations of Job 42:6 should be considered as legitimate possibilities.[51] Whatever Job's final response may be, it must be recognized

---

50. Cf. Crenshaw (*Old Testament Wisdom,* 111): "In the face of such a blustering deity, who would not be speechless?"

51. The major interpretive options are conveniently identified by Newsom ("Book of Job," 628–29) and Habel (*Job,* 577–78). See further T. Tilley, "God and the Silencing of Job," *Modern Theology* 5 (1989) 257–70, who observes that the multiple translation possibilities for Job

as anything but a simple admission of sin. I do not intend to debate the strengths and weaknesses of the various alternatives for rendering this verse. I do want to suggest, however, that one of the recognized translations is particularly consonant with the purpose of the divine speeches as I have discerned it in this essay.

Job's final words in 42:6 may reasonably be translated as follows: "Therefore I retract [my words] and change my mind concerning dust and ashes." Two critical issues must be addressed in order to unlock the meaning of these words. First, the verb *mā'as*, here translated "retract," is active, not reflexive, and ordinarily takes an object. In 42:6 there is no clearly identified object, although one may reasonably assume that an object is implied.[52] Of the alternatives that have been proposed, I am inclined toward supplying "my words" as the object.[53] The specific content of what may be included among Job's "words" is ambiguous, but his previous concession that he has attempted to speak about "things too wonderful" (42:3: *niplā'ôt*) makes it plausible to suggest that the reference is to the wondrous design of God's creation (cf. 38:2).[54] Job had cursed this design as being inimical and meaningless for innocent sufferers like him (Job 3). God had countered with a vision of a creation teeming with a variety of intricately balanced life forces. In response to this revelation, Job may be understood to relinquish his limited discernment of creation's design and to acknowledge that the grander vision he has been granted now requires of him a new assessment.

The key to Job's new assessment is found in 42:6b, where a second critical issue must be addressed. The syntax of the Hebrew words is relatively clear: Job "repents" or "changes his mind" *concerning* (*niḥamtî 'al*) dust and ashes.[55] What is signified is a reversal or a retraction of a previous decision or position. It is the meaning of the phrase "dust and ashes" that

---

42:6 mean that "interpreters make, rather than find, the text which they interpret" (260). He concludes that the text interpreters have typically "made" has had the effect of reducing Job to silence.

52. W. Morrow has discussed the philological data, noting that of nearly 70 occurrences of *mā'as* in the Qal stem, an object is given in all but four of the cases (Job 7:16; 34:33; 36:5; 42:6) ("Consolation, Rejection, and Repentance in Job 42:6," *JBL* 105 [1986] 214).

53. Cf. S. R. Driver and G. B. Gray, *The Book of Job* (ICC; Edinburgh: T. & T. Clark, 1921) 373; M. Tsevat, "The Meaning of the Book of Job," *HUCA* 37 (1966) 91; G. Fohrer, *Das Buch Hiob* (KAT; Gütersloh: Mohn, 1963) 531; M. H. Pope, *Job* (3d ed.; AB 15; Garden City, N.Y.: Doubleday, 1973) 349; Newsom, "Book of Job," 629. See also the following Bible translations: NAB, JPS, JB, TEV.

54. So also Newsom, "Book of Job," 629.

55. On the idiom *nḥm 'al*, as "repent *about/concerning*," as opposed to the more traditional rendering "repent *in*," see Morrow, "Consolation," 215–16; D. Patrick, "The Translation of Job XLII 6," *VT* 26 (1976) 370.

determines finally what Job has decided to relinquish and what he now intends to embrace.

The phrase "dust and ashes" (*'āpār wā'ēper*) occurs but three times in biblical Hebrew: Gen 18:27, Job 30:19, and Job 42:6. In each case it signifies something about the human condition vis-à-vis God. In Job 30:19 Job laments that God has thrown him into the "mire" (*ḥōmer*) of human mortality,[56] where human existence is defined as "dust and ashes." In the context of his suffering Job understands this to mean that he is but one small example of the way in which afflicted humans may be banished from society (30:1–8), scorned and terrorized by their peers (30:9–15) and by God (30:16–23). Job's experience leads him to conclude that as "dust and ashes" he is consigned to live in a world where he cries out to God, and God does not answer (30:20). In Gen 18:27 the phrase "dust and ashes" applies to Abraham. In the context of arguing with God about matters of justice, Abraham acknowledges that as a mere creature of "dust and ashes" he has entered into dangerous territory. Abraham's recognition of his status before God is not dissimilar to Job's in 30:19, except that in Abraham's case he persists in questioning God, and God answers.[57] Indeed, the Hebrew text of Gen 18:22, without the *tiqqûn*, invites a dramatic understanding of God's regard for this creaturely interrogator. It says, "Yhwh remained standing before Abraham."[58] The picture suggests that God, the "judge of all the earth," stands waiting to hear what "dust and ashes" will say on the subject of divine justice. I concur with J. G. Janzen, who observes that in this picture of Creator and creature locked in dialogue over matters of mutual concern, we are given a glimpse of how the divine image may be enacted on earth.[59]

These two images of "dust and ashes" must inform the interpretation

---

56. Cf. Job 4:19; 10:9; 33:6, where the term *ḥōmer* is used with reference to human mortality.

57. For my argument here it is not necessary to resolve the question of whether Job is dependent on Genesis or vice versa. It is sufficient to note that significant parallels between Abraham and Job suggest the likelihood that both texts reflect acute concerns with questions about divine justice that emerged in the postexilic period. See J. Blenkinsopp, who notes that these connections were already noticed by medieval Jewish commentators ("Abraham and the Righteous of Sodom," *JJS* 33 [1982] 126–27; "The Judge of All the Earth: Theodicy in the Midrash on Genesis 18:22–33," *JJS* 41 [1990] 1–12). On the postexilic provenance of Gen 18:22–33 and its connections with Job, see further L. Schmidt, *"De Deo": Studien zur Literarkritik und Theologie des Buches Jona, des Gesprächs zwischen Abraham und Jahwe in Gen 18 22ff. und von Job 1* (BZAW 143; Berlin: de Gruyter, 1976) 131–64.

58. The scribal correction of Gen 18:22 is "Abraham remained standing before YHWH."

59. Janzen, *Job*, 257. See further the similar assessment of this text by E. Ben Zvi: "The text underscores the notion that when the ideal teacher defends the universal order and confronts God with the standards by which God ought to judge the world, he is in fact fulfilling the role God has chosen for him to fulfill" ("The Dialogue Between Abraham and Yhwh in Gen. 18.23–32: A Historical-Critical Analysis," *JSOT* 53 [1992] 39).

of Job's final response to God. Given what God has shown him, Job now changes his mind about "dust and ashes." He previously had concluded that innocent suffering rendered him mute and submissive before a God who permitted neither challenge nor confrontation. In terms of the theology of Psalm 8, he could discern only that to be created in the image of God was more a curse than a blessing. As a human creature a "little lower than God," he was destined for death, not life; for the mire, not for the throne; for the misery of silent servitude, not for the "glory and splendor" of royalty.

God's disclosure of creation's design, however, requires of Job a transformed understanding of "dust and ashes." In God's design creaturely existence may entail undeserved suffering, but it does not mandate silence and submission.[60] Like Behemoth and Leviathan, God endows human beings with power and responsibility for their domains. They are and must be fierce, unbridled contenders for justice, sometimes with God and sometimes against God. As near equals of God their destiny is to live at the dangerous intersection between the merely human and the supremely divine. When humans dare to enact this destiny, their appearance before God as "dust and ashes" confirms their heritage as faithful descendants of Abraham. They may be sure that they do not approach an indifferent God; they approach instead the One who awaits and desires their arrival. They may speak words of praise; they may speak words of curse. They may also move beyond these two levels of discourse to speak words of resistance and protest. But they may not be silent, for silence is unworthy of those who have stood in the divine presence and have learned that creation has been entrusted to them, because they are a "little lower than God." I submit that this is the foundation for the new articulation of faith that Job announces with the words "now my eye sees you" (42:5).

---

60. Janzen's discerning interpretation of Job's transformed understanding of "dust and ashes" is perhaps closest to the view I am offering here, although I depart from him in important ways (*Job,*, 254–59). He suggests that Job's new understanding of "dust and ashes" teaches him that innocent suffering does not belittle humankind. Rather it is the very condition under which the "royal vocation" to image God can be accepted and embraced. In this respect he suggests that Job comes to a new self-understanding of his suffering that bears a resemblance to the suffering servant in Second Isaiah. In response to Janzen one may argue that he invokes the theology of innocent suffering in a way that does not address adequately the primary issue that is at stake in the book of Job. Job does not suffer on behalf of others. His family does not die on behalf of others. His suffering and their death are "for no reason." It is "without cause," and it can hardly be construed in any normal sense as redemptive. I am more inclined to say that what Job has learned is that humankind may image God not by acquiescing to innocent suffering but rather by protesting it, contending with the powers that occasion it, and, when necessary, taking the fight directly to God. It is just such power, courage, and fierce trust that God seems to commend to Job in the figures of Behemoth and Leviathan.

If this view of God's disclosure from the whirlwind has merit, then I suggest that Brueggemann's summons to attend to the "fresh hunches" about God conveyed by Israel's lament tradition, especially as modeled by Job, does indeed invite a new way of thinking about Old Testament theology. More importantly, it invites a Joban way of imaging God in the world, the neglect of which seriously jeopardizes God's purposive design for creation.

– 19 –

The Impossibility of Mourning

Lamentations after the Holocaust[1]

Tod Linafelt

> ...and what is a poet for in a destitute time?
> —FRIEDRICH HÖLDERLIN

"Wozu Dichter in dürftiger Zeit?" asks the poet Hölderlin in his elegy "Bread and Wine": "What are poets for?" or, one might translate, "What good are poets?" In particular, what good are poets in a destitute time? The time evoked by Hölderlin, so the philosopher Martin Heidegger informs us, refers to an era "defined by the god's failure to arrive, by the 'default of God.'"[2] For Heidegger this era is now, is the present: a present that is premature even as it is belated. "We are too late for the gods," he writes, "too early for Being."[3] Yet is this not always the case? Is this era of default not every era? To answer in the negative—that is, to affirm that the past as a former present existed prior to destitution—is to allow for the accomplishment of mourning. It is to put the past behind, and to reapply its force to the present self, thereby attending to the birth of Being, which for Heidegger is only now "just begun."[4] If, however, the past as a former present is viewed as a time no less destitute, then mourning becomes impossible. The past can never be put behind, for it has always been behind, and one attends not to the *birth* but to the *perpetual retreat* of Being. This impossibility of mourning becomes melancholia.

In Freud's original treatment of mourning and melancholia in 1917, he

---

1. An earlier version of this article was presented to the Reading, Theory, and the Bible section at the 1996 annual meeting of the Society of Biblical Literature. I am happy to dedicate it here to Walter Brueggemann, who first introduced me the lament tradition in the Hebrew Scriptures and who remains a mentor of uncommon generosity.

2. Martin Heidegger, *Poetry, Language, Thought* (trans. Albert Hofstadter; New York: Harper and Row, 1971) 91.

3. Ibid., 4.

4. Ibid.

attempted to distinguish between these two states. Though he begins by admitting that "the correlation of melancholia and mourning seems justified
by the general picture of the two conditions," and that they may well be
the product of "the same influences," he contends that, unlike mourning,
melancholia is to be considered "a pathological disposition."[5] Freud writes
that although it is true that "mourning involves grave departures from the
normal attitude to life," we may "rely on its being overcome after a certain lapse of time."[6] This overcoming, the *work* of mourning, proceeds by
way of reality testing, which shows that the loved object no longer exists
and that attachments to the object must be withdrawn. Resistance follows,
but eventually "reality gains the day," and "when the work of mourning is
completed the ego becomes free and uninhibited again"[7] and thus able to
attach itself to a new object. By contrast, melancholia is precisely the failure of the work of mourning; it is the inability of the ego to overcome the
loss of the object, the inability to break off the tie, no matter how much
reality is tested and found wanting.

The Book of Lamentations and the Sense of a Rending

Freud's structure of mourning—presence, loss of presence, presence—is in
fact the converse of the history of interpretation of the book of Lamentations, or at least a certain history of interpretation, one focused on the
figure of Zion in chapters 1 and 2. Rather than absence surrounded by presence, one finds bookends of destitution at both ends of a long and desperate
attempt to stave off the melancholia of sustained absence.

The first of these bookends is the book of Lamentations itself. The destitution, the default of God, is most apparent in chapters 1 and 2, where
Zion is personified as a widow and a mother lamenting her abused and
dying children (see esp. 1:16, 18; 2:20–22). Her rhetoric is acutely urgent,
in particular as it addresses God, from whom the figure of Zion demands
a response on behalf of her children. As Walter Brueggemann has written, "Israel's world is a world of peculiar and persistent dialogical speech
wherein life consists of address and answer."[8] In this instance, however,
the address stands alone without an answer, and the book ends with the
plaintive appeal:

5. Sigmund Freud, "Mourning and Melancholia," in *The Standard Edition of the Complete Psychological Works of Sigmund Freud* (trans. James Strachey, et al.; London: Hogarth,
1954) 14:243.

6. Ibid., 244.

7. Ibid., 245.

8. Walter Brueggemann, *Abiding Astonishment: Psalms, Modernity, and the Making of
History* (LCBI; Louisville: Westminster/John Knox, 1991) 24.

> Why have you forgotten us utterly,
>> forsaken us for so long?
> Take us back, LORD, to yourself, and let us come back.
>> Renew our days as of old.
> For if you have truly rejected us,
>> bitterly raged against us,
> then....
>
>   (5:20–22)[9]

The final phrase of v. 22 is a poignantly appropriate way to end the book of Lamentations, inscribing, via its unfinished nature, the sense of a rending represented by God's nonresponse and the poet's refusal to move beyond lament into praise or a statement of confidence in God. I have translated the final phrase as a conditional statement that is left trailing off, that is, a protasis without an apodosis.[10] The book is simply left opening out into the freighted emptiness of God's silence. By leaving a conditional statement dangling, the final verse leaves open the future of those voicing the lament. It is hardly a hopeful ending, for the implied apodosis is surely negative; nevertheless it does defer that apodosis. By arresting the movement from an "if" to a "then" the incomplete clause allows the reader, for a moment, to imagine the possibility of a different "then," and therefore a different future.

The appeal in Lam 5:20–22, like the appeals made by Zion and the poet in chapters 1 and 2, remains unanswered. The voice of God never sounds in the book of Lamentations; and as Westermann assures us, before any move from lament to praise could be made, "first the most important thing had to occur: God's answer."[11] Without such an answer, the book of Lamentations remains incomplete. Nor is this incompleteness easily imagined as

---

9. Unless otherwise indicated, translations from the Hebrew texts are my own.

10. As virtually all commentators note, it is difficult to know how to render the *kî 'im* with which the line opens. It has been argued that it is possible to take *kî 'im* as meaning "unless," implying that the possibility of what follows has been excluded. But such a use of *kî 'im* occurs elsewhere only when preceded by a clause containing a negative statement. It has also been suggested that the line be read as a question: "Or have you totally rejected us? Are you indeed so angry with us?" But there is no evidence in the Bible of *kî 'im* being used to introduce a question, nor is there any support for taking it to mean "or." Another option, and apparently that chosen by the LXX and the Peshitta, is simply to ignore or delete the *'im*, thus rendering line as "for you have truly rejected us, bitterly raged against us." It has often been noted that one might expect *kî 'im* to introduce a conditional statement, but that the second colon of v. 22 does not seem to state the consequence of the first as would be expected in a true conditional statement. While this is true, it does not rule out the conditional nature of *kî 'im*. Thus I have chosen to translate the line as an *incomplete* conditional statement. See Tod Linafelt, "Surviving Lamentations: A Literary and Theological Study of the Afterlife of a Biblical Text" (Ph.D. diss., Emory University, 1997) 116–19, for a more complete review of the linguistic issues and relevant bibliography.

11. Claus Westermann, *The Psalms: Structure, Content, and Message* (trans. Ralph D. Gehrke; Minneapolis: Augsburg, 1980) 42.

one that is carried to term: it is not an incompleteness that sits well with readers; it is not an incompleteness that evokes assent and allows one to move on, but rather suspends one's reading in a moment of abrupt rending. These questions, doubts, and affirmations of absence bring the book to its unsatisfactory close. The appeals to and the charges against God have gone unanswered. Zion's children remain lost, and God remains absent: the default of God is bound up with the loss of Zion's children. In such a destitute time, Zion's work of mourning can never be accomplished. The book's refusal to acknowledge presence and its refusal to move beyond the lost children to a new object perpetuate its melancholic character.

Although the completion is deferred, its *demand* is not lessened; Zion's rhetoric of survival remains strong, even if unmet. So reader after reader has contributed to the afterlife of the book of Lamentations by attempting to complete the incompleteness by filling the void that exists in place of an ending. The process is a perfect example of what Walter Brueggemann has identified as the "dialectical and dialogical quality" of the bond between Israel and Israel's God.

> Israel's text, and therefore Israel and Israel's God, are always in the middle of an exchange, unable to come to ultimate resolution. There may be momentary or provisional resolution, but because both parties are intensely engaged and are so relentlessly verbal, we are always sure that there will be another speech, another challenge, another invitation, another petition, another argument, which will reopen the matter and expend the provisional settlement.[12]

The history of Jewish interpretation of the book, in its repeated attempts to forestall melancholia by reintroducing the divine presence and by replacing the object of Zion's loss, her children, manifests in a striking way the dialectic between provisional settlement and open-ended exchange. For every answer that is provided is related dialectically to the answerless text of Lamentations, which, though generating these provisional settlements, nevertheless remains as a critique of them.

We may see the dialectic as early as Second Isaiah, written during Israel's exile in Babylon and thus during the immediate aftermath of the destruction described in Lamentations. For example, Isa 49:14–26 appropriates the word pair *šākaḥ* ("forget") and *'āzab* ("forsake") from Lam 5:20:

> Zion said:
> "The LORD has forsaken me,
> my Lord has forgotten me." (49:14)

---

12. Walter Brueggemann, *Theology of the Old Testament: Testimony, Dispute, Advocacy* (Minneapolis: Fortress Press, 1997) 83.

But the poet of Second Isaiah transforms this word pair into an affirmation that God does *not* forget or forsake, putting the following response to Zion into the mouth of the Lord:

> Can a woman forget her nursing child?
> Or have no pity for the child of her womb?
> Even these may forget,
> but I could never forget you. (49:15)

The poet buttresses this assertion with an extended speech by God that pertains nearly exclusively to the return and multiplication of Zion's children (49:16–26). Second Isaiah has chosen the one metaphor for the divine that can perhaps begin to answer the rhetoric of Lamentations: God as a mother who also laments and hopes for the return of her children.[13]

As one moves into postbiblical Hebrew literature this exegetical trajectory continues unabated, evincing the drive to supplement and thus to abrogate the rending encountered as one finishes the book of Lamentations. For example, the narrative expansions in Targum Lamentations (an early translation of the book into Aramaic) intensify the rhetoric about the murder of the children, provide the voice of God in response, and imagine a messianic restoration of Israel in which Zion's children "will gather together from every place where they were scattered on the day of [God's] fierce anger." In the midrash to Lamentations (an anthology of rabbinic commentary on the book), Abraham, Isaac, and Jacob all plead for mercy for their "children" Israel, only to fail to get a response from a God who seems to remain "above the fray." The response in the midrash comes when the matriarch Rachel, standing in for Zion, reproaches God for having allowed the enemies to exile and kill her children. Rachel is, of course, the model of melancholia in the Hebrew Bible, who in Jer 31:15 "refuses to be comforted for her children, because they are not." But in language strikingly similar to Heidegger's notion of the future as the result of the present birth of Being and to Freud's notion of the overcoming of mourning, God in the midrash cites Jer 31:15 and then tells Rachel: "Refrain your voice from weeping and your eyes from tears, for your work shall be rewarded.... There is hope for your future, your children shall return to their own land." Finally, the medieval liturgical poetry of Eliezer ben Kallir draws on these previous biblical and rabbinic texts to fashion its own version of consolation and restoration, its own version of the accomplishment

---

13. For more on the connections between Second Isaiah and Lamentations, see Carol Newsom, "Response to Norman Gottwald, 'Social Class and Ideology in Isaiah 40–55,'" *Semeia* 58 (1993) 73–78; Tod Linafelt, "Surviving Lamentations," *HBT* 17 (1995) 45–61; and Patricia Willey, "Remember the Former Things: The Recollection of Previous Texts in Isaiah 40–55" (Ph.D. diss., Emory University, 1996).

of Zion's mourning: the character of Jeremiah (representing for Kallir the poet of Lamentations) "roars" (*šāʾag*) on behalf of Zion, and God (now decidedly in the fray) "cries out" (*ṣāʿaq*) God's own lament on behalf of the perishing children.[14]

All of these examples from the history of interpretation of Lamentations may be viewed as "survivals" of the biblical book in the full etymological sense of the word *survival* (in German, *Überleben;* in French, *survie*). That is, they "live beyond" the text that generated them, and in fact "overlive" it, imagining a "life in excess" that is commensurate with the excessive textuality they represent.[15] While these supplements are no doubt driven by a genuine impulse to deal with the felt absence that is the core of Lamentations, they threaten to betray the biblical book's refusal to move beyond loss. The settlements they represent can only ever be provisional. For while the triumph of life found in these survivals of Lamentations may embody various readers' need to overcome mourning, the melancholia evoked by the book of Lamentations nevertheless remains.

A Post-Holocaust "Survival" of Lamentations

Alan Mintz has written that the function of Second Isaiah's poetry is "to reconstruct the faculty of hearing, to recreate the conditions under which the reality of divine speech regains plausibility."[16] But can these conditions be re-created in the present context, particularly after the silence of God during the Holocaust? Can the representation of divine speech ever regain plausibility? Is it possible to imagine the triumphant return of Zion's children without betraying the memory of the one million children who did not return from Nazi death camps? Acknowledging these problematics does not, however, lessen the urgency of Zion's demands that remain in Lamentations. Thus the paradox: how to meet the drive for survival in Lamentations, to fill the unbearable whiteness of the blank page that constitutes its nonending, in a way that does not ring false to our present

---

14. Each of these postbiblical texts is given an entire chapter in my dissertation, where one can find both the Hebrew texts and a much more detailed analysis of them. See Linafelt, "Surviving Lamentations," chaps. 4–6.

15. The connotations of survival as "overliving" or "life in excess" are explored with much subtlety by Jacques Derrida ("Des Tours de Babel," *Semeia* 54 [1991] 3–34) and Robert Detweiler ("Overliving," *Semeia* 54 [1991] 239–55). On "survival" in relation to biblical texts, see esp. Hugh Pyper, "Surviving Writing," in *The New Literary Criticism and the Hebrew Bible* (ed. J. C. Exum and D. J. A. Clines; Valley Forge, Pa.: Trinity, 1993) 227–49; and Timothy K. Beal, *The Book of Hiding: Gender, Ethnicity, Annihilation and Esther* (London and New York: Routledge, 1997).

16. Alan Mintz, *Ḥurban: Responses to Catastrophe in Hebrew Literature* (New York: Columbia Univ. Press, 1984) 43.

historical situation. It is in relation to this paradox and these sorts of questions that I turn to Cynthia Ozick's short story, "The Shawl."[17] Unlike the texts considered above, Ozick's story is not explicitly presented as an interpretation of Lamentations. If the trajectory of survival that I have briefly presented above trades in presence, both the presence of God and the presence of Zion's children, "The Shawl" returns to destitution and the default of God. But in my judgment it is no less a survival of the biblical book, for it too allows the book to live beyond its borders, to live again in another context.

"The Shawl" opens with its three main characters—Rosa, Magda, and Stella—on a long, cold march. The reader gradually learns that they are Jews on a march toward a Nazi concentration camp. Rosa is the mother of Magda, an infant as the story begins but a toddler by the end of it. Stella is Rosa's niece. Rosa has managed to keep Magda alive by hiding her in a shawl, nursing her until her milk runs dry, and then sharing her food when they are in a barracks. But Magda's survival is precarious. "Rosa knew that Magda was going to die very soon; she should have been dead already, but she had been buried deep inside the magic shawl, mistaken there for the shivering mound of Rosa's breasts."[18] Once in the camp, Rosa knows that it is only a matter of time until someone would inform on them, or someone "would steal Magda to eat her." In spite of these constant threats, Magda manages to survive, wrapped always in her shawl and sucking on it for the comfort no longer available from Rosa's breasts.

But one day, "Stella took the shawl away and made Magda die. Afterward Stella said: 'I was cold.' "[19] Magda wanders out of the barracks and into the open square, "with her little pencil legs scribbling this way and that, in search of the shawl." Rosa sees too late to stop Magda, who, silent until now, is howling in "the perilous sunlight of the arena."

> A tide of commands hammered in Rosa's nipples: Fetch, get, bring! But she did not know which to go after first, Magda or the shawl. If she jumped out into the arena to snatch Magda up, the howling would not stop, because Magda would still not have the shawl; but if she ran back into the barracks to find the shawl, and if she found it, and if she came after Magda holding it and shaking it, then she would get Magda back.[20]

Opting for the latter, Rosa enters the barracks, tears the shawl away from Stella, and runs into the arena, holding it aloft for Magda to see.

---

17. Cynthia Ozick, "The Shawl," in *The Shawl: A Story and Novella* (New York: Knopf, 1989).
18. Ibid., 108.
19. Ibid., 109.
20. Ibid., 109–10.

Far off, very far, Magda leaned across her air-fed belly, reaching out with the rods of her arms. She was high up, elevated, riding someone's shoulder. But the shoulder that carried Magda was not coming toward Rosa and the shawl, it was drifting away, the speck of Magda moving more and more into the smoky distance.[21]

Magda has been discovered and is carried by a guard toward the electrified fence. The final paragraph of the story reads as follows:

All at once Magda was swimming through the air. The whole of Magda traveled through loftiness. She looked like a butterfly touching a silver vine. And the moment Magda's feathered round head and her pencil legs and balloonish belly and zigzag arms splashed against the fence, the steel voices went mad in their growling, urging Rosa to run and run to the spot where Magda had fallen from her flight against the electrified fence; but of course Rosa did not obey them. She only stood, because if she ran they would shoot, and if she tried to pick up the sticks of Magda's body they would shoot, and if she let the wolf's screech ascending now through the ladder of her skeleton break out, they would shoot; so she took Magda's shawl and filled her own mouth with it, stuffed it in and stuffed it in, until she was swallowing up the wolf's screech and tasting the cinnamon and almond depth of Magda's saliva; and Rosa drank Magda's shawl until it dried.[22]

So the story ends, with a bereaved mother squelching the cry of grief and shock at witnessing the murder of her child.

What then are the connections between this story and Lamentations? At the thematic level, with its emphasis on the mother-child relationship, the threat of an enemy, and the hints of cannibalism, "The Shawl" bears marked resemblances to Lamentations. Attention to the details of the story, however, suggest that there is an even more immediate relationship to be teased out.

For example, two *leitwörte* in the story point the reader to Lamentations. The first of these words is "pity." The absence of pity is repeated three times in the description of the characters situation: "They were in a place without pity, all pity was annihilated in Rosa, she looked at Stella's bones without pity."[23] The English word *pity* has a semantic field in biblical Hebrew that includes the roots *ḥml, nḥm,* and *rḥm.* Just as "pity" is a *leitwort* in "The Shawl," two of these three words for pity are *leitwörte* in Lamentations 1 and 2. The notion of the absence of pity in the face of desperate suffering most immediately recalls the repeated refrain in chapter 1 of Lamentations that Zion has no one to "comfort/pity" (*nḥm*) her. In chapter 2 the poet employs *ḥml* to express the lack of pity from God: the

21. Ibid., 110.
22. Ibid., 110–11.
23. Ibid., 108.

reader is told in 2:17 that God "has destroyed without pity," and in 2:21 that God has slaughtered boys and girls "without pity." Thus the opening chapters of Lamentations and "The Shawl" are both concerned with constructing in the mind of the reader a world in which all hope of pity and comfort are extinguished.

The second common *leitwort* is the "arena" or "the square," encountered in the Ozick story when Magda stumbles out of the barracks in search of her shawl. By the time Rosa sees her, Ozick writes, "already Magda was in the square outside." Ozick contrasts the peril of the arena outside with the safety of the shawl inside the barracks.

> It was the roll-call arena. Every morning Rosa had to conceal Magda under the shawl against a wall of the barracks and go out and stand in the arena with Stella and hundreds of others, sometimes for hours, and Magda, deserted, was quiet under the shawl, sucking on her corner.[24]

It is into the arena that Magda stumbles out, "swaying on her pencil legs," and it is in the arena that she dies.

The semantic range in biblical Hebrew of "arena" or "square" is primarily constituted by the two words *rĕḥōb* and *ḥûṣ*, both of which are key words in Lamentations 2, and both of which are explicitly named as the place where Zion's children are dying. The first, *rĕḥōb*, is twice repeated in 2:11–12, where the poet breaks down in v. 11 over the "babes and sucklings [who] falter in the squares of the city." Verse 12 reads:

> They falter like the wounded,
> in the squares of the town,
> as their life runs out
> in the bosom of their mother.

This verse demonstrates the subtle complexity with which "The Shawl" echoes the biblical book. It does so not only in the choice of the square as the place of the children's death, but also in the description of how the children make their way through the square. In "The Shawl" Magda sways on perilously thin legs, she "flopped onward with her little pencil legs scribbling this way and that," and she "falters" at the barracks opening.[25] The imperiled children are presented in this same way in Lamentations, where the verb *'āṭap*, repeated twice and usually translated as "languished," can mean "to be faint" or "to falter." The image of Magda stumbling to her death in the square echoes the stumbling of Zion's children to their death in the *rĕḥōb*.

---

24. Ibid., 109.
25. Ibid., 109.

The web of allusion extends even further in this verse. In a key paragraph of "The Shawl" (partially quoted above), Ozick sets up a structural opposition between the safety of the shawl and the threat of the open square. The shawl itself, of course, stands in for the bosom of Rosa: it is a surrogate source of nourishment and safety when Rosa's breasts have given all they can or when Rosa is unable to carry Magda with her, as when she must enter the roll-call arena. Thus when Rosa enters the square, she has to "conceal Magda under the shawl." And we are twice told that "since the drying up of Rosa's nipples," only the shawl could keep Magda quiet and therefore safe. Earlier in the story, the identification of shawl with bosom is made even more explicit when we read that Magda would have died had she not been "buried away deep inside the magic shawl, mistaken there for the shivering mound of Rosa's breasts."[26] I explore this at some length because just at the key point of Lam 2:12, where we have already seen a strong correspondence with the story "The Shawl," we are told that the children's lives are running out "in the bosom [ḥêq] of their mother." What is astonishing, in light of the connotations of the bosom/shawl in Ozick's story, is that ḥêq in the Bible quite often indicates a "fold of garment at the breast" (in other words, a shawl). Furthermore, it serves as a place of concealment (as in Prov 21:14 and Job 23:12). Thus the shawl as a surrogate bosom and place of concealment may also be seen as an echo of Lamentations.

The Impossibility of Mourning

If it is true that "The Shawl" picks up on the concerns of Zion for the survival of her children and makes those concerns its own, it is also true that the survival represented by "The Shawl" has been radically transformed. Long gone are the buoyancy of Second Isaiah and the promises of the Targum and the midrash. Absent too is the advocacy of Jeremiah, roaring on behalf of the children as he did in Kallir's medieval poem "In the Fullness of Her Grief." Most conspicuously missing is the voice of God. The only response to Magda's death in "The Shawl" is Rosa's "wolf's screech," a screech cut short by filling her mouth with Magda's beloved shawl.

So the nonending of the story is not unlike the nonending of the book of Lamentations: a mother fails in her attempts to keep her children alive, and the reader is left to fill the silence, or the white space, as best as she or he can. Such a return to destitution, to the default of God renders "The

---

26. Ibid., 108.

Shawl" more nearly akin to the biblical book than are those texts explicitly concerned with its interpretation.

I began this article by defining melancholia as the impossibility of mourning; but that definition is not quite accurate. It is not so much that mourning is *impossible,* but that mourning may prove *impossible to accomplish,* to be done with once and for all. It is not to claim that mourning does not exist, but that mourning always exists. The incorrigibility of mourning does not, contra Freud, imply a pathological state or even one of resignation, since the force of mourning derives precisely from its renunciation. In a recent article, Derrida writes that "the force of mourning develops its maximal intensity, so to speak, only at the mad moment of decision, at the point of its absolute interruption, there where *dynamis* remains virtuality."[27] Derrida goes on to write that one thus works *at* mourning both as an object and as a resource, "working at mourning as one would speak of a painter working at a painting but also of a machine working at such and such an energy level."[28] Melancholia is this perpetual state of interruption, and as such it preserves mourning as force, as virtuality.

Melancholia impugns both an optimism that imagines to have paid its debt to Being, as well as a nihilism that acknowledges no debt to begin with. So these two bookends of destitution trade in absence and abandonment, but an absence that is felt and an abandonment that is resisted. To allow these texts into one's psyche means, to borrow a phrase from Lyotard, "to be inhabited by something to which no answer is ever given."[29] But it also means to expect one nonetheless.

---

27. Jacques Derrida, "By Force of Mourning," *Critical Inquiry* 22 (1996) 177.
28. Ibid., 173.
29. Jean-François Lyotard, "The Survivor," in *Toward the Postmodern* (Atlantic Highlands, N.J.: Humanities Press, 1993) 149.

– 20 –

C(ha)osmopolis

Qohelet's Last Words

Timothy K. Beal

If we are in some sense, like it or not, children of modernity, modernity is likewise in some sense, like it or not, the child of biblical wisdom: on the one hand, confident in the stable, reasonable order of the cosmos and our ability to articulate that order and live according to it; on the other hand, haunted by an unnameable who introduces profound disjunction and disorder, an unnameable who is revealed on the edge between creation and uncreation, cosmos and chaos. Modernity, like biblical wisdom, is haunted by this unnameable, and thus is fraught with tensions between grand visions of a reasonable moral universe and the particular voices and faces that give witness to an otherness that introduces massive ruptures in that vision.

In his essay on the rise and development of the modern Western consciousness, Stephen Toulmin uses the term *cosmopolis* to describe one side—the dominant side—of this tension: the total vision of the coherence of all things, from the stable, reasonable, and predictable order of the *cosmos* to the likewise stable, reasonable, and predictable order of human lives and social relationships (*polis*).[1] The hidden, almost unconscious agenda of modernity, he argues, was to establish a new cosmopolitical vision in the aftermath of an old one that had broken down under the weight of the Thirty Years War and other seventeenth-century theological and political crises. Indeed, Toulmin argues that the modern cosmopolis was in many ways a *theological* response to a *theological crisis*. "The general crisis of

---

1. Stephen Toulmin, *Cosmopolis: The Hidden Agenda of Modernity* (Chicago: Univ. of Chicago Press, 1990) 66–71; concerning the "intellectual scaffolding" of this cosmopolis, see also 107–15. I was first introduced to Toulmin's book by Professor Brueggemann when I was a seminary student in his Old Testament Theology course. I am glad for this opportunity to return the book, so to speak, in an essay that is pervaded by the influence of the one it is written to honor.

the early seventeenth century was, in short, not just economic and social, but also intellectual and spiritual: the breakdown of public confidence in the older cosmopolitical consensus."[2]

> After the catastrophic times from 1618 to 1655, a new and self-maintaining social order was gradually established . . . a new Cosmopolis, in which the divinely created Order of Nature and the humanly created Order of Society were once again seen as illuminating one another. . . . After 1660, similarly, the development of new ideas of social structure placed the highest priority on social stability. This development, too, went hand-in-hand with the evolution of a stable vision of Nature.[3]

In seventeenth-century Europe the grand new vision of cosmopolis, drawing from Newton, Descartes, and others, offered society a way of ordering the chaos, of staving off the floodwaters that threatened to overcome it. It allowed one to envision, and therefore to create and enforce, order against chaos—from heavenly bodies to individual bodies and everything in between. The "hidden agenda" of modernity is, in a sense, *Chaoskampf* (the struggle with chaos).

Like modernity, biblical literature has its visions of cosmopolis. One finds them, for example, in the wisdom discourses of Proverbs and in the "teachings" of Job's friends. These visions find their orientation in traditions of creation and Torah piety: the order of creation is stable, reliable, perceivable, reasonable; the order of society is closely related; keep Torah and you will be blessed; failing this, you will be cursed, driven from the land, flung into the chaos waters of exile.[4]

But biblical literature also articulates disjunction and even breakdown—always necessarily theological—in this cosmopolis. It also offers visions of cosmopolitical order, the moral universe, falling to pieces, the return of chaos (*tōhû wābōhû*) over the order of creation. If the order of creation is precarious, then so are all political orderings that are grounded in an affirmation of that creation. Chaos is reintroduced within cosmopolis: *chaosmopolis*. What is particularly striking in biblical literature—especially

---

2. Ibid., 71.
3. Ibid., 98.
4. On the relation between wisdom and creation in Hebrew Scriptures, see esp. Roland E. Murphy, "Wisdom and Creation," *JBL* 104 (1985) 3–11. Whether one agrees or disagrees with the argument that wisdom influences Deuteronomy (so Moshe Weinfeld, *Deuteronomy and the Deuteronomic School* [Oxford: Oxford Univ. Press, 1972]), it is clear that there are strong relations between Deuteronomic and wisdom traditions. For summaries of recent scholarly research on wisdom, see esp. Roland E. Murphy, "Wisdom in the OT," *ABD* (New York: Doubleday, 1992) 6:920–31; and James L. Crenshaw, "The Wisdom Literature," in *The Hebrew Bible and Its Modern Interpreters* (ed. Douglas A. Knight and Gene M. Tucker; Philadelphia: Fortress Press, 1985) 368–407. On Torah piety and wisdom in Qoh 12:9–14 (the frame narrator's words), see Gerald H. Wilson, "The Words of the Wise: The Intent and Significance of Qohelet 12:9–14," *JBL* 103 (1984) 175–92.

when compared with other polytheistic texts from the ancient Near East—
is that one and the same God appears to be the bearer of both order and
chaos. The biblical God is both chaos monster and monster tamer (akin,
in a sense, to *both* Tiamat and Marduk), both champion and adversary of
the *Chaoskampf*. Chaosmopolis, like cosmopolis, comes from God. We see
it happening in the flood story of Genesis 6–8, and in the story of Babel
in Genesis 11. We see it happening in the "city of chaos" in Isaiah 24. We
also see it happening (and being challenged) in Job, as the individual righteous body in pain boldly calls into question the rightness and justness of
the entire created order and even its Creator.[5]

We also see such a vision of chaosmopolis in the final words of Qohelet
(12:1–8). After recalling a long life of chasing after wind, with the school-
house built on the dual foundations of Wisdom and Torah in splinters on
the ground, Qohelet's last words envision "evil days" on the horizon. The
dominant scholarly understanding of this passage sees it as an allegory, or
at least as a symbolic discourse, on one man's aging and death. Without
denying the presence of that theme in this text, I will argue that the exclusive preoccupation among biblical scholars with this theme has resulted in
neglect of another highly significant dynamic within the text, namely, the
strange inbreaking of elements of proto-apocalyptic discourse in these last
words, and the vision of chaosmopolis that this inbreaking presents.[6]

Finally, I will argue that in these last words envisioning cosmopolitical

---

5. On Job's discourse as a problematizing of the Deuteronomic moral universe, see Timothy K. Beal, "Facing Job," *Semeia: Levinas and the Bible* (ed. Tamara C. Eskenazi and Gary A.
Phillips, forthcoming); on the ambivalence of "blessing/curse" as a fault line running down the
middle of the entire theological discourse of Job, see Tod Linafelt, "The Undecidability of ברך
in the Prologue to Job and Beyond," *BI* 4 (1996) 154–72.

6. I do not intend to argue that Qoh 12:1–8 is apocalyptic according to any generic definition (on which see John J. Collins, "Early Jewish Apocalypticism," *ABD* 1:282; idem,
Apocalypse: The Morphology of a Genre [Semeia 14; Missoula, Mont.: Scholars Press, 1979).
Rather, I intend to draw attention to elements in this text that are strikingly similar to other
prophetic texts commonly believed to be the predecessors to the fully developed apocalypses
that begin to appear in the third century BCE. See the subsequent discussion.
Interpreters have not always neglected the presence of apocalyptic elements in Qohelet's last
words, however; indeed, sometimes such elements have been *added*. John Jarick has shown
how the third-century theologian Gregory Thaumaturgos (d. 270 CE), who is believed to have
been a student of Origen, offers a paraphrase of Qohelet that clearly understands 12:1–7 as
a full-blown apocalypse. See John Jarick, "An 'Allegory of Age' As Apocalypse (Ecclesiastes
12:1–7)," *Colloquium: Australian and New Zealand Theological Review* 22 (1990) 19–27;
see also Jarick, "Gregory Thaumaturgos' Paraphrase of Ecclesiastes," *Abr-Nahrain* 27 (1989)
37–57. Gregory's paraphrase, however, is primarily interested in making Qohelet a more pious
and theologically affirming text. Therefore he highlights and then builds upon the apocalyptic
elements in the text in order to *soften* the theological crisis that the earlier Hebrew and Greek
versions articulate so powerfully and so provocatively. That is, in Gregory's paraphrase, the
apocalyptic vision at the end of Qohelet is made to describe a day of judgment for the un-
righteous, whose fate is sharply distinguished in his text from the assured salvation of the
people of God. In Gregory's text, then, the apocalypse is envisioned along the lines of the wis-

disjuncture and breakdown, Qohelet expresses a longing for the other side of apocalypse, that is, for a justice that is beyond accommodation within the limits of the present cosmological-moral order as articulated in wisdom tradition (or, for that matter, in Deuteronomy) and as problematized in Qohelet's discourse. In this sense, too, Qohelet should not be understood as old-age cynicism on the vanity of life. Rather, in Qohelet's articulation of this chaosmopolis, we find a longing for and a beckoning of what is beyond it.

Qohelet's Last Words

¹ Remember your creator in the days of your youth,
   before the evil days arrive,
      and years approach about which you say,
         "There is no pleasure for me in them";
² before the sun darkens (and the light and the moon and the stars)
   and the clouds return after the rain;
³ on the day when the housekeepers tremble, and men of might go
            crooked,
      and the grinders cease, because they are so few,
         and those watching in the window grow dim,
⁴   and the doors onto the street are shut up;
         when the voice of the grinder is lowered,
      and one rises up at the voice of the bird,
         and all daughters of song are bowed down;
⁵   also they will fear what is high and terrors in the road;
      and the almond sprouts,
         and the locust becomes a burden to itself,
         and the caper berry fails to satisfy;
      for humanity is headed for its eternal home,
         and the wailers go about in the street;
⁶ before the silver cord is snapped, and the golden bowl is
            smashed,
      and the jar by the spring is broken, and the wheel at the cistern is smashed;
⁷   and the dust returns over the land, just as it had been;
      and the life-breath returns to *Elohim*, who gave it.
⁸ "Vapor of vapors," said Qohelet, "the whole of it is vapor."

(Qoh 12:1–8)

Remember...

Following the governing imperative (*ûzkōr*, "remember") the passage can be neatly divided into three subsections, each introduced by *'ad 'ăšer*,

---

dom poems on the fate of the wicked spoken by Job's friends (e.g., Job 15:17–35; 18:5–21; 20:4–29).

"before" (vv. 1b, 2, and 6).[7] The command to remember in v. 1a therefore governs all of what follows in Qohelet's poetic discourse up to
(but not including) his concluding statement in v. 8. Its three subsections each reach back to this imperative: "Remember... before evil days
arrive... [remember] before the sun dims... [remember] before the silver
cord is snapped...."

And yet, what to remember? Strikingly, the object of this most significant
imperative is not entirely clear. The text has *bôr'eykā,* "your creator" (related to *br'*). Yet many scholars believe that this would be inconsistent with
the rather gloomy tenor of the rest of the poem. The most popular emendation is to remove the *'aleph* (the *yod* being merely a fuller spelling) and read
it as *bôrkā,* which could be translated as "your grave," and which is considered to be more consistent with what follows. I do not agree.[8] First of all,
there are no early witnesses that support the reading. Second, the word *bôr*
is used only five verses later (v. 6) in the same poem with clear reference
to "cistern" or "well" (involving a wheel or pulley) rather than "grave."
Third, and most important, the text as it stands ("remember your creator")
is entirely consistent with what follows, so long as the connotation of remembering *bôr'eykā* is understood not as an act of piety or thanksgiving,
but rather as a grave recognition of one's fleeting mortality (cf. a similar use
of the word in Ezek 28:13, 15). To get this sense a little more strongly in
American English, one might translate it as "remember your maker" (as in
"time to meet your maker"). Thus *bôr'eykā* may be understood as a theo-

---

7. On the one hand, 12:1 is actually a continuation of the material beginning at 11:7. First,
11:7, as several factors indicate, is preoccupied with the "goodness" of light ("the light," "the
sun") and vision ("eyes," "to see"), while 11:8 warns one to "remember" (*zkr*) that there
will be many "days of darkness [*haḥōšek*]." Likewise, in 12:1–2, there is the imperative to
"remember" (*zkr*), as well as an anticipation of "evil [or bad] days" and unpleasant years
when the "sun will grow dark [*teḥšak*]," along with "the light, the moon, and the stars."
Moreover, the imperative in 11:9a ("Rejoice, youth, while you are young, and be cheerful-
hearted in the days of your youth") is very like the imperative in 12:1 ("Remember... in the
days of your youth"). Likewise, the confirmation in 11:9b "that [*kî*] in all [*kol*] this, *Elohim*
will bring you into judgment" is very close to the frame narrator's concluding words (12:14a):
"for all [*kî kol*] deeds Elohim will bring to judgment." Finally, *hābel,* "absurdity," occurs in
11:8, 10, anticipating the final thematic phrase in 12:8, "Absurdity of absurdity... the whole
of it is absurdity." Thus 12:1–7 is clearly bound to 11:7–10. On the other hand, there is
good reason to distinguish 12:1 as the beginning of a new movement within Qohelet's poetic
discourse. Whereas there are several imperatives in the verses preceding it ("rejoice," "walk,"
"know," "remove," and "put away," plus the jussive "let him remember"), 12:1 begins with a
single imperative ("remember") upon which the remainder of vv. 1–7 will depend, and moves
some distance, I will argue, from the scope of 11:7–10. See below.

8. Neither do, among others, Robert Gordis, *Koheleth—The Man and His World* (3d ed.;
New York: Schocken, 1968) 340; Michael V. Fox, *Qohelet and His Contradictions* (JSOTSup
71; Sheffield: Almond, 1989) 299–300; Aarre Lauha, *Kohelet* (BKAT 19; Neukirchen-
Vluyn: Neukirchener Verlag, 1978) 209–10; George Aaron Barton, *A Critical and Exegetical
Commentary on the Book of Ecclesiastes* (ICC; Edinburgh: T. & T. Clark, 1908) 185.

logical rendering of transience. R. B. Y. Scott sees no reason that the text should use this term instead of *Elohim* if that is what is meant.[9] But that is *not* exactly what is meant. In this passage, Qohelet is commanding a youth, even while still a youth, to remember his rather precarious status as creature—and, I will argue, the precarious status of the entire created order as well—even before the signs of its collapse become unavoidably clear.

Before Evil Days Arrive

Verse 1b then begins the long, graphic description of what is coming. This is the shortest of the subsections governed by 12:1a, and also the most personal with regard to the youthful addressee. It begins with two verbs, "arrive" (*bô'*) and "approach" or "come upon" (*nāgā'*), which give a sense of inevitability and, at the same time, deferral. The objects of the verbs ("evil days" and years without pleasure) further this sense. "Bad" or "evil" (*rā', rā'āh*) has been a dominant adjective throughout the book, connoting both adversity (e.g., 1:13; 2:17; 7:14; 8:6) and, more commonly, moral or ethical evil (e.g., 4:3, 17; 5:13 [MT 12]; 7:15; 8:3–13; 9:3; 12:14). Here both connotations may well be operative, for evil actions often bring about human suffering, as Qohelet makes clear on other occasions (e.g., 4:1–3). At the same time, "evil days" must here also suggest imminent cosmic calamity, given what follows in v. 2.

With the approach of "years about which you will say, . . . " the duration of this gloomy future is extended, and the experience of it becomes suddenly personal. Whereas in 11:8 Qohelet says that one ought to "rejoice" in all of one's "many years" of life, here he watches for years "about which you will say, 'There is no pleasure for me in them.' "

Before the Sun Darkens

Verse 2 then begins the second and longest subsection (again introduced by *'ad 'ăšer*). It is at this point in the text that the traditional interpretation of Qohelet's final poetic discourse as being strictly about a man's old age becomes highly problematic, as the discourse moves from the breakdown of the body to the ultimate breakdown of cosmopolis. Not surprisingly, then, this is also the point at which allegory or symbolism becomes key for many interpreters. While recognizing the possibility of symbolic and even allegorical meanings that connote human aging and death in this text, I submit that such an approach—when taken as an exclusive hermeneutic—misses at least as much as it captures, and reflects a desire to find more coherence in this powerful description of collapse and decay than actually

---

9. Scott, *Proverbs-Ecclesiastes* (AB 18; Garden City, N.Y.: Doubleday, 1965) 255.

exists in the text. Moreover, that desire reflects a certain androcentrism, narrowing all the imagery down to a focus on the youth as an aging man. As will soon be clear, the descriptions here are much broader, including both cosmic and social dimensions as well.

Indeed, the expansive dimensions of this vision of breakdown are immediately clear in v. 2, for here the imagery is of cosmic calamity. As "evil days" arrive and years approach in which "you" will find no pleasure, the whole created order will begin to go awry. The verse involves two successive descriptions of this. First, the sun and light, which were "good" or "sweet" (*ṭôb*) in 11:7, will "dim" or "grow dark" (*teḥšak*), along with the moon and stars. That is, all the luminaries described in creation (Gen 1:3–5, 14–19) will cease to function as they are supposed to in the cosmic order. Second, "the clouds return after the rain" (v. 2b). This further emphasizes the gloom and darkness described in 12:2a, and denies the commonsense wisdom that sunny skies return after rain. There is no clear sky peaking through, no rainbow. Only rain, then clouds, then rain again.

Contrary to Fox,[10] these images do not exclusively connote something as narrow as human misery or gloom and despair. He is correct insofar as the verb or noun form of *ḥšk* in reference to the sun, light, or day is often used to evoke a sense of cosmic sympathy for misery (e.g., Job 3:4–10); and "groping" or "going" in *ḥōšek* is an image for humanity's vain toil (cf. Qoh 2:14; 5:16; 6:4; Job 5:14; 12:25). This is not, however, the only sense evoked by these images here. As in several prophetic descriptions (esp. in later texts), these images are suggestive of apocalyptic in-breaking of chaos. For example, Joel 2:2 describes "a day of darkness [*yôm ḥōšek*] and gloom, a day of clouds and thick darkness" when the enemy will arrive to destroy the people. The same description occurs in Zeph 1:15. While the term for "cloud" in these passages (*'ānān*) is not the same as in Qohelet, the sense is strikingly similar. Ezek 32:7–8 is perhaps the most suggestive parallel, referring to all the luminaries mentioned in Qoh 12:2, as well as clouds (again, *'ānān*) and *ḥōšek*:

> When I blot you out, I will cover the heavens,
>   and make their stars dark;
> I will cover the sun with a cloud,
>   and the moon shall not give its light.
> All the bright lights of heaven I will darken over you,
>   and put darkness [*ḥōšek*] on your land.[11]

Like Qoh 12:2, each of these texts imagines a rupturing and breakdown of the cosmic order as it is presently known. They envision the undoing

---

10. Fox, *Qohelet*, 300–301.
11. See also the very similar description in Isa 13:10.

of the created order established in Genesis 1—a theme common in proto-apocalyptic as well as apocalyptic texts. On the one hand, of course, one must recognize that the Qohelet passage, unlike the prophetic texts, has no explicit notice that all this will happen by divine agency. On the other hand, the sense of divine judgment is not entirely foreign here either, for it has already been mentioned in 11:10, and will be mentioned again in 12:14. What is important here, however, is to recognize how Qohelet appropriates the imagery common in texts like Joel, Zephaniah, and Ezekiel to describe cosmic chaos, without punctuating so strongly the theological reasoning behind it, and without losing the focus on a particular individual's misery and despair. Much as in Job 3, then, the poetic feat of this passage is to bring individual calamity into contact with total chaos. This being the case, the imperative in v. 1a is to remember not only one's fleeting mortality (i.e., "createdness") but the impermanence of the created order as well.

With v. 3, Qohelet turns attention away from the cosmos and onto the social surroundings, the polis, painting a picture that is remarkably similar to that of the "city of chaos" (*'îr tōhû*) in the proto-apocalyptic text of Isaiah 24. One should note, however, that while this verse shifts the focus, it nonetheless remains rhetorically bound to what has preceded it, as cosmopolis becomes chaosmopolis. The introductory phrase *bayyôm š-* ("on the day when"), first of all, relates what follows in vv. 3–5 to v. 2 (not directly to v. 1a) as an extended temporal clause. Thus vv. 2 and 3–5 are linked together as a unit within the larger poetic discourse. This linkage with v. 2 is strengthened, furthermore, by the recurrence of the verb *ḥšk*, which, given its subject, also recalls 11:7 by way of contrast ("those watching [*ḥārō'ôt*] . . . grow dim" versus "it is pleasant to see [*lir'ôt*] the sun").

Four social collectives are described in this verse, each as the subject of a verb. First, "the keepers of the house tremble." The subject may connote either those who watch over the house (e.g., 2 Sam 20:3) or maintenance people ("housekeepers"). Either way, they are servants. The verb attributed to these subjects, *zw'*, is rare in the Bible. It occurs also in Est 5:9, where Mordecai incurred Haman's wrath when he did not "tremble" before him. In Hab 2:7, it refers to the people's fear as the enemy approaches to destroy them. In its Aramaic form, it occurs in Dan 5:19 and 6:26 [MT 27], both times describing human recognition of vulnerability or threat. The sense in those texts, as here, therefore, is of displaying vulnerability or intimidation in the face of something more powerful or threatening. In any case, it has less to do with a man's old age or "the gradual deterioration of a house"[12]—even if he is the homeowner—than it does with the *house's* vul-

---

12. J. L. Crenshaw, *Ecclesiastes* (OTL; Philadelphia: Westminster, 1987) 186.

nerability (as a socioeconomic unit) in the face of imminent threat. Here again I must emphasize that my point is not to dismiss the connotations of aging and dying altogether, but to broaden the effect of this poetic discourse to include a more pervasive sense of breakdown—from body to polis to cosmos.

Second, "men of might [*heḥāyil*] go crooked." The subject here may suggest either "strong men" or men of social status or power (as in Job 5:5; Ruth 2:1; cf. Est 1:3). Moreover, how one interprets this will determine how one interprets the verb ('wt in *Hithpael*). It may be quite literally that strong men become physically bent over (i.e., old or weakened). This plays into the theme of aging nicely (although it does not refer to a single individual). It must be noted, however, that there are no biblical parallels for such a meaning for 'wt. Indeed, the verb is invariably used elsewhere in terms of "pervert," "make crooked," or "overturn" (often with God as the subject). In this sense, the image evoked is that of social collapse due to corruption; and this in turn would play on the moral/ethical sense of "evil days" in 12:1 (cf. Amos 8:5). This understanding is, furthermore, better in keeping with the use of this verb elsewhere in Qohelet (1:15; and 7:13, with God as the subject: "who can make straight what [God] has made crooked?").

Third, "the grinders cease, because they are few." The verb *bṭl* is a hapax in biblical Hebrew, although it does occur in Aramaic in Ezra 4:21–24 and 6:8. There, as in mishnaic Hebrew, its sense is "to cease" or "to be idle."[13] The grinders, in keeping with the context of the verse, should be understood not as some sort of machines or tools but as female servants (cf. Exod 11:5). The text indicates that they cease their work because they are so few in number. The general sense, then, is similar to the two preceding parts of v. 3, namely, a faltering and breakdown of polis.[14]

Fourth and finally, "those watching in the window grow dim." As already noted, the subject (*hārō'ôt*, "those watching") recalls the pleasant activity of "seeing [*lir'ôt*] the sun" (11:7). Here, however, the seeing, like the sun itself (v. 2), grows dim (*ḥšk*). The darkness overcoming polis matches the darkness that has overcome cosmos. That is, their looks reveal the tenor of gloom and darkness that pervades the poem. As in Lam 5:17, the image further suggests their experience of collapse and desolation all about them.

---

13. Gordis, *Koheleth*, 342; Fox, *Qohelet*, 303.

14. See the various interpretations in Gordis, *Koheleth*, 342–43; Barton, *Ecclesiastes*, 188; Lauha, *Kohelet*, 211–12; and Emmanuel Podechard, *L'ecclésiaste* (Paris: Lecoffre, 1912) 457–59. Gordis, Barton, and Podechard all support the allegorical interpretation of this as a reference to teeth. Indeed, this is to my mind the most plausible element in the allegorical line of interpretation (locust=penis being the most bizarre).

Thus, while covering the entire social spectrum (from slave to free; cf. Isa 24:2),[15] this verse widens the picture of imminent gloom and doom beyond that described in vv. 1–2. The sense is that of rapid consecutive breakdowns, covering the whole spectrum from personal lack of pleasure to social foundering to cosmic disorder.

This sense of consecutive breakdown continues in v. 4 (still part of the long temporal clause introduced by "in the day when" in v. 3). Whereas the images in v. 3 centered primarily around the domestic scene, here the focus moves out into the street (*baššûq*). At this point, the images become more random, offering a collage of scenes depicting despair, terror, anomaly, and death.

While it may be the case, as Anat and Fox assert,[16] that doors onto the street would be shut and grinding mills would be silent during a funeral, there is no reason to assume that this is what is being described here. First, there is no explicit mention in the text of a funeral; second, as of yet there has been no mention of anyone dying; third, the verse does not describe an inoperative grinding mill, but the lowering of the grinder's voice;[17] and fourth, such an assumption makes interpretation of what follows more difficult than it already is (e.g., what does rising to the voice of a bird have to do with such a scene?). Nonetheless, it is quite possible that this line in v. 4 draws from imagery appropriate to a death or funeral.[18]

Verse 5 concludes the extended temporal clause begun in v. 3, as well as the subsection begun in v. 2 with *'ad 'ăšer* ("when"). Like v. 4, it too reads like a collage, with no obvious coherence or unity to its imagery. Such an approach is not without significant poetic effect. For while continuing

---

15. Although tempting, I do not think it is possible to make a perfect chiasm of social status out of this verse, as Crenshaw does (*Ecclesiastes*, 185–86), for it cannot be asserted without question that those looking through the window are women of higher social status (see also Gordis, *Koheleth*, 342). Nonetheless, albeit not with the same symmetry, this verse does indeed cover the social spectrum from low-status servants (keepers of the house and grinders) to privileged free ("men of might" or "greatness").

16. Fox, *Qohelet*, 303; and M. A. Anat, "The Lament on the Death of Man in the Scroll of Qohelet," *Beth Mikra* 15 (1970) 379 (Hebrew, summarized in Fox, 303).

17. Of course "grinder" could here refer to the mechanism, or perhaps even the mill; and *qôl* could refer to its "sound" rather than "voice." Even if this is granted, however, *špl* most probably does not mean "cease" or "close down" here. On the contrary, it often connotes humiliation. Thus with *qôl* as its subject, "lower" is far preferable. Moreover, the reference to "grinders" as female servants in the previous verse should suggest that it refers to a person here as well.

18. There is no explicit subject to the third-person singular verb (*wĕyāqûm*). It is traditional to assume that the subject is "he" who is supposedly aging in v. 3. But "he" has not been mentioned previously; and besides, the old man supposedly described as aging in these verses would be referred to as "you," given the fact that 12:1 establishes this as an address to a young man (in the first person [v. 1b]) to remember his maker before things go from bad to worse. Given this, I suggest that the subject of the verb be taken generically: "and one rises up to the voice of the bird."

to fill out the picture of gloom and calamity with further particularities, it also evokes a sense of randomness and disorientation in the process of its presentation. "They" (presumably "all the daughters of song" who are "bowed down") are fearful in the face of someone or something—it is not clear—higher, that is, more powerful or threatening, and "terrors in the road."[19] Thus this opening line in v. 5 makes explicit a linkage in the text between fear, anxiety, and threat on the one hand, and gloom, lamenting, and death on the other (cf. Isa 24:8).

The verse continues with three images from nature, followed by a *kî* ("for," "that") clause, which concludes the subsection (vv. 2–5). These three images suggest, above all, that even nature is not behaving or producing for humanity as it should.[20] First, the almond "blossoms" or "sprouts"; that is, it goes to seed, and is therefore no good to eat.[21] Second, the locust "is a burden to itself." This is either a counternatural (i.e., anomalous) image (since the locust is a small, light insect), or perhaps suggests that it is weighted down from feeding. Third, "the caper berry fails to satisfy" (cf. Job 40:8); that is, the berry known to stimulate one's (sexual)[22] appetite becomes ineffectual.

After this brief description of nature gone awry, v. 5 (and with it the second subsection) concludes with this cheerful note: "for humanity is headed for his eternal home; and the wailers go about in the street." While Qohelet's poetic discourse is not yet finished (vv. 6–7 will also be governed by the command to remember), this serves as an intermediate motive clause following the lengthy temporal clause of vv. 3–5. It is, moreover, undeniably evocative of a death scene. At the same time, "lamenting" (*sāpad*) can also be an element in the description of more general—even theophanic— calamity, as in Mic 1:8–9.[23] An interesting juxtaposition emerges: the image

---

19. Cf. 2 Chr 35:25 and Ps 35:14. The combination of "song" with "bowed down" would suggest the activity of lamenting. The context here supports this interpretation, even if one does not see this primarily in terms of a funeral. The meaning of *ḥatḥat* ("terror"), a hapax, is related to the verb *ḥātat*, "to be shattered" or "dismayed." Thus it is consistent with the present context, which is pervaded by calamity, disorientation, and mayhem.

20. A very dull book could be written on the questions and problems of translation involved in these three brief descriptions. The discussion of these matters here will be kept to a minimum, since one arrives at a point of diminishing returns very quickly.

21. I am assuming the standard emendation of the verb *nāṣaṣ* ("sprout"), following the lead of LXX (*antheō*), Vulgate, and other translations, along with nearly all modern commentators. I read *haššāqēd* as "the almond" rather than "the almond tree," since this is consistent with its verb and the context (so Gordis, *Koheleth*, 345; though he then reads it allegorically). This is, moreover, the more common sense. The only other instance in which the term means "almond tree" is Jer 1:11: "I saw a rod of an almond tree." There "almond" alone would be especially strange.

22. See Barton, *Ecclesiastes*, 190; and Crenshaw, *Ecclesiastes*, 188.

23. On which see Timothy K. Beal, "The System and the Speaking Subject in the Hebrew Bible: Reading for Divine Abjection," *BI* 2 (1994) 171–89.

of a single subject, "humanity" (*hā'ādām*), going inevitably toward its "eternal home" over against the image of plural subjects, "those mourning" (*hassōpdîm*), "going around"; an inevitable march toward death contrasted against the milling about of mourners, creating a sense of tension between pandemonium and the stasis of death.

Before the Silver Cord Is Snapped

Verse 6 begins the third and final subsection under the governing imperative of 12:1a. As with the other subsections, it is introduced by *'ad 'ăšer* ("before" or "when," recalling again "remember your creator" from v. 1). What follows consists of four subject-verb sets: "the silver cord is snapped[24] ... the golden bowl is crushed ... the jar is broken ... the wheel [or pulley] is crushed." In addition, the last two subject-verb sets include prepositional phrases that locate the demolished objects near water sources—"over the fountain" and "at the cistern." It should also be noted that the verb *rāṣaṣ* ("crush") is used twice, and that two of the subjects are vessels while the two others are something else.[25] The overall picture is clearly that of various functional items which have been demolished and abandoned "at the scene."

Many have interpreted the images of this verse as figurative for death and burial, the most obvious allusion being *bôr*, which can mean "pit" or even "grave" in addition to "cistern."[26] The other objects might then be understood symbolically as funerary items. Given the depiction of cosmopolitical calamity in the previous verses, however, I propose that sustained focus be given to its more literal sense, namely, a description of demolished and abandoned items used in everyday life. The most obvious sense here is of an abandoned occupation site. Indeed, images of smashing and breaking are common in biblical literature, especially in prophetic visions of urban ruin (e.g., Isa 24:10, 12; 30:13–14; Jer 18:6; cf. Deut 28:33; Judg 7:19–20). The image here is somewhat like that of a ghost town—the aftermath of a city of chaos.

Based on this reading, v. 7 follows very nicely, serving both as a conclusion to the entire depiction of collapse and ruin that began in 12:1b,

---

24. Reading the *Qere*.

25. Presumably *galgal* serves some function related to the cistern (or perhaps "pit"), just as the jar would serve some purpose beside or above a spring. For example, it may be a pulley of some sort (so Crenshaw, *Ecclesiastes*, 188). With regard to the silver cord there can be no certainty. It may be safely assumed for the present discussion, however, that it, like the other broken objects, was functional. Crenshaw suggests that it holds the bowl on the wall. Fox (*Qohelet*, 306–7) agrees, although he suggests that the cord was actually holding all three items over a spring at the bottom of a pit. The closest parallel to "cord of silver" would probably be in Est 1:6, which describes the decor of Ahasuerus's palace. Cf. Qoh 4:12 as well.

26. See, most recently, Fox, *Qohelet*, 306–8.

and as a continuation of the image of demolition and abandonment described in the immediately preceding material: "and the dust returns over the land, just as it had been; and the life-breath returns to *Elohim*, who gave it." The symmetry and clarity of this verse are striking—especially when contrasted against vv. 2–6—and they elicit a sense of tension between, on the one hand, the sense of closure established formally by vv. 1 and 7 and, on the other hand, the cosmopolitical mayhem envisioned in between. Each line includes the verb *šûb* ("return"), a prepositional phrase, and a relative clause ("just as it had been" in v. 7a; "who gave it" in v. 7b). Moreover, the subject-verb order is structured chiastically at the beginning of each line (*wĕyāšōb he'āpār...wĕhārûaḥ tāšûb*—"and the dust returns" in v. 7a, "and returns the life-breath" in v. 7b). This chiastic pairing of returns in v. 7—the returning of dust to dust and divine breath to the one who breathes it—represents the last moment in the undoing of creation, for with it Qohelet imagines the separation of the dust of the earth from the breath that enlivened it into a human being in Gen 2:7.

Vapor of Vapors

Qohelet's last line is therefore a fitting conclusion—both to his last words in 12:1–8 and to the book as a whole: " 'vapor of vapors,' says Qohelet, 'the whole of it is vapor.' "[27] Many translators opt for a more figurative and less literal rendering of Qohelet's use of *hebel* (lit. "vapor," "breath," or

---

27. No that the statement here is not entirely identical to 1:2, in that it does not repeat *hăbēl hăbālîm* after "said Qohelet." A few manuscripts, including the Syriac, add the repetition to 12:8, no doubt to make the text more symmetrical.

As mentioned earlier, this verse also serves as a conclusion to the poetic discourse begun in 11:7, as a subset to the book as a whole. In 11:8 he said "all that comes is absurdity [*hăbel*]." By 12:7, everything has returned to stasis, "just as it was." In addition, this verse functions as a transition out of Qohelet's direct discourse and into the frame narrator's. This is done by the inclusion of both "voices" here, reminding the reader that, within the logic of the book, 1:2–12:8 has actually been one extended quotation. Thus, if the prologue and epilogue are frames for the book as a whole, moving the reader into and out of the world of the text, then 1:2 and 12:8 are something like frames-within-frames, moving the reader between Qohelet and the one quoting him.

Of course, Qohelet does not have the last word in the book. Rather, another voice, that of a "frame narrator," follows Qohelet (12:9–14), anxiously covering over the abyss that Qohelet has begun to open. As others have noted, the frame narrator's words in 12:9–14 draw particular themes from Qohelet's discourse—especially the hope for an ultimate divine judgment (cf., e.g., 12:14 and 11:9). Certainly Qohelet expresses some highly ambivalent and tentative hope in an ultimate judgment, but never in such a confident, affirmative fashion as the frame narrator. In vv. 9–14, this narrator pulls together a few theological threads from Qohelet's discourse in order to throw a line between Qohelet in the midst of the flood waters and the solid, dry ground of Torah and wisdom, thereby attempting to make the final lesson of the book the command to fear God and keep God's commandments, and thereby attempting to overwrite the sense of theological tension and ambivalences that pervade Qohelet's discourse. Of course, Qohelet's last words echo beyond the frame narrator's last words. On 12:9–14 and Torah piety, see esp. Wilson, "Words of the Wise."

"breeze," associated with *rûaḥ*, "breath," "wind," or "spirit" in Isa 57:13;
Qoh 1:14; and here in 12:7). Given its close relation with *rûaḥ* in the previous verse, and with creation language generally, however, a more literal
translation is appropriate here. The vapor here is the trace of a trace: the
trace of the breath (*rûaḥ*; 12:7), which is the trace of the one who creates
and uncreates worlds (cf. Gen 1:2, where before creation "a *rûaḥ 'ĕlōhîm*
swept over the deep"; and Gen 2:7, where God's *rûaḥ* turns dust into a
human being). While suggesting the fleeting, transient quality of all creation (from cosmos to polis), then, the vapor also suggests that there are
always traces in creation—and in creation's undoing—of an unnameable
other who is both caught "in the fray" and beyond it. The vapor is not
simply emptiness, but the trace of a haunting presence: a vapor trail of
the divine.

Chaotic Desert

Here in Qohelet's last words the crisis in wisdom's vision of a moral
universe reaches critical mass in a vision of chaosmopolis—an undoing
of creation, a reintrusion of chaos from God upon the divinely ordered
cosmopolis. Chaosmopolis now.

Throughout his discourse, Qohelet has articulated a vision of the world
out of whack, not in sync with the cosmological and moral laws that supposedly derive from it. "The time is out of joint," as Hamlet puts it. Jacques
Derrida reads Hamlet, at the moment he utters this line (which closes the
scene where the specter of his murdered father appeared and addressed
him), as one experiencing profound *disjuncture* in the day-to-day order
of things.[28] This disjuncture opens him to the possibility of a justice—as
relation to the other—that is infinitely beyond the law, and also beyond
simple vengeance or restitution.[29] This moment for Hamlet is, according to
Derrida, apocalyptic, because in this "out of joint" moment (a time that
does not make sense within time), a "chaotic desert"[30] is opened in which
one longs for—and waits for, and beckons—what is beyond the "order of
the day," that is, for a new (always new) relation to the other. Granted,
Derrida's understanding of apocalyptic is a far cry from that of formalist
biblical scholars. But it is insightful and suggestive in its own right nonetheless. Indeed, Qoh 12:1–8 may be understood as "apocalyptic" in two

---

28. Jacques Derrida, *Specters of Marx: The State of Debt, the Work of Mourning, and the New International* (trans. Peggy Kamuf; New York: Routledge, 1994), esp. 3–48.

29. Ibid., 23–28. Derrida derives this formulation of justice as relation to the other largely in conversation with the work of Emmanuel Levinas.

30. Ibid., 28.

senses. First, as I have shown, this text uses imagery and language that is very close to other commonly considered "proto-apocalyptic" texts, such as Joel 2, Ezekiel 32, and Isaiah 24. Beyond these simple literary connections, however, Qohelet's last words are also apocalyptic in a second, more profound, albeit less formal sense: they open a space—most literally a "chaotic desert" (dust and wind)—where otherness might be revealed.

Qohelet's last words offer no simple vision of "the end" as such. Rather, they envision the end as *edge,* threshold—an ending/beginning, between uncreation and creation, chaosmogony and cosmogony. Qohelet's last words give us a glimpse of wisdom's speaking subject on the edge: on the edge of a chaotic desert, the edge of the wasteland, which is the place of a possible new relation to the other, a new creation, a new justice—excessive, beyond law and order, unnameable.

Part Five

Continuing the Dialogue

– 21 –

Theology of the Old Testament

A Prompt Retrospect

Walter Brueggemann

No one can doubt that theological interpretation of the Bible—most especially in the context of a Christian reading—is in a quite new, quite different, and quite demanding interpretive situation. It does not matter to me if that new circumstance is termed "postmodern," though I have used that term to describe it. What counts is a *pluralistic* interpretive community that permits us to see the polyphonic character of the text, and the *deprivileged* circumstance whereby theological interpretation in a Christian context is no longer allied with or supported by dominant epistemological or political-ideological forces. So long as Christian interpretation was dominant and normative, it could count on "intellectual reasonableness" to sustain it. That supportive alliance no longer pertains. Learning to do biblical theology outside the Western hegemony is demanding work, in order that Christian interpretation may come to know something of what Jewish interpreters have long known how to negotiate. Or more briefly, hermeneutical problematics and possibilities have now displaced positivistic claims—historical or theological—as the matrix of theological reflection.

I

As a consequence of that changed contextual reality, theological reflection concerning the Old Testament/Hebrew Bible must perforce move beyond the great twentieth-century achievements of Walther Eichrodt and Gerhard von Rad. Indeed, reading those works now strikes one as remarkably dated, and as largely innocent of the interpretive problems and possibilities that one now must face.

Having said that, however, I must add that no serious interpretive enterprise ever begins de novo, and certainly biblical theological work stands in important and grateful continuity with those contributions. Thus it is

307

my intention to have worked carefully at issues of *continuity and disconti-nuity* with that scholarship, though it is likely that my appropriation and borrowing are more pervasive than I am aware. Eichrodt's effort to organ-ize around the single conceptual frame of covenant was, in his time, an immense gain. It is unfortunate, moreover, that the theological grid of cove-nant got carried away into historical-critical matters with Klaus Baltzer, George Mendenhall, and Dennis McCarthy, because Eichrodt's governing theological insight—namely, that the God of Israel is characteristically a God *in relation*—was better than any of that. That insight, rooted for him in the Christian interpretation of John Calvin, is what Eichrodt sought to exposit.

It is clear that von Rad's work has been much more decisive for me, and indeed my opening section on "core testimony" is willfully von Radian. Von Rad's thesis of *recital* as a fundamental dynamic behind the Old Tes-tament permitted a sense of openness, an acknowledgment of variation and plurality, and an accent upon "the said." All of that I have appropriated, though I have gone further than von Rad with the rhetorical, and have sought to avoid the morass of positivistic history from which von Rad was unable to escape. Thus the continuities with this scholarly work are im-portant to me, and I have the sense that the thesis of *an alternative world voiced in Israel's testimony* is indeed a Barthian impulse on my part, which echoes G. Ernest Wright's thesis of "against."

II

Having said that and having acknowledged debts and continuities with gratitude, I want to suggest now the ways in which I have tried to move beyond those dominant models of the twentieth century, hopefully to con-tribute in a way congruent with our own interpretive context that is outside hegemony, pluralistic, and deprivileged. I will suggest six elements of my exposition that I consider to be *contributions to our ongoing work*.

1. At the outset it has seemed clear to me that a theology of the Old Tes-tament *cannot appeal to "history,"* as evidenced by von Rad's inability to hold together "critically assured minimum" and "theological maximum":[1]

> But our final comment on it should not be that it is obviously an "un-historical" picture, because what is in question here is a picture fashioned throughout by faith. Unlike any ordinary historical document, it does not

---

1. Gerhard von Rad, *Old Testament Theology* (trans. D. M. G. Stalker; 2 vols.; New York: Harper & Row, 1962–65) 1:108.

have its centre in itself; it is intended to tell the beholder about Jahweh, that is, how Jahweh led his people and got himself glory.[2]

I do not for one instant mean to suggest, following Rudolf Bultmann, that there is nothing of "happenedness"; rather, the "happening" is not subject to the measure of modern positivistic categories.[3] The "happenedness" of the theological claims made for Israel's God is in, with, and under Israel's attestation; critical positivistic—and now nihilistic—judgments do not touch those claims. Indeed, Israel's recital and attestation at many points consciously assert a memory and a claim that is counter to dominant history, and our interpretation must attend to that impulse to counter. Thus the problematic is not Israel's claim made for its God, but the flattened criticism that refuses in principle to host such claims.

The issue, then, is not at all a particular claim that should be dissolved into universal assertion, for I have insisted everywhere on the particular and have refused a groundless universalism. The issue rather is particularity that has confidence in its own utterance and that refuses to submit its claim to any universal norm.

2. The counterside of eschewing modernist historical categories is to appeal to *the practice of rhetoric.* I understand Old Testament theology to be reflection upon the uttered faith claims of Israel concerning the God who is given to us precisely in and through those claims. In this regard, the focus upon utterance is congruent with von Rad's approach, which was unfortunately complicated by his appeal to critical history. Beyond von Rad, moreover, I am much influenced by Paul Ricoeur's awareness that utterance is an act of imagination that produces worlds and/or counterworlds.[4] More closely than Ricoeur, I am inescapably instructed by my teacher, James Muilenburg, who understood best about faith and rhetoric, so that in some general way Old Testament theology is "rhetorical criticism."

Such a focus upon rhetoric, in a context outside hegemony—pluralistic and deprivileged—is an effort at nonfoundationalism, an attempt to trade neither upon the stable claims of the Western theological-ontological tradition nor upon the claims of Western positivistic history, either in its

---

2. Ibid., 302.

3. See Walter Brueggemann, *Abiding Astonishment: Psalms, Modernity, and the Making of History* (LCBI; Louisville: Westminster/John Knox, 1991).

4. On the production of worlds, see Peter L. Berger and Thomas Luckmann, *The Social Construction of Reality: A Treatise in the Sociology of Knowledge* (Anchor Books; Garden City, N.Y.: Doubleday, 1967); and Amos N. Wilder, "Story and Story-World," *Int* 37 (1983) 353–64. More directly pertinent for us, see Wesley A. Kort, *"Take, Read": Scripture, Textuality, and Cultural Practice* (University Park, Pa.: Pennsylvania State Univ. Press, 1996) 9 and passim.

maximal or now in its exceedingly minimalist tendency. Israel's rhetoric mediates a God not held in thrall by either mode of Western certitude or control.

3. I have increasingly found thematic approaches to biblical theology wanting, not only because they are inescapably reductionist, but because they are characteristically boring and fail to communicate the open-ended vitality of the text. It is for that reason that I decided, early on, to focus not on substantive themes but on *verbal processes* that allow for dynamism, contradiction, tension, ambiguity, and incongruity—all those habits that belong peculiarly to interactionism.[5] What I hope I have offered is an interactionist model of theological exposition congruent with this believing community that is endlessly engaged with God, a God who is available for the extremities of praise and complaint, which are Israel's characteristic modes of speech in this conflictual engagement. The importance of this move *from theme(s) to process* cannot be overstated for me, because the interactive process seems crucial both to the Subject of Old Testament theology and to the pluralistic, deprivileged context of our own work.

4. More specifically, it is the focus upon juridical language of *testimony* that I hope will be the major gain of my work. I understand that "testimony" as a theme can be as reductionist as any other theme, but I intend it not as a theme but as a process whereby Israel endlessly gives an account of reality featuring the God of Israel as decisive, whether in presence and action or in absence and hiddenness.

It may be that the notion is reductionist because one can, I am sure, claim that not everything is testimony. Except that I think a case can be made that Israel, in all its utterances and writings, stays roughly fixed upon that single and defining claim for Yahweh.[6] Testimony about a single and defining claim permits two maneuvers that are important. There is, on the one hand, immense variation (as one would expect) in the detailed accounts offered the court by witnesses who nevertheless agree on the main point. On the other hand, there is a significant core of agreement among these witnesses, when heard in the presence of other accounts of reality that construe without reference to Yahweh.

It strikes me as odd that the genres of disputatiousness, given often in litigious tone, have not more centrally occupied theological interpreters. I would focus, for many reasons, on Second Isaiah wherein the poetry dis-

---

5. On the remarkable emergence of such interactionism in the twentieth century as a theological and philosophical perspective, see Hans Urs von Balthasar, *Theo-Drama: Theological Dramatic Theory* (trans. Graham Harrison; San Francisco: Ignatius, 1988) 1:626.

6. See the comprehensive perspective on "testimony" by Paul Ricoeur, *Essays on Biblical Interpretation* (ed. Lewis S. Mudge; Philadelphia: Fortress Press, 1980) 119–54.

putes about other gods. But the "speech of judgment" is dominant in the preexilic prophets.[7] The Deuteronomic history, informed as it may be by Deuteronomy 32, proceeds as an extended narrative speech of judgment. The psalms of complaint, culminating in the book of Job, proceed in similar fashion. I believe, moreover, that it is legitimate to conclude from such a core of material that even where the genre is not visible, Israel characteristically makes a case for a Yahwistic construal of reality against other construals of reality. Where the case is not disputatious, it is even there a lesser or softer advocacy for this rather than that. Thus I want to offer this focus on testimony as a gain, as long as it is taken as metaphor and not pressed too hard to a conclusion.

5. The process of litigation that gives great maneuverability allows for a *paradigmatic juxtaposition of core testimony and countertestimony,* a juxtaposition that I count as a major gain of my study. While Israel's utterances make a sustained case for a Yahweh-focused world, and in the face of rivals speak with one voice on the matter (acknowledging many traces of religious phenomenology not fully incorporated into that dominant voice), yet there is vigorous dispute with that unified claim among these advocates. It is my insistence that the counterclaims must be taken seriously as a datum of theological utterance.[8] My impression is that heretofore a coherent way has not been found for such an interface. Even von Rad's "answer" really did not exhibit the remarkable dynamic of that text.[9]

I take the countertestimony to be powerful evidence that Israel is resolved to tell the truth, to tell the truth of its own life, and to tell that truth even if it crowds the large claims made for Yahweh. This is no small matter, for it means that Israel's faith has little patience for religious softness or prettiness or cover-up in the interest of protecting or enhancing God. I am drawn to Jacques Derrida's verdict that, finally, justice is undeconstructible.[10] Or in another mode, Israel's faith will not compromise the undeniable givenness of bodily reality, especially bodily pain or pain in the body politic.

---

7. See Claus Westermann, *Basic Forms of Prophetic Speech* (trans. Hugh Clayton White; Philadelphia: Westminster, 1967).

8. Emil Fackenheim, *To Mend the World: Foundations of Post-Holocaust Thought* (New York: Schocken, 1989) 11, refers to the Holocaust as "the most radical countertestimony to both Judaism and Christianity."

9. I refer to von Rad's rubric, "Israel before Jahweh (Israel's Answer)," as his title for the discussion of the wisdom traditions (*Old Testament Theology,* 1:355).

10. Jacques Derrida, "Force of Law: The 'Mystical Foundations of Authority,'" *Cardozo Law Review* 11 (July/August 1990) 945, has famously averred, "Justice in itself, if such a thing exists, outside or beyond the law, is not deconstructible. No more than deconstruction, if such a thing exists. Deconstruction is justice." Such a verdict seems to me to be quintessentially Jewish in its claim.

Such a procedure of claim and counterclaim is, in my judgment, definitional for theology in this tradition. This procedure appears to be deeply and endlessly open and unresolved, so that finally "claim" will not silence "counterclaim," nor, conversely, can "counterclaim" ever nullify "claim." This disputatious dialectic seems of absolute importance for the character of Yahweh rendered in this text, and consequently for the character of this people that renders and responds to Yahweh.

The refusal to give closure is a defining point of the data. This is a very different read from Bultmann's sorry verdict that the Old Testament is a failure, because the openness is not failure but a rigorous willingness to speak in dispute.[11] Christians exhibit an endless propensity to give closure to the matter in Jesus of Nazareth. I am, however, instructed by Jürgen Moltmann's suggestion that Friday and Sunday constitute a "dialectic of reconciliation," that is, both parts enduring and in force, so that the claim of Easter does not silence the counterclaim of Friday. The dynamic belongs to the process of faith and therefore inescapably to the parties in the process, Yahweh and Israel.

6. Finally, I have tried to extrapolate beyond Eichrodt's covenant the definitional *relatedness* of Yahweh, which I have voiced under the rubric of "Unsolicited Testimony." That is, everything said about Yahweh is said about Yahweh in relation. Yahweh is characteristically embedded in sentences with active verbs that have direct objects for whom the agency of Yahweh matters decisively.

I have, moreover, tried to make the case in some detail that what is said of Yahweh is, mutatis mutandis, characteristically said of Israel as well. Derivatively what is said of Israel as Yahweh's defining partner is said of all partners, so that Yahweh vis-à-vis Israel becomes the model for Yahweh vis-à-vis creation, nations, and human persons. This parallelism that I have suggested is in no way a move away from the privilege and particularity of Israel's status with Yahweh, but is the matrix through which all else is to be understood vis-à-vis Yahweh.

This relatedness that we subsume under covenant is crucial, because it not only draws the human-historical side of reality into the orbit of Yahweh's rule and reality—a point decisive in Calvinist theology since the first pages of the *Institutes*—but the relatedness bespeaks the truth of Yahweh as

---

11. Rudolf Bultmann, "Prophecy and Fulfillment" (trans. James C. G. Greig), in *Essays on Old Testament Hermeneutics* (ed. Claus Westermann; Richmond: John Knox, 1963) 75, has devastatingly expressed triumphalist Christian interpretation: "In the same way faith requires the backward glance into Old Testament history as a history of failure and so of promise, in order to know that the situation of the justified man arises only on the basis of this miscarriage."

much as it voices the truth of Israel or any of Yahweh's derivative partners. That is, Israel can entertain the claim that this relatedness is not always a one-way deal: it does not always move from Yahweh to Israel (and the other partners). Nor is it adequate to suggest, as scholarship has done, that the relation is "bilateral." On occasion, so it seems to me, there is role reversal, so that Israel (or other partners) can take the initiative over against Yahweh, in complaint and in praise.[12] This prospect of role reversal, whereby the lesser party becomes provisionally the dominant party, seems to me a question for further probing, even though the possibility is beyond the horizon of conventional Christian understanding. This possibility is a learning that Christian interpretation may recover from Jewish tradition. It is an evidence of how radical and daring Israel is prepared to be in its dissent from Yahweh, as well as how capable it is in resisting the conventions of perennial Western philosophy.

This sense of relatedness is true to the text in broad outline. In parallel fashion, this construal of holiness represents a powerful alternative to Cartesian reductionism. Thus the interactionist model of holiness offered by Martin Buber and Franz Rosenzweig, and now voiced afresh by Emmanuel Levinas, seems to be thoroughly rooted in the Bible, though it entails a drastic relearning for the dominant theological tradition of Western Christianity.[13] It will be evident that all of these elements I regard as gains are interrelated and of a piece in an interactionist model that refuses to take God either as a fixed object or as an empty cipher. Everything about this theological tradition insists, in the utterances of Israel, that there is Someone on the other end of the transaction who is decisive—even if absent, hidden, or in eclipse.

III

The gains that I suggest are commensurate with what will surely emerge as *points of contention and continued dispute.* I do not imagine that I have been able to see things convincingly through to the end. So I am glad to acknowledge at least four points where the argument is vulnerable, though other such points will surface in our discussion. I regard these as vulnerable points because they propose fresh perspectives for which we lack adequate categories. I incline to think that the vulnerability is only because things

---

12. On the prospect of role reversal, see Walter Brueggemann, "Prerequisites for Genuine Obedience (Theses and Conclusions)" (forthcoming).

13. It is important to recognize that the entire interpretive trajectory from Buber, given new voice by Levinas, is designed precisely to counter the Cartesian claim of autonomy. It is important that this counteroffer is *Jewish*, but it is equally important that it is a *public* claim not addressed simply to Jewish faith.

are not carried through, not because they are wrongheaded. It remains to be seen, of course, whether that judgment turns out to be acceptable to my colleagues.

1. *A nonfoundationalist perspective.* There is now available a huge literature moving in this direction.[14] But no one in the biblical field known to me has tried to make the case as directly as have I. Thus my formulation of the matter leaves me with some considerable uneasiness.

A nonfoundationalist approach is open to criticism from two perspectives. First, it will not satisfy conventional theologians who have cast matters in categories of Hellenistic ontology with the assumption that God is a stable, fixed point. But the insistences out of ancient Israel cannot concede this point, because to do so is to conform the oddity of Yahweh to settled generic categories, a maneuver that is both an epistemological accommodation and an excessive political compromise. Anyone who reflects theologically on this text knows that the God of Abraham, Isaac, and Jacob, to say nothing of the God of Moses and Job, is not easily confused with the God of the philosophers.[15] Second, and more difficult, is my urging that the rhetorical claims for Yahweh in ancient Israel are not fully linked to the happenedness of history as it has been understood in positivistic categories. The current rage of historical minimalism (nihilism?), on the basis of positivistic claims, would love to nullify theological claims for Yahweh on the basis of the negation of historical data. But that is to fall into von Rad's dilemma. I prefer to insist that *history follows rhetoric,* so that the memory uttered is the memory trusted. This is, in my judgment, how it works in a reciting, testifying, confessing community, except that acceptance of the testimony creates a circle of affirmation in which it can be subsequently claimed that the rhetoric derives from the history. The difficulties are acute. I suppose I am more aware of the problem of "history behind rhetoric" than I am skilled at articulating the countercase against that long-standing Western assumption. Rhetoric is indeed "the weapon of the weak."[16] To the extent that ancient Israel lives its life and practices its faith "outside," to that extent its rhetoric is and must be profoundly orig-

---

14. See the brief expression by John E. Thiel, *Nonfoundationalism* (Guides to Theological Inquiry; Minneapolis: Fortress Press, 1991).

15. This claim in the twentieth century has been especially voiced by Karl Barth, "The Strange New World Within the Bible," in *The Word of God and the Word of Man* (trans. Douglas Horton; repr. Harper Torchbooks; New York: Harper & Brothers, 1957) 28–50. See also Martin Buber, "The Man of Today and the Jewish Bible," in *On the Bible: Eighteen Studies* (ed. Nahum N. Glatzer; New York: Schocken, 1968) 1–13.

16. The phrase is from James C. Scott, *Weapons of the Weak: Everyday Forms of Peasant Resistance* (New Haven: Yale Univ. Press, 1985).

inary, the only recourse held by "the weak" to remain outside hegemonic assumptions.

2. *Historical criticism.* The previous point leads to the question of historical criticism, which Brevard Childs has identified as the crisis point for doing biblical theology. I am sure that I have not done well in articulating the delicate relationship between historical criticism and theological exposition. Part of the problem is that I am so deeply situated in historical criticism that it is likely that I appeal much more to such categories than I am aware. And part of the problem is that it is increasingly difficult to say with precision what it is that constitutes historical criticism, given the eruption of methodological alternatives. What now is taken as historical criticism is certainly very different from what it was in ancient days when I was in graduate school.

But the real issue is neither of these two preliminary matters; the real issue is the work and import of such criticism. We must think critically about the Bible, because we live in an enquiring intellectual world. Taken on that basis, criticism is simply being intellectually responsible. A case is readily made, however, that what has passed for historical criticism has in fact been a commitment to something like Enlightenment rationality, whereby criticism has had the negative task of eliminating whatever offended reason and the positive task of rendering the claims of the text compatible with autonomous reason. That way of understanding criticism is supported by the so-called historical minimalists who have made a virtue out of skepticism, thus pushing criticism toward skepticism that is endlessly dismissive of the claims of the text.

The issue is nicely represented in Old Testament theological scholarship by comparing the work of Childs with that of James Barr. Childs has indicated that historical criticism is largely a deficit operation for theological exposition. But Barr, fearing authoritarian obscurantism, will insist that any credible theological claim from the text must be cast in the environs of critical categories. I suspect that what is made of historical criticism depends on what one most fears in the project of interpretation: *a debilitating fragmentation* (Childs) or *an excessive fideism* (Barr). It may be then that we do best to say that criticism is to be assessed dialectically in terms of the interpretive context. I have sought to occupy a mediating position. My sympathies are with Childs, but I do not want to follow him—as I shall clarify in a moment—toward his notion of "canonical," which strikes me as unfortunately reductionist. The issue, in the end, is how the odd claims of this text make their way in an intellectual environment inclined toward domestication and resistant to the scandal of particularity, a particularity that refuses the flattening that becomes predictable and replicable.

3. *Jewish and Christian reading.* Biblical theology in a conventional
Christian context is often deeply supersessionist.[17] The assumption too
often is that the Old Testament moves directly and singularly toward the
New Testament and its christological claims, so that any other interpretive trajectory is excluded in principle.[18] There is no doubt that this is a
deeply vexed question beyond my capacity to address, and that such conventional supersessionist interpretations have contributed powerfully, even
if indirectly, to the anti-Jewish barbarism of the recent past. But it seems
clear that exclusionary reading toward Christology is morally intolerable
as well as theologically problematic.

I suspect that I do not know enough to deal adequately with the issue.
My take on it, while waiting for further instruction, is that as a Christian
I will by conviction and by habit read toward the New Testament. But because the text is endlessly polyvalent and because its Subject is endlessly
elusive and beyond domestication, it is impossible, in my judgment, to pretend a monopolistic reading. Thus my reading toward the New Testament
is done in the midst of other legitimate and valued readings—primarily Jewish—to which I must attend and by which I may expect to be instructed. It
is my expectation that in the long run Jewish reading may also be open to
the (not exclusive) validity of Christian reading, though clearly the issues
are not symmetrical because of the long history of Christian hegemony and
abusiveness. While I do not imagine any easy convergence in these readings, neither will I accept the verdict shared by Childs and Jon Levenson
that we read different Bibles.[19] Rather we must read together as far as we
can read and, beyond that, read attentively in each other's presence. Such a
strategy, to be sure, has much to unlearn and to undo, but we must begin
somewhere. I am encouraged that N. T. Wright has made a powerful case
that the New Testament gospel is the retelling of the story of Israel through
the life of Jesus, a retelling that does not preempt.[20] In all such common
reading the particularity and primacy of Jewish claims are to be affirmed,

---

17. See the analysis of R. Kendall Soulen, *The God of Israel and Christian Theology*
(Minneapolis: Fortress Press, 1996).

18. This perspective has been powerfully advocated by Francis Watson, *Text, Church and
World: Biblical Interpretation in Theological Perspective* (Grand Rapids: Eerdmans, 1994);
and *Text and Truth: Redefining Biblical Theology* (Grand Rapids: Eerdmans, 1997).

19. See Jon D. Levenson, *The Hebrew Bible, the Old Testament, and Historical Criticism:
Jews and Christians in Bible Studies* (Louisville: Westminster/John Knox, 1993) 76–81.

20. N. T. Wright, *The New Testament and the People of God* (Christian Origins and the
Question of God 1; Minneapolis: Fortress Press, 1992); and *Jesus and the Victory of God*
(Christian Origins and the Question of God 2; Minneapolis: Fortress Press, 1996). In a very
different way and from a Jewish perspective, Jon D. Levenson, "The Universal Horizon of
Biblical Particularism," in *Ethnicity and the Bible* (ed. Mark G. Brett; Leiden: Brill, 1996)
143–69, has offered a fresh scenario of an extent to which Jews and Christians may read
together in a way that is seriously theological.

and whatever else follows must follow from that primal affirmation. As I have indicated in my comments on the "Partners" for God, Israel is the defining partner, and whatever else is to be said of other partners is derived from and informed by that claim and relationship. My sense, therefore, is that Christian reading must be done very differently from what we have done heretofore. The barbarism of the twentieth century is not an irrelevance, but is rather a primary datum that requires learning to read (and believe) differently.

4. *Toward the church.* The Christian enterprise of biblical theology, and specifically Old Testament theology insofar as it is Christian, has important responsibilities and limitations. This point is the counterside of my last point concerning the interface between Jewish and Christian modes of theological exposition.

There is now an important insistence, especially by Childs (and, from the side of systematic theology, by Francis Watson), that Old Testament theology must be deeply and exclusively linked to the New Testament because, in Childs's terms, the two testaments are "two witnesses to Jesus Christ."[21] This tendency (i.e., to assume that Christian interpretation of the Old Testament is distinctively and closely focused upon the church's claim for Jesus) assures that no competing or complementary interpretation—even Jewish—warrants any consideration. The several schemes of relation of Old Testament and New Testament—law-gospel, promise-fulfillment, salvation history—may all be utilized, but the common assumption is that the Old Testament awaits the New for a compelling reading.[22] The accent is completely upon the *continuity* between the testaments.

A student of the Old Testament, however, cannot help but notice the *disjunction and disconnection* from one testament to the other, so that the theological claims of the Old Testament do not obviously or readily or smoothly or without problem move to the New Testament. Indeed, if we are to claim some kind of continuity—as any Christian reading surely must—it is a continuity that is *deeply hidden* and *endlessly problematic.* For that reason, and given the intensely and consistently iconoclastic propensity of the Old Testament text, it may be suggested that the Old Testament stands as a critical principle over against any easy claims of New Testament faith, so that the God of Israel is not easily reduced to or encom-

---

21. From this perspective, see also Peter Stuhlmacher, *How to Do Biblical Theology* (PTMS 38; Allison Park, Pa.: Pickwick, 1995).

22. The issues are summarized in a quite conventional way by A. H. J. Gunneweg, *Understanding the Old Testament* (trans. John Bowden; OTL; Philadelphia: Westminster, 1978).

passed by Christian claims.[23] After all of the adjustments from the faith of Israel to the faith of the church there is yet a deep "otherwise," which is uncontained and undomesticated, that must be acknowledged.

If the issue is to struggle with the ill fit between the two testaments, the problem is even more acute when one moves from the claims closely linked to Jesus in the New Testament to the developed dogmatic tradition of the church. It is well known that over the course of his long engagement with the intractable problem of canon, "canon" has meant several different things to Childs. In his *Biblical Theology of the Old and New Testaments,* surely his most mature articulation, the term *canon* has come to refer to the "rule of faith" (whereby Childs seems to mean the christological-trinitarian formula) as the way in which biblical theology is to be done.[24] Such perspective seems to me, in the end, both reductionist and excessively ideational, because it must gloss over the characteristic disjunctions of Old Testament rhetoric that mediate the disjunctive God of Israel. This same inclination is present in the essays collected by Carl Braaten and Robert Jenson in response to Childs.[25]

It seems to me that such a reductionist reading remains in the service of the hegemonic, triumphalist claims of the church, without at the same time recognizing the endlessly subversive intention of the text that is endlessly restless with every interpretive closure, whether Jewish or Christian. My own inclination is more congruent with the recent proposals of Wesley Kort—who considers Calvin's theory of reading as informed by *sicut,* "as if"—to read against every given conviction, to an unfounded (nonfoundational?) alternative that is given only in the text.[26] From Calvin, Kort's sense of Scripture in a postmodern context is that Scripture is too elemental, too primal, and too originary to be administered and shaped by established interpretation and doctrine:

> This is not to say that institution and doctrine are unimportant. The question is one of relative status. Reading the Bible as scripture must lead to an exit from them. For theology this means, first of all, freeing reading from theological determinations, particularly the substitution of doctrines of scripture

---

23. I take this, in a different voice, to be the point of William Stacy Johnson, *The Mystery of God: Karl Barth and the Postmodern Foundations of Theology* (Louisville: Westminster/John Knox, 1997), an insistence that in Barth God's mystery is not finally reduced to theological control.

24. Brevard S. Childs, *Biblical Theology of the Old and New Testaments: Theological Reflection on the Christian Bible* (Minneapolis: Fortress Press, 1993) 67 and passim. A closely parallel argument is made by Stuhlmacher, *How To Do Biblical Theology,* 61 and passim.

25. Carl E. Braaten and Robert W. Jenson, eds., *Reclaiming the Bible for the Church* (Grand Rapids: Eerdmans, 1995).

26. Kort, *"Take, Read,"* 25–36 and passim.

for reading the Bible.... But unity and stability in the church are not necessarily good things, and certainly imposed or abstract unity and stability are not.... But reading the Bible as scripture involves first of all movement away from self and world and toward their divestment and abjection.[27]

It is my sense that Christian reading, long hegemonic in the West, must now face *divestment and abjection* of a social-political-economic kind that is best—perhaps inevitably—matched by a theological divestment as well. Although Israel has long understood that the force of the Holy One requires the exposure of the idols, any long triumphalist interpretation characteristically does not regard its own triumphalism as idolatrous.

Kort is against the stream in much current theological conviction. I think he has it proximately right and am reassured that he finds this guiding motif at the center of Calvin's own perspective. It is Calvin's (and Kort's) *"as scripture"* to which we must attend, in a phrasing parallel to that of Childs that comes to mean something very different. It is this "as scripture" that is *originary* and *undetermined by institutional force* that may help us face the demands of interpretation, for both the wounded and the wounder.

It is evident that such a stance toward church claims, a stance critical but not dismissive, is a complement to my suggestion concerning Christian theology vis-à-vis Jewish faith. The claim of Scripture, endlessly problematic in the history of Christian reading and made poignant for our time by Karl Barth, is that the Holy One of Israel will not be held in church claims any more than in the temple claims of Solomon, for "Even heaven and the highest heaven cannot contain you, much less this house that I have built!" (1 Kgs 8:27).

IV

It will be evident that I have opted for a *process* of testimony, dispute, and advocacy; I trust it will be equally evident why I have done so. The process of adjudication is not formal and vacuous, but endlessly implies *content* about the Subject of that testimony, dispute, and advocacy. The emphasis on the process, however, seems crucial to me because (a) Israel presented its most daring utterance in disputatious process, (b) the God of Israel characteristically engages in precisely such dispute, and (c) such ongoing, respectful disputation is the only interpretive option, in my judgment, in a pluralistic, deprivileged interpretive environment. I do not believe for a minute that deprivileged environment should itself dictate the terms of our exposition; I am, however, convinced that the shape of our interpretive en-

---

27. Ibid., 124, 128.

vironment is oddly congruent with Israel's preferred way to voice its faith. I have suggested, in my book, that the endless negotiation of core testimony and countertestimony, in Christian mode, takes the form of the dialectic of Friday and Sunday.[28] I have, moreover, been deeply moved and informed by the judgment of George Steiner that "ours is a long day's journey of the Saturday."[29] A Christian dynamic of Friday-Sunday regards post-Easter Monday as still under the aegis of Easter joy. In Christian perspective, Monday is very different from Saturday. But serious Christian discernment also knows that the problems of Saturday must continue to be faced on Monday, better faced with Jews who also wait. My attempt at theological interpretation is to engage the reading of our common calling, Saturday issues even on Monday.

---

28. Walter Brueggemann, *Theology of the Old Testament: Testimony, Dispute, Advocacy* (Minneapolis: Fortress Press, 1997) 400–403.

29. George Steiner, *Real Presences* (Chicago: Univ. of Chicago Press, 1989) 232.

– 22 –

Walter Brueggemann:
A Selected Bibliography, 1961–1998

Clayton H. Hulet

The variety and extent of Walter Brueggemann's literary output—from instructional and devotional materials for youth and lay readers to theological and exegetical works for the academy—create a problem for his bibliographers: what items can be excluded to keep a relevant list of his writings from overwhelming the interested reader?

For this list I chose to include all monographs, essays, and articles the reader could expect to peruse at a typical North American library (i.e., either housed in the library or obtained via interlibrary loan). Excluded are book reviews, audio and video tapes of sermons and interviews, translations of his works into languages other than English, books and journals he edited or translated, prefatory comments (such as forewords and introductions), articles published in magazines not appearing in the major bibliographic utilities, and unpublished papers, speeches, and manuscripts.

To make this bibliography interesting and usable to an audience as diverse as Brueggemann's own, I chose to list all published writings by year regardless of size or scope. For each year, monographs are listed first, followed by essays and articles; all are alphabetical by title. This format allows readers to approach Brueggemann's work in a variety of ways, and it provides insights into the development of his interests and his career.

From the 400-word essay "Fatling" (1962) to the celebrated 777-page *Theology of the Old Testament* (1997), this record of Walter Brueggemann's literary work testifies to his creativity and passion, which seem to intensify through the years. Walter Brueggemann's greatest literary work is still ahead. As I write this, his long-anticipated theology of the Old Testament is a few months from publication. And, to be sure, he still has a large measure of untapped energy and unmined imagination in reserve. The bibliography that follows, then, should be viewed as a preliminary, provisional effort.

1961

"A Form-Critical Study of the Cultic Material in Deuteronomy: An Analysis of the Nature of Cultic Encounter in the Mosaic Tradition." Th.D. dissertation, Union Theological Seminary, New York, 1961. 492 pages.

1962

"Arcturus." In *The Interpreter's Dictionary of the Bible,* volume 1. Nashville: Abingdon, 1962. 216.

"Fatling." In *The Interpreter's Dictionary of the Bible,* volume 2. Nashville: Abingdon, 1962. 246.

"Gabriel." In *The Interpreter's Dictionary of the Bible,* volume 2. Nashville: Abingdon, 1962. 332–33.

"Orion." In *The Interpreter's Dictionary of the Bible,* volume 3. Nashville: Abingdon, 1962. 609.

"Thigh." In *The Interpreter's Dictionary of the Bible,* volume 4. Nashville: Abingdon, 1962. 630.

"Tongue." In *The Interpreter's Dictionary of the Bible,* volume 4. Nashville: Abingdon, 1962. 670.

"Wave Offering." In *The Interpreter's Dictionary of the Bible,* volume 4. Nashville: Abingdon, 1962. 817.

1963

"Humor and Faith of the Bible." *Youth Magazine* 14, no. 7 (1963) 19–24.

1964

"The Bible and the Church in Which We Live." *Church School Worker* 15, no. 4 (1964) 9–11.

"The Bible and the God We Serve." *Church School Worker* 15, no. 3 (1964) 7–9.

"The Bible and the History We Face." *Church School Worker* 15, no. 1 (1964) 7–10.

"The Bible and the Persons We Teach." *Church School Worker* 15, no. 2 (1964) 9–11.

"The Miracle and Burden of Being God's People." *United Church Herald* 7, no. 12 (1964) 24–25.

1965

"Amos IV:4–13 and Israel's Covenant Worship." *Vetus Testamentum* 15 (1965) 1–15.

"Biblical Biography: Suggestions on a Method." *Church School Worker* 16, no. 2 (1965) 18–20.

1966

"Tradition Engaged with Crisis." *Theology and Life* 9 (1966) 118–30.

1967

"Hints of Certainty in the Bible." *Children's Religion* 28, no. 3 (1967) 3–5.

1968

Confronting the Bible: A Resource and Discussion Book for Youth. Boston: United Church Press, 1968. 75 pages.

The Renewing Word. Edited by Elmer J. F. Arndt. Boston: United Church Press, 1968. 32 pages.

Tradition for Crisis: A Study in Hosea. Atlanta: John Knox, 1968. 164 pages.

"David and His Theologian." *Catholic Biblical Quarterly* 30 (1968) 156–81.

"Isaiah 55 and Deuteronomic Theology." *Zeitschrift für die alttestamentliche Wissenschaft* 80 (1968) 191–203.

"The Kerygma of the Deuteronomistic Historian: Gospel for Exiles." *Interpretation* 22 (1968) 387–402.

1969

"Amos' Intercessory Formula." *Vetus Testamentum* 19 (1969) 385–99.

"Israel's Moment of Freedom." *The Bible Today* 42 (1969) 2917–25.

"King in the Kingdom of Things." *Christian Century* 86 (1969) 1165–66. Reprinted in *Family Life Today* 3, no. 8 (1977) 8.

"The Trusted Creature." *Catholic Biblical Quarterly* 31 (1969) 484–98.

1970

"Finding a Mature Way to Dissent." *The Living Light* 7, no. 2 (1970) 92–103.

"Of the Same Flesh and Bone (Genesis 2:23a)." *Catholic Biblical Quarterly* 32 (1970) 532–42.

"Scripture and an Ecumenical Life-Style: A Study in Wisdom Theology." *Interpretation* 24 (1970) 3–19.

"The Triumphalist Tendency in Exegetical History." *Journal of the American Academy of Religion* 38 (1970) 367–80. Condensed in *Theology Digest* 19 (1971) 242–46.

1971

What Are Christians For? An Inquiry into Obedience and Dissent. Dayton: Pflaum-Standard, 1971. 124 pages.

"Alternative to Chaos." *United Church Herald* 14, no. 6 (1971) 47.

"Chaos Touched by the Poet." *United Church Herald* 14, no. 12 (1971) 47.

"The Context of Our Many Deaths." *United Church Herald* 14, no. 11 (1971) 47.

"Getting Out of the Calf Business." *United Church Herald* 14, no. 5 (1971) 63.

"The God with the Single Option." *United Church Herald* 14, no. 3 (1971) 55.

"God's Geography in the Age of Aquarius." *United Church Herald* 14, no. 10 (1971) 63.

"The Hinge of Holiness." *United Church Herald* 14, no. 8 (1971) 47.

"Kingship and Chaos (A Study in Tenth Century Theology)." *Catholic Biblical Quarterly* 33 (1971) 317–32.

"Newness and Our Old Identity." *United Church Herald* 14, no. 1 (1971) 47.

"On Faithful Fear and Sound Learning." *United Church Herald* 14, no. 9 (1971) 46–47.

"Power for the Brothers." *United Church Herald* 14, no. 2 (1971) 47.

"Restoration Unlimited." *United Church Herald* 14, no. 4 (1971) 47.

"The Strangeness of Patriotism." *United Church Herald* 14, no. 7 (1971) 13.

"Working for God's Counter-Culture." *The Living Light* 8, no. 1 (1971) 21–35. Condensed in *Theology Digest* 20 (1972) 13–17.

1972

The Evangelical Catechism Revisited, 1847–1972. St. Louis: Eden Publishing House, 1972. 32 pages.

In Man We Trust: The Neglected Side of Biblical Faith. Atlanta: John Knox, 1972. 144 pages.

"Bricks, Bare Feet and Burning Bushes." *United Church Herald* 15, no. 7 (1972) 49.

"The Curious Mix of Power and Delicacy: Some Biblical Reflections on Our Present Dilemma." *The Living Light* 9, no. 2 (1972) 86–95.

"From Dust to Kingship." *Zeitschrift für die alttestamentliche Wissenschaft* 84 (1972) 1–18.

"The Kerygma of the Priestly Writers." *Zeitschrift für die alttestamentliche Wissenschaft* 84 (1972) 397–414.

"Life and Death in Tenth Century Israel." *Journal of the American Academy of Religion* 40 (1972) 96–109.

"The Limitations of Personal Identity." *United Church Herald* 15, no. 6 (1972) 38–39.

"Living Toward a Vision." *Colloquy* 5, no. 7 (1972) 4–8.

"The Maze of Moral Choice." *United Church Herald* 15, no. 5 (1972) 47.

"On Having Only Bitter Herbs to Eat." *United Church Herald* 15, no. 2 (1972) 47.

"On Trust and Freedom: A Study of Faith in the Succession Narrative." *Interpretation* 26 (1972) 3–19.

"Revolting Taxes and the Taxpayers' Revolt." *United Church Herald* 15, no. 4 (1972) 47.

"Weariness, Exile and Chaos (A Motif in Royal Theology)." *Catholic Biblical Quarterly* 34 (1972) 19–38.

"When God Gives Us Clout." *United Church Herald* 15, no. 3 (1972) 47.

1973

"Jeremiah's Use of Rhetorical Questions." *Journal of Biblical Literature* 92 (1973) 358–74.

"Transforming Order into Justice." *Engage/Social Action* 1, no. 11 (1973) 33–43.

1974

"Ethos and Ecumenism: The History of Eden Theological Seminary, 1925–1970." Ph.D. dissertation, St. Louis University, 1974. 284 pages. Revised edition published under same title; St. Louis: Eden Publishing House, 1975. 110 pages.

"Confirmation: Joining a Special Story." *Colloquy* 7, no. 5 (1974) 6–9.

"From Hurt to Joy, From Death to Life." *Interpretation* 28 (1974) 3–19.

"Healing and Caring: Health Care Is an Affirmation About Dignity, Worth and Hope." *Engage/Social Action* 2, no. 7 (1974) 14–24.

"Israel's Sense of Place in Jeremiah." In *Rhetorical Criticism: Essays in Honor of James Muilenburg.* Edited by Jared J. Jackson and Martin Kessler. Pittsburgh Theological Monograph Series 1. Pittsburgh: Pickwick, 1974. 149–65.

"Non-Negotiable Boundaries." *One World* 2 (1974) 26.

"On Coping with Curse: A Study of 2 Samuel 16:5–14." *Catholic Biblical Quarterly* 36 (1974) 175–92.

1975

The Vitality of Old Testament Traditions. Cowritten with Hans Walter Wolff. Atlanta: John Knox, 1975. 155 pages. Second edition; Atlanta: John Knox, 1982. 180 pages.

"How Do We Know a Prophet When We See One?" *Youth Magazine* 26, no. 1 (1975) 50–59.

"Reflections on Biblical Understandings of Property." *International Review of Mission* 64 (1975) 354–61.

"Why Read the Bible? The Possibility of a Fresh Perspective." *PACE: Professional Approaches for Christian Educators* 6 (1975). Reprinted in *Keeping PACE: 25 Years of Theology, Education, and Ministry from PACE.* Edited by Padraic O'Hare. Dubuque, Iowa: Brown-ROA, 1996. 131–37.

1976

Living Toward a Vision: Biblical Reflections on Shalom. Philadelphia: United Church Press, 1976. 201 pages.

"Celebration—A Religious Dimension." *Religion Teacher's Journal* 10, no. 2 (1976) 8–10.

"Death, Theology of." In *The Interpreter's Dictionary of the Bible, Supplementary Volume.* Nashville: Abingdon, 1976. 219–22.

"Eating For or Against Life." *One World* 20 (1976) 23.

"Luke 3:1–4" [expository article]. *Interpretation* 30 (1976) 404–9.

"Presence of God, Cultic." In *The Interpreter's Dictionary of the Bible, Supplementary Volume.* Nashville: Abingdon, 1976. 680–83.

"Reading the Text for Church." *The Christian Ministry* 7, no. 4 (1976) 13–15.

"Yahwist." In *The Interpreter's Dictionary of the Bible, Supplementary Volume.* Nashville: Abingdon, 1976. 971–75.

1977

The Bible Makes Sense. Winona, Minn.: St. Mary's College Press, 1977. 155 pages. Also issued under same title: Atlanta: John Knox, 1977. 155 pages. Revised edition: Winona, Minn.: St. Mary's Press, 1997. 125 pages.

The Land: Place as Gift, Promise, and Challenge in Biblical Faith. Overtures to Biblical Theology. Philadelphia: Fortress Press, 1977. 203 pages.

"An Attempt at an Interdisciplinary M.Div. Curriculum." *Theological Education* 13 (1977) 137–45.

"Biblical Perspective on the Problem of Hunger." *Christian Century* 94 (1977) 1136–41.

"Covenantal Spirituality." *New Conversations* 2, no. 3 (1977) 4–9.

"The Covenanted Family: A Zone for Humanness." *Journal of Current Social Issues* 14, no. 1 (1977) 18–23.

"The Formfulness of Grief." *Interpretation* 31 (1977) 263–75.

"Israel's Social Criticism and Yahweh's Sexuality." *Journal of the American Academy of Religion* 45, no. 3 Supplement (1977) 739–72.

"A Neglected Sapiential Word Pair." *Zeitschrift für die alttestamentliche Wissenschaft* 89 (1977) 234–58.

1978

The Prophetic Imagination. Philadelphia: Fortress Press, 1978. 127 pages.

"The Epistemological Crisis of Israel's Two Histories (Jeremiah 9:22–23)." In *Israelite Wisdom: Theological and Literary Essays in Honor of Samuel Terrien.* Edited by John G. Gammie, Walter A. Brueggemann, W. Lee Humphreys, and James M. Ward. Missoula, Mont.: Scholars Press, 1978. 85–105.

"The Old Testament: Ecstasy and Oppression." In *The Bible and Alcohol and Drugs: A Study Guide.* New York: Commission for Racial Justice, in Cooperation with the United Church Board for Homeland Ministries, Office of Church Life and Leadership, and Office of Communication and Youth Magazine, United Church of Christ, 1978. 5–27.

"Our Heritage and Our Commitment." In *Festival of the Church: Celebrating the Legacy of the Evangelical Synod of North America, September, 1977.* St. Louis: Office of Church Life and Leadership, United Church of Christ, 1978. 3.

"Steps to Better Writing." *Presbyterian Outlook* 160, no. 32 (1978) 6.

1979

Belonging and Growing in the Christian Community. Christian Education: Shared Approaches series. Living the Word, Level 1. Atlanta: General Assembly Mission Board, Presbyterian Church in the United States, 1979. 48 pages.

"Covenanting as Human Vocation: A Discussion of the Relation of Bible and Pastoral Care." *Interpretation* 33 (1979) 115–29.

"The Crisis and Promise of Presence in Israel." *Horizons in Biblical Theology* 1 (1979) 47–86.

"Trajectories in Old Testament Literature and the Sociology of Ancient Israel." *Journal of Biblical Literature* 98 (1979) 161–85. Reprinted in *The Bible and Liberation: Political and Social Hermeneutics.* Edited by Norman K. Gottwald. Maryknoll, N.Y.: Orbis, 1983. 307–33. Revised edition; edited by Norman K. Gottwald and Richard A. Horsley. Maryknoll, N.Y.: Orbis, 1993. 201–26.

1980

Confirming Our Faith. Cowritten with Eugene Wehrli. Edited by Larry E. Kalp. New York: United Church Press, 1980. 256 pages.

"Canon and Dialectic." In *God and His Temple: Reflections on Professor Samuel Terrien's The Elusive Presence: Toward a New Biblical Theology.* Edited by Lawrence E. Frizzell. South Orange, N.J.: Institute of Judeo-Christian Studies, Seton Hall Univ., 1980. 20–29.

"A Convergence in Recent Old Testament Theologies." *Journal for the Study of the Old Testament* 18 (1980) 2–18.

"Covenant as a Subversive Paradigm." *Christian Century* 97 (1980) 1094–99. Reprinted in *A Covenant Challenge to Our Broken World.* Edited by Allen O. Miller. Atlanta: Darby, 1982. 201–8.

"Isaiah 9:2–7" [exegetical article]. *No Other Foundation* 1, no. 4 (1980) 1–6.

"Isaiah 65:17–25" [exegetical article]. *No Other Foundation* 1, no. 2 (1980) 1–4.

"On Land-Losing and Land-Receiving." *Dialog* 19 (1980) 166–73.

"Psalms and the Life of Faith: A Suggested Typology of Function." *Journal for the Study of the Old Testament* 17 (1980) 3–32. Reprinted in *The Poetical Books.* Edited by David J. A. Clines. Sheffield: Sheffield Academic Press, 1997. 35–66.

"*The Tribes of Yahweh:* An Essay Review." *Journal of the American Academy of Religion* 48 (1980) 441–51. Reprinted in *The Bible and Liberation: Political and Social Hermeneutics.* Revised edition; edited by Norman K. Gottwald and Richard A. Horsley. Maryknoll, N.Y.: Orbis, 1993. 228–35.

"Why Study the Bible?" Cowritten with Douglas A. Knight. *Council on the Study of Religion Bulletin* 11 (1980) 76–81.

1981

"The Childs Proposal: A Symposium." Written with Ralph W. Klein and Gary Stansell. *Word and World* 1 (1981) 105–15.

"Genesis 4:13–16" [exegetical article]. *No Other Foundation* 2, no. 3 (1981) 1–4.

"Isaiah 44:1–5" [exegetical article]. *No Other Foundation* 2, no. 2 (1981) 1–4.

"Isaiah 50:4–9" [exegetical article]. *No Other Foundation* 2, no. 1 (1981) 1–5.

"Isaiah 52:7–10" [exegetical article]. *No Other Foundation* 2, no. 4 (1981) 1–4.

"Land: The Foundation of Humanness." *Catholic Rural Life* 31 (1981) 6–11. Reprinted in *The Whole Earth Papers* 17 (1982) 44–46.

"Running the Risk of Prayer." *A.D.* 10, no. 2 (1981) 47–48.

"Social Criticism and Social Vision in the Deuteronomic Formula of the Judges." In *Die Botschaft und die Boten: Festschrift für Hans Walter Wolff zum 70 Geburtstag*. Edited by Jörg Jeremias and Lothar Perlitt. Neukirchen-Vluyn: Neukirchener Verlag, 1981. 101–14.

" 'Vine and Fig Tree': A Case Study in Imagination and Criticism." *Catholic Biblical Quarterly* 43 (1981) 188–204.

1982

1 Kings. Knox Preaching Guides series. Atlanta: John Knox, 1982. 102 pages.

2 Kings. Knox Preaching Guides series. Atlanta: John Knox, 1982. 101 pages.

The Creative Word: Canon as a Model for Biblical Education. Philadelphia: Fortress Press, 1982. 167 pages.

Genesis. Interpretation: A Bible Commentary for Teaching and Preaching. Atlanta: John Knox, 1982. 384 pages.

Praying the Psalms. Winona, Minn.: St. Mary's Press, 1982. 168 pages. Reformatted edition; Winona, Minn.: St. Mary's Press, 1993. 71 pages.

"The Bible and Mission: Some Interdisciplinary Implications for Teaching." *Missiology* 10 (1982) 397–412.

"Genesis 4:3–10" [exegetical article]. *No Other Foundation* 3, no. 3 (1982) 1–4.

" 'Impossibility' and Epistemology in the Faith Tradition of Abraham and Sarah (Genesis 18:1–15)." *Zeitschrift für die alttestamentliche Wissenschaft* 94 (1982) 615–34.

"Isaiah 25:6–9" [exegetical article]. *No Other Foundation* 3, no. 1 (1982) 7–11.

"Response to John Goldingay's 'The Dynamic Cycle of Praise and Prayer.' " *Journal for the Study of the Old Testament* 22 (1982) 141–42.

"Theology and Prophecy." *The Ecumenist* 20 (1982) 92–93.

"Zechariah 2:10–13" [exegetical article]. *No Other Foundation* 3, no. 4 (1982) 1–5.

1983

"As the Text 'Makes Sense': Keep the Methods of Exposition as Lean and Uncomplicated as Possible." *Christian Ministry* 14, no. 6 (1983) 7–10.

"Authority in the Church." *On the Way: Occasional Papers of the Wisconsin Conference, United Church of Christ* 1, no. 1 (1983) 2.

"A Better Governance: Meditations for Advent." *Sojourners* 12, no. 10 (1983) 28–29.

"The Book of Jeremiah: Portrait of the Prophet." *Interpretation* 37 (1983) 130–45. Reprinted in *Interpreting the Prophets*. Edited by James Luther Mays and Paul J. Achtemeier. Philadelphia: Fortress Press, 1987. 113–29.

"Exodus 15:1–11" [exegetical article]. *No Other Foundation* 4, no. 1 (1983) 1–5.

"Isaiah 62:1–4" [exegetical article]. *No Other Foundation* 4, no. 4 (1983) 1–4.

"Isaiah 66:18–22" [exegetical article]. *No Other Foundation* 4, no. 2 (1983) 9–12.

"Psalm 77: The 'Turn' from Self to God." *Journal for Preachers* 6, no. 2 (1983) 8–14.

"Reservoirs of Unreason." *Reformed Liturgy and Music* 17 (1983) 99–104.

"Toward the Breakpoint—and Beyond." In *Social Themes of the Christian Year: A Commentary on the Lectionary*. Edited by Dieter T. Hessel. Philadelphia: Geneva, 1983. 149–58.

"Will Our Faith Have Children?" *Word and World* 3 (1983) 272–83.

"A World in Jeopardy: Meditations for Advent." *Sojourners* 12, no. 11 (1983) 28–29.

1984

Advent/Christmas. Proclamation 3, Series B. Philadelphia: Fortress Press, 1984. 63 pages.

The Message of the Psalms: A Theological Commentary. Augsburg Old Testament Studies. Minneapolis: Augsburg, 1984. 206 pages.

"1 Kings 19:9–18" [exegetical article]. *No Other Foundation* 5, no. 2 (1984) 1–5.

"A Cosmic Sigh of Relinquishment." *Currents in Theology and Mission* 11 (1984) 5–20.

"Futures in Old Testament Theology." *Horizons in Biblical Theology* 6, no. 1 (1984) 1–11.

"On Modes of Truth." *Seventh Angel* 1, no. 2 (1984) 17–18, 23–24.

"A New Creation—After the Sigh." *Currents in Theology and Mission* 11 (1984) 83–100.

"Thesis on Land in the Bible." In *Erets, Land: The Church and Appalachian Land Issues*. Amesville, Ohio: Coalition for Appalachian Ministry, 1984. 4–13. Reprinted in *Catholic Rural Life* 34 (1984) 5–9.

"Unity and Dynamic in the Isaiah Tradition." *Journal for the Study of the Old Testament* 29 (1984) 89–107.

"The Word of the Lord: Thanks be to God." *PACE: Professional Approaches for Christian Educators* 15 (1984). Reprinted in *Keeping PACE: 25 Years of Theology, Education, and Ministry from PACE*. Edited by Padraic O'Hare. Dubuque, Iowa: Brown-ROA, 1996. 34–43.

1985

David's Truth in Israel's Imagination and Memory. Philadelphia: Fortress Press, 1985. 128 pages.

"II Kings 18–19: The Legitimacy of a Sectarian Hermeneutic." *Horizons in Biblical Theology* 7, no. 1 (1985) 1–42.

"The Family as World-Maker." *Journal for Preachers* 8, no. 3 (1985) 8–15.

"Genesis 50:15–21: A Theological Exploration." In *Congress Volume, Salamanca, 1983*. Edited by J. A. Emerton. Vetus Testamentum Supplement 36. Leiden: Brill, 1985. 40–53.

"God's Bias Toward the Poor" [reader's response]. *Christian Century* 102 (1985) 652.

"A Hard Service." *PACE: Professional Approaches for Christian Educators* 15 (April 1985) 1–5. Reprinted in *Keeping PACE: 25 Years of Theology, Education, and Ministry from PACE.* Edited by Padraic O'Hare. Dubuque, Iowa: Brown-ROA, 1996. 34–43.

"Imagination as a Mode of Fidelity." In *Understanding the Word: Essays in Honour of Bernhard W. Anderson.* Edited by James T. Butler, Edgar W. Conrad, and Ben C. Ollenburger. JSOTSup 37; Sheffield: JSOT Press, 1985. 13–36.

" 'Is There No Balm in Gilead?' The Hope and Despair of Jeremiah." *Sojourners* 14, no. 9 (1985) 26–29.

"Isaiah 52:13–53:12" [exegetical article]. *No Other Foundation* 6, no. 2 (1985) 39–43.

"Joshua 24:14–18" [exegetical article]. *No Other Foundation* 6, no. 1 (1985) 22–25.

"Middle Ground Between Two Perils." *Concern* (United Presbyterian Women) 27 (Winter 1985) 20–22.

"O Lord, You Have Deceived Me [Jeremiah 20:7–13]." *PACE: Professional Approaches for Christian Educators* 15 (January 1985) 1–4.

"Old Testament Theology as a Particular Conversation: Adjudication of Israel's Socio-Theological Alternatives." *Theology Digest* 32 (1985) 303–26.

"Passion and Perspective: Two Dimensions of Education in the Bible." *Theology Today* 42 (1985) 172–80. Reprinted in *Theological Perspectives on Christian Formation: A Reader on Theology and Christian Education.* Edited by Jeff Astley, Leslie J. Francis, and Colin Crowder. Grand Rapids: Eerdmans, 1996. 71–79.

"The Prophet as a Destabilizing Presence." In *The Pastor as Prophet.* Edited by Earl E. Shelp and Ronald H. Sunderland. New York: Pilgrim, 1985. 49–77.

"Psalm 100" [expository article]. *Interpretation* 39 (1985) 65–69.

"Psalm 109: Three Times 'Steadfast Love.' " *Word and World* 5 (1985) 144–54.

"A Second Reading of Jeremiah After the Dismantling." *Ex Auditu* 1 (1985) 156–68.

"A Shape for Old Testament Theology, I: Structure Legitimation." *Catholic Biblical Quarterly* 47 (1985) 28–46.

"A Shape for Old Testament Theology, II: Embrace of Pain." *Catholic Biblical Quarterly* 47 (1985) 395–415.

"A Subversive Memory in a Sacramental Container (Exodus 16:31–35)." *Reformed Liturgy and Music* 19 (1985) 34–38.

"Theodicy in a Social Dimension." *Journal for the Study of the Old Testament* 33 (1985) 3–25. Reprinted in *Social-Scientific Old Testament Criticism.* Edited by David J. Chalcraft. Sheffield: Sheffield Academic Press, 1997. 260–82.

"The 'Uncared For' Now Cared For (Jeremiah 30:12–17): A Methodological Consideration." *Journal of Biblical Literature* 104 (1985) 419–28.

"We Cried Out and the Lord Heard and the Lord Saw and the Lord Knew and the Lord Remembered and the Lord Came Down and Saved." *Engage/Social Action* 13, no. 11 (1985) 26–31.

"Words of Lamentation." *PACE: Professional Approaches for Christian Educators* 15 (March 1985) 1–4.

1986

Hopeful Imagination: Prophetic Voices in Exile. Philadelphia: Fortress Press, 1986. 146 pages.

Revelation and Violence: A Study in Contextualization. The 1986 Père Marquette Theology Lecture. Milwaukee: Marquette Univ. Press, 1986. 72 pages.

To Act Justly, Love Tenderly, Walk Humbly: An Agenda for Ministers. Written with Sharon Parks and Thomas H. Groome. New York: Paulist, 1986. 65 pages. Reprinted, Eugene, Ore.: Wipf and Stock, 1997. 65 pages.

"Biblical Authority and the Church's Task of Interpretation." *Prism* 1, no. 1 (1986) 12–21.

"Biblical Faith as Cosmic Hurt" [1982 Weber Memorial Lecture]. *The Bulletin— Moravian Theological Seminary, 1978–1985* (1986) 83–92.

"Biblical Faith as Structured Legitimacy" [1982 Weber Memorial Lecture]. *The Bulletin—Moravian Theological Seminary, 1978–1985* (1986) 71–82.

"The Costly Loss of Lament." *Journal for the Study of the Old Testament* 36 (1986) 57–71. Reprinted in *The Poetical Books.* Edited by David J. A. Clines. Sheffield: Sheffield Academic Press, 1997. 84–97.

"The Earth Is the Lord's: A Theology of Earth and Land." *Sojourners* 15, no. 9 (1986) 28–32.

"Engaging Monopolies." *Seeds* 9, no. 10 (1986) 5.

"Hunger, Food and the Land in the Biblical Witness: The 1986 Zimmerman Lecture." *Lutheran Theological Seminary Bulletin* 66, no. 4 (1986) 48–61.

"Making History: Jeremiah's Guide for Christians Who Know How to Blush." *The Other Side* 22, no. 8 (1986) 20–25.

"Newness Mediated by Worship." *Reformed Liturgy and Music* 20 (1986) 55–60. Reprinted as "A High Risk Invitation" in *Pastoral Music* 11, no. 4 (1987) 28–34. Also reprinted as "Worship: A High Risk Venture." In *Liturgy and Worship.* Access Guides to Youth Ministry series. New Rochelle, N.Y.: Don Bosco Multimedia, 1990. 34–43.

"Prayer as an Act of Daring Dance: Four Biblical Examples." *Reformed Liturgy and Music* 20 (1986) 31–37.

"Proclamation of Resurrection in the Old Testament." *Journal for Preachers* 9, no. 3 (1986) 2–9.

"Psalm 95" [exegetical article]. *No Other Foundation* 7, no. 1 (1986) 50–53.

"Psalm 97" [exegetical article]. *No Other Foundation* 7, no. 2 (1986) 3–6.

"Theological Education: Healing the Blind Beggar." *Christian Century* 103 (1986) 114–16.

"The Third World of Evangelical Imagination." *Horizons in Biblical Theology* 8, no. 2 (1986) 61–84.

1987

Hope Within History. Atlanta: John Knox, 1987. 128 pages.

"Before the Giant/Surrounded by Mother." *Princeton Seminary Bulletin* 8, no. 3 (1987) 1–13.

"The Case for an Alternative Reading." *Theological Education* 23, no. 2 (1987)
    89–107.
"The Commandments and Liberated, Liberating Bonding." *Journal for Preachers*
    10, no. 2 (1987) 15–24.
"Dreaming, Being Home, Finding Strangers; and the Seminaries." *Mid-Stream* 26
    (1987) 62–76.
"The Embarrassing Footnote." *Theology Today* 44 (1987) 5–14.
"Land: Fertility and Justice." In *Theology of the Land*. Edited by Bernard F. Evans
    and Gregory D. Cusack. Collegeville, Minn.: Liturgical Press, 1987. 41–68.
"Psalm 22:25–31" [exegetical article]. *No Other Foundation* 8, no. 2 (1987) 50–
    53.
"Psalm 146" [exegetical article]. *No Other Foundation* 8, no. 1 (1987) 26–29.
"A Response to 'The Song of Miriam' by Bernhard W. Anderson." In *Directions in
    Biblical Hebrew Poetry*. Edited by Elaine R. Follis. JSOTSup 40. Sheffield: OT
    Press, 1987. 297–302.

1988

Israel's Praise: Doxology Against Idolatry and Ideology. Philadelphia: Fortress
    Press, 1988. 196 pages.
To Pluck Up, to Tear Down: A Commentary on Jeremiah 1–25. International
    Theological Commentary. Grand Rapids: Eerdmans, 1988. 222 pages.
"2 Samuel 21–24: An Appendix of Deconstruction?" *Catholic Biblical Quarterly*
    50 (1988) 383–97.
"The Bible and Our Two Loves." *Biblical Literacy Today* 2, no. 4 (1988) 4–5, 11.
"Embracing the Transformation: A Comment on Missionary Preaching." *Journal
    for Preachers* 11, no. 2 (1988) 8–18.
"Getting Ready for God." In *Whose Birthday Is It Anyway? Christmas, 1988*.
    Ellenwood, Ga.: Alternatives, 1988. 20–24.
"Isaiah 37:21–29: The Transformative Potential of a Public Metaphor." *Horizons
    in Biblical Theology* 10, no. 1 (1988) 1–32.
"Jeremiah 23:1–6" [exegetical article]. *No Other Foundation* 9, no. 1 (1988) 18–
    22.
"Jeremiah: Intense Criticism/Thin Interpretation." *Interpretation* 42 (1988) 268–
    80.
"Our Double-Mindedness: Exodus 16:16–21, Luke 12:13–23." *Trinity Occasional
    Papers* (Australia) 6, no. 2 (1988) 71–74.
"Practical Aids to Lectionary Use: First Sunday of Advent (C)—Last Sunday
    After the Epiphany (C)." Written with Kenneth E. Williams and Robert Fort.
    Reformed Liturgy and Music 22 (1988) 167–73.
"Psalm 34:1–8" [exegetical article]. *No Other Foundation* 9, no. 2 (1988) 25–29.
"Second Isaiah: An Evangelical Rereading of Communal Experience." In *Reading
    and Preaching the Book of Isaiah*. Edited by Christopher Seitz. Philadelphia:
    Fortress Press, 1988. 71–90.
"The Social Nature of the Biblical Text for Preaching." In *Preaching as a Social
    Act: Theology and Practice*. Edited by Arthur Van Seters. Nashville: Abingdon,
    1988. 127–65.

"Truth-Telling and Peacemaking: A Reflection on Ezekiel." *Christian Century* 105 (1988) 1096–98.
"A World Available for Peace: Images of Hope from Jeremiah and Isaiah." *Sojourners* 17, no. 1 (1988) 22–26.
"The 'World' of Israel's Doxology." *McKendree Pastoral Review* 5, no. 1 (1988) 5–31.

1989

Disciplines of Readiness. Louisville: Theology and Worship Ministry Unit, Presbyterian Church (USA), 1989. 25 pages.
Easter. Proclamation 4, Series A. Minneapolis: Fortress Press, 1989. 63 pages.
Finally Comes the Poet: Daring Speech for Proclamation. Minneapolis: Fortress Press, 1989. 165 pages.
"The Bible as the Living Word of God." *Perspectives: A Journal of Reformed Thought* 4, no. 7 (1989) 4–7.
"Covenant and Social Possibility." In *Covenanting for Peace and Justice.* Edited by Choan-Seng Song. Geneva: World Alliance of Reformed Churches, 1989. 6–22.
"Genesis." In *The Books of the Bible,* Volume I: *The Old Testament/Hebrew Bible.* Edited by Bernhard W. Anderson. New York: Scribner's, 1989. 21–45.
"The Land and Our Urban Appetites." *Perspectives: A Journal of Reformed Thought* 4, no. 2 (1989) 9–13.
"The Legitimacy of a Sectarian Hermeneutic: 2 Kings 18–19." In *Education for Citizenship and Discipleship.* Edited by Mary C. Boys. New York: Pilgrim, 1989. 3–34.
"Micah 6:1–8" [exegetical article]. *No Other Foundation* 10, no. 1 (1989) 43–46.
"Narrative Intentionality in 1 Samuel 29." *Journal for the Study of the Old Testament* 43 (1989) 21–35.
"A Poem of Summons (Isaiah 55:1–3)—A Narrative of Resistance (Daniel 1:1–21)." In *Schöpfung und Befreiung: Für Claus Westermann zum 80 Geburtstag.* Edited by Rainer Albertz, Friedemann W. Golka, and Jürgen Kegler. Stuttgart: Calwer, 1989. 126–36.
"Power for Life, Present and Concrete." *Presbyterian Outlook* 171, no. 13 (1989) 8–9.
"Praise to God Is the End of Wisdom—What Is the Beginning?" *Journal for Preachers* 12, no. 3 (1989) 30–40.
"Prophetic Ministry: A Sustainable Alternative Community." *Horizons in Biblical Theology* 11, no. 1 (1989) 1–33.
"Psalm 118:19–29" [exegetical article]. *No Other Foundation* 10, no. 2 (1989) 13–16.
"The Psalms as Prayer." *Reformed Liturgy and Music* 23 (1989) 13–26. Reprinted in *The Hymnology Annual,* Volume 2: *An International Forum on the Hymn and Worship.* Edited by Vernon Wicker. Berrien Springs, Mich.: Vande Vere, 1992. 64–85.

"The Rhetoric of Hurt and Hope: Ethics Odd and Crucial." In *The Annual of the Society of Christian Ethics, 1989*. Edited by D. M. Yeager. Knoxville, Tenn.: Society of Christian Ethics, 1989. 73–92

"Seeking Understanding—in a 'Preacher Factory.'" *Presbyterian Outlook* 171, no. 31 (1989) 16.

"Speechifying Among the Baptized." *Presbyterian Outlook* 171, no. 18 (1989) 8–9.

"Teaching as Witness: Forming an Intentional Community." In *The Pastor as Teacher*. Edited by Earl Shelp and Ronald H. Sunderland. New York: Pilgrim, 1989. 28–64.

"Textuality in the Church." In *Tensions Between Citizenship and Discipleship*. Edited by Nelle G. Slater. New York: Pilgrim, 1989. 48–68.

1990

First and Second Samuel. Interpretation: A Bible Commentary for Teaching and Preaching. Edited by James Luther Mays. Atlanta: John Knox, 1990. 362 pages.

Power, Providence, and Personality: Biblical Insight into Life and Ministry. Louisville: Westminster/John Knox, 1990. 117 pages.

"I Samuel 1: A Sense of a Beginning." *Zeitschrift für die alttestamentliche Wissenschaft* 102 (1990) 33–48.

"An Artistic Disclosure in Three Dimensions." *Cumberland Seminarian* 28 (1990) 1–8.

"The Call to Resistance." *The Other Side* 26, no. 6 (1990) 44–46.

"Evangelism in Three Unfinished Scenes." In *Evangelism in the Reformed Tradition*. Edited by Arnold B. Lovell. Decatur, Ga.: CTS Press, 1990. 21–46.

"Hope and Despair as Seasons of Faith." *Liturgy* 8, no. 4 (1990) 77–83. Reprinted in *The Landscape of Praise: Readings in Liturgical Renewal*. Edited by Blair Gilmer Meeks. Valley Forge, Pa.: Trinity Press International, 1996. 172–79.

"Isaiah 40:1–11" [exegetical article]. *No Other Foundation* 11, no. 1 (1990) 4–7.

"Knowing and Making Known." *New Song/Brian Wren Newsletter* 1 (1990) 5.

"Peacemaking: An Evangelical Possibility." *Church and Society* 81, no. 1 (1990) 8–20. Reprinted as "Powered by the Spirit" in *Sojourners* 20, no. 4 (1991) 10–15.

"The Preacher, the Text, and the People." *Theology Today* 47 (1990) 237–47.

"The Social Significance of Solomon as a Patron of Wisdom." In *The Sage in Israel and the Ancient Near East*. Edited by John G. Gammie and Leo G. Perdue. Winona Lake, Ind.: Eisenbrauns, 1990. 117–32.

"Some Missing Prerequisites." *Journal for Preachers* 13, no. 2 (1990) 23–30.

"Sport of Nature." *Cumberland Seminarian* 28 (1990) 9–25.

"A Time Bomb Among the Superpowers." *Pulpit Digest* 71, no. 506 (1990) 15–17.

"When Jerusalem Gloats over Shiloh." *Sojourners* 19, no. 6 (1990) 24–27.

1991

Abiding Astonishment: Psalms, Modernity, and the Making of History. Literary Currents in Biblical Interpretation. Louisville: Westminster/John Knox, 1991. 94 pages.

Interpretation and Obedience: From Faithful Reading to Faithful Living. Minneapolis: Fortress Press, 1991. 325 pages.

To Build, to Plant: A Commentary on Jeremiah 26–52. International Theological Commentary. Grand Rapids: Eerdmans, 1991. 298 pages.

"At the Mercy of Babylon: A Subversive Rereading of the Empire." *Journal of Biblical Literature* 110 (1991) 3–22.

"Bounded by Obedience and Praise: The Psalms as Canon." *Journal for the Study of the Old Testament* 50 (1991) 63–92.

"Creation Faith: The World through Faithful Speech." In *Heavenly News: Understanding the Origin of the Universe.* Washington, D.C.: Washington National Cathedral, 1991. 18–31.

"Genesis 17:1–22" [expository article]. *Interpretation* 45 (1991) 55–59.

"A Gospel Language of Pain and Possibility." *Horizons in Biblical Theology* 13, no. 2 (1991) 95–133.

"Haunting Book—Haunted People (Jeremiah 36; Luke 4:16–30)." *Word and World* 11 (1991) 62–68.

"He's Heavy—He's More Than My Brother." *Pulpit Digest* 72, no. 512 (1991) 5–8.

"History on the Margins." *Sojourners* 20, no. 7 (1991) 18–19.

"Poetry in a Prose-Flattened World." *Preaching* 6, no. 5 (1991) 28–34.

"The Prophetical Books." In *The New Oxford Annotated Bible.* Edited by Bruce M. Metzger and Roland E. Murphy. New York: Oxford Univ. Press, 1991. 862–65.

"Psalms 9–10: A Counter to Conventional Social Reality." In *The Bible and the Politics of Exegesis: Essays in Honor of Norman K. Gottwald on His Sixty-Fifth Birthday.* Edited by David Jobling, Peggy L. Day, and Gerald T. Sheppard. Cleveland: Pilgrim, 1991. 3–15, 297–301.

"Religious Claims, Uncritical Politics" [correspondence]. *Cross Currents* 41 (1991) 283–84.

"Remember, You Are Dust." *Journal for Preachers* 14, no. 2 (1991) 3–10.

"Rethinking Church Models Through Scripture." *Theology Today* 48 (1991) 128–38.

" 'This is Like....' " *Pulpit Digest* 72, no. 509 (1991) 5–8.

1992

Old Testament Theology: Essays on Structure, Theme, and Text. Edited by Patrick D. Miller. Minneapolis: Fortress Press, 1992. 318 pages.

"A Chance for the Center to Hold." *Christian Century* 109 (1992) 710.

"A Choice Amid Doxologies." *Christian Century* 109 (1992) 772.

"Disputed Present, Assured Future." *Christian Century* 109 (1992) 841.

"An 'Eastered' Alternative." In *From Deep Night to Bright Dawn: Theological Reflections, Vision, Faith, Discipleship*. Cleveland: United Church of Christ, 1992. 12–15.

"God's Relentless 'If.' " *Lexington Theological Quarterly* 27 (1992) 124–31.

"A New King and a New Order." *Christian Century* 109 (1992) 963.

"The Old One Takes Notice." *Christian Century* 109 (1992) 867.

"On Writing a Commentary... An Emergency?" *ATS Colloquy* (September/October 1992) 10–11.

"Pain Turned to Newness." *Cathedral Age* 68, no. 2 (1992) 18–19.

"The Practice of Homefulness." *Journal for Preachers* 15, no. 4 (1992) 7–22.

"Praise and the Psalms: A Politics of Glad Abandonment (Part 1)." *The Hymn: A Journal of Congregational Song* 43, no. 3 (1992) 14–19.

"Praise and the Psalms: A Politics of Glad Abandonment (Part 2)." *The Hymn: A Journal of Congregational Song* 43, no. 4 (1992) 14–18.

"A Prayer That Availeth Much." *Christian Century* 109 (1992) 677.

"Psalm 23" [exegetical article]. *No Other Foundation* 13, no. 2 (1992) 21–25.

"Pushing Past into Present." *Christian Century* 109 (1992) 741.

"Rude Interruptions to Faith." *Christian Century* 109 (1992) 899.

"Samuel, Book of 1–2: Narrative and Theology." In *The Anchor Bible Dictionary*, volume 5. New York: Doubleday, 1992. 965–73.

"Scriptural Authority: Biblical Authority in the Post-Critical Period." In *The Anchor Bible Dictionary*, volume 5. New York: Doubleday, 1992. 1049–56.

"The Terrible Ungluing." *Christian Century* 109 (1992) 931.

"Wrangling over Words." *Christian Century* 109 (1992) 804.

1993

Biblical Perspectives on Evangelism: Living in a Three-Storied Universe. Nashville: Abingdon, 1993. 139 pages.

From Despair to Hope: Peacemaking in Isaiah. Cowritten with Vera K. White. Louisville: The Presbyterian Peacemaking Program of the Social Justice and Peacemaking Ministry Unit, Presbyterian Church (USA), 1993. 21 pages.

Texts for Preaching: A Lectionary Commentary Based on the NRSV. Year B. Written with Charles B. Cousar, Beverly R. Gaventa, and James D. Newsome. Louisville: Westminster/John Knox, 1993. 616 pages.

Texts Under Negotiation: The Bible and Postmodern Imagination. Minneapolis: Fortress Press, 1993. 117 pages. Also issued as *The Bible and Postmodern Imagination: Texts Under Negotiation*. London: SCM, 1993. 117 pages.

Using God's Resources Wisely: Isaiah and Urban Possibility. Louisville: Westminster/John Knox, 1993. 89 pages.

"Against the Stream: Brevard Childs's Biblical Theology." *Theology Today* 50 (1993) 279–84.

"A Case Study in Daring Prayer." *The Living Pulpit* 2, no. 3 (1993) 12–13.

"The Friday Voice of Faith: A Serious Theology of the Cross Requires a Serious Practice of the Lament Psalms." *Reformed Worship* 30 (1993) 2–5.

"Jeremiah: Faithfulness in the Midst of Fickleness." In *The Newell Lectureships*, volume II. Edited by Timothy Dwyer. Anderson, Ind.: Warner, 1993. 13–72.

"Narrative Coherence and Theological Intentionality in 1 Samuel 18." *Catholic Biblical Quarterly* 55 (1993) 225–43.

" 'Othering' with Grace and Courage." *The Anglican* 23, no. 3/4 (1993) 11–21.

"The Peace Dividend." *Pulpit Digest* 74, no. 524 (1993) 5–11.

" 'Preaching to Exiles.' " *Journal for Preachers* 16, no. 4 (1993) 3–15.

"Psalm 37: Conflict of Interpretation." In *Of Prophets' Visions and the Wisdom of Sages: Essays in Honour of R. Norman Whybray on His Seventieth Birthday.* Edited by Heather A. McKay and David J. A. Clines. JSOTSup 162. Sheffield: JSOT Press, 1993. 229–56.

"Response to James L. Mays, 'The Question of Context.' " In *The Shape and Shaping of the Psalter.* Edited by J. Clinton McCann. JSOTSup 159. Sheffield: JSOT Press, 1993. 29–41.

"Why Prophets Won't Leave Well Enough Alone" [interview]. *U.S. Catholic* 58, no. 1 (1993) 6–13.

1994

A Social Reading of the Old Testament: Prophetic Approaches to Israel's Communal Life. Edited by Patrick D. Miller. Minneapolis: Fortress Press, 1994. 328 pages.

"The 'Baruch Connection': Reflections on Jeremiah 43:1–7." *Journal of Biblical Literature* 113 (1994) 405–20.

"Biblical Perspectives on Evangelism." *PACE: Professional Approaches for Christian Educators* 24 (October 1994) 14–27.

"The Book of Exodus: Introduction, Commentary, and Reflections." In *The New Interpreter's Bible,* volume 1. Nashville: Abingdon, 1994. 675–981.

"Brueggemann Sees Boogaart." *Perspectives: A Journal of Reformed Thought* 9, no. 4 (1994) 7.

"Cadences Which Redescribe: Speech Among Exiles." *Journal for Preachers* 17, no. 3 (1994) 10–17.

"Crisis-Evoked, Crisis-Resolving Speech." *Biblical Theology Bulletin* 24 (1994) 95–105.

"The Daily Voice of Faith: The Covenanted Self." *Sewanee Theological Review* 37 (1994) 123–43.

"The Density of Conflict: God and Sibling." *The Living Pulpit* 3, no. 3 (1994) 16–17.

"Disrupting the Hegemony in God and in Us." *Witness* 77, no. 4 (1994) 16–19.

"Duty as Delight and Desire (Preaching Obedience That Is Not Legalism)." *Journal for Preachers* 18, no. 1 (1994) 2–14.

" 'I Will Do It . . . But You Go.' " *Journal for Preachers* 17, no. 4 (1994) 27–30.

"James L. Crenshaw: Faith Lingering at the Edges." *Religious Studies Review* 20 (1994) 103–10.

"Justice: The Earthly Form of God's Holiness." *Reformed World* 44 (1994) 13–27.

"The Prophetic Word of God and History." *Interpretation* 48 (1994) 239–51.

"Remembering Rachel's Children: An Urban Agenda for People Who Notice." *Word and World* 14 (1994) 377–83.

"Response to J. Richard Middleton." *Harvard Theological Review* 87 (1994) 279–
    89.
"Six Questions." *Presbyterian Outlook* 176, no. 20 (1994) 6–7.

1995

*Gathering the Church in the Spirit: Reflections on Exile and the Inscrutable Wind
    of God.* Decatur, Ga.: CTS Press, 1995. 60 pages.
The Psalms and the Life of Faith. Edited by Patrick D. Miller. Minneapolis: Fortress
    Press, 1995. 292 pages.
Texts for Preaching: A Lectionary Commentary Based on the NRSV. Year A. Writ-
    ten with Charles B. Cousar, Beverly R. Gaventa, and James D. Newsome.
    Louisville: Westminster/John Knox, 1995. 589 pages.
"Five Strong Rereadings of the Book of Isaiah." In *The Bible in Human Society:
    Essays in Honour of John Rogerson.* Edited by M. Daniel, R. Carroll, D. J. A.
    Clines, and P. R. Davies. JSOTSup 200. Sheffield: JSOT Press, 1995. 87–104.
" 'In the Image of God'…Pluralism." *Modern Theology* 11 (1995) 455–69.
"A Night for Crying/Weeping (Exodus 11:1–10)." In *Preaching Biblical Texts: Ex-
    positions by Jewish and Christian Scholars.* Edited by Fredrick C. Holmgren
    and Herman E. Schaalman. Grand Rapids: Eerdmans, 1995. 76–89.
"Pharaoh as Vassal: A Study of a Political Metaphor." *Catholic Biblical Quarterly*
    57 (1995) 27–51.
"Preaching as Reimagination." *Theology Today* 52 (1995) 313–29.
"Prophets, Old Testament." In *Concise Encyclopedia of Preaching.* Edited by
    William H. Willimon and Richard Lischer. Louisville: Westminster/John Knox,
    1995. 389–91.
"A Shattered Transcendence? Exile and Restoration." In *Biblical Theology: Prob-
    lems and Perspectives.* Edited by Steven J. Kraftchick, Charles D. Myers Jr.,
    and Ben C. Ollenburger. Nashville: Abingdon, 1995. 169–82.
"Two Narratives of 'The Flash Point' (Mark 9:2–8)" [Westminster Abbey Address].
    Peacemaker (Derby, England) (September 1995) 4.
"The Uninflected *Therefore* of Hosea 4:1–3." In *Reading from This Place*, vol-
    ume 1. Edited by Fernando F. Segovia and Mary Ann Tolbert. Minneapolis:
    Fortress Press, 1995. 231–49.

1996

The Threat of Life: Sermons on Pain, Power, and Weakness. Edited by Charles L.
    Campbell. Minneapolis: Fortress Press, 1996. 163 pages.
"A 'Characteristic' Reflection on What Comes Next (Jeremiah 32:16–44)." In
    Prophets and Paradigms: Essays in Honor of Gene M. Tucker. Edited by
    Stephen Breck Reid. Sheffield: Sheffield Academic Press, 1996. 16–32.
"God Wrestling" [transcription]. With Roberta Hestenes, John S. Kselman, Bill
    Moyers, Hugh O'Donnell, Burton L. Visotzky, Renita J. Weems, and Avivah
    Gottlieb Zornberg. In *Genesis: A Living Conversation.* New York: Doubleday,
    1996. 275–317.

"In God's Image" [transcription]. With Roberta Hestenes, John S. Kselman, Bill Moyers, Hugh O'Donnell, Burton L. Visotzky, Renita J. Weems, and Avivah Gottlieb Zornberg. In *Genesis: A Living Conversation*. New York: Doubleday, 1996. 3–37.

"The Loss and Recovery of Creation in Old Testament Theology." *Theology Today* 53 (1996) 177–90.

" 'Placed' between Promise and Command." In *Rooted in the Land: Essays on Community and Place*. Edited by William Vitek and Wes Jackson. New Haven, Conn.: Yale University Press, 1996. 124–31.

"Psalm 73 as a Canonical Marker." Co-written with Patrick D. Miller. *Journal for the Study of the Old Testament* 72 (1996) 45–56.

"A Shifting Paradigm: From 'Mighty Deeds' to 'Horizon' " In *The Papers of the Henry Luce III Fellows in Theology*, volume 1. Edited by Gary Gilbert. Atlanta: Scholars Press, 1996. 7–47.

"The Struggle toward Reconciliation." In *Talking about Genesis: A Resource Guide*. New York: Main Street Books/Doubleday, 1996. 132–134.

"What Christians Are Saying about the Need for Community." Written with Rick Hawksley and the Catholic Bishops of Appalachia. *Green Cross* 2, no. 3 (1996) 24.

1997

Cadences of Home: Preaching among Exiles. Louisville: Westminster/John Knox Press, 1997. 159 pages.

Theology of the Old Testament: Testimony, Dispute, Advocacy. Minneapolis: Fortress Press, 1997. 777 pages.

"Abuse of Command: Exploiting Power for Sexual Gratification." *Sojourners* 26, no. 4 (1997) 22–25.

"Biblical Theology Appropriately Postmodern." *Biblical Theology Bulletin* 27 (1997) 4–9.

"Churches in a Changing Society." *Chinese Theological Review* 11, no. 2 (1997) 36–53.

"Conversations among Exiles." *Christian Century* 114 (1997) 630–32.

"The Cunning Little Secret of Certitude: On the First 'Great Commandment.' " *Church and Society* 87, no. 6 (1997) 63–80.

"Destroy . . . but Not Quite." *The Caregiver Journal* 13, no. 1 (1997) 25–27.

"Exodus 3: Summons to Holy Transformation." In *The Theological Interpretation of Scripture: Classic and Contemporary Readings*. Edited by Stephen E. Fowl. Cambridge, Mass.: Blackwell, 1997. 155–71.

"Follow Your Thirst." *Journal of Stewardship* 49 (1997) 41–48.

"God's Gift of a Neighboring Future." *Reformed World* 47, nos. 3–4 (1997) 143–54. Reprinted in *Debrecen 1997: Proceedings of the 23rd General Council of the World Alliance of Reformed Churches*. Edited by Milan Opocensky. Geneva: World Alliance of Reformed Churches, 1997. 90–101.

"Holy One in Your Midst." *The Living Pulpit* 6, no. 1 (1997) 44–45.

"Isaiah 6:1–8" [exegetical article]. *No Other Foundation* 17, no. 2 (1997) 5–9.

"James Muilenburg as Theologian." *Union Seminary Quarterly Review* 50 (1997) 71–82.

"A Map for a Lost Church?" *The Clergy Journal* 73, no. 6 (1997) 31–34.

"Neighborliness and the Limits of Power in God's Realm: On the Second 'Great Commandment.'" *Church and Society* 87, no. 6 (1997) 81–96.

"Pain Turned to Newness" [Mark 5:24–34]. In *Preaching Jesus: New Directions for Homiletics in Hans Frei's Postliberal Theology.* Edited by Charles L. Campbell. Grand Rapids: Eerdmans, 1997. 259–264.

"Planned People/Planned Book?" In *Writing and Reading the Scroll of Isaiah: Studies of an Interpretive Tradition,* volume 1. Edited by Craig C. Broyles and Craig A. Evans. Leiden: Brill, 1997. 19–37.

"A Response to 'Our Kind of Crowd.'" *Journal for Preachers* 20, no. 4 (1997) 25–26.

"Texts That Linger, Words That Explode." *Theology Today* 54 (1997) 180–99.

"Truth-Telling as Subversive Obedience." *Journal for Preachers* 20, no. 2 (1997) 2–9.

Scriptural Index